The Role of the State

BRICS ▪ National Systems of Innovation

Series Editors: **José E. Cassiolato,** Federal University of Rio de Janeiro, Brazil.
Maria Clara Couto Soares, Federal University of Rio de Janeiro, Brazil.

This series of books brings together results of an intensive research programme on aspects of the national systems of innovation in the five BRICS countries — Brazil, Russia, India, China and South Africa. It provides a comprehensive and comparative examination of the challenges and opportunities faced by these dynamic and emerging economies. In discussing the impact of innovation with respect to economic, geopolitical, socio-cultural, institutional and technological systems, it reveals the possibilities of new development paradigms for equitable and sustainable growth.

Books in this Series

The Role of the State
Editors: Mario Scerri and Helena M. M. Lastres
ISBN 978-0-415-84254-9

FORTHCOMING
Inequality and Development Challenges
Editors: Maria Clara Couto Soares, Mario Scerri and Rasigan Maharajh

The Promise of Small and Medium Enterprises
Editors: Ana Arroio and Mario Scerri

Transnational Corporations and Local Innovation
Editors: José E. Cassiolato, Graziela Zucoloto, Dinesh Abrol and Liu Xielin

Financing Innovation
Editors: Michael Kahn and Luiz Martins de Melo

BRICS ▪ NATIONAL SYSTEMS OF INNOVATION

The Role of the State

EDITORS

Mario Scerri

Helena M. M. Lastres

IDRC | CRDI
Canada

Routledge
Taylor & Francis Group
LONDON NEW YORK NEW DELHI

First published 2013 in India
by Routledge
912 Tolstoy House, 15–17 Tolstoy Marg, Connaught Place, New Delhi 110 001

Simultaneously published in the UK
by Routledge
2 Park Square, Milton Park, Abingdon, OX14 4RN

Routledge is an imprint of the Taylor & Francis Group, an informa business

Typeset by
Bukprint India
B-180A, Guru Nanak Pura, Laxmi Nagar
Delhi 110 092

Printed and bound in India by
Avantika Printers Private Limited
194/2, Ramesh Market, Garhi, East of Kailash
New Delhi 110 065

British Library Cataloguing-in-Publication Data
A catalogue record of this book is available from the British Library

ISBN 978-0-415-84254-9

Contents

List of Abbreviations

ANC	African National Congress
APL	Local Productive Arrangements (Arranjos Produtivos Locais)
AsgiSA	Accelerated and Shared Growth Initiative for South Africa
BASIC	Brazil, South Africa, India, and China
BIPP	Biotechnology Industry Partnership Programme
BNDES	National Bank of Economic and Social Development (Banco Nacional de Desenvolvimento Econômico e Social)
Bolsa Familia	Poor Family Support Pension
BPC/LOAS	Social Benefit/Social Security Act
BRIC	Brazil, Russia, India, and China
BRICS	Brazil, Russia, India, China, and South Africa
CadÚnico	Unified Register of Social Programs
CAE	Chinese Academy of Engineering
CAPES	Coordination of Qualification of Graduate Human Resources (Coordenação de Aperfeiçoamento de Pessoal de Nível Superior)
CAS	Chinese Academy of Sciences
CASS	Chinese Academy of Social Sciences
CEPAL	The Economic Commission for Latin America and the Caribbean (ECLAC)
CIDE	Tax on Intervention in the Economic Field (Contribuição de Intervenção do Domínio Econômico)
CII	Confederation of Indian Industry
CLTD-2020	Conception of a Long-Term Development of the Russian Federation until 2020
CNI	National Confederation of Industry (Confederação Nacional da Indústria)
CNPq	National Council of Scientific and Technological Development (Conselho Nacional de Desenvolvimento Científico e Tecnológico)
COSATU	Congress of South African Trade Unions

COMECON	Council for Mutual Economic Assistance
CPC	Communist Party of China
CSIR	Council for Scientific and Industrial Research
CTA	Aerospace Technical Centre (Centro Técnico Aeroespacial)
DACST	Department of Arts, Culture, Science, and Technology
DAE	Department of Atomic Energy
DBT	Department of Biotechnology
DHET	Department of Higher Education and Training
DOD	Department of Ocean Development
DoE	Department of Education
DOEn	Department of Environment
DoL	Department of Labour
DoS	Department of Space
DRDO	Defence Research and Development Organisation
DSIR	Department of Scientific and Industrial Research
DST	Department of Science and Technology
DTI	Department of Trade and Industry
DTI	Scholarship for Industrial and Technological Development (Desenvolvimento Tecnológico e Industrial)
EMBRAPA	Brazilian Agricultural Research Corporation
ESKOM	Electricity Supply Commission
ESTD	Early Stage Technology Development
EU	European Union
FAIR	Facility for Antiproton Reactor and Ion Research
FAST	Fund for Accelerating Start-ups in Technology
FBA	Federal Budget Allocations on R&D
FDI	Foreign Direct Investment
FERA	Foreign Exchange Regulation Act
FICCI	Federation of Indian Chambers of Commerce and Industry
FINEP	Studies and Projects Funding Agency (Financiadora de Estudos e Projetos)
FNDCT	National Fund of Scientific and Technological Development (Fundo Nacional de Desenvolvimento Científico e Tecnológico)
FPP	Family Pension Programme
FTE	Full-time Equivalent

FUNTEC	Technological Fund
GDP	Gross Domestic Product
GEAR	Growth Employment and Redistribution: A Macroeconomic Strategy
GERD	Gross Expenditure on Research and Development
HEI	Higher Education Institution
HSE	State University, Higher School of Economics (Moscow)
HSRC	Human Sciences Research Council
IBGE	Brazilian Institute of Geography and Statistics
IBSA	India, Brazil and South Africa
ICAR	Indian Council of Agriculture Research
ICICI	Industrial Credit and Investment Corporation of India
ICMR	Indian Council of Medical Research
ICT	Information and Communication Technology
IDC	Industrial Development Corporation
IDRC	International Development Research Centre
IITs	Indian Institutes of Technology
INPE	National Institute for Space Research (Instituto Nacional de Pesquisas Espaciais)
INR	Indian Rupee
INSPIRE	Innovation in Science Pursuit for Inspired Research
IPCA	Inflation Rate
IPEADATA	Database on Brazilian economy
IPRs	Intellectual Property Rights
ISCOM	Iron and Steel Corporation of South Africa
IT-BPO	Information Technology and Business Process Outsourcing
ITER	International Thermonuclear Experimental Reactor
ITIs	Industrial Training Institutes
JIPSA	Joint Initiative on Priority Skills Acquisition
LDB	Law of Fundaments and Guidelines for Education (Lei de diretrizes e Bases da educação)
Lei da Inovação	Law of Innovation
Lei do Bem	Law of the Goods

MCT	Ministry of Science and Technology (Ministério da Ciência e Tecnologia)
MDIC	Ministry of Development, Industry and Foreign Trade (Ministério do Desenvolvimento, Indústria e Comércio Exterior)
MEC	Ministry of Education (Ministério da Educação)
MIIT	Ministry of Industry and Information Technology
MIT	Ministry of Information Technology
MNES	Ministry of Non-conventional Energy Sources
MOE	Ministry of Education
MS&T	Ministry of Science and Technology
MRTP	Monopolies and Restrictive Trade Practices
MS	Ministry of Health (Ministério da Saúde)
MSE	Micro and Small Enterprise
MTE	Ministries of Labour and Employment (Ministério do Trabalho a Emprego)
NACI	National Advisory Council on Innovation
NASSCOM	National Association of Software and Service Companies
NCR (Delhi)	National Capital Region (Delhi)
NCST	National Council of Science and Technology
NDRC	National Development and Reform Committee
NEPAD	New Partnership for African Development
NGP	New Growth Path
NIS	National Innovation System
NMITLI	New Millennium Indian Technology Leadership Initiative
NNSF	National Natural Science Foundation
NRDC	National Research Development Corporation
NRDS	National Research and Development Strategy
NRF	National Research Foundation
NRGES	National Rural Employment Guarantee Scheme
NRH	National Rural Health Mission
NSERB	National Science and Engineering Research Board
NSI	National System of Innovation
OBMEP	Brazilian Mathematics Olympiad of Public Schools
OECD	Organisation for Economic Cooperation and Development
PAC	Programme for the Acceleration of Growth (Programa de Aceleração do Crescimento)

PACTI	Action Plan for Science, Technology and Innovation
PDE	Plan for Development of Education
PDP	Policy for Production Development
PDTA	Programme for Agricultural Technological Development
PDTI	Programme for Industry Technological Development
Petrobras	Brazilian Energy Company
PINTEC	Brazilian Survey on Technological Innovation
PISA	Programme for International Students Assessment
PITCE	Industrial, Technological and Foreign Trade Policy (Política Industrial, Tecnológica e de Comércio Exterior)
PMO	Prime Minister's Office
PNCTI	National Policy of Science, Technology and Innovation
PPP	Public–private partnership
PRDSF	Pharmaceutical R&D Support Programme
PRO-AERO-NÁUTICA	Programme for Financing to Enterprises from the Brazilian Aeronautical Production Chain
PROFARMA	Programme of Support to the Development of the Health Industrial Complex
PROSET	Stimulus to Retention of Human Resources of Interest to Sectoral Funds
PROSOFT	Development of Software Industry and Services Information Technology
PROTVD	Programme of Support to Implementation of the Brazilian System of Terrestrial Digital TV
PRS	Public Research System
PURSE	Promotion of University Research and Science Excellence
R&D	Research and Development
RDP	Reconstruction and Development Programme
Real Plan	Plan for Economic Stabilisation (Plano Real)
RedeSist	Research Network on Local Innovative Production Arrangements and Systems
RGPS	General Regime of Social Security
RHAE-Inovação	Human Resources for Strategic Activities-Innovation

RISDP	Regional Indicative Strategic Development Plan
RMV	Life Monthly Pension (Renda Mensal Vitalícia)
Rosnano	Russian Corporation for Nanotechnology
Rosstat	Russian State Statistical Service
RSA	Republic of South Africa
RVC	Russian Venture Company
SADC	South African Development Community
S&T	Science and Technology
SAEB	The System for Assessment of Basic Education (Sistema de Avaliação da Educação Básica)
SARChI	South African Research Chairs Initiative
SCI	Science Citation Index
SETEC	Secretariat of Technological Development and Innovation
SMEs	Small- and Medium-scale Enterprises
SPR	Scientific Policy Resolution
SPREAD	Sponsored Research and Development
SPRU	Science Policy Research Unit
SSI	Sectoral System of Innovation
STIs	Scientific and Technological Institutions
STPs	Software Technology Parks
STPIs	Software Technology Parks of India
TDDP	Technology Development Demonstration Programme
TELECE-NTROS	Community centres for Internet access
TePP	Techno-Entrepreneur Promotion Programme
TIA	Technology Innovation Agency
TIFAC	Technology Information Forecasting and Assessment Council
TNCs	Transnational Corporations
TV–PROTVD	Brazilian System of Terrestrial Digital
UNDP	United Nations Development Programme
UNFCCC	United Nations Framework Convention on Climate Change
USSR	Union of Soviet Social Republics
USTP	University Science and Technology Park
VA	Value-added
VAT	Value-added tax
VTC	Vocational Technical Centres (Centros Vocacionais Tecnológicos)
WTO	World Trade Organization

List of Figures

List of Tables

Foreword

If there are any reservations about the importance of intensified cooperation between Brazil, Russia, India, China, and South Africa, this book will speedily dispel them. The usual reservations are based on doubts about economic complementarities and fears that all developing countries rely mainly on natural resource endowments and are therefore unable to trade with each other. This book shows that there is ample scope for comparative studies and hence cooperation in science and technology, and hence innovation for the mutual benefit of each.

The book also shows beyond any doubt that the state has a crucial role in sponsoring innovation, directly and indirectly, thereby leading a process that is often well-supported by the private sector. An essential foundation for innovation is obviously strong mathematics and science in schools and universities. However, state institutions are also vital for providing leadership, setting the pace, providing incentives, and in many other ways.

The history of state leadership is particularly striking in post-independence India when Nehru insisted on a modernisation programme which has been built on by succeeding leaders, not least of whom the current Prime Minister. Indeed, the chapter on India is an inspiring story of the deliberate actions by a government in an underdeveloped country striking out to develop science and technology to break through the legacy of backwardness. Would that other countries were equally determined and decisive!

The contrast, the chapter on China, is surprising. China's industrialisation path was initially based on natural resource endowments and has only recently pressed forward with innovation seriously. This may be because the Asian Tigers initially adopted the policy of last-stage assembly in factories introduced from developed countries. This meant that the relevant research and development was denied them for a long time. It seems that China and others first concentrated on the introduction of technology and equipment with short-term efficiency objectives. However, it is obvious that they have caught up and are now capable of designing their own innovation systems which are clearly essential to sustain their high growth rates.

The case of Brazil is of great interest. In recent decades the state has resorted to a variety of institutions to boost science and technological development. Each step reflected a realisation that Brazil ought not to depend on the importation of US capabilities. The establishment of the National Bank for Social and Economic Development (BNDES) is an outstanding example of a country seeking an original approach to the harnessing of capital for industrial investment. The results are astounding and the impact on GDP growth very significant.

The story from Russia is less inspiring, though there too big advances are underway. The South African case is perhaps the least encouraging, though there has been a significant advance in spending on R&D recently. The problems here are very fundamental, starting in the schooling system, and the lack of drive at the universities to promote mathematical sciences. The efforts of the innovative African Institute of Mathematical Sciences are embryonic but influential because its teaching is based on problem solving, and thereby shows what can be done.

The challenge in South Africa is all the greater for the recent revelation by Citigroup Global Markets that it has over US$ 2.5 trillion of non-energy monetary reserves making it the richest nation when assessed by the in situ value of its natural resources. South Africa is in the top 15 countries with gold, iron ore, nickel, and platinum group metal reserves. This poses an enormous challenge for innovative work to ensure that beneficiation follows on exploration, leading to fabrication.

Fundamental to all this is the financial contribution of the state. As we have now learnt with respect to the international financial crisis, the market alone cannot fix a country's inadequacies. According to Ha-Joon Chang, 40 to 60 per cent of R&D in the United States is provided by the state. It is well-known that their university research benefits enormously from their military budget even if the grants are often disguised. However, it is not only the state that has a responsibility. We are informed that in India gross expenditure on research and development is 68 per cent from government sources and 30 per cent from the business enterprise sector. Surely others can learn from this example.

This book raises the platform of discourse on development to a higher level. It escapes from the narrow confines of trade and investment policy, and reaches out to the more remote spaces of scientific innovation. It is an exciting journey.

Ben Turok

Member of Parliament
African National Congress
South Africa
May 2010

Preface

This book is the result of a collaborative effort of several people and institutions. The contributions presented here consolidate the findings of the project 'Comparative Study of the National Innovation Systems of BRICS' sponsored by the International Development Research Centre (IDRC). The project is rooted in a larger research effort on BRICS national innovation systems being developed in the sphere of the Global Research Network for Learning, Innovation and Competence Building Systems — Globelics. The Globelics initiative on BRICS economies brings together universities and other research institutions from Brazil, Russia, India, China, and South Africa. The aim is to strengthen an original and less dependent thought, more appropriate to understanding development processes in less developed countries.

First and foremost, we would like to thank Professor Bengt-Ake Lundvall, the coordinator of Globelics, who supported and promoted the BRICS project from the outset in 2003 and organised the First International Workshop of the BRICS Project in Aalborg, Denmark, in 2006. Without his leadership and enthusiasm the project could not have taken off.

We owe special thanks to project researchers and coordinators for their engagement in project activities and accessibility to overcome difficulties that naturally emerge from the geographical and cultural diversity of BRICS. We are also very grateful to those who provided the necessary administrative and secretarial support that resulted in the good performance of this project, especially Luiza Martins, Fabiane da Costa Morais, Tatiane da Costa Morais, and Eliane Alves who helped in editing activities and whose support was crucial for formatting the manuscript and organising the tables and figures. Max dos Santos provided the technical IT support for the research network.

The core ideas analysed in this book were discussed at international seminars organised in Brazil (2007), South Africa (2008), India (2009), and again in Brazil (2009) under the auspices of the BRICS Project, gathering scholars, academics, policy makers, businessmen, and civil society representatives. Our understanding of this complex theme has evolved considerably thanks to the seminar participants' constructive criticism. We are grateful to them as well as to all the other people not named here who also helped in the implementation of the project.

None of this work would have been possible without financial support. The support given by the IDRC was essential for the completion of this project. We are very obliged to IDRC and their staff for their support. We would especially like to thank Richards Isnar, Federico Buroni, Gustavo Crespi, Veena Ravichandran, Isabel Bortagaray, and Clara Saavedra. We are also grateful to Bill Carman and Michelle Hibber, then IDRC Publishers, for the technical assistance provided in the preparatory work that led to this publication.

Supplementary grants were received from various agencies of the Brazilian Ministry of Science and Technology, especially FINEP, the Brazilian Innovation Agency and CNPq, the National Council for Scientific and Technological Development. In particular, we would like to thank the general secretary of the Ministry of Science and Technology, Dr Luiz Antonio Elias, and the president of FINEP, Luis Fernandes, who have given enthusiastic support to the BRICS project since its inception.

Introduction

BRICS National Systems of Innovation

José E. Cassiolato and *Maria Clara Couto Soares*

Preamble

The world is experiencing significant transformations in its geopolitical and economic constitution. The processes of transformation have accelerated over the last decades. A significant part of the growth potential of the world economy nowadays and for the coming decades resides in some fast-developing countries. Brazil, Russia, India, China, and South Africa (BRICS) have displayed such potential for dynamic change. In a historic rupture with past patterns of development, the BRICS countries are now playing a major role in alleviating the current global crisis whilst revealing new and alternative progressive paradigms.

Much beyond the emphasis given by international agencies to the identification of investment possibilities in the BRICS production structures or to the prospects presented by their consumer markets, our perspective in analysing the BRICS countries is inspired by their significant development opportunities, as well as their several common characteristics and challenges, and the learning potential they offer for other developing countries. Identifying and analysing these opportunities and challenges will help to uncover alternative pathways towards fulfilling their socio-political-economic development potential within the constraints of sustainability.

The central focus of this book series is the National System of Innovation (NSI) of the five BRICS countries. Each book deals with a key component of the innovation system, providing the reader with access to analyses on the role played by the state, the financing, direct investment and the small and medium enterprises, besides approaching a particularly relevant — though still not extensively studied — aspect of the BRICS economies: the challenge of inequality and its interrelations with the NSIs of these countries.

The research endeavour that generated the publication of this book series has gathered universities and research centres from all the BRICS countries, as well as policy makers invited to discuss the outcomes. The research development and the comparative analysis of its results are intended to bring to light the challenges and opportunities of the BRICS countries' national innovation systems from the points of view of these same countries. Part of the effort undertaken was addressed to the construction of a shared methodology aimed at advancing the comprehension of the specificities of innovation systems in each country. This was done in view of the need for improvements in the analytical framework used for the analysis of the national innovation systems located in countries outside the restricted sphere of developed countries. Special attention was paid to the political implications. However, instead of searching for generalisable policy recommendations, it was sought to identify and analyse bottlenecks that are common to the BRICS economies, their complementarities and competition areas, as well as other aspects of major importance for supporting decision makers and that are able to incite reflection about the subject of innovation and development in other less developed countries.

It is worth mentioning that the research consolidated in this publication is rooted in a larger research effort on BRICS national innovation systems being developed in the spheres of Globelics (www.globelics.org, accessed 3 December 2011) and RedeSist (the Research Network on Local Production and Innovation Systems) at the Economic Institute of the Federal University of Rio de Janeiro (www.redesist.ie.ufrj.br, accessed 3 December 2011). Globelics is an international academic network which uses the concept of innovation systems (IS) as an analytical tool aimed at the comprehension of the driving forces that push economic development. It aims to advance the use of the IS perspective on a world basis. Established in 2002 and inspired by renowned scholars from the field of economics of innovation such as Christopher Freeman (1987) and Bengt-Äke Lundvall (1992), the Globelics network has, among others, the purpose of encouraging knowledge exchange between less developed countries, thus fostering mutual learning across innovation research groups in Latin America, Africa and Asia. With this, it is sought to strengthen an original and more autonomous approach to understanding the development processes in developing countries. On the other hand, the focus put by the Globelics network on the study of innovation systems of BRICS results from the recognition that understanding the particular dynamics which connects the knowledge base with innovation and economic performance in each of the five BRICS countries is, today, a precondition for better appreciating the direction that the world economy will be following (Lundvall 2009). It is within such analytical field that the contribution offered by this book series is inserted.

In the following sections we (*a*) present the broad conceptual approach of NSI used as the guiding analytical framework for the research gathered under this book series; (*b*) characterize the increasing importance of the BRICS countries in the global scenario; and (*c*) introduce the five-book collection on NSIs in the BRICS countries.

NSI and Development — A Broad Perspective

One of the most fruitful ways of thinking developed in advanced countries in the last 30 years came from a resurrection and updating of earlier thinking that emphasised the role of innovation as an engine of economic growth and the long-run cyclical character of technical change. A seminal paper by Christopher Freeman (1982) pointed out the importance that Smith, Marx and Schumpeter attached to innovation (ibid.: 1) and accentuated its systemic and national character (ibid.: 18). Freeman also stressed the crucial role of government policies to cope with the uncertainties associated with the upsurge of a new techno-economic paradigm and the very limited circumstances under which free trade could promote economic development. Since it was formulated in the 1980s, the system of innovation (SI) approach has been increasingly used in different parts of the world to analyse processes of acquisition, use and diffusion of innovations, and to guide policy recommendations.[1]

Particularly relevant in the SI perspective is that since the beginning of the 1970s, the innovation concept has been widened to be understood as a systemic, non-linear process rather than an isolated fact. Emphasis was given to its interactive character and to the importance of (and complementarities between) incremental and radical, technical and organisational innovations and their different and simultaneous sources. A corollary of this argument is the context-specific and localised character of innovation and knowledge. This understanding of innovation as a socially determined process is in opposition to the idea of a supposed techno-globalism and implies, for instance, that acquisition of technology abroad is not a substitute for local efforts. On the contrary, one needs a lot of knowledge to be able to interpret information, select, buy (or copy), transform, and internalise technology.

Systems of innovation, defined as a set of different institutions that contribute to the development of the innovation and learning capacity of a country, region, economic sector, or locality, comprise a series of elements and relations that relate production, assimilation, use, and diffusion of knowledge. In other words, innovative performance depends not only on firms and R&D organisations' performance but also on how they interact, among themselves and with other agents, as well as all the other forms by which they acquire, use and diffuse knowledge. Innovation capacity derives, therefore, from the confluence of social, political, institutional, and culture-specific factors and from the environment in which economic agents operate. Different development trajectories contribute to shape systems of innovation with quite diverse characteristics requiring specific policy support.

It is this understanding of the systemic nature of innovation that allows for two crucial dimensions of the SI approach to be explicitly discussed: the emphasis on historical and national trajectories and the importance of taking into account the productive, financial, social, institutional, and political contexts, as well as micro, meso and macro spheres (Freeman 2003; Lastres et al. 2003). Although all of these contexts are relevant for a discussion about development, two in particular should be singled out that are pertinent to this study. One is the financial context, recognised by Schumpeter (1982 [1912]) in his *The Theory of Economic Development*. For him, entrepreneurs, to become the driving force in a process of innovation, must be able to convince banks to provide the credit to finance innovation. In this sense, any discussion about innovation systems has to include the financial dimension.[2] The other is the idea that space matters, that the analysis of systems of innovation should be done at the national (Freeman 1982; Lundvall 1988) and local levels (Cassiolato et al. 2003).

The national character of SI was introduced by Christopher Freeman (1982, 1987) and Bengt-Äke Lundvall (1988) and has been widely used as an analytical tool and as a framework for policy analysis in both developed and underdeveloped countries. As a result, research and policy activities explicitly focusing on SI can be found in most countries and a rapidly growing number of studies of specific NSIs have been produced. Although some authors tend to focus on the NSI in a narrow sense, with an emphasis on research and development efforts and science and technology organisations, a broader understanding of NSI (Freeman 1987; Lundvall 1988) is more appropriate. This approach takes into account not only the role of firms, education and research organisations and science and technology institution (STI) policies, but includes government policies as a whole, financing organisations, and other actors and elements that influence the acquisition, use and diffusion of innovations. In this case emphasis is also put on the role of historical processes — which account for differences in socio-economic capabilities and for different development trajectories and institutional evolution — creating SI with very specific local features and dynamics. As a result, a national character of SI is justified.

Figure 1 is an attempt to show both the narrow and the broad perspectives on NSI. The broad perspective includes different, connecting sub-systems that are influenced by various contexts: geopolitical, institutional, macroeconomic, social, cultural, and so on. First, there is a production and innovation sub-system which contemplates the structure of economic activities, their sectoral distribution, degree of informality and spatial and size distribution, the level and quality of employment, the type and quality of innovative effort. Second, there is a sub-system of science and technology which includes education (basic, technical, undergraduate, and postgraduate), research, training, and other elements of the scientific and technological infrastructure such as information, metrology, consulting, and intellectual property. Third, there is a policy, promotion, financing, representation, and regulation sub-system that encompasses the different forms of public and private policies both explicitly geared towards innovation or implicitly, that is, those that although not necessarily geared towards it, affect strategies for innovation. Finally, there is the role of demand, which most of the time is surprisingly absent from most analyses of SI. This dimension includes patterns of income distribution, structure of consumption, social organisation and social demand (basic infrastructure, health, education).

Figure 1: *The Narrow and Broad Perspectives on NSI*

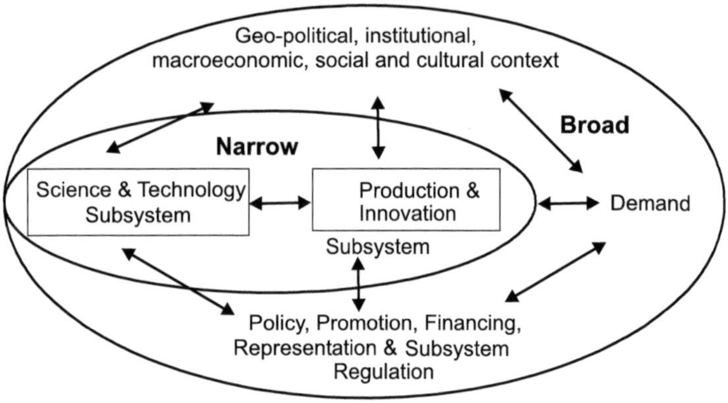

Source: Adapted from Cassiolato and Lastres (2008).

This portrayal of the national innovation system framework is a corollary of an understanding that

- innovation capacity derives from the confluence of economic, social, political, institutional, and culture-specific factors and from the environment in which they operate, implying the need for an analytical framework broader than that offered by traditional economics (Freeman 1982, 1987; Lundvall 1988);
- the number of firms or organisations such as teaching, training and research institutes is far less important than the habits and practices of such actors with respect to learning, linkage formation and investment. These shape the nature and extensiveness of their interactions and their propensity to innovate (Mytelka 2000; Johnson and Lundvall 2003);
- main elements of knowledge are embodied in minds and bodies of agents or embedded in routines of firms and in relationships between firms and organisations. Therefore, they are localised and not easily transferred from one place/context to another, for knowledge is something more than information and includes tacit elements (Lundvall 1988);
- the focus on interactive learning and on the localised nature of the generation, assimilation and diffusion of innovation implies that the acquisition of foreign technology abroad is not a substitute for local efforts (Cassiolato and Lastres 1999);
- national framework matters, as development trajectories contribute to shape specific systems of innovation. The diversity of NSIs is a product of different combinations of

their main features that characterise their micro, meso and macroeconomic levels, as well as the articulations among these levels (Freeman 1987; Lastres 1994).

From the specific point of view of less developed countries (LDCs) the usefulness of the SI approach resides precisely in the facts that (*a*) its central building blocks allow for their socio-economic and political specificities to be taken into account and (*b*) it does not ignore the power relations in discussing innovation and knowledge accumulation. As this book argues, these features are particularly relevant in the analysis of the BRICS countries' innovation systems. As the analysis of economic phenomena also takes into consideration their social, political and historical complexity, policy prescriptions are based on the assumption that the process of development is influenced by and reflects the particular environment of each country, rather than on recommendations derived from the reality of advanced countries. A number of development studies followed these ideas, arguing that technical change plays a central role in explaining the evolution of capitalism and in determining the historical process through which hierarchies of regions and countries are formed. Furtado (1961), for instance, established an express relation between economic development and technological change pointing out that the growth of an economy was based on the accumulation of knowledge, and understood development within a systemic, historically determined, view. Although original, these contributions have a close correspondence with Myrdal's (1968) proposition that: (*a*) contexts and institutions matter; (*b*) positive and negative feedbacks have cumulative causation; (*c*) cycles may be virtuous or vicious, and with Hirschman's (1958) point that interdependencies among different activities are important.

The need to address paradigmatic changes and the problems and options deriving from the upsurge of information technologies led to the outbreak in Latin America in the 1980s of a series of interconnected work from the innovation perspective. Building on Furtado's work on changes associated with the industrial revolution, authors like Herrera (1975) and Perez (1983) analysed the opportunities and challenges associated with the introduction of these radical changes in the region. It was only then that the innovation and development literature started to integrate the empirically validated knowledge about learning inside firms with the contributions stemming from the work of Freeman, Perez, Herrera, and others on new technologies, changes of techno-economic paradigms and systems of innovation. What gave special impetus to this direction was the empirical work focusing on technological capability building as part of a broader national innovation system. The role of government policies in orienting the speed and direction of technological changes was also highlighted (Freeman and Perez 1988).

Development processes are characterised by deep changes in the economic and social structure taking place from (technological and/or productive) discontinuities that cause and are caused by the productive, social, political, and institutional structure of each nation. Development is also seen as a systemic process, given the unequal capitalism development in the world. The recognition of national specificities of these processes is also fundamental. We found the same stress on the national character of development processes in List's work (1841), and on the NSI idea of Freeman (1982) and Lundvall (1988) in Furtado's (1961) discussion about the transformation of national economies where their structural complexity is manifested in a diversity of social and economic forms. For Furtado, it is in this transformation that the essence of development resides: structural changes 'in the internal relations of the economic and social system' (ibid.: 103) that are triggered by capital accumulation and technological innovations. The emphasis on diversity, and the recognition that: (*a*) both theory and policy recommendations are highly context dependent, (*b*) the economy is firmly embedded in society, and (*c*) knowledge and technology are context-specific, conform some general identities.

Furtado (1961) established a direct relation between economic development and technological innovation pointing out that the growth of an advanced economy was based on the accumulation of new scientific knowledge and on the application of such knowledge to solve practical problems. The Industrial Revolution set into motion a process of radical changes based on technical progress that has lasted till now and that is at the root of how the world economy is conformed. In essence, those changes: (*a*) rendered endogenous the causal factors related to growth into the economic system; (*b*) made possible a closer articulation between capital formation and experimental science. Such articulation has become one of the most fundamental characteristics of modern civilisation. As pointed out by Furtado (ibid.), the beginning of such a process took place in the countries that were able to industrialise and create technical progress first, and the quick accumulation made possible in the development of this process became the basic engine of the capitalist system. For this reason, there is a close interdependency between the evolution of the technology in the industrialised countries and the historical conditions on the basis of which such development was made possible. As the behaviour of the economic variables relies on parameters that are defined and evolve into a specific historical context, it is quite difficult to isolate the study of economic phenomena from its historical frame of reference (Furtado 2002). This assertion is more significant when analysing economic, social and technological systems that are different from each other, as in the underdeveloped economies. In this context, underdevelopment may not, and should not, be considered as an anomaly or simply a backward state. Underdevelopment may be identified as a functioning pattern and specific evolution of some economies. Social and economical peripheral structure determines a specific manner under which structural change occurs (industrialisation during the 1950s and 1960s) and technical progress is introduced. Hence different outcomes from those in developed countries are to be expected (Furtado 1961; Rodriguez 2001).

The neo-Schumpeterian perspective also argues that economic development is considered a systemic phenomenon, generated and sustained not only by inter-firm relations, but most significantly by a complex inter-institutional network of relations. Innovation is eminently a social process. Therefore, development — resulting from the introduction and diffusion of new technologies — may be considered as the outcome of cumulative trajectories historically built up according to institutional specificities and specialisation patterns inherent to a determined country, region or sector. Each country follows its own development trajectory according to its specificities and possibilities, depending fundamentally on their hierarchical and power position in the world capitalist system. The more distant underdeveloped countries are from the technological frontier, the larger will be the barriers to an innovative insertion in the new technological paradigm. More serious than technological asymmetries are knowledge and learning asymmetries, with the implication that access, understanding, absorption, domination, use and diffusion of knowledge become impossible. However, even when the access to new technologies becomes possible, most of the time they are not adequate for the reality of underdeveloped countries and/or these countries do not have a pool of sufficient knowledge to make an adequate use of them. This occurs because the learning process depends on the existence of innovative and productive capabilities that are not always available. On this aspect, Arocena and Sutz (2003) argue that there are clearly learning divides between North and South that are perhaps the main problem of underdevelopment nowadays.

The Increasing Relevance of the BRICS Countries

The BRICS denomination was originally used to connect the dynamic emerging economies of Brazil, Russia, India, China, and South Africa as continental countries bearing a strategic position in the continents of the Americas, Europe, Asia, and Africa. The BRICS are also joined by their large geographical and demographic dimensions. Collectively, they were home to 42.2 per cent of the world population as of 2010 representing nothing less than 2.9 billion people. In addition, the five countries account for approximately 30 per cent of the earth's surface, holding significant reserves of natural resources such as energy and mineral resources, water and fertile lands. As well, BRICS countries have 24.3 per cent of world biodiversity; Brazil alone embracing 9.3 per cent of the total (GEF 2008).

Moreover, it is the recent performance of these economies and their macroeconomic indicators that make them more and more the focus of surveillance and analysis. In fact, the BRICS countries display a growing economic importance. In 2000, the five countries accounted for 17.1 per cent of the world GDP in public–private partnership (PPP). Their share increased to 25.7 per cent in 2010, with China and India accounting for 13.6 per cent and 5.5 per cent respectively, followed by Russia (3 per cent), Brazil (2.9 per cent) and South Africa (0.7 per cent) (IMF 2011).

The participation of the BRICS countries in world GDP is expected to rise sharply in the years to come. The impact of the financial crisis and global recession on developed world economy over the last three years has only lent support to this expectation, beyond attracting attention to the BRICS economies' capacity to remain immune or quickly recover from the crisis. Large domestic markets, pro-active investment policies, monetary and tax policies with anti-cyclic capacity, presence of major public banks, and high level of reserves are elements increasingly recognised as having helped at least some BRICS economies to be less affected by the crisis.

While growth slowed in all major regions, China and India continued to grow rapidly in 2009 and 2010 (Table 1). In other BRICS countries the crisis rebounded fast. In Brazil, the GDP fell 0.2 per cent in 2009, but the economy surpassed pre-crisis growth rates in 2010 (7.5 per cent). South Africa showed a GDP decrease by 1.8 per cent in 2009 and had a 2.8 per cent increase in 2010. In Russia, heavily dependent on commodities like oil and gas, the economy has been hit more severely by the global crisis. It experienced shrinking of almost 8 per cent in 2009 but the GDP growth recovered to 3.7 per cent in 2010, beating the developed economies' growth rates. Prospects for 2015 show the five economies representing 29.5 per cent of the world economy.

The economic performance of the BRICS countries has, however, varied widely during the last decades as shown in Table 1. China has maintained its position as the fastest growing economy worldwide. India has also grown significantly and regularly. Brazil has had an irregular performance, well below its potential, but showed an enhancement in the second half of the 2000s. Russia, after the severe 1990s crisis that resulted in a decline of 40 per cent in its real GDP, has recovered and South Africa has had a small improvement in its economic performance that remains below its potential.

These different performances were accompanied by significant changes in the productive structure of the five countries, which reflect dissimilar development strategies.

The competitiveness of China's industrial sector is the main source of the country's impressive economic growth. The share of industry in the composition of China's GDP is unusual and growing: it was around 40 per cent in 1990 and reached 48 per cent in 2009. In contrast, in 2008, 56.1 per cent of the Chinese labour force still remained in rural areas. The relative share of the agricultural sector, which accounted for 30.2 per cent in 1980, is constantly falling, to 11 per cent of GDP in 2009. The share of services grew from 21.6 per cent in 1980 to 41 per cent in 2009.

Really impressive is the mounting share of China's manufacturing sector in world manufacturing GDP (Figure 2). In 1990, it represented 3.1 per cent of global manufacturing GDP, achieving 21.2 per cent in 2009.

Table 1: *BRICS: Average Rates of Growth of Real GDP, 1980–2015 (percentage)*

	1980–1990	*1990–2000*	*2001–2005*	*2006*	*2007*	*2008*	*2009*	*2010*	*2015**
Brazil	2.8	2.9	2.8	3.7	5.7	5.1	-0.2	7.5	4.1
Russia	-	-4.7	6.2	7.4	8.1	5.6	-7.9	3.7	5.0
India	5.8	6.0	6.9	9.8	9.3	7.3	6.5	9.7	8.1
China	10.3	10.4	9.6	11.6	13.0	9.0	8.7	10.3	9.5
South Africa	1.6	2.1	4.0	5.4	5.1	3.1	-1.8	2.8	2.8
Developed Countries	3.1	2.8	1.9	2.8	2.5	0.8	-3.2	3.0	2.3

Source: UNCTAD (2010) for the period 1980–2008 and IMF (2011) for 2009–2015 data. See http://unctadstat.unctad.org/ReportFolders/reportFolders.aspx (accessed 15 March 2011).

Note: * Estimate.

Figure 2: *Manufacturing Sector: BRICS' Share in World GDP, 1970–2009*

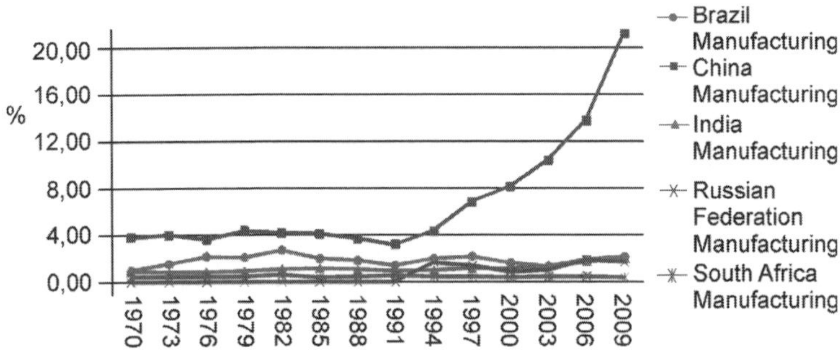

Source: UNCTAD (2009). See http://unctadstat.unctad.org/ReportFolders/reportFolders.aspx (accessed 15 March 2011).

China has diversified its industrial system to a significant degree during the last 25 years and the share of technologically intensive sectors in industrial output in 2009 reached 42 per cent of the total value added by the manufacturing sector. In the other four countries this share is around 15 per cent.[3] In addition, some major differences in the characteristics of the BRICS countries' manufacturing sectors should be noticed.

Brazil has gone through a structural transformation since the late 1980s, with a significant reduction of the share of industry in total GDP (declining from 41.7 per cent in 1980 to 25.4 per cent in 2009) and a high growth of services (from 50 per cent to 68.5 per cent in the same period). It is worth emphasising that agricultural goods that have had an important role in the country's trade surplus were responsible for only 6.1 per cent of GDP in 2009, showing a fall from 9.0 per cent in 1980. In Brazil, as in Russia and South Africa, the products based on natural resources and commodities have a relatively greater share of national GDP than in China and India.

Russia's economic development is heavily dependent on energy and raw material resources. As in Brazil, the contribution of manufacturing sector to GDP in Russia has declined since the 1980s, decreasing from 44.6 per cent in 1983 to 32.9 per cent in 2009. The share of defence-related industrial complex in manufacturing is significant, together with the strong production base in non-electric machines and equipment. The oil and gas industry alone accounts for more than 10 per cent of the gross value added. The share of services in total GDP has grown in the last two decades achieving

62.4 per cent in 2009 while agriculture has decreased its participation accounting for only 4.7 per cent in 2009.

The Indian economy is essentially service-led. Skills in the manufacturing sector are relatively modest and concentrated in non-durable consumer goods and in the chemical-pharmaceutical complex. However, some manufacturing segments in the automobile complex and in certain basic industries have been developing rapidly in recent years. Since the mid-1980s, the contribution of industry to India's GDP has been almost constant and around 26 per cent, but from 2004 to 2009 it increased to 28.3 per cent. India's capacity in the area of services is significant, particularly those linked to information and communication technology (ICT). The share of services in GDP has grown from 39 per cent in 1980 to 54.6 per cent in 2009. Although the agricultural sector is declining in India's GDP, it still represented 17.1 per cent in 2009 (compared to 36.8 per cent in 1980) and constitutes an important determinant of the overall economic growth.

The services sector has also been playing a more important role in the South African economy. The share of this sector in GDP was 45.4 per cent in 1980 and increased to 65.8 per cent in 2009. The development of the financial sector and the growth of tourism have contributed to this growth. Finance, real estate and business services are expanding their share with regard to government services. South Africa's industrial sector is heavily based on natural resources, mainly steel and non-ferrous metals, with some increases in capacity occurring in non-durable consumer goods and the automobile sector. The share of industry-added value in total GDP value decreased from 48.4 per cent in 1980 to 31.4 per cent in 2009. The metal and engineering sectors dominate the manufacturing sector. Although agriculture is responsible for a small share of South Africa's GDP (3 per cent in 2009), it still represents an important source of employment. The minerals and mining sector remains important also with respect to both employment and foreign trade.

The changes observed in the participation of BRICS countries in international trade were even more significant (Table 2). Their share in merchandise trade value more than doubled in the short period of 2000–2010, exports rising from 7.5 to 16.4 per cent and imports from 6.2 to 14.9 per cent. However, the contribution of the five countries varied significantly. The most notable fact is the well-known growth of China in the merchandise trade value: its exports mounted from

3.9 per cent to 10.4 per cent of world exports reaching US$ 1.58 trillion in 2010, and imports increased from 3.4 per cent to 9.1 per cent in the same period.

Table 2: *BRICS: Merchandise Trade Value (in billion of current US$) and Share in World Total, 2000–2010 (percentage)*

	2000		2005		2010	
Exports	*Value*	%	*Value*	%	*Value*	%
World	6,448.57	100.00	10,495.70	100.00	15,174.44	100.00
Brazil	55.12	0.85	118.53	1.13	201.915	1.33
China	249.20	3.86	761.95	7.26	1,578.270	10.40
India	42.38	0.66	99.62	0.95	221.406	1.46
Russia	105.57	1.64	243.80	2.32	400.424	2.64
South Africa	31.95	0.50	56.26	0.54	85.700	0.56
	2000		2005		2010	
Imports	*Value*	%	*Value*	%	*Value*	%
World	6,662.89	100.00	10,800.15	100.00	15,353.26	100.00
Brazil	58.64	0.88	77.63	0.72	191.46	1.25
China	225.02	3.38	660.21	6.11	1,396.20	9.09
India	51.52	0.77	142.84	1.32	328.36	2.14
Russia	49.13	0.74	137.98	1.28	273.61	1.78
South Africa	30.22	0.45	64.19	0.59	96.25	0.63

Source: UNCTAD (2010).

India also experienced a sharp increase of exports, reaching 1.46 per cent of the world total in 2010. Fostered by Chinese growth and commodities boom, the share of Brazil and Russia in world exports grew rapidly from 2000 to 2010, increasing almost four times. South Africa is the only BRICS country that still shows less than 1 per cent of world exports. On the import side, India and Russia increased their share in world imports more than fivefold. Except India and South Africa, the other BRICS countries managed to keep a surplus in their merchandise trade in 2010. In India inflows on account of invisibles have been helpful in financing the growing deficit in merchandise trade.

The BRICS economies have significantly increased their openness to international trade in the last decades. They have raised their exports and imports both in volume terms as a share of GDP, but the level of trade openness has varied quite a lot (Table 3). The greater changes occurred in China and India, particularly since the 1990s when they speeded up their international trade flows. Currently, China, South Africa and Russia are the BRICS economies with the higher levels of openness. The Brazilian economy, despite the liberalisation process in the 1990s, remains the most closed amongst the BRICS countries.

Table 3: *BRICS: Foreign Trade (in million of current US$) and Share of GDP (percentage)*

	Exports + Imports				
Countries	*1970*	*1980*	*1990*	*2000*	*2010*
Brazil	8,719	25,412	61,212	113,762	393,379
China	4,833	38,919	114,71	474,227	2.972.960
India	4,792	28,839	51,144	93,941	540,489
Russia	–	–	349,249	136,973	627,323
South Africa	8,352	50,411	48,6	56,782	161,953
	(Exports + Imports) GDP				
Countries	*1970*	*1980*	*1990*	*2000*	*2010*
Brazil	13.0%	10.3%	14.0%	17.6%	18.8%
China	5.3%	12.9%	29.9%	39.6%	50.6
India	7.9%	15.7%	15.8%	20.4	31.3
Russia	-	-	36.1%	52.7	42.4
South Africa	45.7%	61.2%	43.4%	42.7	44.5

Source: United Nations (2010); World Bank (2011).

The bilateral trade flows between BRICS countries have been relatively restricted. However, since the first half of the 2000s there was a widespread increase of exports and imports flows between the five economies, but particularly a stronger presence of China as an important trade pole for the other four countries (Baumann 2009). In 2009, China surpassed the US as the main trade partner of Brazil and also emerged as the second main trade partner of India and Russia.

The converse does not however hold, as these four economies don't match their respective rankings insofar as they are neither the top import suppliers nor export destinations for China. China exports to Brazil, India, Russia, and South Africa at a more intense pace than it imports from them. In addition, the latter are concentrated on a few primary goods intensive in natural resources while China's exports are much more diversified and led by manufactured goods. Therefore, despite the fact that intra-BRICS trade has increased in recent years, the flows are still restricted in size and unbalanced in terms of the different rhythms and compositions of the BRICS bilateral commercial transactions.

In the last decades, the BRICS countries have been the recipients of significant amounts of foreign direct investment (FDI). Brazil received the greatest share of FDI of all BRICS economies until the first half of the 1980s. Although China has surpassed Brazil since 1985, Brazil continued to be a major destination for FDI during the 1990s, most notably during the process of privatisation that took place during that decade. Since the 2000s Russia and India have been strengthening their relevance as FDI inflow destinations. In 2010, the BRICS countries received 17.6 per cent of global FDI inflows. Especially since 2005, there was a sharp increase of BRICS' FDI outflows. With the exception of South Africa, BRICS countries more than tripled their FDI outflows from 2005 to 2010, raising their participation in the world total from 3.6 per cent to 11.1 per cent in the period.

Table 4: *BRICS: Foreign Direct Investment, Inflows and Outflows Share in the World Totals*

Selected Years

FDI Inflows (%)	*1970*	*1975*	*1980*	*1985*	*1990*	*1995*	*2000*	*2005*	*2010*
Brazil	2.94	4.53	3.53	2.54	0.48	1.29	2.34	1.53	3.90
China	NA	NA	0.11	3.50	1.68	10.96	2.90	7.37	8.50
India	0.34	0.32	0.15	0.19	0.11	0.63	0.26	0.78	1.98
Russian Federation	NA	NA	NA	NA	NA	0.60	0.19	1.31	3.31
South Africa	2.50	0.71	-0.02	-0.80	-0.04	0.36	0.06	0.68	0.13

(*Cont.*)

(*Cont.*)

FDI Outflows (%)									
Brazil	0.01	0.38	0.71	0.13	0.26	0.30	0.19	0.29	0.87
China	NA	NA	NA	1.01	0.34	0.55	0.07	1.39	5.14
India	0.00	0.00	0.01	0.01	0.00	0.03	0.04	0.34	1.11
Russian Federation	NA	NA	NA	NA	NA	0.17	0.26	1.45	3.91
South Africa	0.12	0.44	1.46	0.08	0.01	0.69	0.02	0.11	0.03

Source: UNCTAD (2010).

BRICS countries also followed different development strategies regarding FDI. Particularly remarkable has been the Chinese policy to attract multinational companies since the beginning of the 1990s. Inserted in a broader strategy aiming to expand its technological knowledge and later to strengthen the domestic industries and enterprises, China imposed conditions — such as the establishment of joint ventures and that R&D be carried out locally — that had to be met before the subsidiaries were to operate in China or sell in its markets. Brazil, Russia and South Africa — countries that liberalised their economies with few restrictions — got more portfolio investment, but most of the investment received by the manufacturing sector was used to buy up local companies. In China and India, where the capital account was not liberalised, FDI seems to have been concentrated in new investments in production and innovation.

Other relevant macroeconomic indicators could be added — such as the impressive share of BRICS in international monetary reserves (about 40 per cent of the total) — but the interest in these five emerging economies goes beyond this area. Together with their expanding economic relevance, these countries are claiming a rising geopolitical influence. They have been important players in their geographic areas of influence. However, they are pushing to have an increasing voice in the international high-level decision-making institutions, particularly through reforms in the UN system and in the Bretton Woods organisations. New dialogue spaces bringing together BRICS countries, such as the IBSA (India, Brazil and South Africa), BRICS (Brazil, Russia, India, China, and South Africa), and BASIC (Brazil, South Africa, India, and China) signal concrete steps to move forward the cooperation and coordination within and amongst these countries, which intends to go further than the mere economic sphere.[4]

Their growing leverage in international relations together with other emerging countries is associated with a repositioning of the balance of power on the world stage, which was intensified by the recent world crisis. BRICS countries want to see these changes reflected in the institutions of global governance. Since their economies will probably continue to account for a sizeable portion of the increase in global GDP in the near future, it is expected over time that BRICS will exert increasing financial and political influence, even if limited by their considerable differences and constraints to form a coherent political bloc anytime soon.[5]

The increased influence of these countries took place during a period marked by intense transformations in the global society. One of these remarkable changes is the integration in the economy of a significant portion of previously marginalised segments of the BRICS population. The highly populated China and India led this process in terms of world shares, but Brazil also had an important participation (Soares and Podcameni forthcoming). The present and potential dimension of BRICS domestic markets as well as the policies adopted by some BRICS countries aiming to reduce their dependence on developed countries' consumer markets has been drawing increasing attention in the last years. According to one estimate, two billion people from BRICS will join the global 'middle class' by 2030 (Wilson and Dragusanu 2008) representing a huge impact on the demand profile with expected reflexes on global investments as well as on innovation.

Simultaneously, several hurdles remain for the BRICS to overcome. One of them is the growing social gap caused by the unequal distribution of recent economic growth. While the percentage of the population below the poverty line has decreased over the past 30 years in most of the BRICS countries, inequality is still a major issue for these economies. In fact, the BRICS countries, except Brazil, show a trend of increasing income inequality that — particularly since the 1990s — has been following the rapid economic growth. Moreover, despite the improvements in recent years, Brazil is still among the countries with the worst distribution of income, together with South Africa that found itself in an even worse situation.[6] In addition, India and Russia are among those with the largest percentage of the population living below the poverty line.[7] Furthermore, beyond the income dimension, inequality has a multi-dimensional character in the BRICS countries. This challenge is exacerbated by race, gender, ethnic, and geographic dimensions and therefore demands more integrated solutions (Soares et al. forthcoming).

One of the problems associated with the high poverty levels and the perverse distribution of income is the limited access to quality public services — education, health, housing and infrastructure, safety and security, etc. These problems are common to the five countries, where a significant portion of the population lacks access to essential goods and services, and demand urgent redress. This situation is reflected in poor human development indices in the BRICS countries. Other undeniable challenges faced by BRICS are unemployment, poor quality employment and increasing informality.

Another evident challenge in all five countries is the huge regional disparity in human and economic development. There is also a large gap between the rural and urban population. In general, the wealthier regions are those that are more industrialised. Practically 60 per cent of the total GDP of Brazil originates in the states of the southeast. The Chinese economic development model favours the coastal provinces, while other provinces in the interior are much less developed. In South Africa, economic activity is concentrated in Gauteng province and in the western part of Cape Town. The industrial development of Russia occurred principally around cities such as Moscow, St Petersburg, Nizhny Novgorod, and Ekaterinburg. India also shows significant inequalities between the rich regions to the south and the northern regions of the country as well as between the rural and urban populations. Therefore, regional redistribution of income and access to essential goods and services is another significant challenge that these five countries have in common (Soares et al. forthcoming).

The negative environmental impact of recent growth is another huge challenge to be faced by BRICS countries. According to CDIAC-UN data for 2008, the BRICS countries are responsible for emitting 35.3 per cent of the world's total CO_2.[8] China is ranked as the world's largest emitter, accounting for 21.9 per cent followed by the United States (17.7 per cent), India (5.4 per cent) and Russia (5.3 per cent). South Africa and Brazil are responsible for 1.4 per cent and 1.2 per cent of global emissions respectively, and occupy the 13th and 17th positions internationally. If we take the example of China, we observe that fossil-fuel CO_2 emissions in the country have more than doubled in the 2000 decade alone. Energy efficiency is a big problem in China and energy consumption per product is about 40 per cent higher than in the developed world. Other environmental problems are also critical. For instance, 40 per cent of river and 75 per cent of lake water is polluted leaving 360 million rural people without clean water. As in China, the environmental impacts in other BRICS countries are also mounting.

Other than extending the existing problems in BRICS countries, one general and common issue should be emphasised. This relates to the sustainability of its current growth trajectory. This is true in terms of growing inequality, increasing environmental impacts, as well as regional and other imbalances. However, there are some recent changes that may open better future prospects.

All the BRICS countries have an important role to play in shaping the future of the world economy, but China will probably have a more prominent role in this respect. The Chinese system of innovation has been undergoing some changes in order to address two new proclaimed goals: the building of a 'harmonious growth' and the development of 'indigenous innovations'.[9] The harmonious growth aims at reducing the growing social and environmental imbalances. China's emerging 'high-growth with low-carbon' strategy has been emphasised by recent policy decisions, together with measures directed to reduce rural–urban social gaps. The indigenous innovation goal refers to the efforts to make China less reliant on foreign technology through the building of a new kind of relationship between national and foreign players in the process of developing and using new technologies.[10] China is pursuing these goals especially by linking innovation to domestic needs and by giving increased priority to domestic consumption.[11]

For Brazil, India, Russia, and South Africa, Chinese success may lead to strategies towards strengthening domestic technological capabilities and fostering clean technologies. Nevertheless, the differentiated role of the BRICS countries in the configuration of global power and the global economy will in some way constrain the evolution of BRICS national systems for innovation. In addition, their NSIs are highly dependent on their historical development and on how the different domestic actors interpret global developments as well as how they position themselves in the national and international economies. Yet, more flexibility for setting up new industrial and technological policies may be expected.

Introduction to Books 1–5

This book series attempts to cover five themes that are crucial to an understanding of the National System of Innovation of BRICS. The first book *The Role of the State*, edited by Mario Scerri (South Africa) and Helena M.M. Lastres (Brazil) aims at exploring the relationship between the state and the national systems of innovation in BRICS countries. An evolutionary approach has been adopted in order to capture the nature of the state in the respective countries and thus understand the historical and ideological basis for its role in the evolution of the NSI in the five countries. As a background, it is argued that debates on the role of the state in the development process, especially since the 1980s, have often focused on the apparent dichotomy between market-driven and state-driven development. This is a rather wasteful diversion, since it should be accepted as a starting premise that the state is essential to the structural transformation that is required for development.

The second book addresses an aspect of the NSI that is normally absent from the discussion: the relation between innovation and inequality. The objectives of the book *Inequality and Development Challenges*, edited by Maria Clara Couto Soares (Brazil), Mario Scerri and Rasigan Maharajh (South Africa) were to trace the trends in interpersonal and inter-regional inequality within BRICS in an evolutionary perspective and to analyse the co-evolution of inequality and the innovation system to highlight how the various elements of innovation and the production system and inequality mutually reinforce.

The book is driven to improving our understanding of this issue. The inequality concept is considered in its multi-dimensional character, embracing a phenomenon that goes beyond the mere income dimension and is manifested through forms increasingly complex, including, among others, assets, access to basic services, infrastructure, knowledge, as well as race, gender, ethnic, and geographic dimensions. The book adopts the broad approach of the national system of innovation to analyse the relations between BRICS innovation systems and inequality, departing from a co-evolutionary view.

As shown in the book chapters, innovation can affect inequalities in different ways and through distinct trails that are influenced by national conditions, and shaped by public policy interventions. Although innovation does not constitute the main factor of influence on inequality, it is suggested that distinct strategies for technological change may lead to different outcomes in distributive terms, thus either aggravating or mitigating inequality. Based on this understanding, the book corroborates the hypothesis that inequalities need to be explicitly taken into account in development strategies since the benefits of science, technology and innovation are not automatically distributed equally. Therefore, advancing the comprehension of inter-relations between innovation and inequality may be helpful to find ways to shape the national innovation systems so that they reduce rather than increase inequalities.

The third book aims at analysing the contribution of small- and medium-scale enterprises (SMEs) in the national system of innovation. The objective of the book *The Promise of Small and Medium Enterprises*, edited by Ana Arroio (Brazil) and Mario Scerri (South Africa) is to explore three main research goals. In the first place, to provide an overview of the main characteristics of micro, small and medium firms in the Brazilian, Russian, Indian, Chinese and South African national systems of innovation as a basis to examine the contribution of SMEs to the economy of each country. A second goal is to bring to the forefront crucial issues in the discussion of industrial and technological policies for small firms, including the recent evolution and future trends of policies and instruments, their applicability and coordination, as well as a discussion of the macro-economic, legal and regulatory environment. A final research objective is to draw out initiatives to promote innovation in SMEs that address common bottlenecks in BRICS countries and that can contribute to policy design and implementation by these and other countries.

The fourth book discusses the relationship between transnational corporations and the national system of innovation of BRICS countries. In the book *Transnational Corporations and Local Innovation*, edited by José E. Cassiolato (Brazil), Graziela Zucoloto (Brazil), Dinesh Abrol (India), and Liu Xielin (China) the thesis of technological globalisation is taken with some caution, refuting the idea that R&D activities would be inexorably internationalised.

In fact, technological innovative activities in TNCs have been transformed, in relation with the financialisation of transnational corporations (TNCs), as evidenced by the rise of their intangible assets (which includes R&D, patents, and trademarks) and a reorientation of R&D expenditures towards non-scientific activities and very downstream development.

The book chapters present a detailed presentation of the relation of the position and evolution of TNC in the country. Subsequently, there is a discussion on the local factors affecting innovation by TNCs and local firms in the country. Government policy towards TNCs has been important but as the Chinese experience shows, access to local buoyant markets has also been vital. Other issues discussed refer to how the government protects local companies from the competition of TNCs. Spillovers of TNCs to local BRICS enterprises have also been analysed and the immediate conclusion is that there is hardly any convincing evidence regarding either the existence or non-existence of spillovers. An in-depth analysis of outward FDI has also been conducted.

Finally, the fifth book deals with finance and funding in the national system of innovation. The objective was to analyse institutional character and support instruments for the innovation financing process in BRICS, focusing on institutional structure and innovation policy. This book, *Financing Innovation*, edited by Michael Kahn (South Africa) and Luiz Martins de Melo (Brazil) contributes to understanding the varied approaches to the financing of innovation. It draws on the experience of five diverse countries each of which has undergone dramatic structural adjustment in the last two to three decades. The experience of the BRICS countries presents a unique set of case studies of the transition from largely closed centrally planned and state-driven economic and science policy to a more open and market-led situation. The contributing authors examine the varying approaches to the provision of support to the full range of activities that contribute to innovation ranging from scholarship support to doctoral students, to R&D tax incentives and the provision of seed capital.

The significance of financing investments in innovation has been pointed out as an important structural bottleneck that is yet to be solved by the private financial institutions. If, on the one hand, the internationalisation, deregulation and globalisation of financial markets signals the possibility of resources at lower costs, on the other, the characteristics of investments in innovation such as the length of time needed for development, the uncertainty and the risk, point to the need of setting national institutional arrangements.

Notes

1. This is also true in Latin American countries, where it is being applied and understood in close connection with the basic conceptual ideas of the structuralism approach developed in the region since the 1950s under the influence of the Economic Commission of Latin America and Caribbean. In fact, since the mid-1990s, the work of RedeSist — the Research Network on Local Productive and Innovative Systems — based at the Economics Institute of Rio de Janeiro, Brazil, has been using such a dual frame of reference.
2. See, for instance, Mytelka and Farinelli (2003); Freeman (2003); Chesnais and Sauviat (2003).
3. The following data on BRICS countries' value added by sector (per cent of GDP), 1980–2009 is based on the UNCTAD *Handbook of Statistics* (2010).
4. The IBSA Dialogue Forum was established in June 2003 in Brasilia, Brazil.
   BRIC was formally constituted in June 2009 at a summit of the four countries in Yekaterinburg, Russia. In 2011, South Africa joined the group, which changed its denomination to BRICS.
   BASIC of the G4 was formed during the international climate change negotiations in December 2009 in Copenhagen, Denmark.
5. There are several economic and geopolitical factors that restrict a greater convergence of interests among BRICS countries in multilateral negotiations. The analysis of these constraints goes beyond the limited scope of this concept note, but we could cite the aforementioned relatively low degree of trade complementarities between BRICS as an important one.
6. In 2008, Gini indexes were respectively 0.54 and 0.67 according to Brazilian and South African national institutes of statistics.
7. According to World Bank statistics, the population below poverty line was 28.6 per cent in India and 30.9 per cent in Russia in the mid-2000s.
8. It is important to mention that CDIAC-UN data considers only global carbon dioxide emissions from the burning of fossil fuel, but not emissions from deforestation or other greenhouse gases, including methane.

9. See the AeA research team's 'China's Fifteen-year Science and Technology Plan', in Competitiveness Series, *American Electronics' Association*, Vol. 14, April 2007, p. 2.
10. The US Information Technology Office in Beijing refers to indigenous innovation as a term combining three distinct elements: *yuanshi* (original, or genuinely new); *jicheng* (integrated, or combining existing technologies in new ways); and *yinjin* (assimilated, or making improvements to imported technologies). See http://www.usito.org/ (accessed 8 January 2013).
11. In November 2008, China launched a US$ 584 billion anti-cyclical package. According to the HSBC report on climate change (Robins 2009) almost 40 per cent of the total package resources were allocated to 'green' themes. Among others, it combined the search for a lower carbon pattern with the offering of better transport conditions for lower income people placed in rural areas, fostering a niche for the development of innovations capable of attending to the specificities of this domestic market segment.

References

Arocena, R. and J. Sutz, 2003. 'Knowledge, Innovation and Learning: Systems and Policies in the North and in the South', in J. E. Cassiolato, H. M. M. Lastres and M. L. Maciel (eds), *Systems of Innovation and Development: Evidence from Brazil.* Cheltenham: Edward Elgar, 291–310.

Baumann, R., 2009. 'El Comercio entre los Países "BRICS"', LC/BRS/R.210, Comisión Económica para América Latina y el Caribe (CEPAL), Santiago de Chile, August.

Carbon Dioxide Information Analysis Center–United Nations (CDIAC–UN), 2008. 'Global, Regional, and National Fossil-Fuel CO_2 Emissions'. http://cdiac.ornl.gov/trends/emis/overview.html (accessed 1 March 2011).

Cassiolato, J. E. and H. M. M. Lastres, 1999. *Globalização e Inovação Localizada: experiências de sistemas locais no Mercosul.* Brasília: Instituto Brasileiro de Informação em Ciência e Tecnologia.

———, 2008. 'Discussing Innovation and Development: Converging Points between the Latin American School and the Innovation Systems Perspective', Working Paper no. 08-02, Globelics Working Paper Series, The Global Network for Economics of Learning, Innovation, and Competence Building System.

Cassiolato, J. E., H. M. M. Lastres and M. L. Maciel (eds), 2003. *Systems of Innovation and Development: Evidence from Brazil.* Cheltenham: Edward Elgar.

Chesnais, F. and C. Sauviat, 2003. 'The Financing of Innovation-related Investment in the Contemporary Global Finance-dominated Accumulation Regime', in J. E. Cassiolato, H. M. M. Lastres and M. L. Maciel (eds), *Systems of Innovation and Development: Evidence from Brazil*. Cheltenham: Edward Elgar, 61–118.

Economist, *The*, 2010. 'A Special Report on Innovation in Emerging Markets', 15 April.

Freeman, C., 1982. 'Technological Infrastructure and International Competitiveness', Draft Paper submitted to the OECD Ad Hoc Group on Science, Technology and Competitiveness, Organisation for Economic Co-operation and Development, Paris. http://redesist.ie.ufrj.br/globelics/pdfs/GLOBELICS_0079_Freeman.pdf (accessed 24 September 2012).

———, 1987. *Technology Policy and Economic Performance: Lessons from Japan*. London: Frances Pinter.

———, 2003. 'A Hard Landing for the "New Economy"? Information Technology and the United States National System of Innovation', in J. E. Cassiolato, H. M. M. Lastres, and M. L. Maciel (eds), *Systems of Innovation and Development: Evidence from Brazil*. Cheltenham: Edward Elgar, 119–40.

Freeman, C. and C. Perez, 1988. 'Structural Crisis of Adjustment, Business Cycles and Investment Behaviour', in G. Dosi, C. Freeman, R. Nelson, G. Silverberg, and L. L. Soete (eds), *Technical Change and Economic Theory*, London: Pinter, 38–66.

Furtado, C., 1961. *Desenvolvimento e Subdesenvolvimento*. Rio de Janeiro: Fundo de Cultura.

———, 2002. *Capitalismo Global*. São Paulo: Paz e Terra.

Global Environmental Facility, 2008. 'Index Table — Biodiversity'. http://www.thegef.org/gef/node/1805 (accessed 16 February 2011).

Herrera, A., 1975. 'Los Determinantes Sociales de la Politica Cientifica en America Latina', in J. Sábato (ed.), *El Pensamento Latinoamericano en Ciencia-Tecnologia-Desarrollo-Dependencia*. Buenos Aires: Paidos, 98–112.

Hirschman, A., 1958. *The Strategy of Economic Development*. New Haven: Yale University Press.

Instituto de Pesquisa Econômica Aplicada (IPEA), 2008. 'PNAD-2007: Primeiras Análises: Pobreza e Mudança Social', *Comunicados da Presidência*, 1(9), Instituto de Pesquisa Econômica Aplicada, Brasília.

International Monetary Fund (IMF), 2011. 'World Economic Outlook Database', September 2011. http://www.imf.org/external/pubs/ft/weo/2011/02/weodata/index.aspx (accessed 4 October 2011).

Johnson, B. and B.-Å. Lundvall, 2003. 'Promoting Innovation Systems as a Response to the Globalising Learning Economy', in J. E. Cassiolato,

H. M. M. Lastres and M. L. Maciel (eds), *Systems of Innovation and Development: Evidence from Brazil*. Cheltenham: Edward Elgar, 141–84.

Lastres, H. M. M., 1994. *The Advanced Materials Revolution and the Japanese System of Innovation*. London: Macmillan.

Lastres, H. M. M. and J. E. Cassiolato, 2005. 'Innovation Systems and Local Productive Arrangements: New Strategies to Promote the Generation, Acquisition and Diffusion of Knowledge', *Innovation: Management, Policy & Practice*, 7(2): 172–87.

Lastres, H. M. M., J. E. Cassiolato and M. L. Maciel, 2003. 'Systems of Innovation for Development in the Knowledge Era: An Introduction', in J. E. Cassiolato, H. M. M. Lastres and M. L. Maciel (eds), *Systems of Innovation and Development: Evidence from Brazil*. Cheltenham: Edward Elgar, 1–33.

List, F., 1841. *National System of Political Economy*. New York: Cosimo.

Lundvall, B.-Å. 1988. 'Innovation as an Interactive Process: From User-Producer Interaction to the National System of Innovation', in G. Dosi, C. Freeman, R. Nelson, G. Silverberg, and L. L. Soete (eds), *Technical Change and Economic Theory*. London: Pinter, 349–69.

———, 1992. *National System of Innovation: Towards a Theory of Innovation and Interactive Learning*. London: Pinter.

———, 2009. 'The BRICS Countries and Europe', in J. E Cassiolato and V. Vitorino (eds), *BRICS and Development Alternatives: Innovation Systems and Policies*. London: Anthem Press, xv–xxi.

Myrdal, G., 1968. *Asian Drama: An Inquiry into the Poverty of Nations*. London: Penguin Books.

Mytelka, L. K., 2000. 'Local Systems of Innovation in a Globalized World Economy', *Industry and Innovation*, 7(1): 15–32.

Mytelka, L. K. and F. Farinelli, 2003. 'From Local Clusters to Innovation Systems', in J. E. Cassiolato, H. M. M. Lastres and M. L. Maciel (eds), *Systems of Innovation and Development: Evidence from Brazil*. Cheltenham: Edward Elgar, 249–72.

Perez, C. 1983. 'Structural Change and the Assimilation of New Technologies in the Economic and Social System', *Futures*, 15(5): 357–75.

———, 1988. 'New Technologies and Development', in C. Freeman and B.-Å. Lundvall (eds), *Small Countries Facing the Technological Revolution*. London: Pinter, 85–97.

Ravallion, M., 2009. *The Developing World's Bulging (but Vulnerable) 'Middle Class'*. Washington DC: World Bank.

Robins, N., 2009. 'A Climate for Recovery: The Colour of Stimulus Goes Green', HSBC Global Research, http://www.research.hsbc.com (accessed 2 December 2011).

Rodríguez, O., 2001. 'Prebisch: actualidad de sus ideas básicas', *Revista de la CEPAL*, 75: 41–52.

Schumpeter, J. A., 1982 [1912]. *The Theory of Economic Development: An Inquiry into Profits, Capital, Credit, Interest, and the Business Cycle (1912/1934)*. New Jersey: Transaction Books.

United Nations Conference on Trade and Development (UNCTAD), 2009. *UNCTAD Handbook of Statistics 2009*. Geneva; New York: United Nations. http://unctadstat.unctad.org/ReportFolders/reportFolders.aspx (accessed 15 March 2011).

———, 2010. *UNCTAD Handbook of Statistics 2010*. Geneva; New York: United Nations. http://unctadstat.unctad.org/ReportFolders/reportFolders.aspx (accessed 15 March 2011).

United Nations, 2010. 'United Nations Statistical Databases', United Nations Statistic Division. http://unstats.un.org/unsd/databases.htm (accessed 20 March 2011).

———, 2010. 'United Nations Commodity Trade Statistics Database', United Nations Statistic Division. http://comtrade.un.org/ (accessed 20 March 2011).

Wilson, Dominic and Raluca Dragusanu, 2008. 'The Expanding Middle: The Exploding World Middle Class and Falling Global Inequality', Global Economics Paper no. 170, Goldman Sachs, 7 July.

World Bank, 2010. 'World Economic Indicators Database 2010'. http://data.worldbank.org/data-catalog/world-development-indicators (accessed 25 March 2011).

———, 2011. 'World Development Indicators Database 2011'. http://siteresources.worldbank.org/DATASTATISTICS/Resources/GDP_PPP.pdf (accessed 1 July 2011).

1

The State and the Architecture of National Systems of Innovation

Mario Scerri and *Helena M. M. Lastres*

The series of global financial and economic crises which have been escalating since 2008 have caused shock waves not only in the global economy but also in the stance of economic orthodoxy regarding the ideal relationship between the state and the economy. What is now seen as a singular crisis is very much a product of a particular variety of global capitalism, which is historic in its unprecedented closeness to a neoliberal ideal of the minimal state, both at the global and at the national level. At the very least the crisis is now generally seen as a failure of the global regulatory framework vis-á-vis financial markets, and even in this very limited sense the economic role of the state is now being questioned anew by economists, politicians and global civil society. In the case of evolutionary economics and that branch of it which looks at systems of innovation theory, the role of the state as a shaper and mobiliser of systems has consistently been one of the prominent areas of study.

This book provides a comparative analysis of the relationship between the state and the National Systems of Innovation (NSI) of Brazil, Russia, India, China, and South Africa (BRICS) and this chapter seeks to address four issues which we see as germane to this study. The first, and conceptually the most challenging, deals with the very rationale for placing the role of the state in the development of the NSI as a legitimate object of analysis. In the process of arguing for this rationale, we hope to show that the whole discussion of the location of the state in systems of innovation discourse is quite complex and analytically rich. The second issue concerns the particular varieties of the NSI concept which have been adopted in the individual chapters. Although these five studies in this book generally fall within a broad definition of systems of innovation which goes considerably beyond the sphere of science and technology, there are nonetheless differences of emphasis in the application of this concept to individual cases. The third section provides a succinct comparative treatment of the five country cases. Finally, we outline the basis of future research in the area, arguing that the emergence of the BRICS grouping may have possibly laid the foundation for a new discursive formation in studies on the NSI.

There are several cogent reasons for engaging in the analysis of the relationship between the state and the NSI. Primary among these is the fact that if the fabric of the NSI is an institutional web, it is the Weberian (Mannheim 1947) state with its monopoly on violence and legitimate coercion which sets the foundation of rules and regulations, explicitly as sets of legislation, from which this institutional web emerges. It is this foundation of rules and regulations which shapes the evolution of the various institutional sub-systems which constitute the NSI. On this basis, it is therefore legitimate to claim for the nation state the theoretical position of the defining agent of the NSI. The rationale for the assignment of this primacy to the state in the study of NSI stems at least as strongly from the development of thought in the area of the economics of innovation as it does from empirical observation of the role played by governments in the development of systems of innovation.

We must, however, at the outset introduce a sense of misgiving about the very wording of the title of this book, an articulation which was inescapable but which opens up the discourse in this area to what we feel is a mistaken dichotomy between an entity labelled as the state and another as the NSI. This is a dichotomy which is all-pervasive in economics, whatever the ideological stance towards the state, and which pervades a wide range of development approaches. Whether the role of the state is seen to be circumscribed solely by the need to address the presence of public goods and externalities, as in neoclassical economics, or as formed as the agency of the capitalist mode of production, as in most Marxist literature, or as a Foucauldian account of power exercised through governmentality and biopolitics, or as the possible launch pad of development as in most of development literature, the implicit underlying assumption is that of an organic separation of the *body politic* from the *body economic*.[1] This dichotomy has run throughout most of the economic literature on innovation, as it has through mainstream economics, but this was not a necessary outcome of the body of economic theory which came to be loosely defined under the rubric of innovation. This theoretical objection to the separation of the state and the economy echoes a similar disquiet in state theory at the separation of theories of the state from social theory.[2]

The systemic approach to innovation and to the economy in general, which has been adopted in the heterodox economic literature on innovation, contains the basis for a novel integrated study of innovation systems which has to be understood by looking at the various dimensions of economic systems. This perception allows crucial dimensions of the system of innovation approach to be explicitly discussed: the emphasis on historical and national trajectories and the importance of taking into account the production, financial, social, institutional and political contexts, as well as micro, meso and macro spheres.[3]

There are numerous reasons why innovation theory has yet to provide an alternative general theory of economics, not the least of which is its relatively short history combined with the overwhelming hegemony of neoclassical economic theory. In addition, and as argued by a number of authors, a new framework of thought capable of orienting the analyses of development problems related to knowledge, innovation and learning is also fundamental.[4] In this line it could be argued that the attention the performance of BRICS has attracted in the beginning of the millennium — given not only their share of the world product and trade, their reserves of natural resources and of financial capital, the size of their domestic markets, but also their various challenges — can contribute to reinvigorate the interest in development issues and in the comprehension of how knowledge is acquired and diffused, thus enlarging theoretical contributions and the options for policy prescriptions. In addition, the huge task of reducing imbalances in countries of continental dimensions makes tackling regional and social development a core priority of the policy agenda. There are also opportunities for the development of new policy models which foster sustainable and coordinated development at national, regional and local levels. For those institutions which design and implement policies, the pressure for the elaboration and use of concepts, indicators and models which help to reduce the imbalances, instead of reinforcing them, and which bind economic and social development within a long-term perspective become extremely relevant. This reinforces the need to develop new ways of looking at development issues. Policies emerging from this approach would include players, as well as production and innovation activities with different dynamics and paths, varying from the most intensive in terms of knowledge to those that use indigenous and traditional knowledge, as well as with different sizes and functions, deriving from the primary, secondary and tertiary sectors, operating locally, nationally or internationally. In other words, what is required is the development of new and broader forms of knowledge capable of contemplating the reality of all sorts of economies and societies. The theoretical base of this approach enables a fuller understanding of developing countries with the complexity of their ecosystems, biodiversity and mainly their social communities — including ethnic and cultural formations — and their own forms of interaction with nature and culture.

There is one fundamental tenet which provides the initial departure of the approach adopted here from economic orthodoxy and this is the introduction of ideology in this particular economics discourse. We start from the proposition that theories and concepts are not ideologically neutral and that they are, often implicitly, value-laden. They derive from and reflect specific conditions and points of view. Most available concepts and theories are still limited to a restricted group of activities as the set of legitimate objects of economic analysis, and the actors and regions of concern are mainly located within the contexts of developed economies. This makes a number of activities, actors and regions invisible to both theoretical and analytical lenses. This invisibility is implicit in the exclusion of these agents and dimensions from the policy agenda. This exclusion highlights the importance of fostering the capacity to develop and use contextualised concepts, indicators and analytical and policy models capable of addressing the challenges and opportunities of each context given their geopolitical, institutional, scientific, technological, economic, financial, social, cultural, and environmental dimensions. The development of this capacity should simultaneously enable the association and articulation of these dimensions in an inclusive way. Of course, this is not an easy task. The main challenges involved still relate to the difficulty in working with new concepts, particularly those aiming at capturing and evaluating the creation, use and diffusion of innovation and production capabilities in situations of high levels of inequality and informality. However, as knowledge results from interactive learning processes and pragmatic use has an important learning dimension, we also expect that the analysis of the BRICS innovation systems will shed new light not only on these five countries, but also on this concept itself, contributing to its further development.

Another reason why innovation theory has yet to provide an alternative general theory of economics is the wide span of the definitions of the NSI. These can range from a narrow focus on a network of formal science and technology institutions, at one end, to an incorporation of the whole spectrum of formal and informal institutions which come together in partially planned, but mostly unplanned, networks to provide the setting for innovation. Innovation itself may even be defined in its broadest sense to cover any alteration in economic relationships which is seen to be preferable to what is displaced. Within the context of such a broad approach to the understanding of the evolution and performance of economic systems there is a theoretical scope for the elimination of the false dichotomy between the state and the economy. This scope is allowed by the assumption of specificity and the role of history in determining the shape of innovation systems. The propensity to generalise about any group of agents, be it the state, the private sector, civil society, organised labour, etc., is therefore significantly reduced in an approach which holds contextual specificities to be significant non-trivial determinants of the shape and performance of systems of innovation.

Of course, one could argue that an excessive reliance on specificity as the source of understanding of particular systems also holds the danger that each specific NSI as an object of study is treated *sui generis*, bearing little or no relationship whether of similarity or of categorical difference with the studies of other systems. This would obviously eliminate the legitimacy of comparative analysis and eventually of theory. However, except for extreme approaches of this type, the introduction of specificity into analysis does provide the theoretical space for reconceptualising the nature of the concept of the state in relation to that of the NSI. On the other hand, and in line with the argument developed here, it could be argued that all knowledge is contextual. It could also be claimed that the novel understanding of innovation as a systemic social, political and economic process not only requires advances in theory, but also implies the need to develop a whole new set of indicators and categories to analyse and compare experiences.

Since the introduction of the term, the definition of the NSI concept has varied considerably with often radically different implications for analysis and for policy.[5] Generally, these definitions differ on the basis of two elements of the underlying concept. The first is the definition of innovation. This may range from frontier and radical technological innovations at one end, to one which includes any alteration in economic activity which represents a real or perceived 'better practice' within a specific context, at the other. There is obviously room for a large range of variations in-between these two extremes. The other element is the definition and choice of institutions which may be considered as part of the NSI. The inclusion of formal institutions would range from those strictly concerned with the promotion of science and technology at one extreme to all those institutions that govern all aspects of the economy at the other. These two elements are often interrelated where an increasingly broad definition of innovation implies a widening inclusion of institutions which are considered relevant to the NSI and to innovation policy. We should not see the possible variations of the definition of the NSI as lying across a continuum. At some point the degree of exclusion/inclusion that is adopted results in two fundamentally different concepts, with radically different implications for policy. As the definition of the NSI tends towards the system of science and technology, we have to admit the possibility of the non-existence of the NSI and the imperative to create one in the interest of promoting economic growth and development. If, on the other hand, the definition tends towards the all-inclusive one, the NSI exists whether planned or not, simply by virtue of the binding legal identity of the sovereign state. In this case the possibility of the non-existence of the NSI arises only where the state is under threat due to foreign aggression or civil war. Within the broad definition, the role of policy is not to create but to shape the evolution of the NSI along a path that is more appropriate to the sustainable improvement of the quality of life of the general public. Within the broader definition of the NSI, state policies outside the ambits of science and technology policy may still be seen by the analyst as innovation policies. Thus trade, industrial, labour, education and basic services policies may become a legitimate object of the analysis of the relationship between state and the NSI, even if such policies are not explicitly defined as innovation-related by their designers.

It is also important to bear in mind that the question of whether or not to create an NSI becomes less legitimate as we move from the narrow to the broad definition of the concept. It is more relevant to sub-systems but the broader context and the web of informal institutions which comprise the system exist regardless the nature and extent of planning. More relevant is the discussion of what type of NSI to shape through planning and policy and it is here that, in some cases, policy choice is contaminated by the observation of the structure and dynamics of a specific context. Resulting knowledge is formed (and deformed) by this experience. When applied to a different environment this knowledge ends up frequently inducing the reproduction of behaviours and other elements which, while possibly working well in a specific system, prove to be inappropriate for the local conditions and potentialities of another. The main point here is that context matters both in terms of understanding and promoting innovation. History and specific territorial conditions are essential to explain how production and innovation capabilities are acquired, used and further developed. Analytical models, taxonomies and policy prescriptions that disregard these parameters put their usefulness seriously at risk (Lastres and Cassiolato 2005). In other words, 'general history (social, political and cultural) economic history and industrial history are not only indispensable, but really the most important contributors to the understanding of our problem. All other materials and methods statistical and theoretical are only subservient to them and worthless without them' (Freeman 1982: 8, quoting Schumpeter 1939). In a similar line Lundvall (2006) has argued that to develop a general theory of innovation systems that abstracts from time and space would undermine the utility of the concept both as an analytical tool and as a policy tool. One main conclusion here is that by adding new knowledge derived from the observation of new innovation dynamics and contexts, this book can represent a significant analytical and theoretical contribution with even more fundamental policy implications.

In spite of the width of the range of possible variations in the definition of the systems of innovation concept, the central role of the state in the formation of the NSI is always prominent. Even so, however, the various possible combinations that these definitional options offer open up the possibility of variation in the assessment of the role of the state in the development of the NSI. There is also a strong possibility of a divergence between the analyst's definition of the NSI and its definition by the state. This adds yet another dimension to the analysis of the relationship between the state and the various conceptualisations of the NSI. For the purposes of this study, the broader definition of the NSI is adopted. This definition, which goes beyond the analysis of activities that directly determine technological innovation, captures the overall economic framework which sets the context for innovation. Furthermore, the definition of the economic framework itself is expanded beyond the normal ambit of economic orthodoxy to include all aspects of human capital formation as economic strategy variables. This broad approach is particularly relevant to developing economies where fundamental changes in the underlying institutional infrastructure often form the national development policy strategy framework.

Theoretically, the system of innovation approach with its focus on institutions, formal and informal, provides the broader context within which development economics should properly be based. In this case we have a strong possibility of a convergence between science, technology and innovation (STI) policy and development policy, especially if the broader definition of innovation as any novel and demonstrably superior manner (relative to a specified context) of reallocating resources is adopted. The other two areas of convergence between development economics and innovation theory are the issues of regional disparities and income distribution. In the case of the former, the study of sub-national systems of innovation may enable us to understand the process of regional convergence. In the case of income distribution, we have implications for the process of human capital formation which lies at the core of the evolution of the NSI. The basic assumption of development economics is that of the fundamental inadequacy of economic structures to attain specified development and growth objectives. Consequently, development policy should be designed to engineer the radical structural transformation of the economy in pursuit of the goal. From this perspective, broadly articulated NSI theory with its focus on the institutional foundations of economies provides a comprehensive framework for a coherent approach to development policy.

Even if we accept this argument, we still need to ask about the role played by the state, however defined, in the study of the evolution of systems of innovation. After all, it is widely acknowledged that it is firms which produce, diffuse, adopt, adapt, and even deploy innovation. Firms, however, normally tend to act within a context, determined by market structures, established practices and routines, as well as formal regulatory frameworks. They rarely, except in the most exceptional of cases, act consciously and in a coordinated manner to alter the context in which they operate. This context is, to varying degrees, the product of the 'extra-market' policies, rules and regulations laid down by the state, by regional (supranational) bodies and global protocols. Again, it is in the context of developing economies where there is a recognised need for structural transformation that the role of the state in the development of the NSI becomes paramount. This role should generally be more pronounced than in the case of mature, developed industrial economies where we should be able to assume (at least prior to the current global financial crisis) the underlying institutional framework to be stable, under healthy public regulation and appropriate for growth, stability and international competitiveness.

We can therefore comfortably say that, at least at the national level, the state is fundamental in the promotion and shaping of the development path of the NSI, however that is defined. It is the state which usually lays down the formal institutional underpinning of economic activity, including innovation. The broader the definition of the system of innovation and the further it departs from a science and technology system, the more pervasive and complex is the role of the state. In a fundamental sense we can say that the state is ever present in the articulation and enforcement of the "rules of the game" which govern the way in which innovation occurs, the roles of the various agents who interact in the production of innovation, as well as the effects which emanate from innovations of various forms. The rules of the game introduced by the state often tend to be explicit but they can also be implicit in, for example, unspecified tender grant and procurement policies, labour market practices, environmental considerations, macroeconomic policies, etc.[6] Explicit rules, established through laws and declared practices thus also eventually permeate down to the layer of amorphous sets of routines and practices which are probably a stronger long-term determinant of behaviour than explicit rules. Even the most minimal state imaginable, within an extreme form of neoliberal ideology, still sets the 'rules of the game', by virtue of its absence.

The definition of the NSI adopted in this book is generally broad enough to, at least implicitly, allow for some resolution of the fallacious separation of the state and the system of innovation, or even of the economy. This definition extends significantly beyond the system of science and technology to incorporate a wide gamut of institutions, formal and informal, which affect all aspects of innovation. This certainly covers most functions of the modern state, ranging from those specifically concerned with science and technology, to broader concerns of economic policy, to those areas of state involvement which are often assigned to 'social policy' but which directly affect various aspects of human capital formation. In this sense the 'state' which is considered in relation to the innovation system covers almost the entirety of the state and its sphere of governmentality.

The inclusiveness of this approach is certainly firmly within the essence of the systems of innovation approach which highlights the specificities of the institutional interactions within particular systems as crucial to their analysis. It is here that the nature of particular states and their evolution over time has to be brought in as part of the core of the approach adopted in this book. The introduction of history then opens up to a rich and highly diverse treatment of the five NSIs which form the object of this body of analysis. The common structure of the chapters on the one hand belies the rich variety of the form of the state within and without the national systems which they shaped and which in turn shaped them. On the other hand, without a common structure it would have been extremely difficult to come out with a coherent analytical framework for the analysis of this complex relationship within these very different contexts. This commonality may actually bring to the fore the specificity of these five studies which have been brought together in this book.

The case studies of the five national systems of innovation presented are, by virtue of the core nature of the state within a context of structural transformation, closely concerned with policy, with its intentionality, its consequences, intended or otherwise, and with the various political, economic and historical determinants of policy. In this regard we need to discuss the relationship between innovation policy and other spheres of policy which lie within the specifically delineated terrain of state power. Again, this relationship depends critically on the definition of the NSI which is adopted since the extent of the domain of innovation policy is positively correlated with the breadth of the definition of the NSI. The various studies presented here allude to the degree of integration of policies but again this treatment holds nuances regarding whether we are talking about integration between innovation policy and other policies (macroeconomic, investment, trade, labour, and social policies, to name the immediately obvious) and integration within a definition of innovation policy increasingly broadened to incorporate at the limit all other policy spheres. The significance of these nuances depends both on the analyst's theoretical base and on the official explicit or implicit formulation of innovation policy by the principals of the state. In the specific case of the five systems examined here, all of which are undergoing a rapid process of structural transformation, it is important to assess the relationship between innovation policy and development policy, its convergence or dissonance, and even more fundamentally, the degree of differentiation between the two.

The conceptual foundation of this book thus requires that historical analysis permeates all of the case studies and that specific periodisations are adopted in every case. This periodisation is applied both to the evolution of the role of the state and to the history of the political economy of each country. Again, the degree of convergence of the two areas, the extent to which the evolutionary path of the political economy was affected by the changing role of the state and the degree of convergence, and even possibly the identification, of the two evolutionary paths, differ in each case. This, we feel, makes for a particularly rich comparative analysis of these five very distinct innovation systems.

Certainly, the historical and structural differences of the five economies which are the subject of this book are deep enough to raise the question of the rationale for their grouping within the same body of work. This rationale is loosely based on a number of factors whose peculiar heterogeneity may itself prove to be a valid reason for this grouping of case studies. The immediately obvious rationale is that all five countries have had histories where the very nature of the state has been challenged and altered, often violently, a process which has radically altered the very foundations of the NSI. Second, there is the placement of these five economies on the global political economy topography. Each one of them, in its own right, is particularly influential within a region and as a consequence, its fortunes carry implications at a global level. India and China are now rightly seen as the two emerging economic giants, which, in spite of their significant structural differences, are destined to alter dramatically the very foundations of the world economic order. The sheer size of the Brazilian economy and the diversity of its base place it at the epicentre of the Latin American development thrust and indeed at the forefront of the sustained countervailing centre of development economics over the past four odd decades. The Russian system of innovation emerging as it has from the total repudiation of the Soviet system of innovation constitutes the most dramatic experiment of the radical destruction of the foundations of one of the two most powerful systems of innovation, globally, until the late 1980s. South Africa is not only unique in its emergence from a particular legislated form of racial capitalism but its NSI stands as possibly the regional economic catalyst for the possibility of the development leap of sub-Saharan Africa. It is also worth pointing out that in three of these cases an important dimension was the influence of colonialism in the formation of the nation states and their very birth. These diverse histories also affect the placement of the respective analyses contained in this book within the broad definition of the NSI especially when it comes to the focus on specific policy areas.

Several correspondences exist among the innovation systems analysed in this volume. In terms of ruptures and continuities, South Africa and Russia both went through a sudden and radical transformation of their political systems, with the demise of apartheid and the dissolution of the Soviet Union at around the same time. The effects of those political transformations on the respective NSIs, however, may from a normative perspective be seen as diametrically opposite. In the case of South Africa there is a growing body of literature which sees no significant structural rupture with the previous system of innovation accompanying the radical change in the legal basis of the state. This continuity in the evolution of the NSI is now widely seen as one of the main obstacles to the transformation of the South African political economy to an effective, as distinct from the legal, democracy. In the case of Russia, the opposite is often claimed to be true, that the change in the political order brought in too radical a rupture with the previous system of innovation with the rapid emergence of an extreme form of predatory capitalism. The abruptness of this rupture poses one of the major obstacles to the development of a viable NSI. The evolution of the Chinese and the Russian systems of innovation stand in stark contrast in terms of the ruptures and continuities engendered by the respective changes in their ideological underpinning. Other correspondences exist. Thus India and China are both seen as the emerging economic world powers, through a combination of the size of their economies and liberalisation of their economic policies. The 20th century histories of these two systems, and the radically different structures which emerged from those histories, again lay the basis for a comparison of the implications of policy and ideology for the evolution of NSIs.

The thematic organisation of this and accompanying books in this series is aimed at providing a comparative analysis across the five systems of innovation and in that light there is a loosely defined common structure across the five chapters. Each chapter looks at the nature of the state within the specific NSI and presents an overview of the evolutionary path which led to the current relation between the state and the economic system. In the process of this depiction, ruptures and continuities are identified and the relevant periods of analysis delineated. From this general overview of the evolution of the state, each chapter then focuses on the evolution of institutions and policy frameworks directly concerned with innovation policy, with a particular reference to the relationship between innovation policy and broader economic policy. This analysis requires that the specificities of the particular NSI with its particular national, regional and local production and innovation structures are examined. In the process, the main constraints on the viability of the systems of innovation, in terms of their capacity for reproduction, growth and evolution, are identified.[7]

The chapters follow with a description of explicit and implicit state policy on science, technology and innovation, with a classification of such policies into supply-push and demand-pull categories. Explicit policies are defined as those directly designed to affect innovative activity, specifically related to technological innovations and the deployment of innovation in production. Implicit policies are those which affect sectors which appear peripheral to innovation but which nonetheless form the institutional context within which innovation occurs and which governs its impact on the overall economy.

As mentioned earlier, the particular structures of the five cases determine the specific emphasis on the choice of the relevant policy sets in each case. Thus in the case of India, a mixed economy from its post-colonial inception, with the outward expansion after the liberalisation of the economy in the early 1990s and with a recent reversal of the brain and skills drain, the chosen focus is on STI and industrial policies. In the case of Russia — one of the two former main superpowers (militarily, politically, economic, scientific) — the rapid deterioration of the innovation base with the disintegration of the Union of Soviet Social Republics (USSR) and the Council for Mutual Economic Assistance (COMECON) has created probably the most dramatic transformation of an NSI in recent history. In the Russian case, with a heritage of a broad human capital base the main innovation strategy is to restore and retool the scientific base to attain international competitiveness and the focus of that chapter is on the re-orientation of STI policy to achieve that goal. China's opening up to its particular variety of capitalism is creating a novel model of export-oriented industrial growth which is built on a rapid and radical transformation of its NSI and its policy focus is broad as it seeks to leverage the sheer size of the economy for a development leap in the new world order. Brazil, since the beginning of the 2000s, has struggled to recover its capacity to implement and articulate economic and STI policies, after 15 years of liberalisation that has both impoverished the capacity to design and implement policies and resulted in the destruction of industrial and technological capabilities in sectors such as information and telecommunications and auto parts. In the case of South Africa, the impact of the apartheid legacy is most evident in its systematically impoverished human capital base and the main focus of the South African chapter is on the extent to which post-apartheid economic policy and innovation policy have been congruent and suited for development.

Within this policy framework, the national integration of the innovation system is assessed in terms of the forms of the relationships and interactions of policy between the national and sub-national levels of government. This analysis seeks to identify coordination mechanisms and impediments to coherent coordination mechanisms among the various levels. One particular area of concern in the assessment of the viability of systems of innovation is the development of human capital (or human capabilities). As the definition of the NSI broadens away from that of a system of science and technology, so does that of the relevant human capital base. The centrality assigned to this particular component of the system of innovation rests on the core role which technological capabilities play in the evolution of systems. The long-term investment and appropriability characteristics of human capital development have a particular relevance to the role of the state in shaping the evolutionary path of the system of innovation. Policies in this area, especially when we adopt a broad definition of the constituents of human capital and move it away from an instrumentalist neoclassical definition, could be enhanced if they advanced from the traditional supply-push and demand-pull approach to an effective systemic approach. Finally, each chapter ends with an assessment of the effects of state policy on the respective NSI. Given the complex nature of the relationship between the state and the NSI, this can only be, at best, a tentative assessment taking some specific policy targets as the reference point. On the basis of this assessment, a brief listing of recommendations for the future of state policy in this regard is provided.

At this relatively initial stage of the research on the role of the state and the NSI, as reported in this book, we have five independent chapters for each of the BRICS countries. This constitutes the first assessment of this topic for the five cases but it is as yet only a stage towards a full comparative analysis of the theme across the five systems. At this stage the outlines of such a comparative analysis can only be sketched in this introductory chapter through a summation of the main findings for each country's system of innovation.

At a global level, innovation policy, as distinct from science and technology policy, and the NSI policy framework only entered into the lexicon of national policy makers in the early 1990s and the history of innovation surveys date from that period. Thus, in this sense, innovation policy set within the NSI theoretical framework is generally young. In this book we consider a different measure of age — that of the current form of the systems of innovation themselves, while taking into account those global and regional changes which define the context within which the global economy evolves. In the assessment of the age of a specific form of a system of innovation we have to identify ruptures in its evolution and we have to judge the extent to which a particular rupture represents such a dramatic break that an entirely new phase emerges. The most obvious cause of such radical ruptures is an overthrowing of an established political order which brings about a new legal definition of the nation state and of the NSI. Other, less radical ruptures originate from a paradigmatic change in the ideological base of the political system. Such assessments are obviously inevitably highly contestable but the very fact that they are so makes them a rich ground for research. In terms of this measure of age, therefore, the present form of the Indian system of innovation dates from its independence in 1947. In Brazil it could be said that the only real rupture was colonisation, which started in 1500. All subsequent transformations — independence in 1822 and the inauguration of the republic in 1889 — could be characterised as soft changes, most of them aiming to allow the maintenance of the status quo since they do not entail the radical politico-legal redefinition of the nation state base of the system of innovation. Thus the ruptures, particularly in the case of Brazil but also of China, are relatively 'softer' since they do not entail the radical politico-legal redefinition of the nation state base of the system of innovation. In the case of China, the progressive shifts in economic policy since the late 1970s, culminating in its relatively recent massive emergence on the global markets, dramatic as it may have been, still occurred within the context of a generally stable politico-legal structure. Russia and South Africa possibly constitute the youngest systems whose current structure and form dates from the radical political change of the early 1990s. In the case of Russia the dismantling of the communist state also resulted in the fragmentation of the USSR and of its wider political economic domain within the COMECON region. The total redefinition, not only of the governance system but of the political and geographic terrain of the nation state certainly resulted in the emergence of a new NSI. In the case of South Africa the rift was marked by the demise of apartheid and the creation of the first South African democratic state; there is however a strong sense of reservation, expressed in the chapter on South Africa, about the degree to which the political rupture was accompanied by an equivalent shift in the evolutionary path of the system of innovation. However, and as stressed earlier, one cannot ever ignore the time span of history and the very fact that the old forms which mark these systems' inheritance profoundly affect the shape of the subsequent new forms of systems. The chapters of South Africa and Russia serve as exemplary cases in this sense. They both identify problems which have their origin in the old forms of their respective systems of innovation as main challenges to the development of the current new forms of their systems.

The periodisation discussed in the five chapters also provides the reader with another dimension of age, that of innovation policy. The chapter on Brazil identifies three main enduring deficiencies of innovation policy. These are the excessive focus on technological innovations, the exclusive targeting of the partnership between enterprises and science and technology institutions as the vehicle for innovation and the adoption of the linear model of innovation as the informing vision for innovation policy. It is worth pointing out the aim of consolidating the Brazilian system of innovation, as well as of linking STI, industrial, social, and other policies as main objectives of the policy discourse adopted since 2007, even if it is not yet possible to perceive any effective systemic vision put into practice. In the case of the Russian system of innovation the turmoil of the breakdown of the USSR and the initial swing to a *laissez faire* capitalism retarded the adoption of innovation policy at pace with other industrial countries. The adoption of a comprehensive innovation policy and its integration with other economic policies only started in the mid-2000s. The chapter on Russia identifies a number of current obstacles to the implementation of an effective innovation policy. Generally, these obstacles are due to the relegation of innovation policy as secondary to broader economic policy currently dealing with the impact of the global financial crisis. This has set back the integration of innovation policy into the broader development policy framework. Specifically, the single most significant obstacle to the development of the Russian system of innovation is identified as the low demand for innovation by private sector enterprises, itself perhaps a testimonial to the effects of the unplanned transition to a market economy from the central planning model of the USSR. In the case of India, the overall policy of self-reliance adopted since independence until the liberalisation move in the early 1990s strongly promoted supply-side explicit science and technology policies but the absorption of innovation is also considered to have been retarded by a demand-side failure. Innovation policies are still fragmented and persistent low R&D ratios and low rate of human capital development still pose significant obstacles to the development of the Indian system of innovation. In the three decades since the political shift in the late 1970s, China, starting from a low innovation base has seen progressive shifts transferring science and technology functions from state institutions to enterprises, deepening the indigenous innovation base and moving innovation progressively from cost-reducing to product innovations. The identified constraints to the development of a viable NSI are mainly due to the ongoing process of transition to a market-oriented economy within the context of a single-party socialist governance structure. The main constraints are the lack of integration of the science and technology sector with other sections of the economy and a low human capital base. In the case of post-apartheid South Africa, the first innovation policy articulation was explicitly based on the NSI theoretical framework. However, the overall neoliberal macroeconomic planning framework which was simultaneously implemented, and the policy context which it produced, has prevented the integration of innovation policy with other economic policies. As such, therefore, there is still an absence of a comprehensive innovation policy. The failure to address the crippling human capital deficit inherited from apartheid is probably the single most significant impediment to the attainment of a viable system of innovation in South Africa. Though there is now recognition of this policy failure and a determination to address it in a comprehensive approach, it is still too recent a shift to enable a proper assessment of the significance in practice of this shift. The policy recommendations which are provided in each case flow directly from the respective assessments of the major fault lines in each of the BRICS countries' system of innovation. It is interesting to note the similarities in the recommended policy measures among these disparate political economies which still exhibit a striking number of common features in their national systems of innovation.

Finally, we need to come back to the initial issue of the theoretical validity of the study of the systems of innovation of the BRICS economies. We will have to interrogate the degree to which this study constitutes, along with the other books in this series, the basis for the emergence of a new discursive formation which may provide the scope for an ensuing and expanding distinct field of enquiry.[8] This interrogation will have to proceed in a cascade from general theory to specific application. The general theory in this case is that which underlies the concept of systems of innovation. We can start from the assumption that this body of work already constitutes an established discursive formation which now offers the possibility for the emergence of an alternative theory of economics. The next level will be to enquire whether the grouping of the systems of innovation of the BRICS constitutes an identifiable and uniquely distinct space for the development of the possibility for a distinct body of emerging knowledge. This possibility stems from the combination of three factors — the commonalities in the characteristics of the BRICS systems of innovation, the commonalities of the presence of the BRICS economies in the global economy and their ability to form a new significant economic power bloc of the 'south', the conditions for the possibility that the commonalities among the BRICS systems of innovation constitute a new empirical, but more importantly a theoretical, specificity in systems of innovation theory. The last condition is possibly the most crucial one, given the basis for the inductive origin of the bulk of innovation theory as we know it.

Unlike neoclassical economics, innovation theory, starting from the massive case studies project initiated by the Science Policy Research Unit (SPRU) at Sussex University, and its particular articulation as a system of innovation theory, is decidedly evidence-based theorising. It emerged from a growing sense of disquiet at the failure to explain the residual in growth accounting and gradually grew as its own discursive formation from the growing body of observations in the field. There is consequently always the possibility that a new body of empirical evidence may alter theory and in the process provide the basis for the emergence of a new discursive formation. In a rapidly changing global political economy, the conglomeration of the BRICS systems of innovation as an area of study may well prove to be a case which goes beyond a simple application of an existing body of theory to new empirical terrain. It may affect how we conceive of the theory of innovation systems and open up new theoretical explorations. We hope that this book, and the others in this series, will provide a step in that direction.

Notes

1. One important exception is the work of the so-called Latin American Structuralist School. See, for instance, Furtado (1964).
2. 'Theorizing the state is further complicated because, despite recurrent tendencies to reify it as standing outside and above society, there can be no adequate theory of the state without a theory of society' (Jessop 2008: 1).
3. For details, see Freeman (2003); Lastres et al. (2003); Lundvall (2006).
4. See, for instance, Arocena and Sutz (2003).
5. '[T]he network of institutions in the public and private sectors whose activities and interactions initiate, import, modify and diffuse new technologies' (Freeman 1987).

   '[T]he elements and relationships which interact in the production, diffusion and use of new, and economically useful, knowledge ... and are either located within or rooted inside the borders of a nation state' (Lundvall 2010: 2).

'[A] set of institutions whose interactions determine the innovative performance ... of national firms' (Nelson 1993).

'[T]he national institutions, their incentive structures and their competencies, that determine the rate and direction of technological learning (or the volume and composition of change generating activities) in a country' (Patel and Pavitt 1994).

'[T]hat set of distinct institutions which jointly and individually contribute to the development and diffusion of new technologies and which provides the framework within which governments form and implement policies to influence the innovation process. As such it is a system of interconnected institutions to create, store and transfer the knowledge, skills and artefacts which define new technologies.' (Metcalfe 1995).

6. The literature on technology and development has stressed that economic conditions, in general, and macroeconomic policies, in particular, are important elements shaping microeconomic behaviour and dynamics as far as innovation and technology are concerned. It has been also argued that these so-called implicit policies can assume greater importance than specific technology policies in terms of orienting firms' strategies (Herrera 1975).
7. 'Reproduction is essential for the survival of a system, while (steady state) growth implies that the current shape of a specific system of innovation is well suited to its broader environment. There are various measures that may be used to estimate these two dynamic processes, depending of the breadth of the definition of systems of innovation. They may range from those pertaining specifically to systems of science, technology and innovation to those which reflect the wider political economy. The evolution of systems takes two forms. The first is essentially reactive in the sense that the mutation of the system responds to a changing environment. To use the biological analogy, this type of evolution is Darwinian. The other type, drawing on a Lamarckian analogy, is a conscious mutation, based on feedback effects, which alters the environment within which the system is set; it is initiative rather than reactive.' (Scerri 2009: 37).
8. Variava (1989: 50) describes the conditions for a discursive formation as follows:

'[A] discourse can be seen as a system of possibility which allows statements to be made which will either be true or false. This makes possible a field of knowledge. The rules of discourse ... provide the preconditions for the formation of statements. Foucault formulates four hypotheses in terms of which he attempts to identify and to isolate a discursive formation:

- a discursive formation is identifiable if the statements in it refer to the same object;
- a discursive formation has a regular "style", a common way in which statements are made;
- a discursive formation is identifiable if the concepts in the statements have a constancy;
- a discursive formation exists if all the statements support a common theme, or what Foucault calls in his later books a "strategy", a common institutional or political pattern.'

References

Arocena, R. and J. Sutz, 2003. 'Knowledge, Innovation and Learning: Systems and Policies in the North and in the South', in J. E. Cassiolato, H. M. M. Lastres and M. L. Maciel (eds), *Systems of Innovation and Development: Evidence from Brazil.* Cheltenham: Edward Elgar, 291–310.

Cassiolato, J. E., H. M. M. Lastres and M. L. Maciel (eds), 2003. *Systems of Innovation and Development: Evidence from Brazil.* Cheltenham: Edward Elgar.

Furtado, C., 1964. *Development and Underdevelopment.* Berkeley: University of California Press.

Freeman, C., 1982. 'Technological Infrastructure and International Competitiveness', Draft Paper submitted to the OECD Ad Hoc Group on Science, Technology and Competitiveness, Organisation for Economic Co-operation and Development, Paris. http://redesist.ie.ufrj.br/globelics/pdfs/GLOBELICS_0079_Freeman.pdf (accessed 24 September 2012).

———, 1987. *Technology Policy and Economic Performance: Lessons from Japan.* London; New York: Pinter.

———, 2003. 'A Hard Landing for the "New Economy"? Information Technology and the United States National System of Innovation', in J. E. Cassiolato, H. M. M. Lastres and M. L. Maciel (eds), *Systems of Innovation and Development: Evidence from Brazil.* Cheltenham: Edward Elgar, 119–40.

Herrera, A., 1975. 'Los Determinantes Sociales de la Politica Cientifica en America Latina', in J. Sábato (ed.), *El Pensamento Latinoamericano en Ciencia-Tecnologia-Desarrollo-Dependencia.* Buenos Aires: Paidos, 98–112.

Jessop, B., 2008. *State Power: A Strategic-Relational Approach.* Cambridge: Polity Press.

Lastres, H. M. M. and J. E. Cassiolato, 2005. 'Innovation Systems and Local Productive Arrangements: New Strategies to Promote the Generation, Acquisition and Diffusion of Knowledge', *Innovation: Management, Policy & Practice*, 7(2): 172–87.

Lastres, H. M. M., J. E. Cassiolato and M. L. Maciel, 2003. 'Systems of Innovation for Development in the Knowledge Era: An Introduction', in J. E. Cassiolato, H. M. M. Lastres and M. L. Maciel (eds), *Systems of Innovation and Development: Evidence from Brazil*. Cheltenham: Edward Elgar, 1–33.

Lundvall, B.-Å., 2006. 'National Innovation System: Analytical Policy Device and Policy Learning Tool', Department of Business Studies, Aalborg University, Denmark, 1–19.

———, 2010. 'Introduction', in B.-Å. Lundvall (ed.), *National Innovation Systems: Towards a Theory of Innovation and Interactive Learning*, London: Anthem Press, 1–20.

Mannheim, K. (ed.), 1947. *From Max Weber: Essays in Sociology*. London: Kegan Paul.

Metcalfe, S., 1995. 'The Economic Foundations of Technology Policy: Equilibrium and Evolutionary Perspectives', in P. Stoneman (ed.), *Handbook of the Economics of Innovation and Technological Change*. Oxford: Blackwell, 52–89.

Nelson, R. R (ed.), 1993. *National Innovation Systems: A Comparative Analysis*. Oxford: Oxford University Press.

Patel, P. and K. Pavitt, 1994. 'The Nature and Economic Importance of National System of Innovations', *STI Review*, 14, Organisation for Economic Co-operation and Development, Paris, 9–32.

Scerri, M., 2009. *The Evolution of the South African System of Innovation Since 1916*. Newcastle: Cambridge Scholars Publishing.

Schumpeter, J. A., 1939. *Business Cycles: A Theoretical, Historical and Statistical Analysis of the Capitalist Process*. New York and London: McGraw-Hill.

Variava, R., 1989. 'The Deployment of Racism in South Africa'. Unpublished Ph.D. Dissertation, University of Cambridge.

2

Brazil

Priscila Koeller and *José Luis Gordon*

The adoption of the broad concept of a national system of innovation leads to the discussion on the connection between innovation policy and development policy. Once the political-institutional and geopolitical sub-systems, the sub-systems of policies and representations and the sub-systems of social and economic demand are all comprised in the definition of the national innovation system, it becomes essential to consider the social disparities and heterogeneities in the analyses of innovation policy, in addition to the productive/innovative sub-system.

This connection is even more relevant in a context of underdevelopment, marked by structural (productive and social) heterogeneity. In this case, development policies should determine the strategies that permeate other economic policies. Development policies will necessarily impact the others because if they exist they will manage these structural heterogeneities, and consequently will affect the other policies, and if they are absent, they leave the treatment of these heterogeneities to other policies.

It is worth noting that the concept of development used here emerges from the requisite to overcome the historical conditions of Latin American countries. According to Cassiolato and Lastres (2008), three main characteristics can describe the development process. First, the process is characterised by changes in the social and economic structure. Second, development is a systemic process (this characteristic of development implies the importance of interactions between parts of the national innovation system [NSI] along the learning process). The third attribute of development is the country's specificities in this process, which means that the development process is unique to each country. The Latin American structuralist school — particularly its main contributors, Celso Furtado and Raúl Prebisch — emphasises that the heterogeneity of the social and economic structures in Latin American societies must be considered in the formulation of their development policies. Without this perception, both the structures and the logic that reproduce underdevelopment would persist. These authors identify underdevelopment as an autonomous process, with its intrinsic logic, and not as a stage in a path towards development. Therefore, the development process is not seen as a convergent movement of underdeveloped economies to developed ones. Underdevelopment is considered an autonomous and historical process in a country. The elaboration of specific policies, aimed at breaking the logic that reproduces underdevelopment, constitutes the main role of the state. The requirement of thinking of innovation policy as integrated to development policy, once innovation is recognised as the motor of economic growth, is related to the fact that such growth will not automatically imply development. In order to reach development, the innovation policy must be integrated to the development policy, which should be specific to the context of underdevelopment and, therefore, distinct from the prescriptions provided by developed countries.

Several neo-Schumpeterian authors — particularly Albuquerque, Cassiolato, Lastres, and Viotti, among others in Latin America — have been contributing in recent years to an approach that combines the structuralist and the Schumpeterian schools. This approach makes it possible to include the social issue in the debates on innovation and to start discussing policies that are appropriate for underdeveloped countries. Since 1996, Freeman has claimed that the only way to guarantee that underdeveloped countries will 'reach' those which are developed, in terms of standards of living, is by satisfying two essential conditions: the innovation system should respond to social and economic demands; and the economy should respond to both institutional changes and social policies (Freeman 1996: 34).

In connection with heterogeneities in the social structure, there is also the issue of regional heterogeneity. Particularly in Brazil, regional inequalities are marked by the concentration of productive, scientific and technological structures, as well as of income. Internally, such regions reproduce the social inequalities (of income) and the disparities of the productive structure of the country.

The analysis of innovation policy in Brazil should, therefore, consider the context of underdevelopment and the asymmetries related to it in its productive, social and regional structures. Even when dealing with an explicit innovation policy, with respect to the innovative and productive sub-system, other dimensions of the policy must be considered, especially the social one.

This chapter is structured in five parts. In the first of these, the historical evolution of the innovation policy is presented, with emphasis on the relations and on the dichotomies between state and market, delimiting the period of analysis of innovation policy in Brazil to the post-2006 period.[1] The second part presents a synthesis of the main institutions, programmes and mechanisms of the explicit innovation policy in the ambit of the federal government. The third part discusses the limits and the difficulties in the structure of the national system of innovation in Brazil, considering mainly the implicit policies in the country. The explicit innovation policy is presented in the fourth part, where the implicit policies are also highlighted as well as the difficulty of articulating these with the explicit policy — particularly the policy of education. In the fifth part, we discuss the goals proposed in the scope of the federal government's innovation policy for the period under analysis.

Evolution of the Current Form of State

After World War II — in the 1950s — Brazil experienced a phase where the state guided the development policy based on an industrialisation model that, at first, prescribed the establishment of state enterprises financed by international funds.

This role of the state, which contributed to promote industrialisation, was based on the idea that it was necessary to establish the scientific and technological infrastructure and the industrial foundations in the country. Since the beginning of the 20th century, the state sought to create an organisational infrastructure for R&D restricted mainly to the agricultural and biomedical areas. After this phase, the main concern was establishing sectoral R&D within organisations. Examples of these organisations were Petrobrás (the Brazilian Oil Company created in 1953 as a state-owned enterprise with the main objective of exploring Brazilian oil and which nowadays is the fifth most important oil company in the world), the Aerospace Technical Centre (Centro Técnico Aeroespacial, CTA, established in 1954) and the National Institute for Space Research (Instituto Nacional de Pesquisas Espaciais, INPE, founded in 1961).

Between the end of the 1950s and the beginning of the 1960s, in spite of structuralist arguments, this model was supplanted by a new one based on the attraction of foreign capital enterprises with the purpose of importing industrial technology emerging from the 'second industrial revolution' — the objective, then, was 'skipping development stages'. In order to finance the industrialisation process, the so-called (and well-known) model of imports substitution was adopted.

At that moment, the state employed an innovation policy based on the idea that it would be possible to 'skip stages' for reaching development, relying very much on foreign capital and technology.[2] Such an idea was opposed at that time by the nationalist vision of the structuralist school, which emphasised the importance of embedding technology in the productive structure, and considered underdevelopment as an autonomous process rather than a stage towards development.

On the assumption that the state must lead the innovation policy, the federal government decided to set up another important organisation in order to promote research and development within a strategic field for the country — agriculture. In 1972, based on the experience of the country in this field since the end of the 19th century, the Brazilian Agricultural Research Corporation (EMBRAPA) was created. This enterprise was very important for the development of technologies suited to tropical agribusiness and enabled Brazilian producers to be among the most productive ones in terms of international parameters.

The model of imports substitution industrialisation, in spite of its relative success (once it effectively promoted the industrialisation of the country) and the expressive rates of growth in the gross domestic product (GDP) (Table 2.1), has subsequently been the target of many criticisms. The main downside comes from the fact that the country remained 'closed' for too long, with its enterprises protected against international competition, which resulted in a relative technological backwardness and, consequently, loss of international competitiveness.

Table 2.1: *Real Growth Rate of Gross Domestic Product (GDP), 1950–1980*

Period	*GDP–Real Growth Rate (% p.a.)*	*Period*	*GDP–Real Growth Rate (% p.a.)*	*Period*	*GDP–Real Growth Rate (% p.a.)*
1950	6.80	1960	9.40	1970	10.40
1951	4.30	1961	8.60	1971	11.34
1952	7.30	1962	6.60	1972	11.94
1953	4.70	1963	0.60	1973	13.97
1954	7.80	1964	3.40	1974	8.15
1955	8.80	1965	2.40	1975	5.17
1956	2.90	1966	6.70	1976	10.26
1957	7.70	1967	4.20	1977	4.93
1958	10.80	1968	9.80	1978	4.97
1959	9.80	1969	9.50	1979	6.76

Source: IBGE (Brazilian Institute of Geography and Statistics) website, http://www.sidra.ibge.gov.br/bda/cnt/default.asp?z=t&o=15&i=P (accessed 19 October 2011). Authors' elaboration.

One of the main targets of this criticism was the information technology policy adopted in the 1980s which, rather differently in relation to other segments of economic activity, had its development based on firms of domestic capital. The model has been criticised because it was unable to produce internationally competitive 'information technology', as the domestic production was considered relatively 'obsolete'. However, the critics neglected the building up of human resource capabilities that resulted from this process, as well as the constitution of enterprises that turned the country into a leader in some technologies, such as bank automation.

As a consequence of such criticisms, in the 1990s the market took the leadership of the accumulation process and the state withdrew substantively from the economic environment. From this moment on, neoliberal ideas started ruling the policies of the federal government, also following the global tendency to embrace neoliberalism. In the face of this new logic, measures began to be taken aiming at the reduction of the role of the state in the economy. Privatisation, trade liberalisation and financial liberalisation, among other measures, were implemented throughout this decade. Measures such as the quick withdrawal of non-tariff barriers and suppression of trade tariffs were adopted, without the creation, at least not immediately, of any filter or policy for protecting the enterprises and the economic activities developed in the country.[3] The logic underlying all this was that market failures are less significant than the failures of state intervention.

The consequence of these market-led policies was what became known as the 'two lost decades' — the decades of the 1980s and 1990s — because of their relatively low or even decreasing GDP growth rates, which may be seen in Table 2.2.

Table 2.2: *Real Growth Rate of Gross Domestic Product (GDP) and Inflation Rate (IPCA), 1980–1990*

Period	*GDP–Real Growth Rate (% p.a.)*	*IPCA–Extended Consumer Price Index Growth Rate (% p.a.)*
1980	9.20	99.3
1981	–4.25	95.6
1982	0.83	104.8
1983	–2.93	164.0
1984	5.40	215.3
1985	7.85	242.2
1986	7.49	79.7
1987	3.53	363.4
1988	–0.06	980.2
1989	3.16	1972.9
1990	–4.35	1621.0
1991	1.03	472.7
1992	–0.54	1119.1
1993	4.92	2477.2
1994	5.85	916.50
1995	4.22	22.40
1996	2.20	9.56
1997	3.40	5.23
1998	0.00	1.66
1999	0.30	8.94
2000	4.30	5.97

Source: IBGE (Brazilian Institute of Geography and Statistics) website, http://www.sidra.ibge.gov.br/bda/cnt/default.asp?z=t&o=15&i=P (accessed 19 October 2011). Authors' elaboration.

Furthermore, this policy became known as the 'stop and go' policy, characterised by an environment of high monetary instability and high inflation rates. Thus, whenever the growth rates became positive and exceeded 5 per cent and inflation rates accelerated, plans for stabilisation were adopted for slowing down the GDP growth. In the 1990s, following the 'Real Plan' (*Plano Real*) of 1994 (Plan for Economic Stabilisation), a regime of inflation targeting was adopted with its main instruments being restrictive monetary and fiscal policies, and its unique objective of holding back the inflation rate. We can see in Table 2.2 that the Real Plan succeeded, because after 1995 the inflation rate fell to a new level, although this was accompanied by a low growth of GDP.

In spite of the mediocre growth rates of the economy and a big deficit in the trade balance that accompanied it, the market continued to lead both the accumulation process and the industrial and innovation policy, which continued to be neglected by the federal government until the end of the 1990s.

The federal government returned to the inclusion of innovation in the policy agenda in 1999, although it was restricted to the Ministry of Science and Technology (MS&T). In 1999, sectoral funds were created aimed primarily to finance partnerships between the production sector and the institutions of science and technology. These funds were conceived following the diagnosis that Brazil had attained the consolidation of a wide and competent scientific and technological infrastructure, but was unable to establish an innovative production sector. In order to change this situation, it would be necessary to foster the links between the two segments of the national innovation system. Many analyses show, however, that by the end of 2006 the merit of the sectoral funds was limited to re-establish the budget of the MS&T back to the amounts available in 1995.[4]

With the creation of the sectoral funds, the MS&T started the formulation of the National Policy of Science, Technology and Innovation. The latter has instituted, or designed, mechanisms and instruments that were first implemented in the period 1999–2006. The most important among them, in addition to the sectoral funds, were the mechanisms for equalisation of interest rates and for economic subvention to firms. At the end of 2003, the new federal government of President Lula also launched the Industrial, Technological and Foreign Trade Policy (PITCE — *Política Industrial, Tecnológica e de Comércio Exterior*). For the first time in two decades the federal government was able, again, to make use of the term 'industrial policy'.

In this period, the state again took the lead in innovation policy making, by creating new instruments aiming at affecting innovation strategies of firms and positively influencing economic activity. Nevertheless, we may say that the intervention of the federal government was reticent, since it constituted a modest participation of the state in economic decisions and in defining priorities. Indeed, the PITCE did not set specific mechanisms and instruments for its implementation, which was based on those established by the Policy of Science, Technology and Innovation.

The Policy for Production Development (PDP) launched in the second term of President Lula, on the other hand, aimed at avoiding the problems of coordination shown by PITCE, by creating a structure of governance that was specially concerned with articulating the actions of the various ministries — particularly the Ministries of Science and Technology and of Development, Industry and Foreign Trade.

From a neo-Schumpeterian perspective of innovation policy, the launch of PITCE and PDP by the federal government can be deemed an advance, since it allows a clear reference to a necessary integration between the industrial policy and the scientific and technological policy. Although the National Policy of Science, Technology and Innovation was launched in the period 1999–2002, its political agenda remained restricted to the Ministry of Science and Technology in view of the resistance within the Ministry of Economy towards an industrial policy. This led to some delays in the creation and implementation of instruments that were devised in that period — for instance, the economic subvention.

Although they are seen as advancements, PITCE and PDP still do not incorporate the debate on integration of the remaining policies that comprise other NSI sub-systems as, for instance, educational, macroeconomic and social development policies. These three lines of implicit policies have, in the Brazilian case, significant impacts on the innovation system.

Failing to integrate innovation into these policies makes evident the division that prevails in the ambit of the federal government between the discussions on innovation policy and on development policy. Such a lack of connections leads to missed opportunities with respect to the reduction of structural heterogeneities.

The extent of the academic debate and the advances in innovation policies bring evidence to the relevance of an integrated perspective of NSI, as the aim of the innovation policy is to effectively impact such a system and not only isolated agents. To face this, the integration of the innovation policy to other policies is required, together with actions which take into account the relevance of a development vision that will set the strategic guidelines for such integration. It is not a matter of reproducing an 'old-fashioned' way of policy making, but rather of devising a new way that is appropriate to the local specificities as, indeed, the neo-Schumpeterian school recommends.

Periodisation and analysis of institutions and policies of the state concerned with innovation

The periodisation, starting in the 1990s, established for the innovation policy in the ambit of the federal government, points to the government's choice for policies of a neoliberal character. Within this policy trend, innovation policy as such was not even tolerated (1994–1998) and, when the government decided to adopt one, it seemed inspired by the narrow concept of a national innovation system (practically limited to university–industry relations). In consequence, the innovation policy was restricted to the MS&T without connections to other government policies.

The genealogy of the innovation policy reflects such a neoliberal option by the government which fails to incorporate the advancements of both the academic debate on the innovative process and of policies implemented by other countries. This analysis also reflects the disconnection between the innovation policy and other implicit policies such as education and development, since, during the period studied, no integration was observed. The federal budget shows that only a few ministries have made significant expenditures aimed explicitly at innovation policy.[5]

The present analysis of policies and actions implemented in the ambit of the federal government is restricted to the performance of three institutions — the Ministry of Science and Technology (*Ministério da Ciência e Tecnologia*, MCT); the Ministry of Development, Industry and Foreign Trade (*Ministério do Desenvolvimento,*

Indústria e Comércio Exterior, MDIC); and the Brazilian Federal Agency for the Support and Evaluation of Graduate Education (*Coordenação de Aperfeiçoamento de Pessoal de Nível Superior*, CAPES), subordinate to the Ministry of Education (MEC) —which present the highest expenditures and which hold policies and strategic guidelines that explicitly acknowledge the importance of innovation. The analysis of these departments also comprises their subordinate agencies which played a fundamental role in the implementation of the innovation policy. These institutions — Studies and Projects Funding Agency (*Financiadora de Estudos e Projetos*, FINEP), National Council of Scientific and Technological Development (*Conselho Nacional de Desenvolvimento Científico e Tecnológico*, CNPq), both linked to MCT, and the National Bank of Economic and Social Development (*Banco Nacional de Desenvolvimento Econômico e Social*, BNDES), linked to MDIC — are primarily related to the provision of funds and to the promotion of innovation.

The period of analysis extends from 2006 to 2010.[6] The objective is to understand and critically analyse the main measures adopted as well as the evolution and trends of resource allocation throughout the period in question. In order to do so, the institutions and organisations under analysis will be presented according to their chronology of creation. There is a sequence of main trends in terms of the establishment of the innovation policy: in short, first the importance of science and technology policy (in the 1950s), second, of industrial policy (in the 1960s) and third, of innovation policy in a broad sense (from 2000 onwards). Two important ministries will be presented, the MS&T and the Ministry of Industry; and also CAPES, the agency subordinate to the Ministry of Education. The following descriptions will only highlight the programmes and agencies related to innovation policy.

The Ministry of Science and Technology

The Ministry of Science and Technology was created in 1985, in recognition of the relevance of this issue for the country. It is currently the main department of the federal government responsible for implementation of the explicit innovation policy. In 1999, following a long period without an explicit policy on innovation, a new policy was instituted with the creation of the sectoral funds

— resource funds that would allow the ministry to restore budget resources and to set up the new policy.[7]

In addition, the ministry has a significant participation in the industrial policies, PITCE and PDP, which comprise the explicit innovation policies in the ambit of the federal government.[8]

From 2003 on, the ministry managed to successfully submit a number of Acts to the Congress — for instance, *Lei do Bem* (Law of the Goods) and *Lei da Inovação* (Law of Innovation) — with the purpose of establishing new mechanisms for funding innovation activities, such as economic subventions and interest equalisation, as well as restructuring fiscal incentives for R&D and for innovation. Such mechanisms, although they had been created during the former government, were only implemented as of 2003. They allowed the innovation policy that was designed in the period 1999–2002 to be implemented, based on three main cornerstones:[9] incentives to technological development and to innovation within enterprises; incentives to the creation of technological infrastructure; and incentives to the emergence of new technology-based enterprises. The credit for both these laws and the initiative of implementing the innovation policy belongs to the current government. Table A2.4 (see Annexure) summarises the main legal acts and programmes that allowed the implementation of the innovation policy.

The Law of the Goods is a mechanism for boosting innovation, which seeks to benefit, by means of fiscal incentives, those firms that perform R&D activities.[10] As already emphasised, the main criticism to the concession of fiscal incentives is related to the inadequacy of such a mechanism for changing the long-term strategies of the agents in the production sector, comprising merely a secondary element in the incentive to innovation. In other words, beneficiary enterprises would invest in innovation even without fiscal incentives, once innovation is part of their long-term strategies. In addition, according to Koeller (2007), such incentives are specifically aimed at firms that perform R&D, thus carrying a restricted concept of innovation.

The Innovation Law (Law no. 10.973) was sanctioned in 2004 and had further regulation in October of 2005 through Decree no. 5563. The new law was built upon three cornerstones: the constitution of an environment appropriate to the establishment of partnership relations between universities, technology institutes and enterprises; the incentive to the participation of institutes of science and technology in the innovation process; and the direct incentive to innovation within the firms (Arruda et al. 2006). The innovation law has been further improved by incorporating elements related to the promotion of innovation within enterprises.

The Ministry of Science and Technology consolidated in this period as the main agent in the ambit of the federal government for the design and implementation of the explicit innovation policy. Two agencies subordinate to the MCT are part of this strategy of policy implementation — the Council of Scientific and Technological Development, responsible for the concession of scholarships, and the Studies and Projects Funding Agency, responsible for the concession of financing to research, development and innovation projects.

In terms of results, it can be said that, despite the existence of tax incentives over 10 years, the number of beneficiaries is inexpressive, reaching only about 1,500 enterprises from 1993 through 2009, in a total of 300,000 industrial companies in the country.

Council of Scientific and Technological Development

The Council of Scientific and Technological Development was created in 1951, as the National Research Council, and its mission was related to the promotion of scientific research. For many years, CNPq played the role of coordinator of the National System of Science and Technology, until the creation of the Ministry of Science and Technology in 1985.

Now, CNPq is one of the agencies subordinate to MCT, being responsible for supporting research and providing graduate education aimed at consolidating and expanding both the number of graduate professionals and research in the country. The main instrument used by CNPq for accomplishing its objectives is the concession of research scholarships. These are later allocated according to different modes and directed to various levels of education, from secondary school and college to graduate and postdoctoral studies. Scholarships are divided into two main categories: individual scholarships for studies within the country or abroad, and quota scholarships.

Among the scholarships granted by CNPq, some are aimed to *stricto sensu* masters and doctoral programmes, but there are also some aimed specifically to the advancement of technology. The budget assigned to doctoral studies has presented a growing trend during the period under analysis and it constitutes one of the main expenditures of the agency.

Two programmes — Human Resources for Strategic Activities-Innovation (RHAE-*Inovação*) and Stimulus to Retention of Human Resources of Interest to Sectoral Funds (PROSET) — grant scholarships to professionals who develop R&D projects within enterprises, aiming at settling masters and Ph.D.s in the enterprises, in accordance with the logic established by the explicit innovation policy.

Furthermore, in the scope of individual scholarships for scientific development, some mechanisms of promotion are worth emphasising. One of them is the Regional Scientific and Technological Development, which aims at establishing human resources with qualifications in science, technology and innovation in regions in need of expanding the number of qualified professionals. This programme is also concerned with the matter of competitiveness of enterprises.

This modality of support incorporates, then, two fundamental issues from the point of view of the innovation policy: the question of overcoming regional inequalities and the question of integrating graduate professionals to the business area. A negative aspect of this scheme to promote innovation is the linear approach to the process, which associates innovation to basic research. This perspective permeates the procedures of granting this modality of scholarship, requiring professional qualification at graduate level and restricting the concession of 'scholarships for retaining graduate professionals' to the firms that develop, are applying, or have been granted research projects. Such requirements *a priori* rule out a wide group of professionals and firms that do not hold the mandatory qualifications and are not involved with scientific research, although it does not mean that they are less innovative or less able to produce innovations.

Also noteworthy is the Industrial and Technological Development (*Desenvolvimento Tecnológico e Industrial*, DTI) scholarships programme. This kind of scholarship is granted to professionals who participate in R&D projects carried out within enterprises.

On the other hand, the Scholarship for Internship/Training_in the country is part of the programme Individual Scholarships for Technological Advancement. This is a very important programme for the preparation of professionals in firms that seek to enhance quality. However, as can be seen later in Table 2.3, resources available for this modality of scholarship were gradually reducing and finally ran out in 2007.

Both scholarship programmes — Industrial and Technological Development and Internship/Training — follow the same logic of DTI, binding the concession of grants to the participation of the professional in a research project. It is therefore assumed that the innovation process is necessarily related to research and the fact that a big deal of innovations and technological advancements occur outside research laboratories is neglected. The restriction of these qualification grants to research projects limits the role that this mechanism could play in a firm.

The analysis of criteria for qualification of candidates corroborates the criticism that these scholarship programmes carry a linear vision of the innovation process in their essence. In the case of DTI, the criterion always requires experience in research, development or innovation activities. Tacit knowledge, which is highly important for innovation within companies, is neglected in this form of granting scholarships.

The priority of the agency is still put on the preparation of researchers, which is reflected in the resources allocated for the concession of the several modalities of scholarships — the major amounts of resources are allocated to doctoral and masters scholarships.[11]

Finally, one problem faced by CNPq related to its scholarship policy is the instability of budget resources. The variation of these resources along time is not always positive, which hinders the decision-making, design and implementation of a continued policy, able to produce changes in the strategies of the agents that comprise the Brazilian innovation system.

Studies and Projects Funding Agency

The Studies and Projects Funding Agency was created in 1965 and is subordinate to the Ministry of Science and Technology. The institution is responsible for financing activities aimed at innovation and at scientific and technological advancement, by means of granting both reimbursable and non-reimbursable funds to companies, universities and public or private research centres.

This organisation has a number of programmes for financial support. These are divided into four main categories: (*a*) support to innovation within companies; (*b*) support to scientific and technological institutions (STIs); (*c*) support to cooperation between companies and STIs; (*d*) support to activities in science and technology (S&T) aimed at social development. Each one of these categories comprises a group of programmes targeting different areas aimed at boosting innovation and scientific and technological development.

Most of these programmes are financed with resources from the sectoral funds and are implemented mainly by means of public bids and calls for proposals. The first sectoral funds were created in 1999 and there are currently 16 such funds whose resources are allocated for financing innovation and S&T development.[12]

One may observe an overlapping of financing priorities — programmes are created for supporting various sectors concurrently. This, in fact, indicates the lack of a strategy for the innovation policy. The projects that have been approved apparently do not follow a coherent policy, spreading over a wide range of areas. Thus, in addition to the problems inherent to the operation of such a wide and varied range of programmes, there is the risk of disconnection of supported projects from the guidelines established by the innovation policy.

One of the principles of the sectoral funds is to promote cooperation and to establish partnerships between companies and scientific and technological institutions (universities, institutes, etc.). The resources are released for the STIs and not directly to the companies, as a form of promoting cooperation between different agents of the Brazilian innovation system. All programmes financed with resources of the sectoral funds can only be implemented according to this methodology. As noted by Cassiolato:

> [A] minority of firms is involved in university-industry relations; the studies suggest that, whereas many of the firms maybe do not need to establish cooperation with universities and R&D centres, many [others] do not have the required capabilities, particularly human resources, for establishing the cooperation. Kristensen and Madsen (2003) propose a labour division in the innovation system, in which the large companies specialize in relations with educational and research institutions, while the SMEs exploit the synergies with partners within the value chain (2003: 8).

The existence of qualified human resource in the companies, able to dialogue with the research institutions, is crucial for the success of the cooperation. Small and medium enterprises may have no qualified professionals able to establish partnership relations with researchers, while large companies generally have their own R&D laboratories, and thus cooperation may end up occurring only occasionally. Furthermore, this mechanism of cooperation between the enterprises and the universities and research institutions bears an implicit linear vision of the innovation process, once it both emphasises the importance of research to the detriment of other processes that are significant for innovation, and neglects the participation of other agents of the national innovation system, who may assume a fundamental role in certain innovative processes.

In addition to these programmes, FINEP has another one, quite important for the accomplishment of activities concerning innovation funding. Economic subvention is one of the main mechanisms used by this institution. The resources available through this mechanism are not reimbursable and are granted through public bids. Economic subvention was launched in 2006 and is granted directly to the company. Each year a new bid is launched aiming at supporting a number of enterprises that have interest in investing in innovation projects.

The objective of the subvention can be summarised as follows: 'to significantly enhance the innovation activities and to increase competitiveness of both the companies and the country's economy'.[13] The idea behind this mechanism is to strengthen the enterprises that aim at innovating, by means of granting non-reimbursable funding to those firms that submit innovation projects and that meet the selection criteria of the bid. Although it was designed in 2002, the subvention was implemented by FINEP in 2006. In that year, the resources allocated to this programme were 300 million Reais (0.013 per cent of the 2006 GDP) and 145 companies had their projects approved. In 2008, 450 million Reais were allocated (0.016 per cent of 2008 GDP) to the programme and 206 companies had their projects approved. The analysis of the beneficiary companies and their respective projects demonstrates that the criteria for selection of the projects are not connected to the strategic guidelines set by the innovation policy, particularly in the bids of 2006 and 2007. Most selected projects were classified by FINEP as projects on 'general subjects'. The 2008 bid was the first to detail the kind of project and the policy guidelines for selecting projects, leaving less room for 'general subjects' projects.

In December of 2009, 261 new projects (and 560 million Reais) were approved in this programme, for the three strategic areas of information and communication technology (ICT), health and defence. In the other three priority areas — biotechnology, energy and social areas — submitted projects were not recommended for implementation. However, only 229 million Reais (0.007 per cent of 2009 GDP) were spent, and this expenditure was not for these new projects, it was for projects approved in previous years.

Similarly, the resources expended in 2010 in this programme were related to projects approved in other years and corresponded to 526 million Reais (0.014 per cent of the 2010 GDP). Another bid was launched in 2010, but because of the Brazilian Court of Audit (TCU), which was examining the compliance with existing regulations about the legality of the participation of private non-profit organisations and cooperatives in the process of subvention, dissemination of the bid's results were suspended.

Ministry of Development, Industry and Foreign Trade

In the government of the period 2003–2006, MDIC gained room as a promoter of national development. Policies for industry, technology and foreign trade acquired an excellent position as conditions necessary for development. The ministry is one of the main agents in the implementation of these policies. Some actions and programmes among those implemented by MDIC are directly addressed to innovation. Furthermore, MDIC is the main manager of the Industrial, Technological and Foreign Trade Policy (2003–2007) and the Policy for Production Development (2007–2010).

First, it is possible to highlight the actions/programmes of the Ministry of Development that are more directly related to the innovation process. Table A2.1 (see Annexure) shows some of the actions that the ministry is implementing in the scope of its contribution to the innovation policy. The programmes presented unfold into more specific actions. These involve a range of activities from tax matters to fiscal incentives aimed at small and medium enterprises. These programmes are varied and seek to embrace different niches of the domestic economy.

One of them is the programme for Incentive to Innovation in the Enterprise which has as its major objective, according to MDIC, to provide Brazilian entrepreneurs with an online service for reference regarding the search for solutions of difficulties related to the development of technological innovations. The programme comprises various initiatives that lead to different ways of implementing the policy, as can be seen in Table A2.1.

The main instrument of the programme is the concession of fiscal incentives and its main problem is the fact that it is restricted to larger enterprises.[14] Many authors, like Rothwell (1983), Ergas (1987), Guimarães (2006), and Arundel (2006) emphasise that, although fiscal incentives are used by most countries (except for United Kingdom), the efficacy of such incentives suggests that they are, at best, a secondary element in public support to innovation. The authors affirm that most beneficiary enterprises would have made the investments in R&D irrespective of the concession of the benefit.

On the other hand, the programme Cooperation Enterprise/Technological Institution is based on a model where the enterprises search public R&D organisations aiming at establishing partnerships. This model is based on the assumption that small-sized enterprises are aware of the importance of innovation and interaction with universities and that they have enough capability for establishing cooperative relations. Some problems arise from this assumption. First, many small-sized enterprises do not hold a clear image about the role that universities and research laboratories may play for the growth of the firm. Second, the enterprises that hold this vision hardly have R&D facilities nor are they able to establish partnership relations with R&D institutions. In addition to these findings, one may observe a component of the old linear vision that innovation would result from basic research.

These programmes, although being pointed out by MDIC as initiatives directly aimed at innovation, have no budget resources associated to them, nor any specific tools for their implementation; this makes it difficult to implement effective actions.

The Programme of Micro, Small and Medium Enterprises, created in 2007, is inserted in the objectives of PDP, suggesting that small enterprises are highly important for the development of national production. The ministry's outlays aimed at development of micro, small and medium enterprises have been made since at least 2004, a period that precedes the PDP. Similar to other programmes, there is a high instability of budget resources that vary significantly along the considered years. Such instabilities make both the decision-making and the implementation of continued actions by policy makers difficult.

The policy of Local Productive Arrangements/Systems (*Arranjos Produtivos Locais*, APL), according to the ministry, has the objective of 'guiding and coordinating the governmental efforts in the induction of local development, looking for, in accordance with the government's strategic guidelines, the generation of employment and income and the stimulus to exports'.[15] This would be another form of incentive to small and medium enterprises. Despite the creation of the programme, its implementation faced huge difficulties, given the scarcity of resources and the problems for coordinating the actions with other governmental departments, as well as with banks' and supporting agencies. According to the budget of MDIC, the resources for the APLs were almost nil in the latter years. Thus, although highlighting the importance of these arrangements for national development, and particularly for regional development, the programme has not been effectively implemented.

This programme would target not only the enterprises, but the development of the region around the arrangements. The government claims that: 'The strategic option for operations within APLs results, fundamentally, from the acknowledgement that the policies for boosting small and medium enterprises are more effective when directed to groups of firms and not to isolated firms.' Such a claim, however, seems contradictory to other programmes instituted by the ministry, which have action lines addressed to individual firms, such as the programme of Micro, Small and Medium Enterprises, making it difficult to prioritise resource allocation and to implement effective actions.

The relevance of the Ministry of Development, Industry and Foreign Trade for the explicit innovation policy has unquestionably grown following the implementation of the Policy for Production Development, which was instituted in May 2008. The reason is that the ministry has been appointed for coordinating the policy, having as executive secretariat the National Bank of Social and Economic Development (BNDES), a public enterprise linked to the ministry that undertakes major responsibilities in the implementation of the policy.

The National Bank for Social and Economic Development

The National Bank for Social and Economic Development is one of the major institutions in Latin America for financing investment in production. According to the bank innovation is seen as a strategic issue for the concession of financing: The support to innovation is a strategic priority for BNDES. The aim is contributing to the expansion of innovation activities in the country and to their systematic fulfilment.

There are some lines of support to innovation, as seen in Table A2.2 (see Annexure), that unfold into lines of direct support to innovation and financing lines aimed at the industry, that would indirectly incorporate innovation. The programmes of BNDES present different formats. The Innovative Capital has its focus on the enterprises with the capability for performing innovative activities. The financing is related to the strategy of the enterprise and this is the only programme that imposes this relevant condition. The idea behind this condition is that financing projects of research and development that are not related to a broad strategy of innovation by the firm brings an implicit risk that the project may be discontinued due to crisis or failures. On the contrary, financing an innovative strategy would tend to change the perspectives and strategies of long-term investment of the firms.

The programme of Technological Innovation has its focus on new technologies, at least for the domestic market, and seems to follow the pattern instituted by the programmes of the Studies and Projects Funding Agency presented eralier. Another programme is the Technological Fund (FUNTEC) that presents, according to BNDES, the following premise: to support projects of research, development and innovation in areas of clear relevance for the country. The priority sectors are: health, renewable energies and environment. These are relevant topics for the Brazilian innovation system, since Brazil is a large country with great capacity for expanding the use of renewable energies (solar, wind power, biofuel, etc.), with one of the greatest biodiversities of the planet, and with sensitive deficiencies regarding tropical diseases among others.

The programmes offer interest rates lower than those applied in the market, but conversely to the programmes of FINEP, their financing lines are reimbursable. Technological Innovation shows interest rates of 4.5 per cent per year and Innovative Capital presents an interest rate comprising financial cost, basic remuneration set by BNDES and credit risk rate. It is important to note that there are no budget resources associated to the programmes, which makes their implementation difficult.

The programmes cited earlier were related to innovation and there are other ones associated to industry. The Programme of Support to Implementation of the Brazilian System of Terrestrial Digital TV (PROTVD) is the programme that aims to develop the domestic industry, based on technologies of digital TV, thus including various sectors, such as, for instance, software and the equipment for radio broadcasting. However, the procedures for releasing the financing to interested enterprises are not established yet; furthermore, no measures have been announced about any specific policy aimed at the creation of Brazilian enterprises that could develop such technologies in the case that no firm manifests an interest.

Finally, it is worth mentioning the Programme of Support to the Development of the Health Industrial Complex (PROFARMA). This programme is also one of the lines of BNDES for health. The objectives of the programme are: to expand significantly the participation of national enterprises in the domestic market; to promote the growth of their exports; to strengthen the process of R&D and innovation in the sector; to boost the improvement in quality and the certification of products and processes associated to the sector; to promote the growth and internationalisation of national enterprises of the sector; to promote consolidation of the sector; to promote the dissemination and the growing use of national software both in Brazil and internationally; to strengthen the national operations of multinational software and IT services companies that develop technology in Brazil and/or use the country as a platform for exporting.

Table 2.3 shows the number of projects and resources invested in by BNDES through its innovation funding programmes, in 2007 and 2008. It is possible to note that, during these two years, the programmes did not show a large scale, neither in terms of the number of supported projects, nor in terms of the volume of resources.

Table 2.3: *BNDES: Innovation Funding Programmes, 2007/2008*

	2007		*2008*	
Programmes	*Investment*	*No. of Projects*	*Investment*	*No. of Projects*
Innovative Capital	-	-	2,049,600	1
Innovation R,D&I	105,653,488	7	17,858,400	3
Production Innovation	280,420,966	11	41,814,898	9
Automotive Engineering	-	-	172,320,400	2
Innovation Profarma: Support for the Development of Industrial Health	30,341,802	5	13,055,000	3
Business Prosoft: Development of Software Industry and Services Information Technology	372,796,686	12	321,802,382	9
Supplier Protvd: Support the Implementation of the Brazilian Digital TV	-	-	8,400,909	1
Others: Technological Development	5,873,750	6	44,437,586	5
Total	795,086,692	41	621,739,174	33

Source: Vermulm and Hollanda (2009).
Note: Current values in dollars PPP.

Only information on the total funds invested in these programmes is available for 2009 and 2010, respectively, $788 million (current values in dollars PPP) and $1,924 million (current values in dollars PPP). This means that, at least in terms of resources invested (considered as a percentage of GDP; 0.017 per cent of the 2009 GDP and 0.037 per cent of the 2010 GDP), these programmes are advancing.

Brazilian Federal Agency for the Support and Evaluation of Graduate Education, Ministry of Education

The Brazilian Federal Agency for the Support and Evaluation of Graduate Education was created in 1951, initially in the ambit of the National Campaign for Improving Higher Education. Its main purpose was guaranteeing the existence of specialised human resources, aiming at fulfilling both public and private needs for facing the challenge of development.

CAPES is currently subordinate to the Ministry of Education and one of its roles is to grant scholarships for human resources education at graduate level. Indeed, CAPES, in conjunction with CNPq, has been responsible for the consolidation of the graduate education system in the country and for the preparation and qualification of higher education teaching personnel. As a result, the country has also been improving its position in the ranking of scientific publications, published by the National Science Indicators (NSI), having risen from the 15th position in 2007 to the 13th in 2008, maintaining the same position in 2009.

The merit of CAPES in human resources training and in the consolidation of the educational and research system, along with CNPq, is fully acknowledged. However, there still persists a poor and fragile coordination between this policy and the explicit innovation policy, the absorption of qualified graduate professionals by the production sector being still relatively weak, as already mentioned.

Specificities of the System of Innovation in the Country and its Relationship with the State

The evolution of the Brazilian production structure

By the end of the 1940s, the Brazilian production structure was almost exclusively based on the primary sector. It was only after World War II that the country started its industrialisation process, which was based, then, on the idea of import substitution. It focused, at first, on the establishment of an industry of non-durable consumer goods, in order to meet the demand of an urban working class that was beginning to be formed in the country. After this first period, which lasted until the middle of the 1950s, the productive structure began to become more diverse, with the entry of capital goods in the production of national manufacturers. At the same time, the service sector also started to appear, tending to increase its share in GDP throughout the period. Figure 2.1 presents the share of services, industry and agriculture as a percentage of GDP for the period from 1947 to 2010.

Figure 2.1: *Brazil: Share of Services, Industry and Agriculture in GDP, 1947–2010 (percentage)*

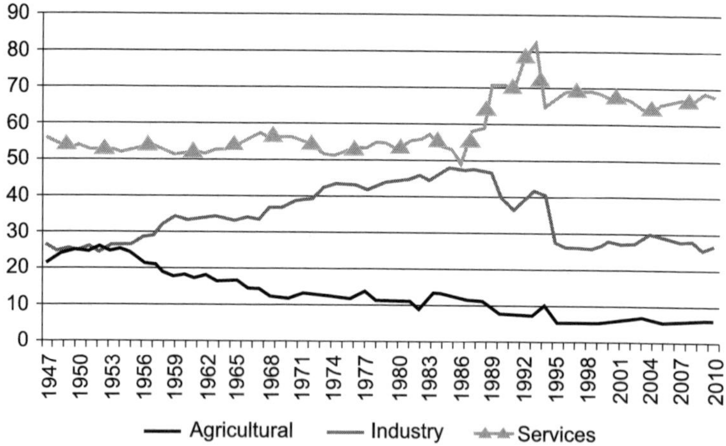

Source: IBGE (Brazilian Institute of Geography and Statistics) website, http://www.sidra.ibge.gov.br/bda/cnt/default.asp?z=t&o=15&i=P (accessed 19 October 2011). Authors' elaboration.

The limited participation of industry in GDP observed in the period 1947–1955, is due to the collapse of the import substitution of non-durable consumer goods in the process of industrialisation. After 1955 until the early 1980s, the process of import substitution began a new phase, including durable consumer goods and capital goods, which marked the growing involvement of industry in GDP, as shown in Figure 2.1. This phase was related to the attraction of foreign-owned enterprises, with the purpose of importing industrial technology.

Based on this policy, in the late 1970s, the country attained a complex and relatively complete production structure, in terms of the sectors that comprise it. Industry was producing petrochemicals, ferrous and non-ferrous metals, fertilisers, paper and pulp and capital goods. Moreover, the country could establish an efficient infrastructure of energy, communications and transport (Cassiolato 1992).

This successful phase ended in 1980, with the Mexican crisis (Ferraz et al. 2003). The 1980s and 1990s represented reduction in capacity for the Brazilian industry in several sectors, with increased industrial concentration in some of them. Moreover, during this period many Brazilian companies were acquired by foreign capital, and several mergers and acquisitions took place, including those resulting from the privatisation process sponsored by the government.

Table 2.4 presents the composition of the industrial output of general industry for the period from 1996 through 2007.[16] The main observation is that the sectors intensive in natural resources, such as oil refining (16.5 per cent), beverages and food (16 per cent) and metallurgy (7.9 per cent), augmented their participation in the total industrial production during these years. The sectors intensive in technology such as machinery and equipment for offices and informatics goods; electronic devices and communication equipment; other equipments (that includes the aeronautics sector) either decreased or maintained their low participation in the total industrial production for the same period.

Table 2.4: *Brazil: Composition of the Industrial Output of General Industry, 1996–2007*

	Years						
Sectors	*1996*	*2004*	*2005*	*2006*	*2007*	*2007–1996*	*2007–2004*
General Industry	100	100	100	100	100.0	Difference in %	
Extractive Industries	2.2	3.4	4.2	4.1	4.0	1.8	0.6
Manufacturing Industries	97.8	96.6	95.8	95.9	96.0	–1.8	-0.6
Beverages and Food	17.2	15.4	15.8	16.0	15.1	–1.3	0.5
Tobacco	1.1	0.7	0.7	0.7	0.7	–0.4	0.0
Textiles	3.3	2.2	2.0	2.0	1.9	–1.3	–0.2
Clothing	2.3	1.3	1.4	1.5	1.8	–0.8	0.2
Leather, Leather Artefacts and Footwear	2.2	1.9	1.6	1.6	1.5	–0.7	-0.4
Wood Products	1.1	1.6	1.4	1.3	1.3	0.2	–0.3
Pulp and Paper Industry	3.7	3.8	3.3	3.4	3.4	–0.3	–0.4

(Cont.)

(*Cont.*)

Sectors	Years						
	1996	*2004*	*2005*	*2006*	*2007*	*2007–1996*	*2007–2004*
Edition, Recording and Press	4.9	2.9	2.9	2.9	2.8	–2.0	–0.1
Oil Refining	7.0	14.0	16.3	16.5	15.5	9.5	2.5
Chemicals	12.7	11.0	10.2	9.9	10.2	–2.8	–1.1
Rubber and Plastic Goods	4.1	3.4	3.4	3.4	3.3	–0.7	0.0
Non-metallic Products	3.4	3.3	2.9	3.2	3.1	–0.2	–0.1
Metallurgy	5.4	9.2	8.1	7.9	7.9	2.5	–1.3
Metallic Products	3.8	3.1	3.6	3.2	3.6	-0.6	0.1
Machinery and Equipment	6.8	5.9	5.2	5.4	5.8	–1.4	–0.5
Machinery and Equipment for Offices and Informatics Goods	0.5	0.5	0.5	0.6	0.6	0.1	0.1
Devices and Machines	2.6	1.9	2.4	2.2	2.6	–0.5	0.3
Electronic Devices and Communication Equipments	3.5	2.3	2.0	2.1	1.7	–1.5	–0.2
Hospital and Medical Devices	0.8	0.7	0.8	0.8	0.8	–0.1	0.1
Assembly and Manufacturing of Motor Vehicles	8.1	7.8	7.9	7.9	8.6	–0.2	0.1
Other Equipments	0.8	2.0	1.7	1.9	2.0	1.0	–0.1
Furniture and Other Industries	2.2	1.6	1.5	1.6	1.6	–0.7	0.0
Recycling	0.0	0.1	0.1	0.1	0.1	0.0	0.0

Source: IBGE (Brazilian Institute of Geography and Statistics) website, http://www.sidra.ibge.gov.br/bda/cnt/default.asp?z=t&o=15&i=P (accessed 19 October 2011). Authors' elaboration.

In summary, the last two decades have not been favourable, to say the least, for industry and agriculture, which have been losing their share in GDP. For industry the situation was even worse, since the sectors most intensive in technology lost share in relation to commodities. Only from 2005 to 2010 (with the exception of 2009, when the Brazilian industry suffered the impacts of the global financial crisis that hit the world in 2008) a small, timid recovery in the share of industry in GDP can be observed, which reflects the reversal in governmental policy, with the reintroduction of industrial policy as the subject, as noted earlier.

The main specificities and heterogeneities of the Brazilian innovation system

The main specificities of the Brazilian innovation system are its structural (and innovative) heterogeneities, which are also reflected in the outstanding regional disparities. The policy for industrialisation adopted until the 1970s could be considered successful once the country got to forge a complex and complete industrial structure in terms of economic activities and size of enterprises.

This infrastructure, however, is largely concentrated in the south-eastern and southern regions of the country. Table 2.5 presents the participation by region in the gross added value, which represents the differences in the production structure of the regions.

Table 2.5: *Participation by Region in the Brazilian Gross Value Added at Basic Prices*

Year	*North*	*Northeast*	*Centre-West*	*Southeast*	*South*
2002	4.82	13.25	9.06	55.73	17.14
2003	4.88	13.03	9.21	54.90	17.97
2004	4.90	12.70	9.10	55.80	17.40
2005	5.00	13.10	8.90	56.50	16.60
2006	5.10	13.10	8.70	56.80	16.30
2007	5.00	13.10	8.90	56.40	16.60
2008	5.10	13.10	9.20	56.00	16.60

Source: IBGE (Brazilian Institute of Geography and Statistics) website, http://www.sidra.ibge.gov.br/bda/cnt/default.asp?z=t&o=15&i=P (accessed 25 October 2011). Authors' elaboration.

Table 2.6 presents the structure of income distribution in the country, marked by considerable disparities that characterise the socio-regional heterogeneity.

Table 2.6: *Per Capita Income by Region*

Regions	*2001*	*2002*	*2003*	*2004*	*2005*	*2006*	*2007*	*2008*
Centre-West	6,590	8,770	8,930	9,350	9,200	9,230	10,210	10,550
North	3,910	4,190	4,220	4,510	4,560	4,740	5,230	5,290
Northeast	2,970	3,230	3,180	3,310	3,470	3,580	3,860	3,880
South	7,640	7,980	8,350	8,560	8,320	8,400	9,480	9,450
Southeast	8,480	9,250	9,070	9,460	9,750	10,040	11,030	10,960

Source: Instituto de Pesquisa Econômica Aplicada (IPEADATA) website, http://www.ipeadata.gov.br. (accessed 1 November 2011). Unit: R$ 2000.

Note: The per capita household income is defined as the ratio between the sum of monthly income of all family members living in the house and the number of family members. It is deflated by the INPC index.

Besides unveiling outstanding social inequalities, the information shows a strong concentration in both the income and production structure in the southern and south-eastern regions. These differences in the production and social structure of the country that distinguish the Brazilian innovation system, somehow determine the path of reproduction, growth and evolution of this system.

Another important specificity is related to the educational system. In the scope of the public system in Brazil, elementary education is mostly under the responsibility of municipalities; states account primarily for secondary education; and higher education is mainly provided by the federal government. The education system is complemented by private schools and universities.

According to the Law of the National Education Guidelines (*Lei de diretrizes e Bases da educação*, LDB), in force since 1966, 'it is the responsibility of the federal government to regulate and monitor higher education institutions, including private ones, and furthermore to promote the distribution of material and financial resources to states and municipalities for them to invest in their secondary and elementary schools' (Dantas 2008: 1).

The major concern of the educational policy during recent decades has been the 'universalisation' of elementary education, a goal that was achieved, with a significant growth in the number of enrolments. The current concern is put on the quality of education, which has proved to be low according to a number of indicators.[17] Figure 2.2 clearly shows the yearly evolution in the number of enrolled students. A significant increase is observed from 1970 to 1997. Subsequently, the beginning of a low decrease in the number of enrolments is observed. However, if this evolution is compared in relation to the Brazilian population in the years 1970 and 1997, the percentage growth is low (respectively 17 per cent and 22 per cent, according to Dantas [2008]).

Figure 2.2: *Evolution in the Number of Enrolments in Elementary Education*

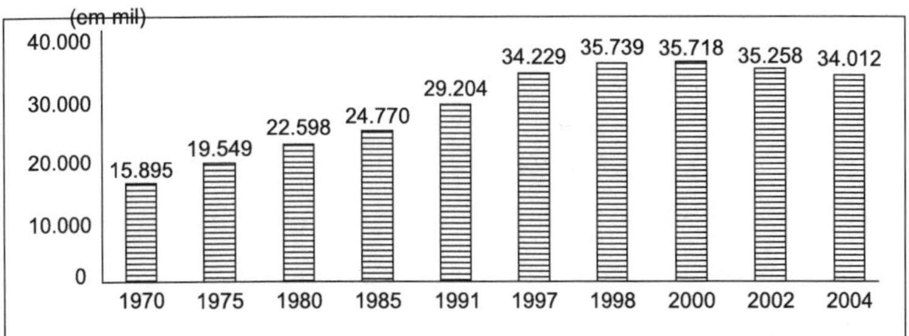

Source: IPEA (2006) in Dantas (2008: 6).

In addition, the rate of conclusion for elementary, secondary and higher education is quite low: 'Only 84% out of practically 100% children at school starting age enrolled in the 1st grade of elementary education get to complete the 4th grade; 57% complete elementary school and only 37% complete secondary education' (IPEA 2006: 129 *sic passim* in Dantas 2008).

The access to quality education also reflects the income concentration prevailing in the country, with private schools, whose students comprise the higher income ranges, being better ranked in the tests that assess quality of education. Differences regarding the education of youngsters according to income ranges are expressive. In the first age range (0–6 years), the access to education by the highest income ranges (50.6 per cent) is very much higher than that of the lowest income ranges (28.9 per cent). In the age range of 7 to 14, quantitative differences decrease. As for the last age range (18–24 years) disparities are again remarkable, with the highest income youths showing greater access to education than those with the lowest income. Such inequality in the access to education in Brazil aggravates existing differences, contrarily to what should happen.

Another fact that reflects the education policy in Brazil is the difference in investment across the education levels — elementary, secondary and higher education. Table 2.7 shows that expenditure per student for public elementary education is much lower than expenditures for higher education. Such disparity, added to the fact that most of the students that access the university pertain to the 5th highest income quintile, as seen later in Table 2.11, emphasises the aggravation of inequality. Dantas (2008:9) claims that: 'Brazil is the country, in the whole world, with the highest investment per student, in relative terms, for public higher education: no other country spends, per student enrolled in higher education (including graduate courses) a sum not even close to the equivalent of per capita GDP.' The expenditure on public higher education is crucial; however, restricted access to this educational level is a major problem to be faced by the public policy.

Table 2.7: *Public Direct Investment per Student*

				Elementary Education			
Year	*Total*	*Basic Education*	*Children's Education*	*1st to 4th Grade or First Years*	*5th to 8th Grade or Final Years*	*Secondary Education*	*Higher Education*
2000	2051	1707	1953	1680	1714	1628	18872
2001	2157	1799	1792	1687	1897	1883	18952
2002	2250	1862	1763	2058	1911	1385	18778
2003	2188	1838	1971	1936	1840	1544	15981
2004	2355	1935	2068	2047	2069	1415	15926
2005	2380	2016	1922	2250	2142	1406	15908

Source: IPEA (2006) in Dantas (2008).
Note: Current values in dollars PPP.

Concurrently, the production sector undergoes a lack of qualified personnel, as shown, for instance, in researches conducted by RedeSist (Research Network on Local Innovative Production Arrangements and Systems) and as signaled by the Survey on Technological Innovation (PINTEC 2005).

In PINTEC 2008, interviewed enterprises indicated either high or medium importance to the lack of qualified personnel as one of the problems and obstacles to the development of innovative activities. In the frequency ranking of mentioned problems, the lack of qualified personnel stands at the third position (57.8 per cent) for industrial companies, behind the problems of economic character (costs of innovation and economic risks). For the enterprises in the segment of services, such a problem has been identified as still more serious: for selected services (publishing, telecommunications, information technology) companies (70.4 per cent), it was the first in the ranking; and for the R&D enterprises (46.7 per cent), this problem stood in the fourth position (it is important to underline that in 2005, it was ranked in sixth position). Although it has not appeared in all economic activities as the main problem or obstacle to innovation, the participation of the enterprises that indicated the lack of qualified personnel as being of high or medium relevance is quite significant (from 46.7 per cent for R&D enterprises to 70.4 per cent for selected services enterprises).

Explicit and Implicit State Policy towards Science, Technology and Innovation

The government of the period 2003–2006 began in a context characterised by inflation acceleration, in spite of the regime of inflation targets that implied the raise of interest rates and a restrictive fiscal policy. In this domestic scenario, the macroeconomic policy for 2003 remained unchanged and tied to the regime of inflation targets, using restrictive fiscal and monetary policies as instruments for reaching the 'target' — in spite of the historical promises of changing the economic policy by the Workers' Party, the winner in the elections. This policy meant the rise of interest rates, rise of economic surplus with reduction of federal outlays, particularly investments, and appreciated exchange rates.

In spite of a negative domestic scenario, there was a favourable context from the international point of view, with increasing demand for commodities boosted by the growth of China and that of the main global economies.

The characterisation of explicit and implicit innovation policies is based on the concept of a broad national system of innovation adopted in this study, as already noted. As implicit policies, which in the case of Brazil have a significant impact, we will consider the macroeconomic policy as well as social development and educational policies. The analysis of the policies, both explicit and implicit, will focus on the period 2003–2010, with emphasis on the period 2007–2009.

Explicit policies

Although retaining the macroeconomic policy of the former administration, in November of 2003 the federal government launched the Industrial, Technological and Foreign Trade Policy, taking a favourable stand towards an industrial policy. The objectives of PITCE were:

> The Industrial, Technological and Foreign Trade Policy seeks, in the short run, to reduce the country's external restrictions and, in the medium and long run, to equate the development of key-activities, so that to generate capabilities that allow Brazil to raise its competitiveness in the international scenario (BRASIL 2003: 9–10).

Thus, the government sought to implement a policy that could provide support to the domestic production sector by means of the strategies presented earlier in this chapter. Many criticisms can be raised against this policy. However, the merit of the government in restoring the importance of the innovation policy is undeniable. Furthermore, such a policy spans several federal institutions, not restricting the issue to the Ministry of Science and Technology, as the former government had done.

Some of the criticisms of the implementation of this policy, as observed by Koeller (2007), concern the difficulties faced in defining its guidelines, besides the problems of coordination that hindered its implementation. Laplane and Sarti (2006: 284) raise further criticisms: 'Until the end of 2005, this process resulted in a quite comprehensive set of initiatives, at very different stages of planning and implementation. There was a huge prevalence of horizontal actions.'

The actions of PITCE were structured according to three axes:

(*a*) **Horizontal action lines**

- (*i*) Innovation and technological development
- (*ii*) International insertion
- (*iii*) Industrial modernisation
- (*iv*) Production capacity and scale

(*b*) **Strategic options**

(*i*) Semiconductors
(*ii*) Software
(*iii*) Capital goods
(*iv*) Pharmaceuticals and medicines

(*c*) **Activities with future perspectives**

(*i*) Biotechnology
(*ii*) Nanotechnology
(*iii*) Biomass/renewable energies

In spite of the establishment of action lines and the choice of strategic sectors and activities that bear future perspectives and that may contribute to the restructuring of the Brazilian production sector, PITCE did not set a governance structure or specific mechanisms for its own operation. Its implementation was through the mechanisms created by MCT for operating the National Policy of Science, Technology and Innovation, particularly the public bids of the sectoral funds and the economic subvention. The overlapping of policies and the fact that these mechanisms were under the coordination of other institutions, not the MDIC, and thus also answered to other political priorities, hindered the implementation, the analysis and the monitoring of PITCE.

Thus, the government of the period 2007–2010 instituted, in May 2008, the Policy for Production Development, for facing the following challenges: to expand the supply capacity; to keep the robustness of the balance of payments; to enhance the innovation capacity; and to strengthen the micro and small enterprises (MSEs). For this purpose, the policy proposed four macro-goals:

Expansion of fixed investment: INVESTMENT/GDP — Goal for 2010: 21 per cent (R$ 620 billion). Situation in 2007: 17.6 per cent or R$ 450 billion. Average annual growth of 11.3 per cent between 2008 and 2010.

Rise in private expenditures on R&D: PRIVATE R&D/GDP — Goal for 2010: 0.65 per cent (R$ 18.2 billion). Situation in 2005: 0.51 per cent or R$ 11.9 billion. Average annual growth of 9.8 per cent between 2007 and 2010.

Expansion of exports: PARTICIPATION IN GLOBAL EXPORTS — Goal for 2010: 1.25 per cent (US$ 208.8 billion). Situation in 2007: 1.18 per cent or US$ 160.6 billion. Average annual growth of 9.1 per cent between 2008 and 2010.

Stimulation of MSEs: NUMBER OF EXPORTER MSEs — Goal for 2010: increase by 10 per cent in the number of exporter MSEs. Situation in 2006: 11,792 enterprises.

For doing this, the government defined 25 priority sectors that would be focused on in this policy. These economic sectors are divided into three main areas: programmes for advancing strategic areas; programmes for strengthening competitiveness; programmes for consolidating and enhancing leadership.

For each of these areas, the policy mechanisms available have been identified, and sorted out according to four types:

(*a*) Incentive mechanisms: credit and financing, venture capital and fiscal incentives;

(*b*) Governmental purchasing power: purchases by the government and by state companies;

(*c*) Regulatory mechanisms: technical, public health, economic, and competition regulation;

(*d*) Technical support: certification and metrology, trade promotion, management of intellectual property, business and human resources capacity building, intra-governmental coordination and liaison with the private sector.

Most of these mechanisms of support to innovation already existed. The policy sought to organise such mechanisms according to the areas and sectors set as priorities, aiming at informing the enterprises, sharing responsibilities among the various institutions and coordinating the various instruments in support of those primary sectors and areas.

Furthermore, indicators for measuring the policy progress in each priority sector or area were identified and goals were set. This represents an advance regarding PITCE which did not establish goals. However, a more meticulous analysis of goals and challenges raises some doubts regarding the criteria that guided their definition: whether they were based on international parameters; whether the background of priority sectors and areas was considered (and, in this case, since a long time there were no specific policies, if adjustments were made accordingly to expected impacts by means of a coordinated use of policy instruments); whether analyses were carried out about the needs and the impacts of the advancement of these sectors and areas on the national innovation system; or whether the country's development strategy was considered. No information was obtained during the elaboration of the present study that could allow the analysis of the criteria used for setting goals and priorities.

The implementation of the PDP began in May of 2008. Therefore, it is still too soon to evaluate its results. Nevertheless, it is possible to highlight some positive aspects, as well as some issues of concern. Among the positive aspects, we may cite the attention on the governance of the policy and on 'sharing responsibilities' among the various institutions responsible for its implementation.

As for the issues of concern, two of them stand out: the first one regarding the high number of sectors and areas considered, besides the possibility of including new segments, as indicated by the policy statement itself.

In terms of official documents, the policy proposal is based on a systemic vision of the production system, as it is clearly stated in the following guideline expressed in the PDP: Systemic Actions — with focus on factors that generate positive externalities for the whole production structure. That is, the idea that the actions undertaken have an impact on other areas of the production structure, besides being dependent, for their accomplishment, on many governmental agencies.

The policy formulation took into account the dialogue with other policy proposals available in ministries, as well as in some organisations of the civil society, such as: the Programme for the Acceleration of Growth (*Programa de Aceleração do Crescimento*, PAC), promoted by the federal government with the objective of overcoming the 'bottlenecks' of infrastructure; PACTI, the Action Plan for Science, Technology and Innovation launched by the Ministry of Science and Technology aiming at enabling the implementation of the National Policy of Science, Technology and Innovation, and that takes responsibility for coordinating some priority sectors and areas defined by the PDP; and policies of the Ministries of Labour and Employment (Ministério do Trabalho a Emprego, MTE), the Ministry of Health (Ministério da Saúde, MS) and the Ministry of Education (Ministério da Educação, MEC); besides the attempt of liaising with the National Confederation of Industry (Confederação Nacional da Indústria, CNI), an institution of the civil society.

In spite of the discourse, the excess of priorities, besides bringing risks of failure due to problems of operationalisation, seems to not ascribe much importance to the systemic character of the innovation process that would imply the choice for segments and economic activities capable of generating changes in the productive and social structure of the country. The innovation policy must reflect, according to Gadelha (2001: 152), the 'systemic character of the entrepreneurial environment and the specificity and diversity of the evolution patterns of industrial structures'.

The second matter of concern regards the mechanisms of the policy, that are the same as those created in former years. In this case, the worries refer not so much to the old instruments, but rather to the way in which they will be implemented, since many problems with implementation have already been identified in previous years.

The liaison with other policies seems to be advancing insofar these are explicitly aimed at innovation. In other words, the connection of the PDP with PACTI seems to be working, since this policy has innovation as one of its objectives. However, in respect to the remaining policies, the liaison is apparently unsuccessful, as for instance with the Education Policy, coordinated by the Ministry of Education, through the Plan for Development of Education (PDE).

The Action Plan for Science, Technology and Innovation for National Development was designed by the MCT with the purpose of both consolidating the national system of science, technology and innovation (S, T & I) and expanding innovation within enterprises. The plan was formulated for the years 2007–2010 and has the following as its strategic priorities: expansion and consolidation of the National System of S, T & I; promotion of technological innovation in the enterprises; R, D & I in strategic areas; S, T & I for social development.

The priorities of the ministry are mainly focused on strengthening the national scientific infrastructure and on technological innovation, being based on the legal framework comprised by the already mentioned Law of the Goods and Law of Innovations.

The main goals presented by PACTI for 2010 were the following:

Investment in R, D & I: 1.5 per cent GDP in R, D & I (1.02 per cent in 2006); 0.64 per cent federal government and 0.21 per cent state governments.

Innovation in the enterprises: 0.65 per cent of investments in R, D & I made by the private sector (0.51 per cent in 2006).

Training of human resources: 95,000 scholarships by CNPq; 68,000 in 2006, with focus on engineering and other areas related to PITCE plus 65,000 scholarships by CAPES.

S & T for social development: 400 Vocational Technical Centres (*Centros Vocacionais Tecnológicos*); 600 new *telecentros* (community centres for Internet access); OBMEP: 24 million students and 10,000 scholarships.[18]

PACTI selected 13 strategic sectors which gain special attention within the policy regarding the development of R, D & I.[19] However, conversely to the PDP, it does not set specific objectives, goals and mechanisms for each sector, showing the horizontal character of the policy. The chosen sectors also make part of PDP (although this latter has been formulated subsequently to PACTI), which expresses the beginning of integration between the various governmental departments explicitly related to the innovation policy.

Similarly to PDP, the mechanisms and the legal framework used by PACTI for implementing its guidelines are: non-reimbursable resources (sectoral funds), financings, venture capital, economic subvention, fiscal incentives (Law of the Goods), human resources training and capacity building, law of innovation. Again, the criticism directed to these instruments is related rather to the way they are implemented and to the lack of coordination between them, than to the mechanisms themselves.

Implicit policies

In the Brazilian case, the social and economic contexts and the policies designed for these two domains of NSI assume a significant relevance either as obstacles or as opportunities for the development and the evolution of the NSI.

As already discussed, the macroeconomic policy that characterised the Brazilian economic environment during the period under analysis — and the beginning of the 2003–2006 and 2007–2010 governments — became an obstacle to the implementation of the innovation policy, once it assumed the characteristics of what Coutinho (2005) called a pernicious macroeconomic regime.

This macroeconomic policy, characterised by the regime of inflation targets — whose current target is 4.5 per cent with a possible variation of two percentage points — adopted as its main instruments the interest rates, which were kept high during the whole period of analysis, and a regime of fluctuating exchange rates and restrictive fiscal policies, with strict goals fixed for primary surplus.

In this context, Laplane and Sarti highlight (2006: 273) that: 'As of 2003, Lula Government has, on the one hand, effectively withdrawn the prevailing veto to an industrial policy, by implementing the

Industrial, Technological and Foreign Trade Policy (PITCE); but, on the other hand, it kept the same regime of economic policy.'

What is emphasised by Laplane and Sarti is exactly the fact that Brazil was able to propose an industrial policy after two decades of banning, which, for being inserted within a pernicious macroeconomic regime, can hardly reach favourable results. The reason is that the high interest rates discourage investments, imposing negative effects also on the investments in innovation activities.

Furthermore, the regime of fluctuating exchange rates has occasionally over-appreciated exchange rates, stimulating imports to the detriment of the domestic production sector. This movement creates a vicious circle insofar as the lack of investments in innovative activities leads to losing competitiveness, thus increasing the stimulus to imports, particularly of goods with greater value added and of more intensive technology. Consequently, it leaves to the domestic production sector the production of commodities and of goods and services of lesser value added and less intensive in technology. In brief, it jeopardises the production restructuring required for social and economic development.

The restrictive fiscal policy has significantly reduced investments by the federal government, thus hindering investments with infrastructure which became bottlenecks to production. This policy reduced the budget available to ministries for policy implementation, by allocating the resources as contingency reserves, thus affecting also the budgets aimed at the innovation policy.

Such a policy resulted in a slowdown of GDP real growth rates, with a reduction in GDP real growth rate, from 2.7 per cent in 2002, to 1.10 per cent in 2003; returning to growth in 2004, with a rate of 5.70 per cent, fostered especially by a favourable international context, as we may see in Table 2.8.

In the Brazilian case, the macroeconomic policy, seen as an implicit policy, became one of the main obstacles to the evolution and growth of the national innovation system. Thus, conditions were placed for the reproduction of an asymmetric system that hampers the integration of the innovation policy with the other policies. The reason was the choice in favour of a restrictive macroeconomic policy as of 1994, which has as its main adjustment variables the interest rates and the exchange rates.

The option for this macroeconomic policy, which subsumes a neoliberal perspective, prevented the adoption of a development policy and hindered the adoption and implementation of a broad innovation policy — that is, one that would embody the advances of the systemic vision. Therefore, it restricted this policy to a narrow vision about the NSI — defined as explicit innovation policy.

Table 2.8: *Real Growth Rate of Gross Domestic Product (GDP), Inflation Rate (IPCA), Interest Rates, 2001–2008*

Period	*GDP: Real Growth Rate (% p.a.)*	*IPCA: Extended Consumer Price Index Growth Rate (% p.a.)*	*Interest Rate (TJLP % p.a.)*
2001	1.30	7.67	9.5
2002	2.70	12.53	9.9
2003	1.10	9.30	11.5
2004	5.70	7.60	9.8
2005	3.16	5.69	9.8
2006	3.97	3.14	7.9
2007	6.09	4.46	6.2
2008	5.16	5.90	6.1
2009	–0.64	4.31	6.0
2010	7.49	5.91	5.9

Source: IBGE (Brazilian Institute of Geography and Statistics) website, http://www.sidra.ibge.gov.br/bda/cnt/default.asp?z=t&o=15&i=P (accessed 25 October 2011). Authors' elaboration; and BNDES website, http://www.bndes.gov.br/SiteBNDES/bndes/bndes_pt. (accessed 1 November 2011). Authors' elaboration.

Note: References for GDP values: for 1995–2006, National Accounts System Reference 2000 (IBGE/SCN 2000 *Anual*); for 2009 and 2010, preliminary results estimated from Quarterly National Accounts Reference 2000.

From 2003 on, with particular emphasis on 2004 and 2005, the domestic market began to get stronger, mainly because of the social development policy established by the government, whose main programme was the Bolsa Familia (Poor Family Support Pension).

The establishment of 'Bolsa Família' was specifically addressed to the Brazilian social context, characterised by deep income inequalities, which also reflect the significant regional and intra-regional disparities. In 2009, Brazil presented a GDP of US$ 1,998,985 billion (in dollars PPP) and a per capita GDP of US$ 10,344.22 (in dollars PPP). Even so, there were 39.6 million poor people and 13.4 million indigents in 2009 in Brazil.[20] The heterogeneous social structure, with strong income concentration, affects the patterns of demand and consumption. Existing regional differences and disparities of purchasing power result in a broad heterogeneity in the national pattern of demand, thus affecting the production structure.

The production structure often presents, within the same plant, distinct production methods, in order to comply with different consumption patterns. In order to break up these differences that allow reproduction of the underdevelopment process, it will be necessary to set policies, among which should be those of income transfer, aiming at including population into the market.

These policies can be regarded as opportunities for producing the required changes in the productive structure, if they are integrated to a policy of social and economic development. They should have innovation as one of their main guidelines, being therefore integrated also to the innovation policy. As for this latter, it should not be restricted to technological innovation, but rather should also consider other kinds of innovations such as organisational, in processes, etc., thus incorporating the systemic vision of the innovation policy.

'Bolsa Família', the federal government's programme aimed at income transfer, assumes a key role for the enhancement of domestic demand. According to the Ministry of Social Development and Food Security:

> Family Pension Programme (FPP) is a programme for direct transfer of income with conditionalities that benefit families in situation of poverty (monthly per capita income between R$ 60.01 and R$ 120.00) and in situation of extreme poverty (monthly per capita income below R$ 60.00), in conformity with Law 10836, of 9 January, 2004 and the Act no. 5209 of 17 December, 2004.[21]

The programme establishes the following conditions for families to access the benefits: Families with monthly per capita income of up to R$ 137.00 appropriately registered in the Unified Register of Social Programmes (CadÚnico) are entitled to benefit from the Family Pension Programme.[22]

Table 2.9: *Evolution of Benefits of RGPS, BPC and 'Bolsa Família' (Poor Families Pension), 2000–2007 (Million Benefits/ Families)*

	2000	2001	2002	2003	2004	2005	2006	2007	2008	2009	2010
General Regime of Social Security RGPS (1)	17.5	17.9	18.9	19.5	20.5	21.1	21.6	22.1	22.8	23.5	24.4
Conti-nuing Social Benefit/ Social Security Act - BPC/ LOAS (1) (2)	1.2	1.3	1.6	1.7	2.1	2.3	2.5	2.7	2.9	3.2	3.4
Family Grants — Bolsa Família (3)	-	-	-	3.6	6.6	8.7	10.9	11.0	10.5	12.3	12.8

Source: Ministry of Planning, Budget and Management website, http://www.planejamento.gov.br (accessed 1 November 2011). Ministry of Social Development and Fight against Hunger website, http://www.mds.gov.br (accessed 1 November 2011). Ministry of Social Security website, http://www.mpas.gov.br (accessed 1 November 2011). Authors' elaboration.

Note: More than 60 per cent of these benefits had values equal to one minimum wage.

(1) Issued benefit.

(2) Does not include Life Monthly Pension (*Renda Mensal Vitalícia*, RMV).

(3) Family supported.

The programme has been effectively improving the purchasing/consumption power of lower income families, thus impacting even the country's structure of income distribution. The Gini Index for Brazil, of 0.54 in 2009, has presented a positive, although slow, evolution towards income de-concentration.

Thus, policies for social inclusion play a very important role in the formation of the Brazilian system of innovation. Social policies are not restricted to income transfer; health and education policies, for instance, are also important for the formation of the NIS.

The NIS also comprises the sub-system of capacity building, which integrates the scientific, technological and educational perspectives. This sub-system is fundamental for the NSI, being included both by the broad definition of NSI and by its strict concept. The capacity and capabilities of the agents in the economy depend to a large extent on their education level. The assimilation, learning and use of knowledge as input to innovation depend on these characteristics of the agents. When the agents present better qualifications, at the levels of both basic and higher education, the learning process becomes easier in view of their enhanced capacity for assimilating and disseminating new knowledge.

Based on this diagnosis, the federal government, through the Ministry of Education, developed the Plan for Development of Education (PDE). The programme can be organised according to four main lines: basic education, higher education, vocational education, and literacy.

PDE was formulated based on a systemic concept, where the various territorial and social dimensions are taken into account for the implementation of the programme. Therefore, the territorial and the educational matters are interconnected through the notion of educational arrangement. It can be said that the programme is founded on the following assumptions: (*a*) systemic vision of education, (*b*) territoriality, (*c*) development, (*d*) collaborative regime, (*e*) accountability and (*f*) social mobilisation.

These assumptions are meant to support the elaboration of a programme that seeks to reduce educational disparities in the country and, thus, intends to reduce social and territorial inequalities. The idea of a systemic model is helpful insofar as it does not isolate the various education levels. Furthermore, it connects education to territorial and development matters and highlights its potentiality to contribute to social matters and equity in the country. Thus, it is sought to build an education system that is connected to the multiplicities prevailing in the country.

Despite the appropriate discourse to meet the country needs, the PDE is still very recent for evaluating its results. The programme was launched in 2007, and its implementation was gradual throughout the country and was only completed, according to the original schedule, at the end of 2010.

Nevertheless, the main indicator available for monitoring the PDE is the Index of the Basic Education Development (*Índice de Desenvolvimento da Educação Básica*, IDEB) — which is based on two major national assessments — School Census and Evaluation System of Basic Education (SAEB). This indicator is biannual and the latest available data, for 2009, demonstrate compliance with the targets set for this year.

Outcomes of State Policy and State Institutions on the NSI

There is a great deal of difficulty for assessing the outcomes resulting from the innovation policy and the efforts by federal government institutions responsible for its implementation in the period 2003–10. Such difficulty stems from the complexity in identifying and detaching the causality relation between innovative advances in the production sector and explicit and implicit policies.

Still, the impact of implicit policies, especially the macroeconomic policy, on the NSI is evident. This policy reflected on an economic environment unfavourable to investments, because of high interest rates and overestimated exchange rates that were adopted in this period.

On the other hand, the analysis of the goals of explicit policies becomes restricted to the goals of the government policies in the period 2006–2010, since the governmental policies of 2003–2006 — the PITCE and the National Policy of Science, Technology and Innovation (PNCTI) — did not define goals and indicators for evaluation. This means that the goals and indicators set for the PDP specially its macro objectives and PACTI will be considered.

Before analysing the compliance with the goals in 2010 — the target date of the policies — it is worth highlighting that almost all of them are input goals. That is, they refer to expenditures in R&D, investments, infrastructure building or scholarship grants, except for the goals related to exports that refer to outcomes such as participation in global exports. Specifically regarding innovation, the main goal refers to both rise in participation of R&D private investments and rise in investments in R&D in relation to the GDP.

The systemic vision of the innovative process is neglected, once innovation is associated exclusively to R&D and the policy fails to recognise that the learning process, the main tool of innovation, may occur through varied forms. Besides the systemic vision, the characteristics of the national production system and of the social structure also seem to be ignored. The existing heterogeneity, distinct characteristics of consumption, income concentration, and regional disparities that would lead to further measures, to other kinds of 'efforts' and, consequently, goals, were not taken into account.

Thus, the Action Plan is limited to a small sphere of action possibilities. In no moment was it sought to strengthen the learning process and knowledge building in enterprises, so that they would be able to improve their innovative capacity. The intangible factors of the enterprises gain no prominence in the policy of the ministry. In a society where tacit knowledge is relevant for innovation, policy should contain mechanisms and tools aimed at its main input (knowledge). Furthermore, in restricting innovation to the technological feature it reduces the possibilities of action a great deal.

Although the arguments point to the lack of indicators able to provide responses to the systemic vision, and this is why the goals are still linked to traditional indicators, the counter-argument is that, in fact, the proposed measures are still based on a linear vision of the innovation process and the goals and indicators only reflect this reality.

As to the progress towards goals, the current situation of indicators proposed by the two policies PACTI and PDP which together represent the explicit innovation policy in force, can be summarised as follows:

Action Plan on Science, Technology and Innovation for National Development — PACTI[23]

- Investment in R, D & I/GDP (%): 1.5 per cent GDP on R, D & I in relation to GDP (1.02 per cent in 2006), 0.64 per cent federal governments and 0.21 per cent state governments — according to the Ministry of Science and Technology, in 2010 the indicator was 1.16 per cent (preliminary data).
- Innovation in firms: 0.65 per cent of investment in R, D & I made by the private sector (0.51 per cent in 2006) — according to the Ministry of Science and Technology, in 2010 the indicator was 0.55 per cent (preliminary data).

- Formation of human resources: 95,000 scholarships by CNPq; 68,000 in 2006, focus on engineering and other areas related to PITCE, and 65,000 by CAPES — according to the Ministry of Science and Technology, the indicator for 2009 was 70,601.

Policy for Production Development — PDP[24]

- Expansion of fixed Investment: INVESTMENT/GDP — Goal for 2010: 21 per cent. Situation in 2007: 17.6 per cent — According to the Brazilian Institute of Geography and Statistics, the indicator was 18.4 per cent in 2010.
- Rise of the private expenditures in R&D: PRIVATE R&D / GDP — Goal for 2010: 0.65 per cent (R$ 18.2 billion). Situation in 2005: 0.51 per cent or R$ 11.9 billion — according to the Ministry of Science and Technology, in 2010 the indicator was 0.55 per cent (preliminary data).
- Expansion of exports: Participation in Global Exports — Goal for 2010: 1.25 per cent. Situation in 2007: 1.18 per cent. According to the Brazilian Central Bank it was 1.36 per cent in 2010.

As already emphasised, there are 25 sectors that should be served by the PDP. The aim is to establish a policy for strengthening these sectors, by means of a horizontal policy. Thus, these macro objectives permeate such sectors, which gain special attention in order for the goals to be reached. The instruments applied in the implementation of these macro objectives, as detailed earlier, are: accelerated depreciation, funds for emerging enterprises, FINEP resources (R$ 6 billion between 2008 and 2010 — under responsibility of BNDES).

The data indicate that the goals of investments in R&D were not reached as much considering expenditures in the country as a whole, as taking into consideration only the expenditures by the enterprises. In spite of a growing trend of these indicators, such growth proved to be slow. The proposed investment goals also presented a growing trend and the exports goal was reached. It is worth stressing that exports had a significant increment due to increases in of both demand and prices of commodities in the global market. It does not necessarily mean that such increment resulted from the PDP. The two indicators, as well as the indicators of investments in R&D, are subject to international conditions, which have been unfavourable since 2008 (particularly following the second half of the year).

Conclusions and Recommendations Targeting Improvements in the NSI with Specific Emphasis on the Role of the State

The role of the state in the Brazilian innovation system was crucial for the formation of a scientific and technological infrastructure as well as for the industrialisation of the country. In recent years, particularly from 1999 on, the federal government has assumed a pro-innovation stand by designing and implementing a specific policy for promoting innovation.

As discussed in this study, the explicit innovation policy adopted in the period 1999–2002 was still restricted to the Ministry of Science and Technology, and was opposed to the macroeconomic policy then in force. Only after 2003 has this policy been incorporated by other ministries, particularly by the Ministry of Development, Industry and Foreign Trade. Even so, as it was discussed here, the general guidelines remain the same in both periods.

Although this policy has targeted the enterprises, its evaluation suggests that the mechanisms and instruments created for promoting innovation within enterprises have some characteristics that hinder the advance of NSI. Among them, some stand out:

(*a*) a bias towards technological innovation, prioritising the mechanisms for support to research and development, to the detriment of other important innovative activities — thus ignoring (or neglecting) the heterogeneity of the production structure, which entails distinct levels of capacity.

(*b*) a focus on partnership relations between enterprises and scientific and technological institutions, which makes the integration of the other agents participating in the innovation process difficult.

(*c*) implementation forms still based on a linear model of innovation.

In 2007 and 2008, further changes were made in the policy: new guidelines were designed and priority sectors and areas were selected. The governance structure of the policy was modified, but, at the same time, there was the maintenance of old instruments and mechanisms, although proposing a connection between them. The already discussed establishment of goals for this new policy indicates a progress, since in the former policy there were practically no short-term goals. Even so, these goals raised concerns regarding the implementation of such instruments and mechanisms, since they were expressing a linear vision about the innovation process. They possibly only were reflecting the lack of more appropriate indicators, pointing out the need for investments by the policy in the formulation of new indicators. However, a concern remained as to whether the goals would only be expressing the lack of audacity by the explicit policy of innovation.

From the perspective of the implicit innovation policy, the conclusion is that the linear vision hinders the liaison between the explicit policy and the other policies. Particularly in the Brazilian case, three implicit policies are noteworthy: the macroeconomic, the educational and that of social development. The analysis demonstrates that the need for integration surpasses the matter of 'taking advantage of opportunities'. Non-integration became an obstacle to the explicit policy of innovation, preventing or hindering the accomplishment of outcomes. Moreover, the evaluation indicates that integration between policies is crucial for the social and economic development of the country.

On 2 August 2011 the 'Plano Brasil Maior' (Brazilian Major Plan) was launched, establishing industrial policy, technology, services, and foreign trade of the federal government for the period 2011–2014. The new policy sets out some changes in the legal framework for innovation among which are public procurement and the protection of domestic industry. Despite these changes, it is too early to assess the implementation and results of this policy.

Notes

1. The period before 2006, particularly 1995 to 2006, was the subject of the first report of the BRICS Project.
2. The model of industrialisation adopted had the structuralist approach as its fundamental framework, with special emphasis on the ideas of the Brazilian economist Celso Furtado who proposed by that time the idea of 'embedded technology' (or technical base) in the production structure. In the debate of the 1960s the Latin America structuralist school pointed out the need to adapt technologies, which would later be called internalisation of technical advance.
3. After the first impact of economic liberalisation, *ad hoc* regimes were adopted protecting those segments with major weight — either

economic or political — for example, the automotive regime, which protected the automobile industry, and the protection to the textile sector.

4. See, for instance, Pereira (2005).
5. In considering expenditures with research, development and innovation by ministry, the study opted for ministries that are not sectoral, given the difficulties for identifying such expenses in sectoral ministries. Furthermore, previous data surveys have shown that in most sectoral ministries such expenditures were not significant.
6. The analysis was based on information available on the websites of the ministries and related departments. In these sources, we looked for identifying programmes, actions and instruments that made explicit reference to the innovation policy. In addition, information on budget execution was organised for these ministries and departments, in some cases for specific programmes, for the whole period of the analysis, including the estimates for 2009. Again, it is worth recalling that the former period (1995–2005) makes up part of the first report of BRICS Project.
7. As mentioned before, the innovation policy of the period 1995–2006 was discussed in the previous report of BRICS Project.
8. According to the concept of innovation policy used in this study.
9. See 'Uma Visão Geral', Ministério da Ciência e Tecnologia, Secretaria de Desenvolvimento Tecnológico. Brasília, 2006 and 'Relatório de atividades 1999, Diretrizes para 2000', Ministério da Ciência e Tecnologia, Secretaria de Desenvolvimento Tecnológico. Brasília, dezembro 1999; and 'A Política Brasileira para a Inovação na Década dos 1990s', mimeo.
10. According to MCT, the Law of Goods (Law no. 11.196, of 21 November 2005), in its Section III, automatically authorises the use of fiscal incentives by the juristic persons that accomplish technological research and development of technological innovation. Among these incentives, it's possible to highlight income tax deductions for expenditures with R&D activities, which may reach a value of up to twice the expenditures of the firm. The other incentives are: income tax deduction, reduction of tax on industrialised products, accelerated depreciation of equipments, accelerated repayment, credit of income tax withheld at source on money remittance to other countries for payment of royalties; reduction to zero of the rate of income tax withheld at source in money remittances to other countries. All these incentives are bound to the implementation of R&D activities.
11. The masters' and doctorate education is very important for a country. Policies for preparing researchers should not be discontinued. However, this should not be the only way for implementing a policy for scholarship granting if the aim of the policy is to induce innovation in the production sector.

12. See Table C in the Annexure.
13. FINEP's website http://www.finep.gov.br/pagina.asp?pag=30.80.30 (accessed 15 May 2009).
14. In the Brazilian legislation, fiscal incentives are granted only to firms that declare actual rather than projected profits for purposes of corporate income tax.
15. MDIC's website http://www.desenvolvimento.gov.br/sitio/interna/interna.php?area=2&menu=300 (accessed 12 May 2009).
16. There was a structural break in series between 2007 and 2008 due to change in the National Classification of Economic Activities (CNAE) which was launched in the version 2.0 following the International Standard Industrial Classification of All Economic Activities (ISIC) rev. 4. Therefore, it is not recommended to compare for the whole period since 1996.
17. Programme for International Students Assessment (PISA), created by OECD; The System for Assessment of Basic Education (*Sistema de Avaliação da Educação Básica*, SAEB) of MEC; among others.
18. Brazilian Mathematics Olympiad of Public Schools.
19. Areas bearing future possibilities: biotechnology and nanotechnology, information and communication technologies, health products, biofuels, electricity, hydrogen and renewable energies, petroleum, gas and mineral coal, agribusiness, biodiversity and natural resources, Amazonia and semi-arid, meteorology and climate changes, spatial programme, nuclear programme, national defence and public security.
20. The lines of extreme poverty or indigence shown on *Ipeadata* are estimated based on a methodology developed by the commission IBGE-IPEA-CEPAL that defined a list of basic needs foods which satisfy the nutrition requirements for each Brazilian region. From the information about the total amount of calories per day, the amount consumed and the unit price, the expenditure was calculated for each product and its sum, resulting in the line of extreme poverty per person. The line of poverty is defined as twice the line of extreme poverty. (*Ipeadata*, http://www.ipeadata.gov.br. The Ipeadata site is provided and managed by the Institute of Applied Economic Research (Ipea), Brazil. According to the site Ipeadata, it is committed to providing high quality information from reliable data sources).
21. See the website of the Ministry of Social Development and Fight against Hunger, http://www.mds.gov.br/ (accessed 29 October 2009).
22. The family income is calculated by adding the monthly incomes of all individuals of the household (such as wages and retirement pensions). This value must be divided by the number of people who live in the household, thus resulting in the per capita income of the family.
23. The other indicators are not available yet.
24. The other indicators are not available yet.

References

Albuquerque, E., 2007. 'Inadequacy of Technology and Innovation Systems at the Periphery', *Cambridge Journal of Economics*, 31(5), 669–90.

Arruda, M., S. Hollanda and R. Vermulm, 2006. *Inovação Tecnológica no Brasil: A indústria em busca da competitividade global*. São Paulo: Anpei.

Arundel, A., 2006. 'Innovation Indicators: Any Progress since 1996?: Or How to Address the "Oslo Paradox": We See Innovation Surveys Everywhere but Where is the Impact on Innovation Policy?' Paper presented at the conference 'Blue Sky II: What Indicators for Science, Technology and Innovation Policies in the 21st Century', Organisation for Economic Co-operation and Development, The U.S. National Science Foundation, Industry Canada and Statistics Canada, 25–27 September, Ottawa.

Brasil, 1990. 'Política industrial e de comércio exterior: Diretrizes gerais', Ministério da Economia, Fazenda e Planejamento, Secretaria Nacional de Economia, Brasília.

———, 1998. 'Nova Política Industrial — Desenvolvimento e Competitividade', Presidência da República, Brasília.

———, 2002. 'Livro Branco: Ciência, Tecnologia e Inovação: Resultado da Conferência Nacional de Ciência, Tecnologia e Inovação', Ministério da Ciência e Tecnologia, Brasília.

———, 2003. 'Diretrizes de Política Industrial, Tecnológica e de Comércio Exterior', Casa Civil da Presidência da República; Ministério do Desenvolvimento, Indústria e Comércio Exterior; Ministério da Fazenda; Ministério do Planejamento; Ministério da Ciência e Tecnologia; Instituto de Pesquisa Econômica Aplicada (IPEA); Banco Nacional de Desenvolvimento, Econômico e Social (BNDES); Financiadora de Estudos e Projetos (FINEP); Agência de Promoção das Exportações (APEX) Brasil, Brasília, 26 November.

———, 2006. 'Relatório de Gestão do Ministério da Ciência e Tecnologia — Janeiro de 2003 a Dezembro de 2006', Ministério da Ciência e Tecnologia, Brasília.

———, 2008. 'O Plano de desenvolvimento da educação: Razões, Princípio e Programas', Ministério da Educação, Brasília.

———, 2011. 'Plano Brasil Maior — Inovar para competir, competir para crescer, Plano 2011/2014', Governo Federal, Brasil.

Brazilian Institute of Geography and Statistics (IBGE), 2008. *Estatística do Cadastro Central de Empresas 2006*. Rio de Janeiro: Brazilian Institute of Geography and Statistics

Cassiolato, J., 1992. 'The Role of User-Producer Relations in Innovation and Diffusion of New Technologies: Lessons from Brazil'. Ph.D. Thesis, Science Policy Research Unit, University of Sussex.

Cassiolato, J., 1999. 'A Economia do Conhecimento e as Novas Políticas Industriais e Tecnológicas', in H. M. M. Lastres and S. Albagli (eds), *Informação e Globalização na Era do Conhecimento*. Rio de Janeiro: Campus, 164–90.

Cassiolato, J., 2003. *Notas Preliminares sobre Sistemas de Inovação e Cooperação*. Rio de Janeiro: Mimeo.

Cassiolato, J. and H. M. M. Lastres, 2005. 'Sistemas de Inovação e Desenvolvimento — as implicações de política', *São Paulo em Perpectiva*, 19(1): 34–45.

———, 2008. 'Discussing Innovation and Development: Converging Points between the Latin American School and the Innovation Systems Perspective', Working Paper no. 08-02, Globelics Working Paper Series, The Global Network for Economics of Learning, Innovation, and Competence Building System.

Conferência Nacional de Ciência, Tecnologia e Inovação, 2006. '3ª Conferência Nacional de Ciência, Tecnologia e Inovação: síntese das conclusões e recomendações', Ministério da Ciência e Tecnologia, Centro de Gestão de Estudos Estratégicos, Brasília.

Coutinho, L. G., 2005. 'Regimes macroeconômicos e estratégias de negócio: uma política industrial alternativa para o Brasil no século XXI', in H. M. M. Lastres, J. E. Cassiolato and A. Arroio (eds), *Conhecimento, Sistemas de Inovação e Desenvolvimento*. Rio de Janeiro: Editora UFRJ/Contraponto, 429–48.

Dantas, M., 2008. 'O Drama da Educação Pública No Brasil', Research Paper no. 26/08, Projeto BRIC´s, Rede de Pesquisa em Sistemas e Arranjos Produtivos e Inovativos Locais (RedeSist), Rio de Janeiro.

Ergas, H., 1987. 'The Importance of Technology Policy', in P. Dasgupta and P. Stoneman (eds), *Economic Policy and Technological Performance*. Cambridge: Cambridge University Press, 51–96.

Ferraz, J. C., D. Kupfer and M. Iootty, 2003. 'Made in Brazil: Industrial Competitiveness 10 Years after Economic Liberalization', *Latin American Studies Series*, Institute of Developing Economies–Japan External Trade Organization (IDE–JETRO), 4: 32–85.

Freeman, C., 1977. 'Aspects of Public Policy for Innovation', in G. Boyle, D. Elliot and R. Roy (eds), *The Politics of Technology*. London: Longman and The Open University Press, 76–87.

———, 1982. 'Innovation and Long Cycles of Economic Development', Paper presented at the 'International Seminar on Innovation and Development at the Industrial Sector', Economics Department, University of Campinas, 25–27 August, Campinas.

———, 1992. 'Formal Scientific and Technical Institutions in the National System of Innovation', in B.-Å. Lundvall (ed.), *National Systems of Innovation: Towards a Theory of Innovation and Interactive Learning*. London: Pinter, 169–90.

Freeman, C., 1996. 'The Greening of Technology and Models of Innovation', *Technological Forecasting and Social Change*, 53(1): 27–40.

Gadelha, C. A. G., 2001. 'Política industrial: uma visão Neo-Schumpeteriana Sistêmica e Estrutural', *Revista de Economia Política*, 21(4): 149–71.

Guimarães, E., 1996. 'A Experiência Recente da Política Industrial no Brasil: Uma Avaliação', *Textos para Discussão*, 409, Instituto de Pesquisa Econômica Aplicada, Brasília, April.

———, 2006. 'Políticas de Inovação: Financiamento e Incentivos', *Textos para Discussão*, 121, Instituto de Pesquisa Econômica Aplicada, Brasília, August.

Guimarães, V., F. Peixoto, J. Cassiolato, and H. Lastres, 2007. 'Reformas estruturais, ciclos de criação e destruição de capacidade produtiva e o pensamento de Celso Furtado', in J. Sabóia and F. Carvalho (eds), *Celso Furtado e o Século XXI*. Rio de Janeiro: Instituto de Economia da Universidade Federal do Rio de Janeiro, 167–80.

Koeller, P., 2007. 'O Papel do Estado e a Política de Inovação'. Research Paper no. 02/2007. BRICS Project — A Comparative Study of National Innovation Systems of Brazil, Russia, India, China and South Africa, Projeto BRIC´s, Rede de Pesquisa em Sistemas e Arranjos Produtivos e Inovativos Locais (RedeSist) and Instituto de Economia, Universidade Federal do Rio de Janeiro.

Koeller, P. and J. E. Cassiolato, 2009. 'Achievements and Shortcomings of Brazil's Innovation Policies', in J. E. Cassiolato and V. Vitorino (eds), *BRICS and Development Alternatives: Innovation Systems and Policies*. London: Anthem Press, 35–72.

Laplane, M. and F. Sarti, 2006. 'Prometeu Acorrentado: O Brasil na Indústria Mundial no Início do Século XXI', in Ricardo Carneiro (ed.), *A Supremacia dos Mercados e a Política do Governo Lula*. São Paulo: Editora UNESP, 271–91.

Lundvall, B.-Å. (ed.), 1992. *National Systems of Innovation: Towards a Theory of Innovation and Interactive Learning*. London: Pinter.

———, 2010 [1992]. 'Post Script: Innovation System Research Where it Came from and Where it Might Go', in B.-Å. Lundvall (ed.), *National Innovation Systems: Towards a Theory of Innovation and Interactive Learning*. London; Anthem Press, 317–49.

Lundvall, B.-Å., B. Johnson, E. Andersen, and B. Dalum, 2002. 'National Systems of Production, Innovation and Competence Building', *Research Policy*, 31(2): 213–31.

Ministério da Ciência e Tecnologia, 2009. 'Plano Estratégico', Ministério da Ciência e Tecnologia, Brasil. http://www.mct.gov.br/index.php/content/view/15854.html (accessed 1 June 2009).

Pacheco, C., 2006. 'Ciência, Tecnologia, Inovação e Geração de Riqueza', in '3ª Conferência Nacional de Ciência, Tecnologia e Inovação: síntese das conclusões e recomendações', Ministério da Ciência e Tecnologia, Centro de Gestão de Estudos Estratégicos, Brasília.
Pereira, N., 2005. 'Fundos Setoriais: Avaliação das Estratégias de Implementação e Gestão', *Texto para Discussão*, 1136, Instituto de Pesquisa Econômica Aplicada, Brasília.
Pesquisa de Inovação (PINTEC), 2003. *Pesquisa Industrial de Inovação Tecnológica 1998–2000*. Rio de Janeiro: Instituto Brasileiro de Geografia e Estatística.
———, 2005. *Pesquisa Industrial de Inovação Tecnológica 2001–2003*. Rio de Janeiro: Instituto Brasileiro de Geografia e Estatística.
———, 2007. *Pesquisa Industrial de Inovação Tecnológica 2003–2005*. Rio de Janeiro: Instituto Brasileiro de Geografia e Estatística.
———, 2010. *Pesquisa Industrial de Inovação Tecnológica 2008*. Rio de Janeiro: Instituto Brasileiro de Geografia e Estatística.
Prebisch, R., 1964. *Dinâmica do desenvolvimento latino-americano*. Rio de Janeiro: Fundo de Cultura.
Reinert, E., 1996. 'The Role of Technology in the Creation of Rich and Poor Nations: Underdevelopment in a Schumpeterian System', in D. Aldcroft and C. Ross (eds), *Rich Nations, Poor Nations: The Long Run Perspective*. Cheltenham: Edward Elgar, 161–88.
Rothwell, R., 1983. 'The Difficulties of National Innovation Policies', in S. Macdonald, D. M. Lamberton and T. Mandeville (eds), *The Trouble with Technology: Explorations in the Process of Technological Change.*. London: Pinter, 202–15.
Vermulm, R. and S. Hollanda, 2009. *Os novos instrumentos de apoio à inovação: uma avaliação inicial*. Brasília: Centro de Gestão e Estudos Estratégicos–Associação Nacional de Pesquisa e Desenvolvimento 2008.

Annexure

Table A2.1: *MDIC Programmes Related to Innovation*

Programme	*Action/Instrument*	*Methods of Operation*
Incentive to innovation within firm		Related to computing of net profit, actual profit and tax on the net profit
	Tax incentives	Tax on industrialized products — IPI
		Accelerated depreciation
		Income tax withheld at source
		Sharing laboratories and equipment
	Cooperation enterprise / Technological research institution	Technology transfer
		ICT partnership/Company
	Cooperation company/ Technology institution	
	Incentives for business software	
		Centre-west, north and northeast
	Incentives for industries of hardware and automation	Other regions of the country
		Acquisitions made by CNPq
	Grant for innovation in enterprise	
Project in cooperation with the European Union		

(*Cont.*)

(*Cont.*)

Programme	*Action/Instrument*	*Methods of Operation*
	Project network technology centres and Brazilian SMEs	
	Project support international insertion of Brazilian SMEs	
Local productive arrangements — APLs		
Micro, small and medium enterprises		
	Productive development policy	

Source: MDIC website, http://www.desenvolvimento.gov.br/sitio (accessed 1 November 2011). Authors' elaboration.

Table A2.2: *BNDES Programmes Aimed at Innovation*

Innovation
Innovative Capital Line
Technological Innovation Line
Technological Fund — FUNTEC
CRIATEC Programme
Industry
Programme for Support to the Implementation of the Brazilian System of Terrestrial Digital TV — PROTVD
Programme for Financing to Enterprises from the Brazilian Aeronautical Production Chain — PRO-AERONÁUTICA
Programme for Support to the Development of the Health Industrial Complex — PROFARMA
Programme for the Development of Software and Information Technology Services Industry — PROSOFT

Source: BNDES website, http://www.bndes.gov.br/SiteBNDES/bndes/bndes_pt (accessed 1 November 2011). Authors' elaboration.

Table A2.3: *Brazil: Legal Framework of Innovation Policy*

Laws	*Main Objective*
1993 — Law 8.661	Created tax incentives to foster enhancement of the technological capacity of manufacturing and agricultural enterprises taking part in one of the programmes: Programme for Industry Technological Development (PDTI) and Programme for Agricultural Technological Development (PDTA).
1997 — Law 9.532	Reduced the tax incentives established by Law 8.661/93, by approximately 50%.
2000 — Law 10.168	Created a tax: Tax on Intervention in the Economic Field, *Contribuição de Intervenção do Domínio Econômico* (CIDE), to finance the programme *Programa de Estímulo à Interação Universidade-Empresa para o Apoio à Inovação.*
2001 — Law 10.332	Re-established the tax incentives created by Law 8.661/93. Also instituted the grant for enterprises taking part in the PDTI or PDTA, and mechanisms for subsidising interest rates.
During the period 1999–2002, 12 sectoral funds were created	Provided support for the development of R&D projects in partnership between scientific and technological institutions and enterprises. The funds related to the following sectors: petroleum and natural gas, energy, water resources, transport, mineral resources, aerospace, telecommunications, information technology, health, aeronautics, biotechnology and agribusiness. There were also the *Verde-Amarelo* funds, Amazon Fund, and funds for infrastructure.
2004 — Law of Innovation Law 10.973	Aimed at promoting interaction between scientific and technological institutions of the federal government and enterprises. This law also created new tax incentives for the innovative process within firms, establishing a grant for enterprises taking part in a project under the *Fundo Nacional de Desenvolvimento Científico e Tecnológico* (FNDCT).
2004 creation of two further sectoral funds	Related to the naval and coastal sector and to the Amazonian area; aimed at developing new technologies and stimulating the innovative process.
2005 — *Lei do Bem* — Law 11.196	Also related to tax incentives for technological innovation. This law replaced Law No 10.637 (2002) and its main instruments are: tax exemption, accelerated depreciation and the possibility of grants

(*Cont.*)

(*Cont.*)

Laws	*Main Objective*
	for researchers and graduates (masters and doctors). The difference between this new law and the former is that the mechanisms for tax incentives became automatic; previously, it was necessary to participate in the PDTI or the PDTA.

Source: Presidência da República website, http://www4.planalto.gov.br/legislacao/legislacao-1/leis-ordinarias (accessed 1 November 2011). Authors' elaboration.

Table A2.4: *Brazil: Total Scholarships in the Country and Abroad Granted by Federal Agencies 1997–2008*

		In the Country			*Abroad*		
Year	*Total (A=B+E)*	*Total (B=C+D)*	*CNPq*	*CAPES (D)*	*Total (E=F+G)*	*CNPq*	*CAPES*
1997	37.4	34.9	13.3	21.6	2.480	1.1	1.4
1998	35.0	32.9	11.7	21.1	2.140	791	1.3
1999	32.9	31.0	11.2	19.8	1.855	596	1.3
2000	32.0	30.3	11.5	18.7	1.772	562	1.2
2001	37.2	34.4	12.0	22.4	2.794	716	2.1
2002	38.1	35.1	11.8	23.3	2.955	744	2.2
2003	39.7	36.8	12.3	24.5	2.859	460	2.4
2004	41.9	38.9	13.6	25.3	3.003	499	2.5
2005	44.2	40.9	14.8	26.1	3.297	403	2.9
2006	48.6	45.0	16.1	28.9	3.578	347	3.2
2007	52.1	48.4	16.8	31.5	3.740	487	3.2
2008	62.6	58.9	17.9	41.0	3.740	526	3.2

Source: MCT (Ministry of Science and Technology) website, http://www.mct.gov.br/index.php/content/view/2050/_b__i_Bolsas_de_formacao_e_pesquisa_b__i_.html (accessed 1 November 2011). Authors' elaboration.

3

Russia

Tatiana Kuznetsova

Russian history is full of contradictions in the evolution of its innovation system, its state policy and its position in the world.[1] Russia as a successor of the USSR is known for its contribution to global science and technology (S&T). During its long history the basic elements of science and an innovation system were put in place under political and economic objectives which led to the acceleration of S&T to serve military requirements and industrialisation. Intensive investment was made in R&D facilities and equipment, and it became possible to carry out research in the most important scientific areas. As a result, the very specific — but at the global cutting edge — S&T sector and national system of innovation (NSI) were created (Gokhberg 2003).

In the USSR the government was spending about 4 per cent of the country's budget on R&D. In certain years total R&D expenditures amounted to 3 per cent of the GDP. According to official statistics, even in 1990 (the last and not the best year in the history of the USSR) 2 per cent of the GDP was allocated to support the R&D sector. 'Science and related services' employed about 4 million people (including almost 1 million researchers); the share of researchers in the economically active population was one of the highest in the world — more than 200 R&D personnel per 10,000 employed.[2] Though R&D potential during that period was mainly concentrated in a few major R&D centres, an active regional policy was pursued. All large regions (the Soviet republics) had academies of science, universities, big R&D centres, informational centres, etc.

Advanced research, cutting-edge technologies, innovations have radically changed the way of life the world over, and continue to do so. Many experts agree that losing the pace of S&T development was one of the main reasons leading to the collapse of the USSR. Here we refer specifically to the relationship between science, the NSI as a whole and the state. This covers the organisation, management and the support for S&T development. It concerns the efficiency of mechanisms for the reproduction and use of R&D potential and the application of R&D results in the economy.

Against the background of the overall stagnation of the Soviet economy, its painful inability to adopt and implement R&D results and new technologies, the opportunities to mobilise additional resources required to sustain a high S&T level began to shrink. One might think that in a planned economy it should not be a problem to create optimal conditions for regulating the S&T and innovation activities sphere but this was not the case. Due to predominating centralised management, the conditions for pursuing an S&T and innovation policy were extremely adverse. In reality nothing except direct government intervention into the activities of specific research institutes or enterprises encouraged S&T progress. Indirect motivation and promotion of S&T and innovation activities practically haven't been used at all.

Immediately after the collapse of the USSR the S&T complex faced a systems crisis, and some of its consequences still haven't been overcome yet. According to official statistics, gross domestic R&D expenditures (GERD) just in 1990–1995 dropped by four times (in constant prices); federal budget allocations (FBA) on R&D dropped five times; the number of R&D personnel two times.[3] Despite the subsequent improvement, by 2009 GERD had increased to just 75 per cent of the 1991 level (and to just half of the 1990 figures). R&D expenditures as a share of GDP in 2009 amounted to 1.24 per cent (2005–2006 — 1.07, 2007 — 1.12, 2008 — 1.04 per cent); expenditures per researcher were $40.1 thousand (several times less than in many developed countries).[4] The S&T potential is still unevenly distributed across the country's territory (in certain respects the situation became even worse). In 2009, 21 per cent of all R&D organisations were located in the city of Moscow (and almost 28 per cent of them in Moscow together with the Moscow region), with a further 10 per cent in St Petersburg.

Practically until the disintegration of the USSR and even a few years afterwards, its system of innovation existed in narrow scientific-technological space. Scientific results and innovations were created and introduced (as a rule) on the basis of the centralised decisions of the government, and in the areas connected to the state's interests. Note that the term 'national system of innovation' was never used in the USSR, and the actual NSI was not considered worthy of research or of a special government policy.[5] Only during the last years of the painful transformations of the economy, the state and society, has a comprehension of a key role of innovations, and the necessities of a wider understanding of NSI as a system of national institutes been emerging.

The wide understanding of innovation and the new approach to NSI have been fixed in key documents of a state policy only in the beginning of the current century. Most of them were adopted by the government of the Russian Federation. Among them were the basic direction of the Russian Federation's policy on S&T development until 2010 and subsequent period (2002), R&D and Innovation Development Strategy in the Russian Federation until 2015 (2006) and the Ministry of Education and Science (MES) basic report 'The Development of Innovation System of Russian Federation' (2008) documents.

The position detailed in these documents are consolidated and widened in the main official initiative at the current stage (2008) — 'Conception of a Long-Term Development until 2020' (CLTD 2020).[6] This document reflects the world trend connected with increased importance of long-term socio-economic and S&T development priorities, affected both by global trends and limitations and national specificities and potential. International experience suggests that understanding these trends and taking them into account when developing national policies is necessary to select adequate policy tools which would allow the implementation of national concepts and priorities in the environment of open economy and international competition. The importance of speeding up the country's 'leap' becomes even more apparent against the background of the global financial crisis and its manifestation in the Russian Federation.

All segments of the NSI and all economic actors feel an urgent need for a systematic representation of the country's R&D and innovation system, as well as an improvement of appropriate government policies. This is due to the fact that all of them feel the pressure of a whole host of legal, administrative, financial, and other limitations and barriers which hinder their efficient operation and hamper the economy's transition to innovation-driven development, which, in turn, are the strategic objectives of the country's development policy.

A major result of the CLTD (including the long-term forecast of socio-economic and S&T development prepared in the course of this work) and other documents is the consensus arrived at by the society and economic community regarding the unquestionable need to shift the national economy from heavy reliance on raw material exports to innovation-driven, socially oriented development.

Note also another aspect important in the context of the study. In effect for the first time in Russia, the Concept documents use the modern definition of NSI which comprises the following:

(*a*) interlinked structures engaged in production and/or commercial exploitation of knowledge and technologies and;

(*b*) a set of legal, financial and social institutes which ensure interaction of educational, R&D, entrepreneurial and non-profit organisations in all spheres of the economy and social sector.

For example, CLTD 2020 is based on three main elements:

- Policy framework — the conception brings together the key policy directions and establishes connections between NSI development policies and other spheres: education system development, progress of high-tech sectors, environment protection strategies, health system development, regional development strategies, etc.
- 'Roadmap' for reforms — this component of the CLTD 2020 sets out the structure of each direction as well as a basic plan of action. For NSI it is represented by six initiatives including development of human resources for innovation, infrastructure support, stimulation of demand for innovation, and others. For the first time in the history of Russia this document confirms the invariance of its transition to an innovative model of development and submits the restrictions, opportunities and directions of this transition so much in detail.
- Target indicators — a statistical tool for tracking the main macro effects to monitor the progress of the reforms. There are several indicators proposed to refer to the NSI development goal: GERD-to-GDP ratio, labour productivity, share and other indicators for the high-tech industries, etc. Some of them can be seen in Table 3.1.

Table 3.1: *The Key CLTD Target Indicators for NSI Development*

(%)	2007	2020
GERD to GDP ratio	1.12	2.7
Labour productivity growth rates	6–7	9–10
Share of high-tech sectors in value added	10.9	17–19
Share of high-tech products exports in the world's total	0.3	2.0
Share of innovative products in total sales	5.5	25–35
Share of industrial enterprises engaged in technological innovation	13.3	40–50
VA of innovation sector to GDP	10–11	17–20

Source: GRF (2008a).

In spite of the inevitable adjustment of the indicators presented in the table — and of the other target CLTD 2020 indicators — due to the effects of the global financial and economic crisis, in the long term the suggested ways and means to ensure sustainable increase of the population's standard of life, improve national security, achieve dynamic growth of the national economy, secure a better position on the global arena should remain valid and develop further. Russia's political leaders repeatedly made statements to this effect, speaking about plans to sustain the level of support to R&D and high-technology sectors.

Evaluation of the Current Form of State and Its Position in Relation to NSI

In the USSR (and in Czarist Russia before 1917) R&D was developed as a government sub-system, and concentrated in government-owned structures such as institutes and universities. In terms of the scale of the S&T complex, the USSR was quite comparable with the USA but its development was accompanied by numerous ambiguous and controversial phenomena which ultimately eroded that positioning. In 1989 the Soviet R&D sector comprised more than 4.6 thousand organisations including research institutes, design bureaus, higher education institutions, and enterprises. It employed over 4 million people, or almost 4 per cent of the national workforce. Fourteen out of every thousand workers were researchers (Centre for Science Research and Statistics 1992).

During that time the scientific community and the society generally became convinced that universal, comprehensive government support (funding, planning, supervision, etc.) was natural and necessary. Until about the late 1970s scientists and university teachers received sufficiently high (by Soviet standards) salaries and their professions enjoyed a high prestige in society. Then the situation deteriorated dramatically.

The combination of two key factors — reliance on permanent patronage by the government and gradual worsening of the majority of the researchers' material situation — partially explains why a proportion of the scientific community, a rather appreciable one, did not accept the liberal market reforms of the early 1990s. Up to a point this attitude is still there. For example, a study of researchers' opinions regarding the current state of the R&D sphere and efficiency of various government policies suggests that about 50 per cent of the scientists still remain quite sceptical about the prospects of a national system of science and those of their own career development. Among the least appreciated government initiatives are those on privatisation and incorporation of R&D organisations, the limitation of their business activities (as part of downsizing and restructuring of the public R&D sector) and other institutional changes.[7]

In any country society's needs are met, economic potential grows and national security is achieved through development of the S&T sphere. During the 1980s, when the efficiency of the Soviet S&T complex was obviously declining, according to the then president of the USSR Academy of Science, G. Marchuk, in 40 per cent of the 400 priority S&T development areas Soviet scientists were either the leaders or on par with the top world level. In other areas the lag was apparent. In 1980–1988 the share of R&D results which were better than the top world level dropped from 9 to 4 per cent, and of those on par with it from 34 to 22 per cent (Avdulov and Kulkin 1996; *Scientific–Technical Progress in the USSR* 1990).

After the disintegration of the USSR when wide ranging reforms including privatisation and market liberalisation were being undertaken, the Russian economy and the Russian state changed dramatically. The state became more democratic; market institutes, elements of a civil society (which are not always accepted 'canonical' forms) gradually began to develop. All this occurred in a background of economic crisis — deep contraction of output with GDP as well as industry output declining by roughly 50 per cent (1990–1995). The collapse of the Soviet Union, and the transition to a market economy radically affected the inherited national S&T system.

However, the reforms of the S&T system and other sectors of the Russian economy were much different in terms of speed and depth, in favour of the latter.

These developments prompted the government to turn to international experience. Modern mechanisms for supporting the S&T and innovation sphere attracted a lot of attention, though not per se but rather in the context of an open (or not so open) contest of the two systems — socialist and capitalist. The Soviet leaders had to admit that some of the Western countries had more advanced S&T potential, developed more efficient mechanisms for application of R&D results to production, and that their governments were more successful in encouraging research and innovation activities. Analysis of international experience revealed not just factors due to the differences between the economic systems but also certain significant socially neutral elements of S&T organisation, a sensible combination of direct and indirect management and promotion techniques.[8] Attempts to develop and implement similar components under the 'brand name' of 'self-financing R&D sector' were made in the USSR and then in Russia after the mid-1980s.

At the beginning of the 1990s the situation in the S&T sphere started to develop along a worst-case scenario. The share of internal R&D expenditures dropped to 0.7–0.8 per cent of the GDP, and then for several years remained under 1 per cent — a typical level for countries which practically do not develop (or do not have at all) their own S&T potential. The radical transition to market economy affected all sectors of the economy and all spheres of social life, and the effects had profoundly different scales and sometimes different directions as well. Due to a very large number of reasons (identified in the course of this study), the R&D sector was among those which have been largely negatively affected by the market reforms and their consequences.

If market reforms of the overall Russian economy were generally implemented during the 1990s, in the R&D sphere this process still remains unfinished. Accordingly, if in the overall economy in the 2000s only 3.3 per cent of organisations and enterprises were publicly owned, the appropriate figure for the R&D sector was over 70 per cent (Rosstat 2008: 349; HSE 2011a: 28). As owner of the major share of the R&D sector's property and in effect the only solvent customer of R&D products, the state (on behalf of the government) could have implemented a tough 'top down' reform in this sphere at the very beginning of the market reforms period. That was the case in almost all Eastern European and Baltic countries. However, due to various reasons a different way was chosen — allowing the R&D sphere to self-adapt to the new environment.

Table 3.2: *R&D Institutions by Ownership (percentage)**

	2000	2002	2004	2005	2006	2007	2008	2009
Total = 100%	4099	3906	3656	3566	3622	3957	3666	3537
Public	71.6	72.1	73.2	73.8	73.2	71.3	74.1	75.1
Federal	67.2	67.7	69.0	69.6	69.2	67.0	69.9	70.8
Voluntary Associations	1.5	0.8	0.7	0.8	0.8	0.9	0.8	0.7
Private	9.5	11.7	11.5	11.8	13.9	16.1	13.9	13.4
Joint**	15.5	13.5	12.8	11.8	10.3	9.7	9.4	8.8
Private and Joint, Total	25.5	25.2	24.3	23.6	24.2	25.8	23.3	22.2
Joint***	1.4	1.5	1.4	1.3	1.2	1.57	1.1	1.1

Source: HSE (2009a); HSE (2011a).
Note: * Municipally-owned and cooperative organisations are not listed due to their very small number (in 2009 there were 14 and three such organisations, respectively).
** Without foreign participation.
*** With Russian and foreign participation.

Analysis of the data in Table 3.2 makes the failure of this strategy quite evident. The data clearly shows that during practically the whole period of reforms privately owned R&D organisations did not have opportunities, motivation or prospects for successful development. Rare examples of corporate science's success rather confirm than refute this argument. The non-profit private R&D sector in Russia is even weaker. About 1 per cent organisations brand themselves as private non-profit institutions in this sector. As a rule most of them are financial mediators, which are not engaged in research in practice.

The S&T system which developed under the Soviet 'rules' had three special characteristics: it was very large, centrally directed and government-financed (Kiseleva et al. 1991; Kuznetsova 1992). These features were ill-suited to a market economy and it was not surprising that the system of S&T underwent a system crisis and posterior deep stagnation. In principle, the same could be said about a wider sphere than the S&T complex — the NSI.

The period of 1999 to the middle of 2008 may be considered as a period of stability and socio-economic recovery. However, this growth was not based on real labour productivity or innovation. The Russian science sector and the NSI are still mostly inefficient. There is a striking imbalance between resources devoted to research activities (carried out mostly in government institutions outside of the higher education sector and industry) and the innovation performance.

A specific feature of the Russian situation is the fact that the government's influence over R&D and the NSI was predominant under both the 'totalitarian Soviet regime' and in democratic Russia, as well as during various crises and periods of economic growth. In the early stages of the reform it was believed that restructuring the R&D sector would be impossible without overcoming the negative heritage of the USSR — namely the highly militarised, government-controlled nature of this sphere, weak links with the international scientific community, and insufficient connections with innovation, industry and education. The result of the 20-year period of reform is paradoxical — a lot of good things inherited from the Soviet era were abandoned and rejected while the 'Soviet' R&D model's features that the reformers were set to transform still largely remain in place.

Here are three examples to illustrate the point:

(*a*) Shares of R&D organisations controlled by various government agencies (including state academies of science) have changed, but the approach to the management of science is still based on the same government supervision principle. Government agencies provide more than 50 per cent of R&D funding — just like they did 15–20 years ago. Approximately 13 per cent of all R&D spending was provided for the basic support of the Russian Academy of Science's institutes.

The share of funding allocated through tenders is growing slowly. For example, only 15–16 per cent of total R&D expenditures were allocated through target programmes. This figure includes the inflow from public R&D foundations also.[9] In total these foundations allocate about 7 per cent of civil R&D expenditures. About 2 per cent more came in grants (to support young and outstanding scientists, scientific schools, etc.). Of course, in the federal budget the share of funding allocated through tenders is much higher, at about 37 per cent.

Furthermore, this approach is quite likely to become even more pronounced.[10] The evidence of that is the invariably high share of public funds in the R&D expenditures (65.5 per cent in 2009); the predominant share of research institutes among the R&D (53.1 per cent), and of academic institutes in the public R&D sector (almost 70 per cent). Another proof is the results of modernisation of the academic sector (more truly — the absence of evident results) and creation of large government-owned S&T corporations (see later). Public administration's efforts to coordinate initiatives in the S&T and innovation sphere in most cases amount to just 'declarations of intent'.

(*b*) The R&D sphere in the USSR was indeed highly militarised, and the reasons of that are well-known. Before the collapse of the USSR domestic science began to lag behind other countries in many civilian areas which determine the modern S&T 'image' of the world. However, drastic reduction of government military orders in the 1990s can hardly be seen as a good solution to the problem. Damage was done not just to the military but to civilian R&D as well as to all innovation and technological chains and networks. Some of the enterprises which were vital for the country's economic and geopolitical interests have been closed down. Moreover, military products and technologies happened to be one of the few things Russia could 'boast' of in the international markets.

Today Russia remains a country with a high military potential, and, obviously, to support it, it should develop military R&D. Despite the substantial losses suffered by the sector the chances of its future expansion remain rather high.

(*c*) Despite substantial efforts to promote innovation activities (see later), real changes are very slow to materialise. At first (in the beginning of 1990) the progress was hindered by objective factors — the long period of recession and low demand for locally produced innovations from industry. Today the situation is gradually changing. Enterprises, R&D organisations, research centres, higher education institutes all feel the need for joint innovation activities. However, the laws on the promotion and support of S&T and the innovation sphere are incomplete, insufficiently thorough, or are poorly enforced.

Accordingly, only a small share of Russian enterprises

- are engaged in innovation activities (near 3,000 or 9.4 per cent from the total in 2009);
- produce innovation products (appropriate output amounts to just 5.5 per cent of the total output of industrial enterprises engaged in innovation activities);
- participate in networks and cooperation. The share of industrial enterprises participating in joint R&D projects (on a regular basis) in the total number of enterprises engaged in technological innovations is 33.2 per cent; the share of enterprises which are buying new technologies is 37 per cent; transferring new technologies, 3 per cent; using feedback information from consumers of their products, 11 per cent.

Twenty-seven per cent of technological innovations conducted by industrial enterprises are based on R&D; 7.2 per cent are achieved through industrial design, and less than 1.5 per cent through acquisition of new technologies. A major share of total expenditures on technology (51.2 per cent) is spent on the acquisition of machinery and equipment.

Public R&D organisations and higher education institutes still have problems with setting up small enterprises to transfer their R&D results and technologies to the real economy, with securing and exploiting intellectual property rights, and undertaking joint projects with industrial enterprises. Lots of small enterprises have to go through the same 'sieve' of tax returns and tax inspections as large companies (which can afford to hire numerous accountants, financiers and planners). However, the tax regime for them is extremely volatile.

Succession between the USSR and Russia in the S&T sphere and the NSI on the one hand increased the stability of the new 'object' — the Russian S&T sector — even in the situation of the very hard transition crisis of the 1990s. On the other hand, conservation of the archaic organisation and support system had significantly hindered the reform of the S&T sector to suit the needs of market economy. Today the Russian S&T sector is structured mostly in the same way as it was 20 or 30 years ago. In effect we're talking about the same segments of the S&T network — academic research institutes, higher education institutions and their associated R&D organisations, R&D divisions of industrial enterprises. The difference is that in today's Russia they operate in a market environment, and include a small number of newly emerged privately owned organisations.

It can be argued that today the fate of Russian R&D and NSI still remains in the hands of the government. In recent years this position was considered unfashionable and absolutely irrelevant by a lot of Russian liberal experts and officials. However, it is reflected in many government decisions, in the orders (instructions) of the president of the Russian Federation to the Russian government, ministries and various agencies. In particular these orders concern creation of large national (public) research centres and research universities; adoption of joint funding and cooperation mechanisms between public and private sectors to finance innovation projects; creation of a favourable tax environment for R&D and innovation activities; development of the 'territories' favourable for innovation, etc.

In spite of the necessary (and inevitably promoted by the very 'rules' of a market economy) trend towards reduced government participation in various spheres of socio-economic activities, in reality the role of the state is still very high in any country. The innovation activities of business being supported by the state, is a key factor of the country's competitiveness and sustainable economic growth. In today's Russia the government has sufficient resources (as well as adequate power) to sustain and develop the S&T potential, and to increase its contribution to achieving national objectives.

Periodisation and analysis of institutions and policies of the state concerned with innovation

The evolution of Russian S&T and innovation policies post-USSR can be divided into four main stages for convenience.

The first one was a period of 'marker romanticism' in the early 1990s, driven by the vain hopes of reformers for quick and automatic transfer to a market economy. However, these high initial plans were not met. Multiple mistakes in planning the market reforms and corresponding actions resulted in a deep systemic crisis within the Russian NSI — the dramatic funding fall, the shedding of human resources, the disbanding of scientific organisations during the first wave of privatisation. The consequences of this crisis have not been overcome even now.

In the next stage ('market formalism', the middle and end of 1990s) the S&T sphere fell into deep stagnation. Formally, it was subjected to the same market transformation as all other sectors of the economy, but the real shifts here were lagging far behind the overall economic reforms. Government initiatives were reduced to urgent measures to slow down the definitive disintegration of the S&T complex.

In the early 2000s, during the third period (the stage of 'market pragmatism') important strategic decisions were outlined for the future or were just started. Practical actions were planned and carried out mainly based on the criteria of economic expediency and budgetary savings. However, the strategy of postponing decisions for national science and NSI resulted in serious risks and narrow focus on the short and medium-term programmes and projects at the expense of long-term ones.

The fourth stage, lasting from the mid-2000s to the present day, is characterised by a complex set of measures adopted by the government. Their key aim is the transition towards an innovative model of national economy. All measures of the current period can be divided into three groups. The first one is the creation of a structured NSI policy framework. The second is the implementation of the policy mechanisms for efficient regulation in the main areas of government activity: national priorities, performance-based budgeting, restructuring the government R&D sector, human resources and infrastructure development, etc. During that period yet another cycle of programme development actions took place, producing documents describing a platform and the main development areas — for the medium and long (10 years) terms. The last one is a complex period of anti-crisis and post-crisis activities.

Tables 3.3 and 3.4 provide some quantitative data describing Russia's development during these periods, based on official statistics. They show that during the period of reforms the Russian R&D sphere became one of the areas negatively affected by the market transformation of the economy. The evidence is well-known — the unprecedented decline of funding and of the number of R&D personnel (until the mid-1990s), worsening of the 'scientific climate' and environment in which R&D organisations operated, deterioration of material basis and the country's position in international high-technology markets.

Development trends of an economy in transition are quite different from the laws of a developed market. In any country going through a transitional period the government must increase targeted impact in certain areas, take over some medium- and long-term obligations. In that sense the Russian situation in the 1990s can hardly be considered unique. Since the level of government interference was traditionally quite large in this country, transformation of the science and education sphere would probably have been painful even without the crisis. The 'revision' of the traditional national priorities, the government's refusal to carry on with many of its previous obligations led to corrosion of the previous motivation factors (the defence interests, prestige, etc.). In effect, at the initial stage of the reform period science and innovation have been excluded from the list of strategic priorities, which later on has been judged the reformers' very grave error. Consequences of these decisions are still being felt in Russia (Kuznetsova and Kitova 2003).

Table 3.3: *Main Development Indicators of the S&T Complex, 1990–1999 (The First and Second Periods)*

	1990	*1991*	*1992*	*1993*	*1994*	*1995*	*1996*	*1997*	*1998*	*1999*
1*	10.9	7.3	3.2	3.1	2.9	2.5	2.7	3.0	2.6	2.9
2	2.0	1.4	0.7	0.8	0.8	1.0	1.0	1.0	1.0	1.0
3		25.8**	11.2**	9.9**	6.3**	5.03**	4.3**	6.02**	1.8	1.9
4	–	1.85**	0.94**	0.91**	0.66**	0.24**	0.6**	0.8**	0.24	0.24
5	258	227	213	186	162	160	150	144	134	136
6	–	–	–	32.2	23.1	22.2	23.2	20.0	21.4	24.7
7	–	–	–	27.8	40.3	31.6	33.6	46.0	23.8	19.52
8	–	–	–	–	–	–	–	–	–19.9	– 283.2
9	4646	4564	4555	4269	3968	4059	4122	4137	4019	4089
10	449	400	340	299	276	325	342	299	240	289

Source: HSE (2007); HSE (2009a).

Note: * 1: Gross Domestic expenditures on R&D (GERD) at constant 1989 prices (billion roubles); 2: GERD as a percentage of GDP; 3: Federal Budget Appropriations (FBA) on civil S&T at constant 1991 prices (million roubles); 4: FBA on civil S&T as a percentage of GDP; 5: R&D personnel per 10,000 employment; 6: patent applications by resident applicants in Russia (thousands); 7: patents granted (thousands); 8: technology balance of payments (million US dollars); 9: R&D institutions; 10: among them industrial enterprises.

** Total Federal Budget Appropriations on S&T at constant 1991 prices (million roubles) as a percentage of GDP.

Table 3.4: *Main Development Indicators of the S&T Complex, 2000–2006 (The Third and Fourth Periods)*

	2000	*2001*	*2002*	*2005*	*2006*	*2007*	*2008*	*2009*
1*	3.3	3.9	4.3	4.6	4.9	5.6	5.5	6.1
2	1.05	1.18	1.25	1.07	1.08	1.12	1.04	1.24
3	2.0	2.35	2.65	4.16	4.54	5.5	5.7	7.5
4	0.23	0.26	0,28	0.36	0.36	0.4	0.6	0.5
5	138	136	133	122	122	135	128	126
6	28.7	30.0	29.2	32.3	37.7	39.4	41.9	38.6
7	17.6	16.3	18.1	23.4	23.3	23.0	28.8	34.8
8	20.6	–153.8	–361.0	–564.8	–595.0	–796.0	–1254.0	–1001.0
9	4099	4037	3906	3566	3622	3957	3666	3536
10	284	288	255	231	255	265	255	265

Source: HSE (2009a); HSE (2011a).

Note: * 1: GERD at constant 1989 prices (billion roubles); 2: GERD as a percentage of GDP; 3: FBA on civil S&T at constant 1991 prices (billion roubles); 4: FBA on civil S&T as a percentage of GDP; 5: R&D personnel per 10,000 employment; 6: patent applications with the indication of Russia in Russia (thousands); 7: patents granted (thousands); 8: technology balance of payments (million US dollars); 9: R&D institutions; 10: among them industrial enterprises.

During the first and second stages the development of the R&D sphere was irregular and controversial, mostly due to problems with public funding. The allocated resources and the reaction of the sphere in general didn't match the declared objectives. At the same time reduction even of the small amount of funding promised by the government became common practice.

Despite the crisis, important documents have been developed during that period, summarising the experience of the first years of reforms and defining key principles and approaches to the management of science. These include The Doctrine of Russian Science Development (1996), the federal law 'On Science and the State S&T Policy' (1996), The Concept of Reforming Russian Science in 1998–2000 (1998). A large amount of work was undertaken to implement previously non-existent forms, mechanisms and relations determining the model of science adequate for a market economy.[11] All this has been done in a uniquely short space of time. For the first time in Russian history documents were published to define objectives and areas of the national S&T policy; a legal framework for international S&T cooperation was developed; attempts to restructure academies of science were made.

By the mid-1990s the management model for the Russian R&D sphere started to look similar to the models used by other developed countries (formally, in terms of principles and approaches adopted). However, its practical implementation was inconsequential and contradictory. Accordingly, the actual effect of even the most progressive ideas did not match the expectations and the S&T sector's contribution to the nation's development in terms of the emergence of a modern NSI seemed incomparable to its true potential. The R&D sphere's social rating dropped, and the public perception of its role in the country's development became more sceptical. The public image of 'science falling to pieces' in itself was a serious barrier hindering implementation of the reforms (Shuvalova 2007). The stratification of the academic community became more pronounced, the level of their social and political activity dropped. In effect it amounted to the lobbying of interests of specific groups, projects, programmes representing group or personal interests.

After 2000 Russian government policy became more oriented towards promoting innovation and sustainable economic development. The favourable market situation and macroeconomic and political stability allowed the development and implementation of a wide range of measures to put together a modern NSI and support high-technology sectors of the economy. The ultimate goal of these steps was defined as technological modernisation of industry, exploitation of national competitive advantages (including the R&D potential) to increase the population's standard of life, competitiveness and national security.

It is not easy to identify the precise boundaries of this period due to the beginning of the world crisis (in the end of 2008) and the real perspective of its continuation (the second wave). Thus the start of the fifth period for Russian R&D is more than uncertain.

Specificities of the system of innovation in the country and its relationship with the state

Despite the high rate of economic growth achieved in the 2000s — regarding many indicators reflecting development levels and prospects — Russia is not catching up with the world leaders (see Table 3.5). Low (compared with other developed countries) levels of such indicators as R&D expenditure calculated as share of GDP, scientists' publication activity, innovation activities of enterprises, remained practically unchanged throughout the period of market reforms, including the years of economic growth. Due to a host of objective reasons (very often external to R&D, innovation and even production spheres) companies still are not really interested in the intellectual component of the innovation process. Within the structure of technological expenditures the accent is placed on acquisition of machinery and equipment, in most cases foreign-made. Successful R&D organisations have to work increasingly for foreign companies and international organisations. Higher education institutes are still regarded as non-serious players in the innovation sphere.

Table 3.5: *Parameters of Productivity: Loss of Competitive Positions (International Comparisons)**

Indicators	*Russia vs. Some Other Countries*
Publication in world scientific journals (publication activity)	Russia: 1.8, 16th position in the world (1995 – 7, 1980 – 3)
	China: 15.1, 2nd position (1995 – 1.6, 14 position)
Technology export	Russia: 0.6 bln $, Austria: 7.3 bln $, USA: 89.1 bln $
Patents applications by resident applicant	Russia is lagging behind Japan 9 times, USA 11, Korea 4 times
Share in the world hi-tech market	Russia: 0.3%
	Singapore, Korea, Taiwan: 4–8%
Innovative activity of enterprises	Russia: 9.4%
	EU: from 24% (Latvia) to 80% (Germany)
Share of innovative products in total sales of industrial products	Russia: 1.93%
	Germany: 2.18, Finland: 2.76, Sweden: 3.18%
Share of innovative products (new to the market or new to an enterprise) in total products of industry	Russia: 2.5% Germany: 25.5, Finland: 23.7, France: 20.7%

Source: HSE (2011a); HSE (2011b); HSE (2011c).

Note: * Russia: 2009; other countries: 2007–2009.

Most of the Russian industries remain technologically obsolete while the overall economy still has a serious structural misbalance — which makes its position in the international markets very vulnerable and unstable. The national economy is largely based on mining, processing and exporting fuel, and a few traditional manufacturing sectors (see Table 3.6).

Table 3.6: *Certain Characteristics of the Russian Economy (by Industry) 2010*

	Agriculture	*Manufacturing*	*Mining*	*Wholesale and Retail Trade*
Share in the total number of enterprises and organisations (%)	4.0 (-)	8.3 (-)	0.4 (+)	37.1 (-)
Share in the total turnover of all enterprises and organisations (%)	1.5	21.7	7.1	42.0
Industrial production index	88.7	111.8	108.2	104.5
Share in the total output (%)	4.2	24.6	7.1	15.8
Share in the total added value (%)	4.4	14.5	8.9	18.1
Productivity growth	89.3	109.0	101.3	98.5
Share in total exports	2.3 (+)*	5.7 (+)**	68.8*** (-)	-
Share in total imports	15.9 (-)	44.5 (-)	2.6 (-)	-

Source: Rosstat (2011: 38, 313, 315, 345, 346, 354, 371, 411, 511, 713, 766).

Note: «+» – Growth in the last 2–3 years; «–» – decline in the last 4–5 years
* Food stuffs and agricultural materials
** Machinery, equipment and vehicles
*** Only minerals

So far there are no major technological breakthroughs achieved by Russian industry, nor significant implementation of R&D results which are typical to any innovative economy. Innovations hardly affect Russian economy. At the same time innovation activities are hindered by various barriers engendered by the overall macroeconomic context and the institutional environment. The low level of the latter is evident in all industries, and in all kinds of innovation activities — technological, organisational and marketing innovations.

The potential to achieve dynamic, sustainable and innovative economic growth is limited, on the one hand, by the very weak interest the Russian business sector displays in technological and non-technological innovations alike, and on the other by insufficient productivity of Russian science, lack of a critical mass of innovative projects attractive to investors. Factors such as an insufficiently developed competitive environment and lack of motivation for enterprises to develop and implement new technologies, should certainly be taken into account too.

Some data in support of these conclusions has been included in Table 3.5. For a deeper understanding of Russia's 'innovation paradox', we provide a few additional estimates:[12]

- In 1995–2009, the number of organisations engaged in technological innovations has doubled (from 1,363 to 2,761), but in the last two–three years it remained practically unchanged. In 2009 the number of organisations engaged in all types of innovation activities in industry was 2,682, in manufacturing 2,256 and in the service sector, 644.[13]
- Innovation activities are different in various industries. On the aggregate level, minimum innovation activities (for all types of innovations) are registered in mining (approximately 7 per cent) and maximum in manufacturing (12–13 per cent).
- It is a well-known fact that innovation activities largely depend on the specialty and technological level of production. In Russian high-technology industries, the overall level of innovation activity amounts to about 30 per cent, in medium-technology industries to 13–20 per cent and in low-tech industries to 2–11 per cent.
- In high-tech service sectors (communications, ICT) this figure reaches 10–15 per cent, but the overall innovation activity level in the service sectors remains low.
- A vast majority of innovative enterprises and organisations (86.5 per cent) belong to the manufacturing industry, in particular, production of food, machinery and equipment, electrical equipment, medical equipment and instrumentation, radio, TV and communication equipment, etc.
- Large, economically sound organisations with sufficient financial, human and intellectual resources are the most active in the innovations field. Half of the industrial enterprises engaged in technological innovations employ a staff of more than 500.

- The share of small enterprises engaged in technological innovations varies around 4 per cent. The most active are small enterprises manufacturing medical equipment and instrumentation, pharmaceuticals and computer hardware.

The current S&T development in Russia is still affected by rather conflicting trends. On the one hand, the government R&D funding is growing (FBA on civilian R&D in 2004–2009 grew by 2.45 times in real prices). About 34.6 per cent of the government funds are allocated to support basic research. Financial support of R&D through contracts, programmes and tenders has also grown. The number of researchers (369,000, 49 per cent of R&D personnel in 2009) has nearly stabilised: the rate of its reduction was within 1 per cent from 2003. The number of people employed by private research institutions is increasing (29 per cent increase since 2000). However, the level of government support still lags behind the world's economic leaders. Evidence of that is provided by certain financial indicators given in Tables 3.7 and 3.8.

Table 3.7: *The Role of the State in R&D (Some Statistical Indicators)*

Funding	*Organisations*	*Personnel and Fixed Assets*
FBA on civil R&D: 2.23% of federal budget expenditures (2009)	75.1% of R&D organisations are owned and established by federal and regional governments	78.9% of R&D personnel work in government organisations (federal and regional)
FBA on civil R&D: 0.56% of GDP (2009)	GERD by ownership of R&D institutions (public ownership): 74.3%	86.9% of R&D fixed assets are public
Government contribution as source of R&D funding: 66.5%		

Source: HSE (2011a).

On the other hand the stagnation in the S&T sector is evident. It stems from both insufficient demand for and underdeveloped supply of R&D and technologies. Private business does not show much interest in innovation. Since 2000 the innovation activity has remained at the level of 9–10 per cent.[14] The EU economies' figures are significantly higher. Investment in innovation is considered by private businesses to be more risky and less profitable than investment in mining and quarrying activities. Demand for R&D comes mostly from the government, and the federal budget remains the key source of R&D funding (in 1998–2007 it grew threefold in real prices).

As it has already been mentioned, on the national economy level, the overall effect of R&D and innovation activities is almost invisible. Only high-technology sectors show progress. Unfortunately, their success — relatively higher levels of innovation activity and effectiveness — so far has been unable to change the 'state of affairs' of innovation in the Russian economy, and this effect is limited by the number of working enterprises, number of staff and the actual output. Advanced tools to support and encourage R&D and innovation activities, create innovative infrastructure, upgrade and adjust development institutions, are not used to their full potential in Russia; their conceptual, methodological, organisational, legislative, and law enforcement support is fragmentary, incomplete and occasionally even controversial in nature.

Table 3.8: *Expenditures: A Little to Invest, a Little to Receive? (R&D Funding in Russia)*

	Positive Trends	
Increase of GERD	1998–2009 — more than 19 times	
	At constant prices — more than 2.5 times	
Government Budget Appropriations on R&D (PPP)	Russia*: 23 bln $ (2009)	Far from USA (7 times lower), but very close to Germany and Japan; more than in France and in Great Britain
	Negative Trends	
	Russia	**Other Countries (2007–2009)**
GERD as a Per cent of GDP	Russia: 1.07% (2006), 1.12% (2007), 1.04% (2008), 1.24% (2009)	Israel: 4.77%; Japan: 3.44%; USA: 2.79%; China: 1.54%
GERD (PPP)	Russia: 23.0 bln $ (2009)	15 times lower than in USA; 6 than in Japan; 5 than in China; 1.5 than in Britain

Source: HSE (2011a); HSE (2011b); HSE (2011c).
Note: Russia: Civil R&D.

Due to the fact that the organisation and management of R&D and innovation activities (including reliance on government support) still retain a number of specific features, there are the following short-

and medium-term risks:

- further reduction of entrepreneurs' demand for R&D products; weakening of cooperative interdisciplinary links throughout the whole R&D and innovation cycle;
- limitations hampering efficient development of knowledge-generation environment may remain in place (regarding all kinds of resources and periods of time); the range and development level of scientific results may deteriorate;
- reduced level (quality) of staff training and retraining for innovation-driven economy (science, education, high-technology sectors);
- reduced appeal of the NSI for international contacts and cooperation;
- reduced quality and effectiveness of R&D, lower novelty level of Russian innovation;
- further slowdown of innovation activities;
- reduced range (and shares) of non-government funding sources, increased pressure on the federal budget.

Analysis of the latest science and innovation policy documents creates an impression of structural wholeness and completeness, on par with the best international practices. The wording of their general provisions and principles corresponds with the approaches adopted in developed countries. However, the progress regarding their further, more detailed development (objectives, techniques, mechanisms) is quite slow. Many support measures still and inevitably include an excessively large element of direct financial support (mostly from the federal budget). Measures to promote research and innovation, develop infrastructure, modernise development institutions are not fully implemented.

It is obvious that S&T and innovation in Russia as well as in other developed countries are based on a rather complex relationship between those who provide knowledge, those who control and regulate this process, and those who apply the results. Taking account of negative factors hampering innovation activities in Russia, the primary fields for government S&T and innovation intervention may be listed as follows:

(*a*) promotion of technology transfer (protection of intellectual property rights, building innovation infrastructure, organisational innovation, etc.);

(*b*) creating a favourable environment for S&T and innovation activities, direct support to S&T;

(*c*) development of public–private partnership (PPP) (cooperation), motivating of private business to co-fund and participate in projects initiated by the government;
(*d*) promotion of innovation activity and improvement of innovation climate (support to efficient innovators, creation of a competitive environment, improving legislation);
(*e*) increasing level of professional education, for example, in the field of innovation management;
(*f*) ensuring the prospects of the long-term sustainable technological development.

The practices of developed countries prove that all efforts to create these as well as other frameworks to work out relevant transformation schemes and procedures (including the fundamental reforms of the government S&T sector) appear to be even more effective than direct budget subsidies to S&T activities. In any case this effectiveness depends on adequacy of goals, real substance and the scale of the government's initiatives.

For example, we can examine the appearance in Russia of the system of various foundations for S&T support that were created in the middle of the 1990s. On the one hand, these (rather new for Russian practice) institutional initiatives in fact are based on the government (direct or indirect) subsidies. On the other hand, the spreading in Russia of the idea of competitive support to scientific teams has already played a noticeable role in promoting scientific activities.

The practical measures provided by the government on reorganisation of national science and NSI during the last 15 years did not always have a positive effect. They had not resulted in deep science integration into market economy and increasing impact on the social and economical progress. As a result, many parts of NSI nowadays still retain the features left from the centralised economy, while relevant and efficient policies are lacking. Changes in the situation will strongly depend on the success of measures aimed at improving the overall business environment, the stability of the economy, and the rule of law.

Today, we can assert that in Russia some success can be observed mostly within the groups of policy agenda mentioned earlier under (*a*) and (*b*). Some positive shifts exist within integration of science and education, creation of research universities, introduction of courses for the training of skilled managers for high-tech sectors etc.

(group of policy actions under [*e*]). For the other mentioned issues the Russian government does not so far demonstrate a deep interest in a real improvement of the innovation process. The modest success of S&T and innovation policy (and even the collapse of some parts of it) is to a certain extent determined by the lack of coordination between different elements of such policy, between government bodies dealing with S&T and innovation issues, etc.

In general, specific actions in the areas described in groups (*c*)–(*f*) are planned as part of the CLTD 2020 strategy (as well as other strategic documents mentioned earlier). Their implementation started in 2009 and is continuing at present. Implementation of government policies described in the Long-Term Development Concept will ultimately allow dealing with the main systems problem of the Russian S&T complex — inefficient use of resources allocated to the R&D sector combined with insufficient demand for innovations by businesses. This should lead to increased quality and supply of domestic R&D products and technologies, and increased demand by the real sector of the economy for technologies and innovations.

Explicit and implicit state policy towards science, technology and innovation

Effectiveness of the Russian S&T and innovation government policy is largely determined by the fact that Russia needs to deal with a whole host of problems immediately — those connected with the generation of new ideas, their transformation into high technologies and finally, production of actual goods and services. Constraints hindering acceleration of these processes take place at both ends: among customers and suppliers of R&D products (Gokhberg and Kuznetsova 2010a; Gokhberg and Kuznetsova 2010b).

In the USSR the national S&T policy was shaped under very strict ideological control, and in the situation of an appreciably closed S&T sphere. Creative freedom was allowed and even encouraged (especially in natural sciences, engineering and technology), but the opportunities for research, exchange of ideas and results were either a priori limited or could be made so at any time due to some ideological consideration or an official's whim. Academic mobility of scientists was almost not encouraged at all, though as early as the 1970s it was accepted the world over as a major factor and a sign of innovation-based economies.

After the collapse of the USSR the ideological limits and the closed nature of the S&T sector were overcome quite easily, maybe even too easily, from the point of view of sustaining the S&T complex and the national security. Abandoning the management and behavioural stereotypes which affected the country's social, economic and political development and life of its citizens, had turned out to be much more difficult. In effect the S&T sphere in Russia was (and still is) incorporated into the non-manufacturing sector and funded out of the state budget, mainly according to the leftover ('residual') principle and the 'achieved level' of appropriations. Thus, in the years of prosperity, rather significant public funds are channelled into this sphere, in effect without any analysis of these expenditures' efficiency. In the periods of crisis or stagnation the S&T sector is the first candidate for reduced government support. Usually the cuts are applied equally to all relevant budget articles, again without analysing the efficiency of appropriate recipients and the results they produce.

A negative effect of such an approach is the risk that the S&T potential's structure might deteriorate. The larger, traditional areas (and established R&D structures) get increasingly bigger government appropriations while many of the new, breakthrough S&T areas do not receive adequate funding. In this section we'll show how the Russian government is trying to deal with these negative effects. However, advancing in the right direction is turning out to be very difficult to achieve.

Overcoming the industrial approach to management of the R&D sphere also appears to be hard. The lengthy period of extensive development of the Soviet R&D sector allowed many of the ministries and government agencies to set up and maintain their own networks of R&D organisations, funded out of the government budget but working mostly to satisfy the needs of specific appropriate industries. Departmental approach as a management principle cannot be good or bad per se. However, its domination in the overall system of organisation, planning and funding of R&D activities resulted in fragmentation of R&D organisations and structures, which in turn led to the dissipation of resources, duplication of work, monopolistic practices, expenditures-based and extensive development of the R&D sphere, and an inability to deal with interdisciplinary and inter-industry tasks in sufficiently quick and flexible ways. As was already noted, the drawbacks of this approach have not been overcome in Russia yet. Furthermore, now they are manifesting in new ways — unlike anything seen in the USSR. In particular, goals and objectives of the national S&T and innovation policy (developed primarily by the MES) quite often clash with valid laws regulating the economic activities, and with the general civil legislation which defines the overall environment for R&D organisations (i.e., where this policy is implemented), which are developed primarily by the ministries of finance, economy and industry. The loser is always the S&T sphere and the NSI in particular.

Even further, in the course of modernisation of the budgeting process (see later for more) a quite decentralised (between ministries and government departments) scheme for planning R&D appropriations and distributing responsibilities for the sector's advancement has developed. Basic research is the responsibility of the state academies of science; the S&T sector as a whole and the development of appropriate legislation is the responsibility of MES; state S&T programmes are developed and implemented by the Federal Agency for Science and Innovation (at present abolished); R&D components of major goal-oriented programmes are the responsibility of the Ministry for Economic Development (MED); certain expenditures not related with programmes are administered by the Ministry of Finance. Technology implementation zones, venture funds, development of breakthrough (critical) technologies are responsibilities of MED and MES; Ministry of Information Technologies and Communication and MES are responsible for creation of technoparks; property of federal R&D organisations is managed by the Agency for Public Property Management; regional and local authorities allocate land to build innovative facilities, etc.

These inter-departmental barriers hinder complex, efficient restructuring of the S&T sphere, implementation of integrated R&D and the innovation cycle, development of common understanding among government officials regarding how much resources the state should allocate to advancement of science, and exactly how these resources should be spent. Nevertheless, the contemporary economic potential of the Russian economy is high enough to launch the NSI reforms and complete the transition of the S&T and innovation sector.

As was noted in the report 'Innovation-Driven Development as the Basis for Modernisation of the Russian Economy' (HSE 2008) prepared with the participation of Institute for Statistical Studies and

Economics of Knowledge (ISSEK) experts, there are two approaches to development and evaluation of national S&T and innovation policy:

(*a*) narrow approach which only takes into account a set of decisions affecting (directly and indirectly) R&D and innovation processes;

(*b*) and a wider approach, when decisions are evaluated taking into account the whole range of national goals (including technological modernisation, development of human capital, adjustment of development institutions, positioning of the country as a global power).

In the first case, recommendations and suggestions should cover traditional policy areas: government funding of organisations, enterprises, programmes, and projects (including promotion of cooperation and networking of innovation actors); legal framework, development of infrastructure and appropriate linkages. Certain progress has been made in Russia in this area during the years of reform. Now the accent should be placed on extending the range of available tools and mechanisms.

In the second case there's the need to discuss and adjust approaches to developing a better understanding of the role science and innovations play in the economy, and the S&T and innovation policy plays in the public administration system. It was noted earlier that inefficient government policy became a significant obstacle hindering development of R&D and NSI in Russia. However, the opposite is also true — the state of R&D and innovation activities largely determines available options for policy development and for increasing its efficiency.

By now the main directions of S&T and innovation policy in Russia, the reforms of science and NSI are the following:

National Priorities Setting

In Russia the efforts to select S&T priorities were first launched at the federal level in the middle of the 1990s, and have since been continued on a regular basis. National S&T priorities are formulated in two lists — priority S&T areas and critical technologies.[15] The list of priority S&T areas for the Russian Federation sets the general trends of the country's S&T development and represents the S&T areas deemed to provide new technologies and facilities to contribute to the development of national economy and society.

They are specified in the List of Critical Technologies of the Russian Federation, which serves as a background for making decisions on concentrating public resources in the most important areas of science, technology and innovation and on implementing the available S&T potential.

The first list of eight priority areas was approved by the Government Commission on Scientific and Technological Policies in 1996. In 1999 it was submitted to a large-scale examination by more than 1,000 leading experts. That analysis revealed an urgent need to reconsider the system of priorities, concentrating on 'breakthrough' directions. In 2000–2001 new lists of nine S&T priority areas and 52 critical technologies were developed; in 2006, eight (34); in 2010, six (26). The aim of their formulation consisted in the optimisation of the number of priority areas, so as to concentrate resources in the most important fields of innovation.

As already mentioned, in 2002 the Russian president approved the basic directions of the Russian Federation's policy in S&T development. This document has become an important element of Russia's social and economic development strategy, with its goals of innovation-based economic development, creating of an effective national innovation system and making science and technology one of Russia's key priorities. The S&T priorities and critical technologies approved within that document resulted in the list of research areas that was still too broad to become real targets for selecting technologies for priority government support and for private investment. That was the reason for Russia's MES to organise the revision and correction of the lists immediately. This was done in 2003–2004, and then in 2007–2008. The revision of S&T priorities was carried out during a period of sustained economic growth and great improvement of the state government system. Within the process officials and experts modified the list of priority areas considerably. They took into consideration that it should cover the current international technological development priorities, on the one hand, and the innovation development potential defining the formation of new global markets on the other.

This is particularly true for information technologies, the nanosystems industry and new materials and living systems, national security, etc. Efficient use of available S&T potential and practical implementation of R&D results already achieved in these areas will increase Russian enterprises' competitiveness in domestic and international markets in the medium term.

International experience shows that long-term sustainable development is achievable only through high entrepreneurial and innovation activities both in production and service sectors, diversification of production and a greater share of sophisticated and hi-tech products. So concentrating resources in the areas where Russia's competitive advantages can be exploited helps to accelerate innovation based on latest research outcomes and technologies, which is now a key factor determining the competitiveness of a national economy. This is particularly important for Russia because of its present strong dependence on the international markets for fuel and mineral resources.

The S&T priorities (as well as the critical technologies set) are a powerful tool for innovation policies and especially resources distribution. All NSI development instruments and initiatives (including policies discussed later) are based on the national priorities system. Target-based budgeting and performance evaluation are the mechanisms most closely related with them.

Restructuring Government R&D Institutions

Domination of the government-owned budget-funded institutions in the S&T sector remains one of the most painful problems facing Russian science. Various types of commercial and non-profit organisations were allowed during the transition period of the Russian economy, but there was a minimal change at the level of the state R&D organisations. As it was mentioned earlier, over 70 per cent of all R&D organisations in Russia are public-owned and 39 per cent belong to the state sector (though many R&D institutions de facto belong to the state sector being formally placed by statistics services in the business sector). After federal executive agencies got the right to establish new institutions at the beginning of the 1990s, their number even grew by 1.5 times.

Russia has a huge system of state academies, a legacy of the former USSR. The most unusual feature of their legal status is their 'mixed' nature, which combines elements of government institution, public association and some other forms (e.g., corporation and alliance). Another specific feature is the fact that academies act as holdings, 'owning' non-profit organisations. Therefore, as government institutions, academies have control over a number of various organisations and enterprises. The creation of an institution (academy) consisting of many other institutions (research institutes) causes property conflicts and is not in fact allowed by Russian civil laws. However, under the Federal Law 'On Science and the State S&T Policy' (1996), state academies are an exception, organised exactly in this way. Finally, an important feature of state academies' status is that they operate as government institutions. Academies receive and manage government funding provided by the state to support their research institutes. They can manage and control institutions, create and close them.

This 'mix' of various organisational, legal and administrative forms has no precedent in other countries, and remains a big problem for the Russian government. The most worrying issue is the mismatch between performance and economic results in the R&D carried out by the academies and the amount of their public funding. There are other problems as well: inefficient monitoring of the use of federal property and public funds, along with insufficient transparency in the allocation and use of financial resources. One should mark that in general at least 26 per cent of all public funds allocated for civil S&T go to state academies.

In 2005 the special programme for modernisation of the structure, functions and funding mechanisms in the academic R&D sector was adopted. The aim was to streamline the network of academic organisations and to introduce some new organisational forms for R&D. It was supposed to be implemented by 2008, but it did not happen in full. The resistance of the academy's top management was strong enough to preserve the academy's autonomy (operational and budgetary). Therefore, the plans for more radical changes are still far from final realisation. The longer academies resist innovation, the more negative the consequences are for the academic system collapse.

The large number (and proportion) of government-owned R&D institutions makes Russia very different from other industrially developed countries. State R&D institutions funded by the government have to keep budget limitations. They have almost none of the rights (or responsibilities) needed for adequate economic operations. While claiming large amounts of public money, they cannot guarantee that these resources will be used efficiently. In such conditions the performance of the entire government S&T sector is affected. A similar situation is found in the other social sectors of the Russian economy (education, culture, health care, etc.), showing the need to design and implement new, more flexible, autonomous and independent organisational forms.

To meet this challenge, it was decided to create a new kind of government institutions to operate in the social sphere. The new flexible model is known as 'autonomous institution' which is adopted by the federal law 'On Autonomous Institutions' (2006a). Unlike existing budget-funded institutions, the new structures will not be funded through fixed budgetary institutional grants; but they will receive funding from various sources (including the government). This would increase their responsibility for the expected results. At the same time they will remain government-owned entities. Autonomous institutions will have certain autonomy and independence in attracting (and spending) funds from non-government sources, including credits and investments. It will give them new development opportunities, not available for 'traditional' budget-funded institutions.

The prospects for transition of the government-owned R&D organisations into the new form are outlined in 'R&D and Innovation Development Strategy in the Russian Federation until 2015' (2006b). At least 250 R&D institutions and higher education institutions (HEIs) should move to the new status over a fairly short period of time. Taking into account the period planned for this institutional transformation, the task looks quite complicated.

Large national R&D centres are also expected to operate this way. CLTD 2020 includes creation of several such centres whose objective will be to provide S&T support to high technology sectors of the Russian economy. Another aspect of institutional reforms is related to the integration of science and education. To this end, a special law on integration can be mentioned as well as initiatives stimulating R&D activities in HEIs. The new federal law 'On Changes to the Selected Legal Statements of the Russian Federation Concerning the Integration of Education and Science' (2007a) was adopted to boost S&T and innovation activities at universities and to establish closer linkages between HEIs and research institutions. The new law legalises existing models for such integration and provides a scope of efficient measures including a subset of necessary regulations. These regulations should help to eliminate the existing institutional barriers for fruitful integration.

Unfortunately the adopted law can be characterised as a sort of compromise between the government, the university community and the research institutes. As a result, it does not fully satisfy any of these entities. It just solves some evident problems of integration.

Further amendments are required to make the interaction between science and education not only possible, but also efficient.

Another part of the integration policy is support for the best 'innovative HEIs' and 'research universities'. The National Priority Project 'Education' contains specific policy measures to this end. An important component of this scheme is the government of the Russian Federation's statement entitled 'Support Measures for Higher Education Institutions Implementing Innovative Education Programmes' (2006c). It is devoted to the distribution of competitive grants for developing university innovation (including human resource development, unique R&D and innovation projects, improvement of innovation infrastructure, acquisition of research equipment, etc.). There were 57 winners in 2006–2007. Each of them received funding in the range of US$ 6–30 million for two years depending on the scale of projects. The average annual R&D expenditure of the grant-recipients was a little bit more than US$ 4,000 per member of R&D and teaching staff but the difference between minimum and maximum amounts was very high. This means that only some winning universities are actually able to develop large-scale innovation projects.

However, the scheme marks the first government experiment with the earmarked support for research universities as centres of excellence. The main challenge for today is to continue this practice on a regular basis.

In addition, in 2007–2010 within the framework of integration seven large national universities were established by presidential decrees and 29 leading higher education institutes transformed into research universities.

Evaluation of the Performance of R&D Units

The efficient restructuring as well as current operation of the state-funded R&D institutions also requires a set of comprehensive tools for performance evaluation. Such mechanisms are widely present in many countries and show positive effects. During the post-Soviet period, state funding of the state R&D entities was not based on the estimates of their efficiency and the results of their activity. As a result, positive dynamics of expenditure on R&D from the budgetary sources was followed constantly by negative dynamics of the output indicators.

To improve the situation the Russian government adopted the statement 'On the System of Civil R&D Organisations Performance Evaluation' (2009). The main goals of this system are comprehensive planning and funding for the R&D projects, optimisation of the network of R&D organisations and benchmarking for non-public R&D organisations. The plan is to organise regular surveys (every five years) and support the database containing statistical information about R&D institutions. So-called evaluation commissions are represented by involved interest groups — such as state executive bodies, business, academies, scientific community, NGOs, etc. The key evaluation criteria are put together in order to show the relationship between resources (inputs) and results (outputs).

Output is measured by:

- R&D results (publication activity, project results, etc.);
- commercialisation and application of the results (patents, start-ups, etc.);
- scientific involvement (international contacts, joint projects, etc.).

The further criteria relate to human capital (quality and structure of personnel, salaries, etc.), tangible and intangible resources (equipment, facilities, etc.) and financial sustainability (incomes and expenditures structure, debts, etc.). The final criterion shows the potential for further development. A typical report by an evaluation commission consists of a conclusion on the performance against the key criteria and recommendations. Every R&D organisation should be assigned to one of three groups by performance — from 'outsiders' to 'leaders'. The recommendations therefore can vary from closure (for 'outsiders') to special support (for 'leaders') respectively. The evaluation system will apply not only to the state-funded R&D institutions but also to other NSI components including the innovation infrastructure institutions.

Innovation Infrastructure

There are many different forms of innovation infrastructure in Russia. In the state policy context we'll stop on the presentation of three important elements — technoparks, science cities and special economic zones (SEZs). Technoparks are micro-level instruments for technology transfer, while science cities and SEZs are macro-level mechanisms for balancing the responsibilities of local and federal authorities in the knowledge transfer (and support) activities.

There are several tens of technoparks in Russia, although only some have official licenses. Technopark policies are full of hidden problems. First of all, multiple 'white spots' in the legislation dramatically weaken the commercialisation capability of universities and R&D institutions.[16] State universities or government R&D institutions are limited in creating and directing supporting of SMEs. A state university can create a start-up, but cannot provide any funding or facilities for it. That is why Russian technoparks do not operate independently but only as a part of the 'host organisation's' structure. They lack performance monitoring and mechanisms for the diffusion of best practices. They also suffer from underdeveloped business consulting mechanisms.

The response to these negative factors is 'industry and manufacturing special economic zones' (see later). This makes it possible to significantly reduce tax pressure and attract investors. There also exist other solutions such as business incubators and mechanisms to provide financial support for start-ups; providing conversion and commercialisation mechanisms for defence 'dual-purpose' technologies, etc. Other initiatives are connected with new legal mechanisms. One should mention three main directions —provision of federal lands for technoparks on a competitive basis (both for ownership and for long leasing); direct investments in technopark infrastructure by government bodies; creation of favourable conditions for technoparks investment (construction sites, transport and housing infrastructure funding) sharing expenditures between federal and regional authorities.

An important instrument of the interaction between federal and local authorities takes the form of so-called 'science cities' or technopolises.[17] Russian science cities are the 'oldest' secret communities created in the 1930–1970s in the USSR in order to solve major state defence problems by R&D and new technologies. About 70 cities, settlements and outlying districts were ranked as science cities in previous years. Twenty-nine of them were located within the Moscow Region. About 40 per cent of national S&T potential is still concentrated in the science cities today.

These cities are populated mainly by researchers and their families. 'Mono-orientation' towards scientific activity and specific tasks explains the lack of 'traditional' infrastructure elements, such as industry (in some cities) and the agricultural complex. Therefore, after a dramatic decrease in state support in the 1990s these cities faced extremely difficult economic and social problems.

To improve the situation it was decided to 're-inventory' all former Soviet science cities. The science city concept and special state support mechanisms are regulated by the federal law 'On the Status of Science City in the Russian Federation' (1999). According to the text of this document, the science city is a municipal entity of the Russian Federation with a particular urban science and production complex. This complex consists of institutions carrying out research, development and innovation activities, and training of personnel in accordance with the national priorities in science and technology.

The science city status is confirmed by the president of the Russian Federation for a period of 25 years. The president approves the priorities determined by the government for the science city as well as the state programme for science development which specifies the form of federal support for science cities in accordance with their specialisation. Science city funding, along with logistical and maintenance support, is provided from the federal budget, the regional and local authorities budgets, and other funding sources in accordance with the constituting instrument.

Obninsk and Dubna were the first to obtain the official science city status in the Russian Federation (2001–2003). They are famous for the world's first nuclear power station and the Joint Institute for Nuclear Research (both founded in 1950s). The successful science cities are located in the most populated regions. Today there exist another 12 settlements (officially recognised in this respect in Russia after 2003). Among them are the world renowned Zjukovski (scientific support of aircraft manufacturing), Koltsevo (bio-tech), Korolyov (scientific support of spacecraft manufacturing), Michurinsk (bio-tech, agriculture), etc. Nine of them are located in the Moscow region.

Since 1999, the issue of state support for science cities has been much discussed. Problems for discussion include the state's responsibilities, efficient infrastructure creation and use, mechanisms for transition to autonomous grant-free development, etc. The creation of incentives and favourable conditions for transforming of these regions into centres of high technology and advanced R&D is considered to be a major task for the science city policies. The law on the status of science cities regards investments tax credit as the main support measure. For example, it was planned that the Obninsk administration should have the right to spend at least 50 per cent of tax revenues on the innovation infrastructure development during the first five years. However, this mechanism was later rejected. The reason for this rejection was related to the total absence of industrial activity in a number of cities. There was no industry, so no considerable tax revenues were spent on innovation development.

Finally it was decided to use internal resources of research organisations for the intensive production of R&D. Science city status presumes additional federal funding targeted specifically for the implementation (on a competitive basis) of innovation projects. The main problems today are lack of mechanisms to transfer federal funding to specific scientific projects and regulation potential (legal rights) of local authorities.

In general, science cities are supposed to attract considerable investment as venture business centres and as hubs of science, education, technological excellence, and integration.

There also exist special mechanisms to promote the development of industry-oriented science cities and innovation-active regions. One is the 'special economic zone'. This instrument was introduced in Russia in 2005 by the special federal law, 'On Special Economic Zones in the Russian Federation'. Special zones are the Russian Federation territories defined by the government, where a special regime for entrepreneurial activity applies. They are intended to promote high-technology industries.

There are three types of such zones — industrial (special tax preferences, favourable investment regime); technology and innovation (out of the customs zone, favourable for imports/exports) and recreational zones (special conditions for tourism). Special economic areas can be created on land owned by the government and/or municipalities. However, official initiatives aimed for innovation infrastructure development (as well as other mechanisms discussed earlier) do not guarantee growth in demand for and/or supply of innovation.

Particular NSI elements created directly to compensate missing actors providing demand for (and investment in) innovation are the Russian Venture Company (RVC) and several state corporations. They act as intermediaries, guarantors and sponsors in the public–private partnership mechanisms.

The Public–Private Partnership Mechanisms

The Russian high-tech sector is still unable to absorb enough investment and to find demand for innovation as well. To solve the problem the Russian government established the Russian venture company (RVC) in 2006. Another part of resources should be mobilised by state corporations. Seven state corporations (such as Russian Corporation for Nanotechnology, State Corporation for Nuclear Energy, etc.), were founded in 2007–2008 to support hi-tech sectors.

The role of RVC is to promote venture investment and financial support for S&T throughout the country. The resources for RVC capitalisation are allocated from the Investment Fund of the Russian Federation. In 2008 the authorised capital stock amounted to 28.2 billion roubles (about 775 million Euro). RVC invests in regional and industry venture companies (in the form of so-called closed end investment funds established under the Russian legislation and regulated by the Federal Service on Financial Markets). A special management company manages each fund. These companies compete for the right to sell fund investment shares to RVC. Funding can be provided only for the projects corresponding with the critical technologies.

Once the venture fund has acquired all its funding, the fund management company can start investment activities: launch innovation companies in the areas of microelectronics, information technologies, telecommunication technologies, biotechnologies, medical technologies, environment-friendly energy, and nanotechnologies. The management company team of each fund can finance from 10 to 15 innovation companies for several years. Thus, the output can be up to 15 venture funds and up to 150 innovation companies.

State corporations act as financial instruments to insure concentration and distribution of resources in the areas in line with the state interests and priorities. The need to create such a corporation was expressed in 2007 by the Russian president in his annual message to the Federation Council of the Federal Assembly of Russian Federation. As a rule, they are founded by special federal laws proclaiming the legislative basis, organisation principles, creation and activity goals of state corporations.

For example, the Russian Corporation for Nanotechnology (Rosnano, the Federal Law 'On the Russian Corporation for Nanotechnology' 2007b) addresses the growing challenge arising from the rapid development of new technologies on the nanoscale and enjoying direct budgetary support. Three key directions of

Rosnano activity are related to assistance to the state policies in the sphere of nanotechnology, development of the innovative infrastructure for nanotechnologies and achievement of projects aimed at creating innovative nanotechnologies and nano-industries. In order to achieve its goals, three main functions are carried out: R&D, nanotechnology education and financial support for innovative projects. The first two functions are provided by financial support of the R&D and nanotechnology education projects. The third function includes support of the entire innovation cycle, from project evaluation, financing and provision for commercialisation and production.

At the starting point its five-year budget it had more than 130 billion roubles (about 3.7 billion Euro). Due to its special status, the corporation is not government property and has outside control from executive bodies. The director is appointed by the Russian president only. Operational and stable support for the projects should considerably boost their efficiency. However, such 'freedom' may also lead to an unforeseen abuse. In the opinion of many Russian experts, this fact could lower expected effects from the activity of the company. Their arguments were acknowledged as completely serious, and Rosnano was transformed into another commercial company (a joint stock company with government share).

Another problem already faced by Rosnano is the lack of human resources in this field. That is why education activities there are closely tied with R&D. However, the whole NSI requires constant reproduction and development of human resources (see later).

From 2010 Russia shows visible progress within two more directions of R&D and innovation policy—creation of technological platforms (23 have been organised already) and innovation programmes of big public companies (the government has bound them to develop such programmes).

Human Resources for S&T and Innovation

Relatively high levels of human capital development, high education and skills parameters of the labour force are among the important competitive advantages of the Russian economy (Gokhberg et al. 2009). The need to sustain and increase them is declared in all key documents on the national policy of the Russian Federation (including the long-term CLTD concept, see earlier). Important practical steps in this area have already been taken by the government

(The Federal Programme 'Science and Education Manpower for Innovation Russia', 2008). This promising programme should improve and develop human potential for R&D and innovation activity in HEIs and R&D institutions. It is designed for the period 2009–2013. Its proclaimed aim is to provide institutional support of the development of efficient human resources in the S&T, education and innovation sphere. In order to achieve this goal, it is proposed to attract and involve young talent and highly skilled professionals in S&T and innovation projects and to consolidate excellent and competitive scholars in the best universities and R&D institutes. To this end, the programme includes a number of actions and instruments: centres of excellence for science and education, system of grants for young promising scientists and teachers, special schemes to attract young promising scientists and teachers from abroad, grants for innovation infrastructure development, etc. All these initiatives are going to be implemented in spite of the current financial crisis. The programme budget amounts to 90.5 billion roubles, or about 2.6 billion Euro (88.9 per cent will come from the federal budget). The share of R&D funding is expected to be 73.6 per cent. The programme includes three main directions and 20 tasks.

The programme calls for significant shifts in the S&T human capital sub-system. Among them — annual support of up to 450 centres of excellence; decrease of the average researcher's age by 34 years by 2013; increase in the number of top-level researchers by 2–3 per cent; increase in the number of top-level university teaching staff by 4–6 per cent; increase in Russia's share in world scientific publications by 1–1.5 per cent. One of the goals of the programme is to stimulate and develop non-government funding of supported projects. Therefore projects attracting support from the business sector and NCOs should have an advantage.

Sustainable development of the S&T complex and strengthening of its innovative orientation should be based on an efficient regulation system, including direct funding and indirect motivation. Indirect motivation techniques include tax breaks, discounts and special procedures for property depreciation.

In the conclusion of this section we'll discuss two more items characterising mainly the external conditions of scientific and innovative activity, namely budgetary and tax reforms.

Budgetary Reforms

Most of the industrially developed countries are trying to find more efficient mechanisms and forms of government support for R&D.

The complexity of the problem is explained by the obvious need for such support and by strictly limited resources. The solution found by the Russian government in the current situation looks quite realistic. It is based on a more efficient budgetary resources allocation together with institutional reforms in R&D and the innovation sphere.

Today the federal budget for civil S&T is almost equally distributed between direct and competitive funding. The main portion of the competitive funding stream goes to the federal goal-oriented programmes. Almost a half of the civil S&T budget is still allocated in government R&D institutions under academies of science and under state ministries and agencies. This funding stream is not based on S&T priorities or on performance of R&D institutions. This is the sphere where new mechanisms for evaluation and institutional reform are to be implemented.

The appropriate budgetary legislation was developed in Russia throughout the whole reforming period. The Budgetary Code of the Russian Federation was adopted in 1998, though the country put in place a framework for 'normal' regulation of budgetary relationships. However, the restructuring of the budgeting process did not start for six years. Only in 2004 was the concept of budgetary process restructuring approved. It was based on four key principles:

- separation of existing and newly approved expenditures;
- limiting approved expenditures to objectives clearly defined in advance, according to government policy priorities;
- targeting and programming planning techniques application;
- developing a system of real and target indicators to evaluate performance of government agencies.

Russia has also entered into a new stage of public funds management — mid-term performance-oriented budgeting. All its principles were applied in the 2006 budget, when a prospective three-year financial plan was developed alongside the traditional one-year budgeting projections.

Under the new classification, R&D expenditure is divided into basic and applied parts, which in turn are split into sections. Basic research expenditure comes under the 'general issues' section. Applied research expenditure is mostly accounted for under all other sections of expenditure functional classification — in order to support R&D for education, economy, defence, etc. One of the most important elements of the development of the budgeting process was the restructuring of budget classification and accounting. Under the 'Concept of Budgetary Process Restructuring', the new classification was brought in line with the main functions of government agencies and with international standards for accounting and public finance statistics. The streamlining of the general budgeting process should encourage development of a flexible and dynamic NSI as one of the top national priorities. It should be noted that the potential for streamlining the budgeting process in the R&D sector exists at all its stages — budget expenditures planning, shaping the budget and adjusting appropriation (allocation of funds to recipients), funding of R&D organisations (financial management techniques), legal framework, etc.

During 2010–2011 the process of deep revising was started again.

As long as the state remains the largest R&D 'sponsor' as it will be for the foreseeable future, the Russian government is planning to continue reforms in three directions:

- more concentration on the national priorities;
- optimisation of the funding structure;
- new principles of the budgetary funding.

Concentration on the national priorities requires that direct government support of applied research and technologies should be reduced to a certain minimum, supporting those most relevant to the national priorities only. Foresight is considered to be the most useful tool for national priorities setting. It is a highly discussed topic among Russian scientists and officials. The first project for practical implementation of foresight technology in Russia was launched in 2006–2008 (the second was finished in 2010; the third has just begun).

Optimisation of the funding structure is an important measure both when the total GERD is growing, as well as when it is falling (for example, due to the negative effects of the world crisis). A dramatic change in the structure of the government expenditures is expected. Funding should be re-allocated in favour of target programmes and state R&D foundations. However, a large-scale reallocation is impossible before the reform of the R&D sector.

A crucial principle of the forthcoming restructuring of R&D funding is a transition from subsidies towards credits, while moving along the innovation 'chain' (basic research — applied research — development — implementation of innovations — consumption of innovation products).

New principles for budgetary funding can be defined as liberal funding and competition. The share of so-called basic funding in the R&D budget (funds allocated to particular organisations for specific purposes regardless of their performance) should be decreased. However, each government-owned R&D organisation having survived after the restructuring of the government R&D sector should receive enough public money to meet its actual needs. The so-called package funding practice known in many countries is also being considered in Russia. It would provide a certain freedom of financial management and increase the operation flexibility of R&D institutions (Gokhberg 2003).

Streamlining the mechanisms of joint innovation programmes and project funding is an important element of the budgeting process. Improvement in this area requires creation and development of legal instruments regulating cooperative agreements in the R&D sector and NSI, grant support and long-term government orders for R&D, technologies and innovation. These forms are used to establish public and private sector partnerships and apply the R&D potential efficiently in all developed countries. Using such tools and mechanisms, developing standards and frameworks for independent expert evaluation would improve the whole system of government funding in general, promote a practical shift towards projects and programme funding, increase financial transparency and streamline procedures for making and spending profits, as well as sharing the risks of R&D and innovation activity.

In the context of the current debate, the federal budget can be said to have four main functions:

- *Ideological* (as a programme providing financial support for S&T and innovation reforms) including evaluation of the prospects of this sphere in Russia, the role of the government in its preserving and developing (i.e., as it is declared in CLTD 2020). Ideological function in our context means that the budget reflects the structure and 'ranking' of national targets and the attitude of the state and its leaders to national science.
- *Political* (as a strategy and a set of measures to mobilise and allocate financial resources). It is based on the creation integration of a hierarchical system of national objectives. This function involves the: (*a*) coupling of designations, (*b*) specific decisions of the authorities, (*c*) quantitative parameters of budget obligations for the 'science block', etc.

- *Economic* (as a financial plan to support sectors of the economy). This is concerned with the preservation and development of S&T and innovation by increasing effective demand for and commercialisation of R&D products and technologies.
- *Management* (as a procedure to establish objectives, structure, techniques and mechanisms for managing financial flows, monitoring and evaluating results). It includes coordination, succession and transparency of budgeting process stages, realistic nature of obligations.

Despite all the changes, budgets have not yet become an effective government policy tool, and do not fully carry out functions crucial for developing Russia's R&D and innovation sector. The fourth function is implemented most widely (perhaps even too strictly; the third one is implemented partially while there is still little evidence of the first and the second. To improve this situation the reform should extend outside the budgetary sphere, taking the form of broad institutional reforms.

Some Other Examples of Implicit Measures

Currently Russian S&T and innovation policy is being shaped in an incomplete legal framework for R&D and innovation activity. Taxation laws still do not include provisions that would make an efficient system of tax breaks and benefits, similar to those existing in all developed countries. Inconsistency of legal reforms, lack of continuity of legal provisions brought about a situation where many of the previous norms of tax legislation that have proved their efficiency did not find a place in the Tax Code of Russian Federation (1998, with subsequent amendments). That, in turn, caused problems hindering radical growth of innovation activity and efficient use of the country's intellectual and economic potential. For example, according to the current tax code, R&D expenditures are subtracted from revenues when the tax base is calculated, which encourages organisations to make them. At the same time tax legislation in effect does not encourage activity of R&D organisations participating in practical implementation of knowledge and technologies, or organisations funding R&D and innovation projects.

The work on developing taxation rules for S&T and the innovation sphere in Russia started in the mid-1990s, and was completed in general in 2007 — with the adoption of a number of laws and regulations aimed at reducing the tax burden for innovative enterprises. In 2008 tax breaks provided by the latest amendments to the Tax Code became valid. The most important of them are new rules for calculation of VAT, profits tax and overall simplification of the taxation. For example:

- Profits generated via sales of intellectual property rights (inventions, utility models, etc.) have been exempted from VAT, as well as earning generated by licensing intellectual property. A list of tax-exempted services supporting development of new/improved products was also approved.
- Regarding profits tax, the number of R&D foundations whose money does not have to be included in calculation of the tax base has been increased.
- Other improvements included more favourable accelerated depreciation conditions, additional breaks for organisations contributing to the Russian Technological Development fund, as well as to industrial and inter-sector R&D foundations.
- The list of expenditures not to be included into taxpayers' taxable income under the simplified taxation system includes expenditures on acquisition of exclusive intellectual property rights, patenting and R&D.
- As already noted, more breaks are provided for residents of special economic zones and companies oriented towards exporting information and communication technologies.

It should be noted that compared with the legislation regulating taxation of innovation activities in developed foreign countries, the Russian tax system even after adoption remains insufficiently wholesome and coordinated. The mentioned taxation innovations will contribute to creating a more favourable innovation climate, but they won't play a crucial role in changing private businesses' investment strategies regarding R&D and innovation activities. The new tax breaks are just not big enough (in the context of the overall economy and the S&T and innovation sphere). Problems with property and land taxes for R&D organisations remain unsolved (appropriate tax breaks have been cancelled in the new Tax Code). The lack of such breaks is particularly painful to large R&D organisations engaged in applied research and development.

The new round of tax legislation development began in 2009, although it was slowed down due to problems created by the global financial crisis. Now this process still continues. Its focus is on innovation and innovation-friendly taxation instruments which will help to create a more favourable innovative climate. For example, the government introduced tax benefits for entities investing in R&D and priority S&T areas, such as bio- and nanotechnology, nuclear energy and new types of transport systems; easier conditions for compulsory social security payments for employees of companies whose main economic activities are ICT development, engineering and R&D, etc. (Gokhberg and Kuznetsova 2010a).

Outcomes and Impact of State Policy and State Institutions on the NSI

The preceding analysis of statistical data and various government policies clearly shows that traditional troubles of the Russian S&T and innovations sphere have not been dealt with yet, which makes the 'innovation shift' envisaged in the long-term CLTD 2020 strategy (and other strategy documents) even more complex and important. That is true for development of target indicators as well as designing the overall government S&T and innovation policy. Note that in the process of that shift government agencies have to deal with an increasingly large 'management object' — the growing S&T and innovation activities sphere, which makes decision-making significantly harder and requirements to the quality of such decisions more strict (see Table 3.9).

Relevant government policy should be developed keeping in mind the following objectives:

- to eliminate/temper the existing negative trends.
- to deal with the tasks typical to catch up with leading development models. As experience of foreign countries shows, approaches, tools and mechanisms used for such purposes don't always match.
- to ensure breakthroughs in the sectors of the Russian economy which determine the country's role in the global economy — mainly low- or medium-low research-intensive, with an obsolete technological basis. Mining and energy industries, other basic sectors need a deep modernisation and radical increase of their technological level. Equally important is ensuring major progress in restructuring of the R&D sector itself.
- to develop a new social model, radical restructuring of the institutional environment and legal regulations aimed at promoting R&D and innovation, entrepreneurship, private

investment. The actual Russian experience shows that change is slow to come in these areas, doesn't happen in a systematic way and faces serious opposition at the middle and lower levels of the management hierarchy.

Table 3.9: *Scope of S&T and Innovations Sphere and Amount of Financial Support it Received in 2009*

Indicator	*Value*	*Change Compared with 1995*
R&D institutions	3536	Reduced by 11 times
HE institutions, total state and municipal	1134 660	Increased by 1.17 times (compared with 1999) Increased by 1.01 times (compared with 1999)
R&D personnel (head-count, thousands)	742.4	Reduced by 1.4 times
R&D fixed assets, bln roubles	705.0 (in constant prices – 43.3)	Reduced by almost 2 times
Industrial enterprises engaged in technological innovation*	About 3,000	Increased by almost 1.5 times
Patent applications, thousands	38.6	Increased by 1.7 times
GDER, bln roubles	485.8 (in constant prices – 6.1)	Increased by 10 times (compared with 1999) Increased by 2.1 times (compared with 1999)
FBA on civil R&D, bln roubles	219.1	Increased by 19 times (compared with 1999)
at constant prices	7.51	Increased by 3.9 times (compared with 1999)
FBA on higher education, bln roubles**	280	Increased by 12 times (2008/2000)
Expenditures on technological innovation (total), bln roubles	327.9	Increased by 7.6 times
– from government budget	About 14 bln roubles	NA
Venture companies, bln roubles (2007)	30	NA

(*Cont.*)

(*Cont.*)

Indicator	*Value*	*Change Compared with 1995*
RVC (initial payment of the Government)	15	
Nanoindustry and nanotechnology (initial payment of the Government), bln roubles	130	NA
Volume of "nanoproducts", bln. roubles	112	

Source: HSE (2011a: 24, 36, 69–71, 233, 274); HSE (2011b: 9–11, 37, 39); HSE (2010: 68, 350–51); HSE estimates.

Note: * Mining, manufacturing industries, power generation and distribution, gas and water supply, communications, etc.

** Consolidated budget of Russian Federation and public non-budgetary foundations.

The following issues are crucially important for increasing efficiency of the Russian government S&T and innovation policy:

- variety and integrated nature of management and development tools;
- coordination and harmonisation of various policy tools and areas across the levels of the hierarchy;
- targeted design of laws, programmes, strategies to deal with specific (global and national) challenges;
- ensuring optimal balance of direct supervision and control on the one hand and promotion and motivation of R&D and innovation activities on the other;
- regular monitoring and assessment of government policy's efficiency, to adjust the management and decision-making process accordingly.

Conclusions and Recommendations Targeting Improvements in the NSI with Specific Emphasis on the Role of the State

This chapter has represented an overview of the Russian S&T and innovation sphere, emphasising the most recent trends and policies. Russian history is full of contradictions as well as the evolution of its science, innovation system, the state's policy and positions in the world. In the USSR the innovation system existed in a narrow scientific-technological space. Scientific results and innovations were created and introduced on the basis of the centralised decisions of the government, and in the areas connected to the main interests of the state. The term 'national system of innovation' was never used in the USSR, and the actual NSI wasn't considered worthy of research or special government policy. It is only in the last few years during painful transformations of economy, state and society in Russia that a comprehension of a key role of innovations and the necessity of wider understanding NSI as a system of national institutes has emerged. The wide understanding of innovation and the new approach to NSI have been fixed in key documents of the state's policy.

The analysis in this study allows us to make several important (in our opinion) conclusions regarding possible ways to improve the domestic S&T and innovation system (with specific emphasis on the role of the state):

(*a*) After the disintegration of the USSR when wide-ranging reforms including privatisation and market liberalisation were being undertaken, the Russian economy and the Russian state changed dramatically. The state became more democratic; market institutes, elements of a civil society (which are not always accepted 'canonical' forms) gradually began to develop. Within that process the Russian S&T and innovation sphere reached a turning point in the arduous transformation from a centrally controlled and administered structure to a flexible system operating in the free-market environment. Unfortunately the reforms of S&T and NSI were lagging behind the transformation in other sectors of economy.

Though the transition towards a demand and supply balanced system is not complete, the demand for R&D has already shifted and the institutions meeting it are themselves going through changes towards more efficient and accountable forms. Initiatives aimed for stimulation of demand for R&D and innovations, and for PPP development will have a temporary effect. In the long run institutions — such as Rosnano or RVC — will not be able to replace the traditional market actors that ensure the demand for R&D and innovation. At the same time Russia still lacks high quality supply from R&D institutions. One of the reasons for this is that institutional reforms in the Russian R&D sector are incomplete too.

(*b*) Many experts believe that the current state of Russian R&D and NSI, the barriers and limitations hindering their rapid restructuring and successful development which remained intact for many years, are in a way the end result of inefficient, illogical, inconsequential, and uncoordinated initiatives pursued by various government branches, lack of coordination between ministries, agencies, various legislation, etc. The accumulated negative impulses constitute a serious obstacle not just for practical implementation but even for the theoretical design of an efficient policy including appropriate institutions and mechanisms.

However, the opposite is also true: the current state of the science and innovation sphere creates objective limitations on development and implementation of an efficient policy.

(*c*) It is shown that the Russian S&T and innovation policies transition can be divided into four main stages. The fourth (the current) stage lasting from the middle 2000s to now is characterised by complex activities of the government aimed at the transition towards an innovative model of national economy. One can easily imagine two main dimensions of the policy making activities. The first one is creation of a structured NSI policy framework. The second is the implementation of the policy mechanisms for efficient regulation in the main areas of government activity: the national priorities, performance-based budgeting, restructuring the government R&D sector, human resources and infrastructure development, etc.

This stage of rather stable recovery of NSI was interrupted in 2008 by the painful economical and financial crisis. The consequences of this crisis in Russia have not yet been overcome and are not entirely obvious. What is obvious is that further research in this area is required.

(*d*) The history of reforms of S&T and NSI in Russia shows that they cannot wait for a full economic transition. Innovation activities themselves can contribute to the restructuring of enterprises and industrial change, as well as to the improvement of education, science, health care, and environment. It is crucial to speed up all these reforms in the complex.

Future policy actions in this field will be coordinated with a complex framework including three key components: the development of the S&T sector (and the supply of innovation); increasing demand for innovation; and human capital development. Simultaneously the future of the Russian NSI certainly depends on the reform of the entire economic system and the overall macroeconomic situation. It is evident that an economy based solely on oil and natural gas export is unable to follow an innovation growth trajectory. Accordingly, enterprises can be encouraged to compete and play a central role in directing R&D and innovation only after broad structural shifts in the economy.

In addition, it is obvious today that the important and vital reforms of S&T and NSI cannot wait for a new era of prosperity (after the crisis period). It is critical for Russia (as well as for other counties) to make the following choice — to invest in the future, for example, to continue its efforts in supporting science and innovation activities, or to stop them. The second scenario means a serious risk to worsen the position in the world science and technology development coming out of the current crisis. The leaders of the world economy understand this dichotomy, and demonstrate rather good examples of the first approach.

There is a lot still to do to encourage the contributions of science and innovation, especially in the fields of public policy and reorganisation of the R&D sector. The S&T and innovation policies should be driven by complete priority of complex and dynamic reforms, aimed at efficient innovation and support to the best performers.

(*e*) Progress in the field of S&T and innovations achieved in developed countries is based on a complex system of interaction between all major actors: (*i*) generating various kinds of knowledge (R&D and educational organisations, large companies, small and medium firms, etc.); (*ii*) monitoring (controlling) the flows of this knowledge (and flows of resources) and (*iii*) ensuring their practical implementation. Efficiency of the whole process in each country is determined by the specific way these actors interact as components of the collective knowledge-generation and utilisation system.

Analysis of domestic and international experience suggests that the government's role in this process amounts to creating conditions for the following:

- enterprises and R&D actors (including science and higher education institutions) are motivated to participate in innovation activities (emergence of efficient proprietors, competitive environment for producers and consumers of knowledge, development of cooperative relations between them);
- increased education level of management and easier access to information required for R&D and innovation activities;
- transfer of technologies (including creation of enterprises utilising new technologies);
- organisation of the very process of knowledge creation and dissemination based on advanced forms and mechanisms including cooperation between private and public sector organisations (PPP) in the R&D and innovations area, etc.

(*f*) Effectiveness of Russian S&T and innovation policy is largely determined by the fact that Russia needs to deal with a whole host of problems immediately — those connected with the generation of new ideas, their transformation into high technologies and finally, production of actual goods and services. Constraints hindering acceleration of these processes take place at both ends: among customers and suppliers of R&D products. Nevertheless, the contemporary economic potential of the Russian economy is high enough to launch the NSI reforms and complete the transition of the S&T and innovation sector.

(*g*) The development of the Russian S&T and innovation policy should be ultimately aimed at dealing with the key problem of the country's NSI — inefficient use of resources allocated to the R&D sector combined with insufficient demand for innovations by businesses.

Relevance of this problem increases even further in the situation of the global economic crisis and the changes it brings about. Note that government initiatives to support and promote demand and supply in the S&T and innovations sphere should be accompanied by a serious effort to widen the range and increase efficiency of tools and mechanisms used, including various forms of partnership between the state, business and science. This would certainly help to put together a system of long-term S&T development goals and map the ways of accomplishing them (as it has been already done in frameworks of CLTD and other strategic documents).

(*h*) To increase the real sector's demand for R&D products and technology in the situation of financial crisis and post-crisis recovery, a sensible combination of targeted government policy to promote innovation activities and an overall improvement of instructional environment for entrepreneurship plays a very important role. So far this environment is by no means perfect: administrative, legal and other barriers hindering emergence and functioning of modern market institutions and competitive climate still remain in place in Russia, and occasionally even grow.

Accordingly, measures planned or already on line seem to be particularly important to the country. Among them:

- the promotion of a national network of development institutes (social, financial, etc.). These should provide funding and other support to innovation projects at all stages, as well as to innovation infrastructure and to small and medium companies engaged in technology (and other R&D products) transfer, production of innovative products/services;
- the modernisation of technological apparatus (basis); development of new technical management (technical regulation) tools;
- the improvement of the situation with enforcement of new regulations in the area of intellectual property protection and use;
- the development of the preferential credits system, government guarantees and other forms of risk sharing between the state and the business. This is especially relevant to high technology companies (including small and medium firms) exporting high-tech products/services;
- the creation of new opportunities to implement results of the national technological foresight analysis (this work

was launched on a full scale in Russia in 2007) in public administration, including development of target federal programmes, initiating long-term projects, etc.

(*i*) As to improving the quality and increasing supply of R&D results available to the real sector of the economy, measures which have been implemented during several recent years still remain crucial in Russia. These are aimed at completing the restructuring of the public R&D sector and increasing its efficiency.

The following priority steps are envisaged to achieve significant progress in this area:

- to create a centre of excellence network (based on the existing or new components of the Russian NSI — large R&D organisations and universities), on national, industrial, regional and inter-regional levels; provide special government support to them; promote their networking and cooperation;
- to carry on with measures aimed at improving conditions for integration of science, higher education and business, regardless of organisational structures and operational modes of the participants;
- to implement and actively use in public administration a system for assessing efficiency and effectiveness of R&D organisations (the system for evaluation of R&D units' performance); to improve implementation of appropriate procedures, indicators, criteria, etc.;
- to increase opportunities for R&D organisations and universities to participate in commercial (entrepreneurial) activities, including establishment of small innovation firms and partnerships;
- to work on improving institutional structure of R&D network, by increasing the share of autonomous (public and non-profit) organisations, etc.

(*j*) To widen the range and increase efficiency of government policy tools, efforts are envisaged to increase efficiency of the public–private sector partnership mechanisms. Since in Russia this policy area remains to a certain extent exotic, accent should be placed mainly on using various ways to motivate and encourage potential participants of such partnerships established to prepare and implement large-scale innovative projects.

The following must be done in this area, and as quickly as possible:

- eliminate the remaining limitations on investment of public funds in authorised capital of innovative companies. In a wider context, fund-raising mechanisms to finance innovation projects from all possible sources must be improved (including government budgets, non-budgetary funds, venture capital, foreign investments, etc.). Such mechanisms are necessary to create large-scale and mass supply of new technologies and innovations in Russia;
- increase the amount of government-backed credit to organisations implementing innovation projects;
- make government procurement more innovation-oriented;
- improve the quality of expert evaluation and tender procedures;
- provide financial support to patenting by Russian inventors (both in Russia and abroad), and a number of other initiatives.

(*k*) Government policy is a major factor and an impulse promoting development of the Russian NSI model which would ensure efficient use of the country's R&D and innovation potential to speed up economic growth and improve the quality of life. However, Russian experience sometimes provides examples when government initiatives turn into serious barriers. The economic crisis has already made 'inefficient zones' in the Russian R&D and NSI spheres more evident. One would like to hope that dealing with the existing problems won't be postponed 'until better times' yet again, like it was done 20 years ago.

Accordingly, incorporation into various international S&T initiatives (projects, programmes, alliances, foundations) becomes increasingly important to Russia. In the modern global economy participation in international coalitions and networks (in particular, in the framework of the BRICS project) not only opens access to modern management techniques, practical experience accumulated during design and implementation of crisis management measures, advanced ideas for development and implementation of government policies, but also enables countries to protect their own interests in a more efficient way, develop joint approaches, identify niches for S&T cooperation and expansion on the international markets.

Notes

1. The chapter was prepared with the use of the results of the National Research University 'Higher School of Economics' (HSE) Basic Research Programme.
2. According to the industrial classification adopted in the USSR (*Scientific–Technical Progress in the USSR: Statistical Abstracts* 1990).
3. GERD 1990 is 5 times larger compared with GERD 1995 (in constant prices). Sources (here and after, except specially stipulated cases): the statistical data books published by HSE.
4. For example, expenditures per researcher in Germany amount to about $ 238,000, in the USA, $ 233,000, in Korea, $ 173,000. Sources: HSE (2005); HSE (2007); HSE (2009a); HSE (2009b); HSE (2010); HSE (2011a); HSE (2011b); HSE (2011c). For figures for foreign countries, data for 2007–2009, or the nearest available, is given.
5. The most current (but not adopted) documents are 'Innovative Russia — 2020' (Ministry of Economics 2011); 'Strategy 2020: New Model of Economic Growth — New Social Policy (prepared by expert groups, 2011).
6. In the USSR this lack of usage occurred not only among governments, but among the majority of experts and in the scientific community too. However, it needs to be pointed out that the dissolution of the USSR came about just as the NSI concept was entering the language of policy makers worldwide.
7. Survey of about 3,000 Russian scientists 'Assessment of Scientists' Working Conditions and Appeal of a Career in Science', conducted by the HSE in 2007 (Kuznetsova 2008; Gokhberget al. 2010).
8. There was no question of implementing any major changes in the USSR, nor could anybody raise such an issue.
9. Russian Foundation for Basic Research, Russian Foundation for Support of Small Enterprises in R&D Sector, Russian Foundation for Research in Humanities.
10. Especially in the period of crisis.
11. In particular, foundations to support R&D and small innovative enterprises were created; decisions such as to privatise and commercialise certain segments of the S&T sector taken and partially implemented;

contract-based system adopted; a number of measures to protect and commercialise intellectual property undertaken, etc.

12. See Gokhberg and Kuznetsova (2009: 30, 32); HSE (2011c).
13. Communication, activities involving the use of computers and ICT, wholesale trade — these industries are subjected to ongoing monitoring by Russian innovation statistics.
14. Measured by a ratio of the number of enterprises engaged in technological or other innovation to the total number of enterprises.
15. Priority S&T areas are deemed to be subject areas of S&T with potential for making a major contribution towards providing the country's security, faster economic growth, greater competitive capacity of Russian companies through development of the technological foundations of the national economy and R&D-intensive production facilities. Critical technologies are considered as sets of technological solutions that create potential for further development of various technological areas, possess a broad range of innovative applications in various sectors of economy and as a whole make the greatest contribution to the resolving of the major problems of implementing scientific and technological priorities.
16. These are relations that are not regulated or are poorly governed by current legislation.
17. A typical science city is a large up-to-date research and industrial complex, including HEIs, research institutions, as well as residential area provided with cultural and recreation infrastructure. The international concept of science cities is to concentrate the scientific potential in advanced and pioneer fields, using a favourable environment for creative R&D activities.

References

Avdulov, A. and A. Kulkin, 1996. *Structure and Development Trends of Russia's S&T Potential.* Moscow: Editorial URSS.

Centre for Science Research and Statistics (CSRS), 1992. *R&D in the USSR: Analysis and Statistics.* Moscow: Centre for Science Research and Statistics.

Gokhberg, L., 2003. 'A New Innovation System for the New Economy', background material for a presentation at the First Globelics Conference 'Innovation Systems and Development Strategies for the Third Millennium', 2–6 November, Rio de Janeiro.

Gokhberg, L. and I. Kouznetsova, 2009. 'Innovation in the Russian Economy: Stagnation before Crisis?', *Foresight*, 3(2): 28–46.

———, 2010a. 'New Innovation Policy in the Context of Economy Modernization', *Journal of New Economic Association*, 7: 141–44.

Gokhberg, L. and I. Kouznetsova, 2010b. 'Russian Federation', in United Nations Educational, Scientific and Cultural Organization, *UNESCO Science Report 2010: The Current Status of the Science around the World*. Paris: United Nations Educational, Scientific and Cultural Organization, 215–33.

Gokhberg, L., T. Kuznetsova and S. Zaichenko, 2009. 'Towards a New Role of Universities in Russia: Prospects and Limitations', *Science and Public Policy*, 36(2): 121–26.

Gokhberg, L., G. Kitova, T. Kuznetsova, and O. Shuvalova., 2010. *Social Portrait of the Russian Scientist*. Moscow: Editorial HSE.

Government of Russian Federation (GRV), 1996. 'On Science and the State S&T Policy', no. 127, Russian Federation Law Reports, 23 August 1996.

———, 1998. 'The Concept of Reforming Russian Science in 1998–2000', no. 453, approved on 18 May 1998, Government of Russian Federation, Moscow.

———, 1999. 'On the Status of Science City in the Russian Federation', no. 70, 7 April.

———, 2005. 'On Special Economic Zones in the Russian Federation', no. 116, 22 July.

———, 2006a. 'On Autonomous Institutions', no. 174, 3 November.

———, 2006b. 'R&D and Innovation Development Strategy in the Russian Federation until 2015', no. 1, approved by the Inter-ministry Commission for Science and Innovation Policy, 15 February, Moscow.

———, 2006c. 'Support Measures for Higher Education Institutions Implementing Innovative Education Programmes', no. 89, approved on 14 February 2007, Government of Russian Federation, Moscow.

———, 2007a. 'On Changes to the Selected Legal Statements of the Russian Federation Concerning the Integration of Education and Science', no. 308, 1 December.

———, 2007b. 'On the Russian Corporation for Nanotechnology', no. 139, 19 July.

———, 2008a. *Long-Term Social and Economic Development to 2020: A Policy Framework*. Moscow: Government of Russian Federation.

———, 2008b. 'The Federal Programme: Science and Education Manpower for Innovation Russia', no. 440, approved on 7 April 2008, Government of Russian Federation, Moscow.

———, 2009. 'On the System of Civil R&D Organisations Performance Evaluation', no. 312, approved on 8 April 2009, Government of Russian Federation, Moscow.

Higher School of Economics–State University (HSE), 2005. *Science in Russian Federation*, Data Book 2005. Moscow: Higher School of Economics–State University.

Higher School of Economics–State University (HSE), 2007. *Science, Technology and Innovation in Russia and OECD Countries*, Data Book 2007. Moscow: Higher School of Economics–State University.

———, 2008. *Innovation-driven Development as the Basis for Modernisation of the Russian Economy*. Moscow: Institute of World Economy and International Relations.

———, 2009a. *Science Indicators*, Data Book 2009. Moscow: State University–Higher School of Economics.

———, 2009b. *Indicators of Innovation*, Data Book 2009. Moscow: State University–Higher School of Economics.

———, 2010. *Education in the Russian Federation*, Data Book 2010. Moscow: State University–Higher School of Economics.

———, 2011a. *Science Indicators*, Data Book 2011. Moscow: State University–Higher School of Economics.

———, 2011b. *Indicators of Innovation*, Data Book 2011. Moscow: State University–Higher School of Economics.

———, 2011c. *Russian Innovation Index*, ed. Leonid Gokhberg. Moscow: State University–Higher School of Economics.

Kiseleva, V., T. Kuznetsova and B. Kuznetsov, 1991. *The Analysis of Science Potential: International Comparison*. Moscow: Nauka.

Kuznetsova, T., 1992. 'The Problems and Conditions of Scientific Policy', *Studies on Soviet Economic Development*, 3(6).

———, 2008. 'Science and Technology Policy in Assessments of Russian Scientists', *Foresight*, 2(3): 44–53.

Kuznetsova, T. and G. Kitova, 2003. 'The Effect of Science Policy without Mutual Understanding: Correlation of Theory & Practice', *Studies of Science*, 3(19): 63–75.

President of Russian Federation, 1996. 'The Doctrine of Russian Science Development', no. 35, approved by the president of the Russian Federation, 13 June, Moscow.

———, 2002. 'The Basic Directions of the Russian Federation's Policy on S&T Development until 2010 and Subsequent Period', no. Pr-576, approved by the president of the Russian Federation, 30 March, Moscow.

Russian Federal State Statistics Service (Rosstat), 2008. *Statistical Yearbook of Russia: 2008*. Moscow: Government of Russian Federation.

Shuvalova, O., 2007. 'The Image of Science: People's Perceptions of S&T Achievements', *Foresight*, 2: 50–59.

State Committee on Statistics of the U.S.S.R., 1990. *Scientific–Technical Progress in the USSR: Statistical Abstract*. Moscow: Finance and Statistics.

4

India

V. V. Krishna

India is now counted among the leading emerging economies of the world with a vast network of science and technology (S&T) and research and development (R&D) institutional structure. It is among the top ten nations of the world for Science Citation Index (SCI)–based scientific publications for the decade 1996–2006 and second among BRICS countries. The total number of papers almost doubled from 20,514 in 1996 to 40,062 in 2006. India spent around 1.13 per cent of GDP for R&D as a whole in 2007. India's national aggregate gross expenditure on research and development (GERD) was about INR 413 billion (US$ 29.5 billion) in 2007–2008. A dominant proportion of GERD, around 68 per cent, is met by the government sources and 30 per cent from the business enterprise sector. In purchasing power parity (PPP) terms it works out to be about INR 1,660 billion. India ranks higher as compared to countries such as Brazil, Mexico and South Africa but is behind China which spent US$ 110 billion in R&D in PPP terms in 2006, and the United States at almost US$ 291 billion in 2006.

India has been experiencing a high growth rate of GDP which was 9 and 9.2 per cent for the two years 2005–2006 and 2006–2007, respectively, with an average of 6.9 per cent for the seven-year period from 2000–2001 to 2006–2007. Much of India's recent growth is driven by innovations in high technology manufacturing in drugs and pharmaceuticals, in skill-intensive services in software, telecommunications, engineering, automotive, gems and jewellery sectors, and to a lesser extent in medical services. Science and technology developments in space technology with capabilities to launch commercial satellites and un-manned missions to the moon, nuclear technology, pharma research capabilities in drug discovery and commercialisation, information and communications technology (ICT) software, biotechnology in health and agriculture, and the emerging capabilities in automotive research and telecommunications have contributed to the country's emergence as an important 'knowledge power' from Asia.

India's national system of innovation (NSI) is constituted by: (*a*) public research system of national laboratories under major science agencies and in-house laboratories in public sector enterprises; (*b*) institutions of higher learning and universities; (*c*) business enterprises both local and foreign; (*d*) civil society agencies and bodies; and (*e*) institutions and policies of government which formulate and implement social, economic, monetary and science, technology and innovation policies among others.

The current structure of India's NSI as we see it today has evolved from the post-independence period after 1947. State mediation and the role of government support in the development of science, technology and higher education has been a crucial aspect of India's current NSI. It has its roots in the 1950s when political leadership led by Jawaharlal Nehru had given top priority to science and technology institution building. The Scientific Policy Resolution (SPR) of 1958, India's first S&T Plan of 1974; and Science and Technology Policy Statements in 1983 and 2003 recurrently emphasised building national and local capacities in science and technology and attaining self-reliance in some crucial sectors of the economy.

This chapter on the role of the state in the evolution of India's NSI is specifically conceptualised and structured from a historical perspective covering three different phases from 1947 to the current era. In approaching the role of the state in the evolution of NSI in India, the theoretical framework outlined here selectively draws on three sets of literature, namely, on NSI, S&T policies and those that specifically deal with state mediation through S&T policies. As noted, this chapter on the role of the state in the evolution of NSI in India adopts a historical perspective. Since India underwent a long period of British colonialism, much of modern India's policy of state mediation in science and technology for industrialisation and development is shaped from the roots of its colonial struggle for not only political independence but technological independence. For this reason, we begin looking into the role of state mediation from this perspective in the upcoming section.

Role of State and NSI: Evolution in Three Phases[1]

> Establishing a Sanskrit School under Hindu pundits . . . can only be expected to load the minds of youth with grammatical niceties and metaphysical distinction of little or no practical use . . . But as the improvement of the native population is the object of the government, it will consequently promote a more liberal and enlightened system of instruction, embracing Mathematics, Natural Philosophy, Chemistry, Anatomy, with other useful sciences, which may be accomplished with the sum proposed by employing a few gentlemen of talent and learning, educated in Europe, and providing a college furnished with necessary books, instruments and other apparatus (*Raja Rammohan Roy's Letter to the Governor General, 1823*).

> Indians are incapable of any original work in natural science . . . If indeed it exists as yet in this variety of human race . . . so let us exercise a little discretion with our weaker brethren and not expect them to run before they can walk (*H. B. Medlicott, Head, Geological Survey of India, 1880*).

The role played by the state in the evolution of science, technology and innovation policies and institution building is intimately connected with the colonial context. As is well-known, India was under colonial rule for over three centuries. British colonialism is generally seen by Indian historians to have impacted on Indian politics, economy and society in both constructive as well as destructive or dysfunctional ways and manifestations. In the domain of language and teaching of science and technology, Indian intellectual elite argued for modern science and technology courses to be introduced in colleges with an emphasis on English rather than Indian classical languages as argued by Raja Rammohan Roy from as early as the 1830s (see earlier quote). In several ways Indians were successful in higher education and in the introduction of science and technology courses.

The first modern universities in India which introduced English language teaching were established as early as 1857 in Madras,

Calcutta and Bombay. In the domain of science and industry, whilst the British created over a dozen colonial scientific enterprises such as railways, geology, trigonometry, surveys, public works, botanical gardens, among other sectors, the structure and functions of these scientific enterprises came to be defined in terms of 'colonial science'. There was a division of labour between centre (Britain) and periphery (colony). While the former was assigned the role of scientific synthesis, the latter was relegated more towards survey research and data gathering rather than professionalisation of science and technology. Above all, there was considerable discrimination in the organisation and recruitment of scientists to high positions as the quote of H. B. Medlicott, head of the Geological Survey in the 1880s reflects.

As argued elsewhere, the period from the late 19th century marks a break with colonial science (Krishna 1997a). This period is associated with the creation of a series of support structures in science and technology. Parallel to colonial science, there emerged a stream of early science policy efforts and its role in nation-building in the form of 'national science' during the 1880s and 1940s. This was a phase where elite Indian scientists such as M. N. Saha, P. C. Ray, J. C. Bose, Mahenderlal Sircar, among others, forged a close alliance with political elite (Jawaharlal Nehru and M. K. Gandhi, etc.) towards formulating science policies for nation-building, creating a local national science and technology institutional base including educational institutions in parallel to colonial science enterprises. A number of basic research–oriented science institutions and academic groups in universities and colleges, which were established outside colonial science enterprises, gave an identity to Indian science in the international scientific domain during the 1920s and 1940s. The most significant were the two Nobel Prizes given to Indians in literature and physics by the 1930s.

National or independence movements against colonial powers have taken root in various other Latin American and African countries. However, the specificity of the Indian case is that the intellectual struggle against colonial science policies led to the creation of a local and national base in science institutions that worked towards the formation of an Indian science community which became an integral part of the political struggle as well (Krishna 1997a). Thus even before independence in 1947, the struggle against colonialism and colonial science led to a number of conceptual frameworks and views such as the role of science and technology in nation-building, self-reliance in science and technology, and above all, the importance of modern science and technology institutions in the development of the country.[2] All these views and frameworks on science policy for development, which were the result of the pre-independence struggle, came to play a central part in the state policies which made science and technology important factors for development led by Jawaharlal Nehru — India's first Prime Minister — in 1947 (Krishna 1997a).

We will explore the role of the state in the evolution of the NIS in three phases. The first phase is conceptualised to begin with India's independence in 1947 lasting up to 1970. The second phase began in the early 1970s and lasted until the late 1980s. The third begins with new economic reforms and the liberalisation era in 1991 and continues into the 21st century.

1947–1970: Policy for the sciences and self-reliance

This is the phase in which the role of Nehru and his initiatives in science policies dominated and has left a lasting impression on the development of science and technology in the country, which even reverberates currently in its various manifestations. From the perspective of a science policy framework, this period reflects a phase of 'policy for the sciences' during which the main emphasis was on creating a basic infrastructure for science and technology in the country including the expansion of the university sector for the supply of required S&T human resources. Nehru's views and a framework on science policy with its roots in the pre-independence period resonated unbounded optimism over science and development and assigned a major role for state mediation even before independence which is evident from two important observations cited here. Speaking at the Indian Science Congress in 1938 he stressed (Krishna 1997a: 237):

> It is science alone that could solve these problems of hunger and poverty, of insanitation and illiteracy, of superstition and deadening custom and tradition, of vast resources running waste of a rich country inhabited by starving people.

The Congress Party's manifesto which was issued for the first national government declared in 1945 underlined the prime role of the state in science and the development of the country (Krishna 1997a: 237):

> Science in its instrumental fields of activity has played an ever increasing part in influencing and moulding human life . . . Industrial, agricultural and cultural advance, as well as national defence depend on it. Scientific research is, therefore, a basic and essential activity of the State and should be organised and encouraged on the widest scale.

While Nehru obtained the party's legitimation for assigning an important role of state mediation and governance of science and technology development, the government led by him after 1947 further legitimised the role of the state as it accepted the recommendations of the A. V. Hill Committee Report submitted in 1944. According to this report and the model of science advocated, all science and technology institutions and science agencies including national laboratories were to be placed under the overall control of a government body or ministry.[3] Nehru created the Ministry of Scientific Research and Cultural Affairs in 1948 and took on the portfolio himself. The building of S&T infrastructure with new universities, science agencies and national laboratories came under the control of this ministry. Towards establishing infrastructure and building institutions in S&T, Nehru deemed it very important to bring scientific elite and science leadership closer to the government. He used his annual full-day attendance at the Indian Science Congress every year after 1947 to strengthen his association with the scientific elite and science community where he issued major science and technology policy statements and intentions of the government.[4] As early as 1948, addressing the annual Indian Science Congress, he called upon scientists by observing that, 'in India there is a growing realisation of this fact that the politician and the scientist should work in close cooperation'.

In contrast to Gandhi's religious and rural focus on development, Nehru's modern, liberal image and his explicit support and orientation towards modern science and technology development made him a 'messiah' of Indian science and the science community right from the beginning. The Gandhian model did have some influence in this phase but could not gain legitimacy as an alternative. This close 'alliance between science and politics', inaugurated by Nehru, which is in a large measure relevant even today, played an important part in building science and technology institutions. Nehru's close alliance with the science elite extended to S. S. Bhatnagar in industrial research, Homi Bhabha in atomic energy establishment, P. C.

Mahalanobis in the Planning Commission and D. S. Kothari in the defence establishment.

The period between 1948 and the 1960s, during the development phase of a policy for the sciences, witnessed rapid expansion of major science agencies such as the Council of Scientific and Industrial Research (CSIR) which has a network of 38 national laboratories currently in physical, biological, mechanical, and chemical sciences.[5] Department of Atomic Energy (DAE), Defence Research and Development Organisation (DRDO), Indian Council of Agriculture Research (ICAR), and Indian Council of Medical Research (ICMR) are some of the other major science agencies created during this phase. In the higher education sector, from 30 universities in the late 1940s, about 95 universities including specialised institutions such as the five Indian Institutes of Technology (IITs) were established in this phase.

Table 4.1: *Growth of Major S&T Institutions in Terms of Funding and Manpower in India*

	R&D Budget (US$ PPP)			*S&T Manpower*			*No. Lab./Ins.*
Scientific Agency	*1958–59*	*1965–66*	*1972–73*	*1958–59*	*1969–70*	*1972–73*	*1970*
DAE	16.3	42.1	33.5	1067	7441	7910	4
CSIR	10.7	29.7	32.8	3512	9515	8979	34
DRDO	3.1	20.4	33.8	1500	7003	9691	37
ICAR	7.8	13.4	39.8	1500	8400	5023	24
ICMR	1.07	2.2	3.2	1001	1585	1021	8
Space (DoS)	-	-	24.3	-	-	3694	
Subtotal	38.97	107.8	1257.2	8580	33944	36318	107

Source: Rahman et al. (1973: 44, 116–17); Department of Science and Technology (1975: 5).

Note: DAE: Department of Atomic Energy; CSIR: Council of Scientific and Industrial Research; DRDO: Defence Research and Development Organisation; ICAR: India Council of Agriculture Research; ICMR: Indian Council of Medical Research; and DoS: Department of Space.

Compared to the main locus of Indian science in the academic settings during the 1920–1940s, the expansion and locus of science in the post-independence period shifted to these mission-oriented science agencies under government control. The post-war 'science push' or innovation chain model triggered considerable optimism in the organisation of science under the leadership of Nehru and closely associated elite scientists like Homi Bhabha, S. S. Bhatnagar, Mahalanobis, J. C. Ghosh, among others. The spirit of policy for the sciences perspective was clearly reflected in the Scientific Policy Resolution (SPR) passed in the Parliament in 1958 which in fact provided legitimation for the expansion of public sciences in India for the next three decades or so. The aims of the scientific policy were:[6]

- to foster, promote, and sustain, by all appropriate means, the cultivation of science, and scientific research in all its aspects — pure, applied and educational;
- to ensure an adequate supply, within the country, of research scientists of the highest quality, and to recognise their work as an important component of the strength of the nation;
- to encourage, and initiate, with all possible speed, programmes for the training of scientific and technical personnel, on a scale adequate to fulfil the country's needs in science and education, agriculture and industry, and defence;
- to ensure that the creative talent of men and women is encouraged and finds full scope in scientific activity;
- to encourage individual initiative for the acquisition and dissemination of knowledge, and for the discovery of new knowledge, in an atmosphere of academic freedom; and,
- in general, to secure for the people of the country all the benefits that can accrue from the acquisition and application of scientific knowledge.

The SPR clearly reflected the perspective of the policy for the sciences. Implicit in it was the view that once the infrastructure for modern S&T and congenial conditions for R&D are created, personnel trained and institutionalisation of science is completed, the S&T system will feed into solving the developmental problems of India and tackling poverty. What was also stressed was the need to develop indigenous technological capabilities. As the explanatory note of SPR drew attention, building science and technology infrastructure can make up for shortages in raw materials by technology-based alternatives and by providing skills which can generate revenues in exports. The vision contained in the SPR clearly pointed out that a country of India's dimensions aspiring to become industrialised will have to pay a heavy price for importing science and technology in the form of plant and machinery, professional personnel and technical consultants. Hence, the SPR argued for building infrastructure in S&T which can greatly reduce the drain on outward capital flow during the early and critical stages of industrialisation. The perspective of self-reliance resonated quite forcefully in the Third and Fourth Five Year Plans stretching from 1961–1966 and 1967–1974, respectively:

> a basic objective in the strategy of development is to create the conditions in which dependence on external assistance will disappear as early as possible (and) replacement of imports is essentially a question of developing the necessary capacity for production within the country (Planning Commission 1961: 26–27).

> the (Fourth Plan) seeks to enlarge the area of self-reliance in terms of financial resources and technological *inputs* (Planning Commission 1972: vi–vii).

In all its ramifications, the policy for the sciences, which mainly focused on building infrastructure and strengthening state control, existed in relative isolation to economic and industrial policies in this phase up to 1970. These policies mainly emphasised a thrust towards self-reliance and import-substitution and highly regulated controls on import of technology and private foreign investment. The 1962 conflict with China and subsequent conflicts in 1965 and 1971 with Pakistan further reinforced the state commitment towards self-reliance in technology, and the state's aversion of import dependence basically meant a further thrust to import-substitution in industry as well as its technological requirements. The Fourth Five Year Plan, referred to earlier, had specific directions for the expansion of public sector enterprises:

> [T]he public sector should increasingly base itself on domestic know-how. The public and private sector have both been ready to look for foreign collaboration and not only for financial but for technological resources. We should rely more and more on our own machinery and technical know-how even though it may entail some initial risks and difficulties.
>
> Self-reliance in the technological sense implies the existence and effective functioning of indigenous organization for design, construction and engineering projects as well as capability for design and development of machinery, equipment and instruments indigenously manufactured (Government of India 1972: vi–vii and 48).

The command public sector enterprises in railways, fertilisers, steel, pharmaceuticals, among other industries, followed these import-substitution and self-reliance policies and made efforts to develop technology through promoting in-house R&D units. India had to depend on technology transfer from abroad for a range of industrial sectors in the 1940s and 1950s but by the mid-1960s onwards the policies turned towards tightening import of technology in favour of developing indigenous technological capabilities in these sectors. Almost all these sectors established in-house R&D units or laboratories towards this end but India did not evolve any national science and technology plan until the early 1970s and only in the early 1980s did India issue her first technology policy statement. Arguably, these two documents also reiterated India's commitment to the long-standing 'inward looking' policies of import-substitution and self-reliance. In large measure, these economic and industrial policies de-emphasised export promotion and the liberal import of technology. The government created the Monopolies and Restrictive Trade Practices (MRTP) in 1969 and the Foreign Exchange Regulation Act (FERA) in 1973 to control foreign inflow of firms and liberal financing. Banks were nationalised in 1969 which were directed by the state to focus on and support small-scale industry; within a short period of 10 years from the 1960s to 1970s items reserved for small firms increased from 51 to 147 (Sridharan 1995). Among the various policy measures introduced in this phase, the most significant one, which was designed to strengthen India's technological capabilities while fostering import-substitution and self-reliance, was the 1970 Patent Act. It was amended in 1970 which then reduced the duration of patents from 16 to 14 years, and seven years for food- and drug-related patents. For over three-and-a-half decades, India was able to increase her pharmaceutical technological base and capabilities through reverse engineering in drug development and commercialisation.

1970s to 1990s: Science and technology in policy and redefining self-reliance

The efforts invested in building infrastructure in science and technology institutions and higher education continued in this phase with renewed emphasis. The second layer of science agencies such as the Department of Space (DoS), Department of Electronics (DoE),

Department of Environment (DoEn), Department of Biotechnology (DBT), and Department of Ocean Development (DoD) were created in this phase (see Table 4.3). In higher education, another 55 universities were established bringing the tally of total universities to around 145 by the end of this phase in 1990. Compared to China, India had a much larger visibility in the international scientific world of publications throughout from 1980 to the early 1990s. For instance, in 1990 India published 10,103 science publications measured in SCI, whereas, China published 6,509.[7] As Table 4.2 shows, India's stock of human resources increased more than four times between 1970 and 1990 from 1.147 to 4.811 million.

Table 4.2: *Growth of the Total Scientific and Technical Manpower, 1950–2000*

Category of Personnel	*Stock (Thousand)*							
	1950	*1955*	*1960*	*1965*	*1970*	*1980*	*1991*	*2000*
Engineering Degree Holders	21.6	37.5	62.2	106.7	185.4	221.4	546.7	969.5
Engineering Diploma Holders	31.5	46.8	75.0	138.9	244.4	329.4	873.9	1456.0
Science Postgraduates	16.0	28.0	47.7	85.7	139.2	217.5	482.0	767.1
Science Degree Holders	60.0	102.9	165.6	261.5	420.0	750.5	2430.3	3837.7
Agriculture Postgraduates	1.0	2.0	3.7	7.7	13.5	96.5*	168.4*	231.2*
Agriculture Degree Holders	6.9	11.5	20.2	39.4	47.2	–	–	–
Medicine Degree Holders	18.0	29.0	41.6	60.6	97.8	165.4	310.3	403.4
Total	155.0	257.7	416.0	700.5	1147.5	1780.7	4811.6	7664.9

Source: Department of Science and Technology (1999, 2002).
Note: *Including graduates.

Table 4.3: *Public R&D Expenditure of Major Science Agencies, 1990–1991, 1998–1999 and 2000–2001*

Figures in US$ (PPP)

Science Agency	*1990–1991*	*1998–1999*	*2000–2001*	*2004*
DRDO (Defence)	756,66.0	2421.2	2129.26	1952.85
DOS (Space)	429.1	1595.2	1728.73	1691.42
DAE (Atomic Energy)	306.1	880.7	NA	2715.00
ICAR (Agriculture)	306.8	888.4	1577.68	1079.28
CSIR (Industrial Research)	276.7	750.8	924.00	811.42
MOEF (Environment & Forest)	180.0	397.89	894.73	NA
DST (All S&T)	133.1	314.7	769.89	840.00
DBT (Biotechnology)	45.8	99.47	148.94	195.00
DOD (Ocean)	30.8	89.26	177.68	142.14
ICMR (Medical)	49.4	90.73	154.73	705.71
MIT (ICT)	36.6	65.36	80.00	358.51
MNES (Non-Conventional Energy)	17.7	9.47	NA	NA

Source: Department of Science and Technology (2002, 2004), R&D Statistics; for 2004 see India's Emergence as Global R&D Centre, Working Paper R2007:012, Swedish Institute of Growth Policy Studies, Sweden.

This phase characterises a trend of science and technology policy and redefining self-reliance. The former clearly reflected the inputs of science and technology and its expectations in the policy as well as political and economic processes of development. Various processes of S&T planning beginning with the creation of the National Commission on Science and Technology (NCST) in 1972 and the launching of India's first Science and Technology Plan (1974–1979) which made explicit reference to attaining indigenous technology capacities in various sectors differentiate the earlier phase of science policy. For the first time after independence, planning in S&T came into policy discourse and action. Having established a good deal of infrastructure in S&T, political and economic expectations of science and development increased, together with some visible impacts justifying science and technology policy. India entered the nuclear and space 'clubs' by the 1980s and notwithstanding various criticisms, experienced relative success in the 'Green Revolution' and 'White Revolution'. Having established technological capabilities in some high technology areas such as space, nuclear, pharmaceuticals and green revolution technologies, the government realised that a 'water tight' compartmentalised framework on self-reliance and import-substitution of the previous phase was no more tenable for the 1980s and beyond. The old policy regime which was often referred to as 'nationalist technological policies' of the 1960s was out of date in the 1980s as India had already initiated the indigenisation programmes from defence, space and military industrial projects to pharmaceuticals and the whole public sector enterprises in power, steel, fertiliser, railways, among others. There prevailed a serious concern of the increasing technological gap with industrialised countries and the need for 'catching up' within a perspective of endogenous technological capability. As far as India could maintain the balance of her endogenous technological base, it was thought wise to liberalise import of technology and open up to export regimes. This was important as India's dependence on foreign technology increased as the era of the 1980s came into sharp policy focus over new technologies such as micro electronics, information technologies and biotechnology.

In an effort to reformulate the framework for self-reliance and import substitution they were re-defined, which had definite implications for public research institutions and industry. These concerns were further articulated in economic policies contained in India's Sixth Five Year Plan (1980–1985) and the 1983 Technology Policy Statement. The re-defined terms of the Sixth Plan observed that 'self reliance, as should be obvious, but often is not, does not necessarily mean, self-sufficiency in all sections of the economy'. It went on to assert further, 'however, self-reliance can no longer take the form of indiscriminate import-substitution . . . export promotion is as much a part of the drive for self-reliance as efficient import-substitution'.[8] Similarly, the Technology Policy Statement of 1983[9] sought to make it clear that import of technology and foreign investment in this regard, will continue to be permitted only on a selective basis. Further, the policy document stressed that 'there shall be a firm commitment for absorption, adaptation and subsequent development of imported know-how through adequate investment in Research and Development to which importers of technology will be expected to contribute' (Technology Policy Statement 1983).[10]

As the country entered the decade of the 1980s it was entangled in a double bind situation. On the one hand, new technologies such as biotechnology and ICT and material sciences posed new challenges for their absorption and diffusion forcing the government to lift restrictions on international technology transfer. On the other hand, the critiques increasingly pointed to the failure of S&T for development and the removal of poverty. Despite a number of visible achievements, much of the 'grand optimism' over science and development of the earlier phase began to erode during this phase, also on account of the 1973 oil crises and the rise of appropriate technology and people science movements (Krishna 1997b). As the criticism from various quarters mounted to question the optimistic role of S&T for development envisaged during the earlier phase, the government geared up to formulate appropriate responses. As the basic needs agenda came into sharp focus, the government again responded, this time with the new policy agenda of 'Technology Missions' around the mid-1980s. These were time-bound regulated schemes for tackling the basic needs through redirection of science and technology inputs in water, immunisation, oil-seeds, telecommunications, leather and literacy. The period from the mid-1980s to the 1990s was one of considerable political instability coupled with the challenges of new technologies. The main industrial and S&T policy agenda towards the 1990s remained focused on how to open up and liberalise the Indian economy. Actually the process of liberal economic policies and deregulating industry began from the Rajiv Gandhi regime in 1985 when a number of restrictions on MRTP and FERA companies were lifted and a large number of products reserved for small- and medium-scale enterprises (SMEs) were taken out from the list. In this phase, globalisation became a reality which mounted considerable pressure on the political system to embark on new economic reforms from the early 1990s.

1991–2000: New economic reforms and turn to decentralised S&T policies[11]

With the coming of the new Congress government under P. V. Narasimha Rao and Dr Manmohan Singh (presently India's Prime Minister) as the finance minister, the government embarked on what has come to be known as New Economic Reforms from June 1991. The main feature of this reform process was the New Industrial

Policy (1991) with a major departure from the earlier era. Indian economic policies, compared to China's economic reforms from 1978, introduced a series of liberal economic policies with a focus on export promotion, selective privatisation, foreign direct investment and unprecedented encouragement to the private industrial sector in power, transportation, mineral exploration, electronics and telecommunication, pharmaceuticals, and ICT.

By the time the government announced a Science and Technology Policy in 2003, there had been a notable shift in the formulation and execution of S&T policies from the earlier phases. Even though the government did not abandon the concepts of self-reliance in S&T and drive towards endogenous technological capabilities, their meaning got somewhat broadened within the framework of global competitiveness and export promotion. The Ministry of Industry in 1991 declared:[12]

> [while] government would continue to follow the policy of self-reliance, there would be greater emphasis placed on building up India's ability to pay for imports through its own foreign exchange earnings. At the same time, foreign collaboration would be welcomed in investment and technology in order to increase exports and expand the production base requiring higher technology (Planning Commission 1991).

In contrast to the S&T policy statements (such as in 1958, 1986 and 2003; and the 1974 S&T Plan) which covered a range of subjects and sectors of economy in a somewhat overarching structure, the last decade witnessed a shift towards what may be characterised as a turn to decentralised S&T policies.[13] Compared to previous phases when bureaucratic-elite scientists (for example, people like Homi Bhabha, S. S. Bhatnagar, Vikram Sarabhai, M. G. K. Menon, among others) in alliance with political leadership wielded considerable power in articulating and shaping national S&T policies encompassing several sectors, the last decade witnessed a remarkable shift in the way that S&T policies were formulated and implemented at the level of different sectors. A notable change in the Indian S&T policy-making in the 1990s was the end of the domination of physicists of the 1950s to 1970s era. Technocrats such as Sam Pitroda, chemists such as R. A. Mashelkar, biologists such as P. Balram, P. M. Bhargava and S. K. Bhan, and bureaucrats-cum-strategic scholars such as K. Subrahmanyam, among others, come to influence and shape public policies in S&T. With the economic growth around the 6.9 per cent average for the period 2001 and 2006, there was a rise of private industry sectors in telecommunications, software, media and entertainment, pharmaceuticals, automotive, high technology manufacturing, among others; business enterprises came to influence decision making in policy formulation in the last decade. For instance, business captains such as Rahul Bajaj (three-wheeler auto sector); Ratan Tata and Keshub Mahindra (auto sector); Narayana Murthy and the software sector association — NASSCOM; Ambani brothers (petrochemicals and telecommunications); Mittal brothers (telecommunications); Baba Kalyani (industrial forging); representatives of private industrial houses and their associations such as FICCI and CII for instance, etc., came to influence and participate in science, technology and innovation policies as never before in contemporary history. The government at the same time created more space for private business enterprises as a part of the economic and market strategies of public–private partnerships in various infrastructure and development programmes in the last decade. Also, the civil society representatives and science and technology-based activists have all come to influence and shape the S&T policies which are formulated and implemented at the sector level. In other words, even though the government issues overall national S&T policies from time to time, there is no one 'centre of gravity'. There are multiple actors and agencies at the level of different sectors that have come to play a significant role in shaping S&T policies and the economy as a whole with respect to specific sectors. After 2003, the government did not issue any major overarching S&T policy statement and at the same time various government science and technology departments, ministries and science agencies together have issued over 20 to 25 major policy measures in about 10 sectors of the economy. Table 4.4 summarises some of the most significant policy measures and initiatives in different sectors during the last few years.

It may be noted that this shift towards a decentralised mode is mainly concerned with science, technology and innovation policies and institutional measures concerned with economic and knowledge-based growth sectors of the Indian economy. However, what is left intact without any significant change, as in the previous phases, is the mode of articulation and implementation of innovation-related policies which have societal implications such as environment, climate change, human development, national security, etc. Such

Table 4.4: *Sector-based Science, Technology and Innovation Policies: Tier Two, 1990s to 2009*

Sector	*Main Policies/Initiatives*
Pharmaceuticals	Pharmaceutical Policy 2002 2005 Patent Act (1970 Act amended)
Biotechnology	Biological Diversity Act 2002 Bioinformatics Policy 2004 Biotechnology Industry Partnership Programme (BIPP) 2007–2008 Small Business Innovation Research Initiative (SIBRI) 2008
ICT Software	Software Technology Parks (STP) Policy Initiative, DOE (1990) Creation of Ministry of Information Technology (1999) National Task Force on ICT in the Planning Commission (2006) Information Technology Act 2000; and Amendment 2008
Nuclear Energy	Indo-US Nuclear Deal 2008, Atomic Energy Commission
Space	Satellites Launch Missions, Department of Space Chandrayan Mission 2008–2009
Agriculture	Protection of Plant Varieties and Farmer's Rights Act India (2001) National Seed Policy 2002 National Agriculture Innovation Project (2006)
Telecommunications	New Telecom Policy 1999 Broadband Policy 2004
Rural Development	National Rural Employment Guarantee Scheme 2007 Jawaharlal Nehru Urban Renewal Mission National Rural Health Mission
Industry	Pharmaceutical R&D Support Programme 2004 Home Grown Technology Programme Fund for Accelerating Start-ups 2008 New Millennium India Technology Leadership Initiative 2003 National Innovation Project for Industry 2008 Programme on Cluster Development, Ministry of Industry National Automotive Testing and R&D Infrastructure Project

Source: Compiled from official websites of various government departments and ministries.

overarching policies which cut across various economic and social sectors of the economy are enacted and implemented mainly at the level of the Prime Minister's Office (PMO) and its constituent or closely networked bodies and institutional units such as the National Planning Commission, Principal Scientific Advisor to the government that advises the central cabinet of ministers led by the Prime Minister, etc. For example, India's national position and policy on climate change, skill development council, overarching trade and economic relations and energy, among others, are initiated and articulated at the PMO. Thus it is more reasonable to conceptualise the change and shift taking place in science and technology policies in the current decade after the 1991 reforms in terms of a two-tier decentralised mode. The first tier overarching mode operates at the highest level of the PMO and its closely related bodies. The second tier operates more in a decentralised mode at the levels of various sectors of economy mainly steered by relevant ministries and their respective departments.

Table 4.5: *Science, Technology and Innovation Policies: Tier One, 1990s–2009*

Overarching Policies at PMO	*Overarching Policies at National Planning Commission*	*Office of Principal Scientific Advisor to the Government*
PM Council on Climate Change	With Plan Steering Committee on S&T, energy, environment, etc.	Evolving policies, strategies and missions for generation of innovations and support systems for multiple applications
PM National Council on Skill Development; The Energy Coordination Committee	Policies on inclusive development in the 11th Plan on employment guarantee, health, urban renewal, infrastructure, education, water, irrigation, rural telephony, rural electrification, etc.	Evaluation and review studies on various science and technology-related matters; Reports on optimal use in S&T resources; development of instrumentation; utilisation of human resources, etc.
The National Knowledge Commission: Reports on reforming higher education, national innovation		Creation of missions and also undertake multi-departmental, multi-institutional projects in strategic, technology and other areas of economic/social relevance

Source: Author's elaboration.

Turn to innovation in S&T policy discourse: 2003

The post-1991 reform agenda of the government which clearly set its policy tone towards outward-looking strategy compared to previous regimes was gradually cemented in the policy discourse throughout the 1990s and particularly after the dawn of the new millennium. As Mukherjee (2009: 92) draws to our attention, Dr Manmohan Singh in 1995 clearly envisaged and underscored the changing economic context; 'India's tryst with globalization has become irreversible — no matter which government came to power after the elections of 1996'. Globalisation in India was closely associated with the country's high technology and knowledge capabilities assuming an increasing share in global software services and its exports. India's drive in export of software services as well as in non-high technology sectors such as gems and jewellery gave a new dimension of strategic economic advantages in exports and globalisation as never before. At the same time, it became clear that there are several sectors of both high technology and those that are SME based which have a high potential provided the government introduced appropriate innovation policy measures. India's relative success in ICT software, biotechnology, pharmaceuticals since the 1990s in a large measure demonstrated the importance of policies and the role of the state in injecting dynamism at the level of sectors. Even though perspectives underlying a sectoral system of innovation did not figure in the formal science, technology and innovation policies, the question of why and how certain sectors of Indian economy exhibited more dynamism and growth compared to others drew the attention of policy makers at the Planning Commission.

The year 2003 assumed considerable significance for the turn towards innovation in the S&T policy discourse. Two important developments signalled this important turn. First was the massive exercise in technology forecasting in about 20 sectors undertaken by the Technology Information Forecasting and Assessment Council (TIFAC) of the Department of Science and Technology (DST), Ministry of S&T, under A. P. J. Abdul Kalam and Y. S. Rajan. This resulted in a volume titled, *India 2020 — Vision for the New Millennium* published in 2003. They explored both the weaknesses and strengths of India, as a nation, and offered their version of how India can emerge to be among the world's first four economic powers by 2020. Inherent and central to their argument was the attention given to innovation as an important concept, tool and a strategy which had considerable policy impact since the late 1990s when the exercise on forecasting began at TIFAC. As Mr Kalam assumed the office as India's president, the volume had a radiating impact on India's S&T policies in the five years beginning 2002.

Second, the Science and Technology Policy Statement 2003 (hereafter S&T Policy 2003) which was issued by the government in 2003 clearly reflected the changing economic scenario of globalisation and underscored the importance of innovation. Part C of the document made explicit the 'strategy and implementation plan', wherein, it clearly articulated the need for 'integration of the programmes in socio-economic sectors with R&D activities' on the one hand and 'promoting close and productive interaction between private and public institutions in science and technology' on the other hand. The S&T Policy 2003 goes on to underline the importance of strengthening 'enabling mechanisms that relate to technology development, evaluation, absorption and upgradation from concept to utilization'. While the objectives outlined in the S&T Policy 2003 drew attention to strengthening infrastructure for science and technology in academic institutions, new funding mechanisms for basic research, human resource development, strengthening technology transfer mechanisms between industry and science and intellectual property, among other things, the two most important objectives of the policy clearly spelled out the turn to innovation as follows:[14]

> The transformation of new ideas into commercial successes is of vital importance to the nation's ability to achieve high economic growth and global competitiveness. Accordingly, special emphasis will be given not only to R&D and technological factors of innovation, but also to the other equally important social, institutional and market factors needed for adoption, diffusion and transfer of innovation to the productive sectors. . .
>
> Innovation will be supported in all its aspects. A comprehensive national system of innovation will be created covering science and technology as also legal, financial and other related aspects. There is a need to change the ways in which society and economy performs, if innovation has to fructify.

In continuation of the reform process initiated in 1991 by Dr Manmohan Singh as India's finance minister, the Atal Bihari Vajpayee government, in all its ramifications, continued many of those reforms until Dr Singh again assumed charge as Prime Minister in 2004. The reforms accelerated growth in various sectors of the Indian economy affecting foreign trade and investment, and fiscal reforms affecting liberalisation and foreign ownership of firms. Since 2004 the government has initiated a wide range of initiatives targeted at specific sectors such as software, telecom, biotech and pharma, automotive, among others. Since 2003, the Indian Parliament has ratified a number of laws giving protection to intellectual property rights (IPRs) and in 2005 it passed a patent regime that is compliant with the World Trade Organization (WTO) standards followed the world over.

Contemporary Structure and Organisation of India's National System of Innovation[15]

Actors and agencies of India's NSI

India's national aggregate gross expenditure on research and development was about INR 413 billion (US$ 29.5 billion) in 2007–2008. In absolute terms, Indian GERD witnessed a substantial increase of 60 per cent from INR 249 billion (US$ 17.78 billion) in 2004–2005 to INR 413 billion (US$ 29.5 billion) in 2007–2008. As a proportion of GDP, it witnessed an increase from 0.8 per cent of GDP in 1992–1993 to 1.13 per cent in 2003–2005. However, it registered a marginal decrease to 1 per cent for the period 2004–2007 as estimated by government sources. Notwithstanding the current ongoing economic downturn, the Prime Minister, Dr Manmohan Singh, announced in January 2009 that the government is committed to increase 2 per cent of GDP for R&D.

A dominant proportion of GERD, around 68 per cent, is met by government sources and 30 per cent from the business enterprise sector.

Except for making the idea of creating NSI explicit in the S&T Policy 2003 statement, India is yet to formally define her NSI as such. However, the structure and network of relationships and institutional arrangements exist both in the formal and informal sense between different actors.[16] Such a structure of an innovation system is mainly constituted by: (*a*) public research system (PRS); (*b*) private business enterprise and transnational corporations (TNCs), Indian and foreign; (*c*) higher educational institutions (HEIs); and (*d*) state mediation through public policies. We shall briefly explore various facets of the structure and organisation of India's NSI and then devote a separate section to the importance of state mediation.

Public Research System

This comprises national laboratories under a dozen science and technology agencies from the areas of space, atomic energy, agriculture, industrial research, etc. (see Table 4.1), and in-house R&D laboratories in large public sector enterprises in steel, fertilisers, railways, power, transport and aviation, chemicals, petroleum and energy, etc. The PRS is India's main actor of NSI as it accounted for 68 per cent of GERD in 2007 and 69 per cent (159,000) of the total 230,000 R&D personnel of the country in 2005.[17] Out of the total 230,000 R&D personnel, 71,300 (31 per cent) work in major science agencies such as CSIR, DAE, DBT, etc., 32,200 (14 per cent) work in universities and 55,200 (24 per cent) in government-based public sector enterprises and state government laboratories.

Private Business Enterprises and TNCs

This is the second major actor of the Indian innovation system which accounted for 30 per cent of GERD in 2007 and 31 per cent of total R&D personnel (71,300) of the country in 2005. In 1990–1991 the private sector accounted for 13.8 per cent of GERD which increased to 20.3 per cent in 2001–2002 and to 30 per cent in 2006.[18] The corresponding figure for GERD shows an increase from 2.4 billion Euros in 2002 to 5.5 billion Euros in 2005.

In recent years the business enterprise sector assumed considerable importance with the global competitive edge in pharmaceuticals, automotive, software, telecommunications, and biotechnology. Whereas the international economic crises created ripples in the US and European markets and industry insofar as the auto and IT sectors are concerned, a more optimistic market scenario emerged in the Indian case. In the midst of the crises, Tata launched the world's cheapest small car, Nano, into the Indian market on 23 March 2009 with an advanced booking for over 120,000 cars.[19] The second Indian auto firm, Mahindra and Mahindra also launched its indigenous new model of 'Scorpio' — a semi-utility vehicle. Indian automobile production from 5.3 million units in 2001–2002 grew to 10.8 million units in 2007–2008. In 2006–2007, the Indian automotive industry provided direct employment to more than 300,000 people and contributed 5 per cent of India's GDP.

The other sector which witnessed robust growth and expansion is telecommunications. The Indian telecom market was one of the fastest growing markets in the world in 2009 in terms of subscribers, a little behind China. China stands at more than 800 million telecom subscribers and India at more than 500 million.[20] This figure in 2012 stands at 900 million. In January 2009 alone India added 15 million subscribers. The third sector which witnessed a reasonable growth despite economic crises is India's IT industry which contributed to over 5.8 per cent of India's GDP in 2008–2009. The industry grew by 28 to 29 per cent in the last few years but has slowed down in 2008–2009. For instance, among the top 20 firms operating in the IT sector in India, all big Indian firms such as Tata Consultancy Services, Wipro, Infosys, HCL, and Tech Mahindra-Satyam witnessed modest growth rates between 15 to 20 per cent during 2007–2008 and 2008–2009.[21] Despite the slowdown, the Indian IT-BPO sector grew by 12 per cent in 2008–2009 to reach US$ 59.5 billion in aggregate revenue.

The trend of the global R&D flows to India is sustained and growing in the situation of an economic downslide. About 260 global TNCs operate their R&D centres or laboratories in India in the Bangalore, Hyderabad, Delhi, Pune, and Chennai regions. Bangalore is the most preferred destination for foreign R&D centres which accounts for 45 per cent of the firms, followed by NCR (Delhi) with 22 per cent.

The rise of the business enterprise sector as an important actor of NSI is also evident from various Indian firms which followed the Tatas who acquired the UK steel firm Corus, and Mittal's acquisition of the Belgian-French firm Arcelor.

Higher Educational Institutions

With over 400 universities with 18,000 affiliated colleges, much of the recent dynamism witnessed in the knowledge-based and high technology sectors of the Indian economy is the result of human resources, skills and the vast institutional base already created in the higher educational sector. In an effort to sustain this dynamism the government increased the higher education budget by three times in 2009–2010. However, R&D in HEIs in India is a weak link in India's NSI which accounts for a mere 14 per cent of R&D personnel compared to 55 per cent of total R&D personnel of the country in PRS. Higher education R&D is less than 8 per cent of GERD. However, universities accounted for over 52.2 per cent of

India's total 28,603 SCI-based publications in 2005 which makes the sector a very important actor of the innovation system.[22] In 2006 the government set up the National Knowledge Commission to assess, plan and recommend the knowledge challenges of the 21st century. Three major developments in the higher educational sector are: (*a*) increase India's competitive advantage in the fields of knowledge by expanding the existing 400 universities to 1,500 by 2015; (*b*) 15-year career support programme through scholarships from high school to Ph.D. level; and (*c*) promote university–industry links and partnerships. The Knowledge Commission's tenure continued with the new government in 2009 and its operations are being expanded.

According to various estimates and data from authentic sources, India produces about 2.5 million graduates every year, of which 300,000 are engineers and 150,000 IT professionals. This is in contrast to 70,000 engineers in USA, 33,000 in Germany and 600,000 in China. However, according to Farrel et al. (2005), with 14 million young university graduates (with seven years or less of work experience) India's talent pool is estimated to be the largest in the world, overlapping the Chinese talent pool by 50 per cent and that of USA by 100 per cent.[23]

Innovation governance system

The innovation governance structure in India mainly comprises three main actors or agencies which are hierarchically interconnected and networked. The top most body is the Indian Parliament which consists of the upper house (*Rajya Sabha*) and lower house (*Lok Sabha*). The former is constituted based on political party representation which in a way is an indirect representation of the people in Parliament. The latter is a directly elected body of the people's representatives every five years. All acts and policies of innovation need the ratification of Parliament which generally operates through a committee system. Committees are of two kinds — standing committees and ad hoc committees. The former are elected or appointed every year or periodically and their work goes on, more or less, on a continuous basis. The latter are appointed on an ad-hoc basis as need arises and they cease to exist as soon as they complete the task assigned to them. Much of the work on science and technology-related issues including innovation is first examined by the standing committees and then taken up for ratification by the Parliament. For example, currently an innovation-related bill namely, 'The Protection and Utilisation of Public Funded Intellectual Property Bill, 2008' is pending for the ratification of Parliament in 2012.

At the second level, the PMO, in consultation with the Planning Commission and other concerned ministries and departments formulates, initiates and implements various innovation-related policies. For example, the initiative to launch policies on climate change which seek to implement eight national missions from solar energy to green technologies in the manufacturing sector originated in the PMO's office. This office is supported by the Principal Scientific Advisor, the Science Advisory Council to the Prime Minister. In 2006–2007 the PMO also constituted a National Knowledge Commission in the advisory role. At this level, the Planning Commission plays an important role as it formulates and creates a framework for innovation policies and related aspects. For instance, the Steering Committee on S&T for the 11th Plan played an important role which was chaired by the head of the Scientific Advisor Council to the PMO.

At the third level various ministries from science and technology to industry, human resource development and other sectors have the legal mandate to launch and implement various programmes and schemes on innovation based on the broad framework on innovation and related matters given by higher bodies. The Ministry of S&T has two important bodies, the Department of Science and Technology and the Department of Scientific and Industrial Research, which mainly administered and implemented innovation programmes and schemes on behalf of the government. The ministry-level bodies also coordinate and co-opt various business enterprises, industries and NGOs and their representative associations in a range of innovation policy-related matters.

Main objectives

There is no formal national innovation policy or statement announced by the Indian government so far but various other policy documents on science and technology for development and on economic growth have made reference to innovation policies. The policy documents which are important from a national perspective and relevant to the coming five years are listed in Table 4.4. The term innovation has become an important concept and more often is used in a generic reference to various aspects of development and implementation of economic and industrial policies in the country. The most formal usage of the term is found in two draft policy documents being circulated by the Ministry of Science and Technology.[24]

The term innovation is referred to as *a pro*cess for incremental or significant technical advance or change, which provides enhancement of measurable economic value, and shall include: (*a*) introducing new or improved goods or services; (*b*) implementing new or improved operational processes; and (*c*) implementing new or improved organisational or managerial processes. Measurable value enhancement or economic significance may include one or more of the following: (*i*) increase in market share; (*ii*) competitive advantage; (*iii*) improvement in the quality of products or services; (*iv*) reduction of costs.[25]

Other policy documents refer to innovation in a somewhat similar meaning but stress is laid on the aspect of new knowledge or inventions or advances in knowledge from national laboratories and the way in which it gets commercialised or used by society, industry or any clients. The policy documents listed in Table 4.6 underline objectives which form a basis or a broad framework of India's innovation policies. It must be noted that much of the policy discourse in these documents focuses more on creating an enabling ecosystem for innovation or what can be termed as an innovation potential or capacity in various institutions and organisational structures.

The major objectives which relate to creating this innovation potential or capacity are as follows:

- Prime Minister Manmohan Singh has set the goal of attaining 2 per cent of GDP for R&D from the current level of 1.3 per cent.[26] The objective here is to encourage the business enterprise to double its contribution to GERD from the current proportion of 30 per cent GERD.
- Use 'technology foresight' to make the right technology choices and introduce 'coherent synergy' in our S&T efforts. Technology foresight helps in the selection of critical technologies for development at any point of time.
- In an effort to accomplish the goal of a knowledge-based society and economy, the government has given top priority to both elementary and school-level education as well as higher

education. The goal is to attain 6 per cent of GDP for education in the 11th Five Year Plan period. This plan has earmarked a four times increase in education in the plan period. In terms of pragmatic goals, the aim is to increase the enrolment ratio in higher education from the current level of 11 per cent to 15 per cent in the coming five years. The National Knowledge Commission set this goal for 2015.

- To create a total of 1,500 universities by 2015 by reconstituting 18,000 existing under-graduate and post-graduate colleges; reform higher education to infuse quality, excellence and accountability.
- To effectively implement an education budget of INR 3 trillion (or US$ 214 billion) in the 11th Five Year Plan Period (2007–2012); this is a fivefold increase over the 10th Plan. To increase the share of education from 7.7 per cent to 20 per cent by the end of the plan period.
- To strengthen the human resource skill base, particularly in nuclear, space and new technologies such as biotechnology and genetics, nanotechnology and ICT, in universities and other institutions in higher education.
- To strengthen vocational education, a new Skill Development Mission under the supervision of the Prime Minister with an outlay of 4,509 million Euros or INR 31,2000 million. To aim at opening 1,600 new Industrial Training Institutes (ITIs) and polytechnics, 10,000 new vocational schools and 50,000 new Skill Development Centres. A Skill Development Corporation will also be created by the government with the active participation of the private sector to give special training to young men and women, workers and technicians.
- To enhance India's competitiveness in micro, small-and medium-scale enterprises by making R&D in national laboratories relevant to the needs and demands of this sector. The government goal is to expand some novel R&D and innovation schemes (in DBT, DST, DSIR and other science agencies) to achieve this important goal. The overarching goal is, however, to realise the aim of inclusive development through appropriate research policies.
- To foster research and innovation policies to accomplish the goal of a Second Green Revolution through national

agriculture innovation policy and introduce a systemic basis of research and innovation in agriculture and its extension.

- To strengthen India's intellectual property, particularly in public research institutions and the higher educational sector. The overall aim is to boost entrepreneurship and innovation potential dormant in universities and national laboratories.
- To promote international science and technology collaboration by participating in international 'mega projects' as an 'equal partner' to enhance India's international reputation in big science.
- The Prime Minister's pronouncement on climate change is that India is committed not to exceed the per capita emission levels of developed countries. The objective is to establish an effective, cooperative and equitable global approach based on the principles of common but differentiated responsibilities and capacities in the United Nations Framework Convention on Climate Change (UNFCCC). The national action plan on climate change hinges on the development of institutional mechanisms. The objective is to establish eight national missions (solar energy, enhanced energy efficiency, sustainable habitat, water mission, sustaining Himalayan ecosystem, Green India, sustainable agriculture, and strategic knowledge on climate change).

Main challenges confronting India's NSI

Enhancing Innovation Potential in New Technologies

Sustaining the success achieved so far and extending its scope for the coming decade depends on developing innovation potential with public–private partnerships. Here, the challenge is to create an environment enabling R&D in the public–private research systems including higher education and manage public–private partnerships which determine the effectiveness of innovation in new technologies.

Second, university–industry partnerships assume considerable importance given the nature of science-based innovation in sectors such as aerospace, bio-pharma, automotive, and material sciences. The most important challenge is the introduction of an IPR regime common to universities and public research systems. It also entails reorganisation of research teams to foster networks between universities and other important actors. Third, India has a vast higher educational structure in science and engineering but the main challenge is to make science and engineering more attractive to students.

Building Technological Capabilities and Competitiveness of the Manufacturing Sector

As India's manufacturing sector is growing and expanding into high technology sectors such as bio-pharmaceutical and automotive sectors, its ability to compete both at the domestic and international level is dependent on the firms and their enabling environment. Challenges facing the sector concern training, infusion of skills and upgrading techniques to enhance technological capabilities, maintaining quality and institutionalising international standards in manufacturing.

Second, technological capabilities of firms are related to their R&D and technological intensities. The proportion of business R&D in the national GERD is quite low compared to other countries. A closely associated problem has been the slow diffusion of existing technology from the public research systems to the manufacturing industry as a whole.

Reconfiguration of Formal and Informal Sectors via Inclusive Innovation

Inclusive innovation concerns primarily 80 per cent of the total workforce in the informal sector dominated by house-based micro, small- and medium-scale enterprises ranging from handicrafts to a range of manufacturing goods.

A multipronged approach to reconfigure the formal and informal sectors of economy and manage the transition from rural-based agriculture to an urban and semi-urban industrial-based economy with appropriate strategies of inclusive innovation is the overarching challenge facing the country in the coming decade. Imparting skills to participate in the industrial economy, promoting and diffusing local grassroots innovations and making new technologies such as ICT and telecommunications appropriate to the needs of this sector are some of the current major challenges. The future of India's development and economic progress of the country depends on the challenges of innovation in the rural and semi-urban sectors.

Government Initiatives in Strengthening NSI, 1990s–2009

New research policy developments: Supply side-1

The thrust of new research policies in contrast to innovation policy measures is to leverage the strengths of the public research system (national laboratories and higher educational institutions) to enhance capacities for science-based innovation in new technologies (such as nanotechnology, biotechnology and telecommunications and information technology) with appropriate measures to increase the human resource supply in higher educational institutions. It may also be pointed out that India's NSI till about recently in the 1990s was dominated by supply-side research policies. It is only in the last decade with the emergence of innovation as an important feature in the S&T policy discourse after Science and Technology Policy, 2003, that the government became proactive to promote innovation policy measures.

Further, the strategies of new research policies are also directed to what is known as 'inclusive innovation strategies' which are geared to enhance the competitiveness of small- and medium-scale enterprises and build appropriate linkages between the formal (or modern) S&T systems and rural sectors of economy. India's 11th Plan (2007–2012) finalised by the Planning Commission indicated an increase in the education budget by four times and the science and technology, including R&D, budget by three times the level of 2006–2007 during the plan period. However, the annual budget statement of the finance ministry increased the education and science and technology budget by only 25 per cent for the year 2008–2009. Some important elements of these policies may be specified as follows.

National Science and Engineering Research Board (NSERB)

In an effort to keep the scientific knowledge base up-to-date, a globally competitive basic research environment is essential to maintain a healthy innovation ecosystem in the country. This is given high priority by the government as it set up a NSERB in December 2008 to enhance the level of basic research. As the Prime Minister underlined recently, 'the Board will be an autonomous body and would have freedom to establish modalities of funding research as well as for creating facilities and structures that would help improve the quantity and quality of scientific research in the country'.[27] NSERB is expected to control a budget of INR 10 billion annually to open a new window for funding to researchers in public research institutions and industrial enterprises (Jayaraman 2008).

Innovation in Science Pursuit for Inspired Research (INSPIRE)

A second major recent initiative by the government has been the launching of a new scheme, INSPIRE, through DST which provides scholarships to attract talents to science. It is said to establish a vertical link between different stages in the pursuit of a career in science. It targets the whole learning pyramid from young learners to senior researchers. It is a very significant programme which aims to cover one million young learners. The government allocated INR 21,000 million in the 11th Plan (2007–2012).

Widening Higher Education and Research Base

Given the importance of the emerging knowledge base economy and future demand for highly skilled human resources, the government gave a major boost to widening the higher education and research base in 2009. A fourfold increase in the budget of higher education and scientific research in the 11th Plan period will establish a range of higher educational institutions and national research laboratories.[28]

The 11th Five Year plan's focus on giving special emphasis to education is reflected in the 2009–2010 budget for higher education to implement four new IITs, six Indian Institutes of Management and 14 Central Universities. INR 21,300 million (US$1521.4 million) was allocated for this expansion in the 2009–2010 budget in addition to INR 20,100 million (US$ 1,435.7 million) to higher education.

Promotion of University Research and Scientific Excellence (PURSE)

In an effort to strengthen the scientific research base in universities and further encourage performing universities, the government announced the PURSE scheme which grants INR 100 million to universities over their normal budget for three years. The special grants are based on the competitive basis of the university's publications in SCI-based journals with high impact factors.

Public–Private Partnerships in Science Education for Innovation and Excellence in Research

The Ministry of Science and Technology launched a special fellowship programme in doctoral research in computer sciences and medical electronics in association with the software companies association in 2008.

Biotechnology Industry Partnership Programme (BIPP)

The Department of Biotechnology has launched a public–private partnership (BIPP) programme for high risk discovery and innovation and accelerated technology development especially for futuristic technologies. The scheme is aimed at enhancing global competitiveness in new technologies in agriculture, energy, environment, and human health. The government provides 30 to 50 per cent funding and the rest is met by the industry partner.

The Protection and Utilisation of Public Funded Intellectual Property Bill, 2008

After the Cabinet approval in October 2008, the Ministry for S&T introduced this Bill in the upper house of the Parliament in December 2008. The Bill gives right of ownership to public research institutions and universities for R&D output leading to intellectual property and authorises these institutions to institute technology transfer and innovation units for R&D commercialisation. Researcher(s) who created intellectual property, the research group or department involved and the funder are entitled for one-third each of the rents and royalties generated out of the intellectual property commercialisation under this Bill. Scientists and faculty will be allowed to set up centres for entrepreneurship and innovation from the intellectual property developed.[29]

The New Millennium Indian Technology Leadership Initiative (NMITLI)

This scheme is meant for fostering partnerships between public research systems and industry and at the same time to enable these partnerships to attain global leadership positions in a few selected niche areas. CSIR evolved 57 projects in which 80 industry partners and 270 R&D groups from different institutions are involved with a budget of over INR 5,000 million (US$ 357.14).[30]

Launching of Nano Mission

The nano mission as an initiative launched in May 2007 came into operation in 2008. It is an umbrella programme with a budget of INR 1,000 million (US$ 71.42 million) for five years for developing research capacities in nano science and technology in training, human resource skills, basic research, international cooperation, and innovation. Under this initiative, close to 130 research projects have been funded in 2007 to 2008.

The national Nano Science and Technology Mission created in 2007 with INR 10 billion continued to draw support in 2009 for its implementation to enhance innovation potential. Six new R&D centres in the public–private partnership mode have come up with a budget of INR 1 billion. About 50–60 science and technology institutions, including existing IITs and NITs will be involved in building nano clusters across the country to create the ecosystem for undertaking extensive research in nanoscience and applied nanotechnology to develop applications for industrial products, agriculture, health care and safe drinking water, among others. Eleven centres of excellence have already been established in 2008–2009 in different specialised departments of universities in India. Six major public–private partnership programmes have already been instituted with leading Indian and foreign firms.

India–EU Partnerships in S&T

At the international level India has forged international cooperation in nuclear energy, physics, space and communication technologies with USA and the European Union since 2006. India has become a partner in the Framework 7 of EU since 2007 in the following projects:

(*a*) India is member of the European Union's International Thermonuclear Experimental Reactor (ITER) nuclear fusion energy project.

(*b*) India recently joined the satellite-based navigation system, Galileo Project (European version of USA's Global Positioning System) and is a member of Framework Programmes FP7 for 2007–2012.

(*c*) India and the European Union also decided to embark on joint scientific projects, including those in strategic fields, after holding their first ministerial science conference in the

Indian capital, New Delhi, on 10 February 2007. India also signed a pact with the EU to participate in the proposed Facility-for-Antiproton-and-Ion-Research (FAIR) project aimed at understanding the tiniest particles in the universe.

(*d*) Indian S&T international cooperation has a budget of over 48 million Euros. Much of this budget is being spent on EU-related programmes in S&T.

Innovation policy measures 1997–2009: Supply side-2

Indian science and technology policies for a long period have relied more on input-oriented research policies leaving the R&D downstream connectivity to either enterprises which interacted directly with research institutions or a centralised body called National Research Development Corporation (NRDC). This body was a sort of depository for technologies and R&D results developed in national laboratories which had the mandate to commercialise technologies. The NRDC did not play any significant role either in start-ups or R&D commercialisation. Over 70 to 75 per cent of technologies deposited in NRDC lie idle on its shelves. Second, the role of S&T policies was confined to the 'supply side' of training highly skilled human resources in higher educational and specialised institutions who found their way into industries and business enterprises.

Since the 1990s, a series of initiatives and programmes were introduced by DST, DSIR, CSIR, and other governmental science agencies beginning with the creation of software technology parks of India (STPIs). India has taken a number of steps in the last few years to promote various policies and programmes for innovative start-ups both at the federal government and state government regional levels. From the point of view of sectors, ICT software and biotechnology are the two main areas which have attracted considerable attention. Market failure perspective to fund and support new innovative firms fits well to the Indian context. Hence, the role of government- and public-supported financial institutions has become significant.

Start-ups, spin-offs and early stage technology development (ESTD) all fall into more or less the same category. Ministry of S&T through DST and DSIR has initiated a number of such schemes and programmes as shown in Table 4.6.

Table 4.6: *Ministry of S&T Main Initiatives and Programmes, 1990–2008*

No.	*Scheme/Programme/Initiative*	*Launched by Govt./Private & Organisation*	*Area/Sector*
1	Small Business Innovation Research Initiative (SBIRI) (2007–2008)	Govt./ Department of Biotechnology	Biotechnology and related fields
2	NASSCOM-ICICI Knowledge Park Fund (2008)	Private	ICT software
3	Fund for Accelerating Start-ups in Technology (FAST) (2008)	DSIR	All areas
4	Lockheed Martin India Innovation Growth Programme (2008)	Private/FICCI	All areas
5	Pharmaceuticals R&D Support Programme (PRDSF) (2004)	Govt./DST	Pharma and drug development
6	Techno-entrepreneur Promotion Programme (TePP) (1998)	Govt./DSIR, TIFAC	All areas
7	Technology Development and Demonstration Programme (TDDP) (1993) & Technology Development Board (1996)	Govt./DSIR	All areas
8	Home Grown Technology (HGT) Programme (1992)	Govt./DST, TIFAC	All areas
9	Sponsored Research and Development (SPREAD) (1989)	Govt./DST	All areas–research-industry links
10	Technology Development & Utilization Programme for Women (2007)	Govt./DST	All areas for women
11	New Millennium Indian Technology Leadership Initiative (NMITLI) (2003)	CSIR–Public–Private Partnership	All areas
12	Innovation and Entrepreneurship Programme (from 1990s)	All IITs and UGC	All areas
13	Encouraging and Development of Commercialisation of Inventions and Innovations: A New Impetus	Govt./DSIR	All areas for start-ups
14	The Protection and Utilisation of Public Funded IPR Bill (2008)	Govt./Ministry of S&T	All areas/ public research institutions

(*Cont.*)

(*Cont.*)

No.	*Scheme/Programme/Initiative*	*Launched by Govt./Private & Organisation*	*Area/Sector*
15	Encouraging and Development of Commercialisation of Inventions and Innovations: A New Impetus	Support to Innovative Start-ups Incl. Gazelles	Department of Scientific and Industrial Research, Ministry of S&T
16	The Protection and Utilisation of Public Funded Intellectual Property Bill (2008)	Knowledge Transfer and IPR issues in public/ academic/non-profit institutes	Department of Science and Technology & Department of Biotechnology, Ministry of S&T
17	Biotechnology Industry Partnership Programme	Strategic research policies	Department of Biotechnology, Ministry of S&T
18	National Rural Employment Guarantee Scheme (NRGES)	Support to the creation of favourable innovative climate & horizontal measure in support of financing	Ministry of Rural Development
19	National Rural Health Mission (NRH)	Support to the creation of favourable innovative climate & horizontal measure in support of financing	Ministry of Health and Family Welfare

Source: Compiled from formal websites of various science and technology ministries and departments.

Impact of public support to innovation: Demand side

India's economic growth during the last decade-and-a-half is associated with the dynamic growth of various sectors of economy ranging from aerospace industries, ICT software, pharmaceuticals, auto, petrochemicals, and high technology services. India's GDP grew at an average of 4.5 to 5 per cent for the decade 1993–2004 and accelerated to over 8.8 per cent for the succeeding five years from 2003–2004 to 2007–2008. Growth has also been associated with a jump in exports in skill-intensive manufacturing and services which in turn can be related to a spurt in innovative activities in these sectors. This has resulted in some visible quantifiable gains in reducing poverty and raising the living standards of the middle class in the country. While the poverty level according to the Planning Commission has fallen from 36 per cent to 27.8 per cent in 2004–2005, there has been a tremendous rise in the purchasing power of the Indian middle-class population triggering manufacturing industries and consumer goods. From a macro national perspective it may be said that there has been a combination of research, educational, industrial, fiscal policies and innovation policies contributing to growth and dynamism. Impact of these policies on macroeconomic indicators has certainly taken a long time in the Indian case.

The phase after 1991 is marked by liberal economic policies and opening up of a number of sectors such as pharma, ICT software, chemicals, aerospace, among others, for international competition. Export promotion and developing technological capabilities associated with it were channelled to take advantage of globalisation. Much of the innovation strategy in this phase during the last 15 years was invested in creating an enabling innovation ecosystem. This includes expansion of higher education, R&D base and creating a host of programmes and schemes to foster technology transfer and commercialisation of R&D from public labs to industry. There are various sectors which have witnessed dynamic growth and one can see a combination of the pre-1991 and post-1991 impacts of research, educational and innovation policies.

In the case of pharmaceuticals and drugs, India's patent policies of the 1970s which had protected patents for only seven years enabled technological capabilities in reverse engineering in drugs and chemicals together with the oriented basic research inputs.[31] However, these capabilities have taken a long time since the 1970s–1990s to have some visible impact. By 2000 India became the fifth largest drug producer in the world and in the last five years India's drug industry has certainly progressed from reverse engineering to the drug discovery path. Most importantly, 80 per cent of the essential drugs required by the country and parts of South Asia are produced in India. Between 1981 and 1995, CSIR, India's major R&D organisation with 38 national labs registered only nine US patents in drugs, but during the decade after 1995 to 2005 it obtained nearly 280 US patents in pharma and related fields. Similarly, five leading private Indian pharma firms did not obtain any US patents till 1995, but during 1996 and 2005 each one of them obtained 15 to 20 US patents per year. The Department of Science and Technology's half dozen innovation policy measures certainly contributed to this growth of the pharma sector which is now aiming towards global networking and a global competitive edge in pharma. A good example is the DST technology commercialisation grant to Shanta Biotech, Hyderabad for the development of Hepatitis-B and A vaccines which reduced the cost per dose by 70 to 80 per cent.

Similar is the case with India's growth in the software sector. Virtually starting from scratch in the 1980s the sector became dynamic by the late 1990s. Currently, over three million professionals work in this sector contributing to 6 per cent of India's GDP. The Ministry of Communication and Information Technology is the lead agency for formulating policies in the ICT sector. However, given the dominant role of the business enterprise in software exports, its association, NASSCOM, also plays a lead role in the formulation of research and innovation policies in ICT. The government, through its generic policies, has focused on developing skilled human resources with the expansion of the higher education sector.

Policies to build software technology parks in Bangalore, Hyderabad, Pune, Chennai, Delhi, and Gurgoan and other parts paid off very well. In 2008, 70 per cent of the software exports were from these five major software parks.[32] In a large measure the public–private partnerships in higher education, software technology parks and in e-governance and e-commerce contributed to the growth and dynamism of this sector.

In the auto sector, as already noted, Tata launched Nano in India with 120,000 bookings and the Mahindras launched their new model, UTE 'Scorpio' in the midst of the international auto crisis. Both have benefited from the government's tax incentives of the R&D scheme. In the case of telecommunications, there are currently about 500 million subscribers expanding at the rate of 6 to 10 per cent per month. This is again the result of the government creating an enabling environment and satellite connectivity for convergence technologies and the market's expansion.

The aerospace sector of India which is dominated by the dynamic growth of space technology and innovation has witnessed remarkable progress and world recognition in the capabilities to design and launch satellites.[33] In 2008 the space sector opened up for public–private partnerships in R&D and innovation. The success of launching *Chandrayan-1* for landing experimental instruments on and around the orbit of the Moon led to the high priority being given to space science and technology development.

The case of innovation in the manufacturing sector is revealed by two important surveys. The first is from the World Bank, 'The India 2006 Enterprise Survey', and the second is the innovation study undertaken by India's National Knowledge Commission. The World Bank Survey of 2006 in about 4,000 firms reveals some interesting features of innovation in the manufacturing sector which are as follows (Dutz 2007):

- In India 40 per cent of firms had developed a major new product, while 62 per cent had upgraded an existing product line. The criteria suggest that Indian firms have more innovation outputs than firms in China, but less those in Brazil, South Korea and Russia. The report comments that China's low scores are due to active copying than developing new products;
- Creation-oriented enterprises are concentrated in drugs and pharma, auto components and garments;
- Absorption of knowledge is likely to enable productivity rather than creation of new knowledge. The most important channel for absorbing existing knowledge is through the use of new machinery and equipment, followed by hiring key professionals;
- For most enterprises in India, the acquisition of global knowledge is expected to be more important for productivity than is the creation of domestic knowledge.

India's National Knowledge Commission survey report on innovation has come out with the following four important sets of findings for large enterprises and SMEs in India (National Knowledge Commission 2007).

Increase in Growth and Innovation

(*a*) 'Innovation Intensity' (i.e., the percentage of revenue derived from products/ services which are less than three years old) has increased for large firms and SMEs, with SMEs registering a greater increase in innovation intensity than large firms. Forty-two per cent of the large firms and 17 per cent of the SMEs are also 'Highly Innovative' firms (i.e., firms that have introduced 'new to world' innovations during the course of business in the last five years).

(*b*) Nearly half of the large firms and SMEs attribute more than 25 per cent of change in the following factors to innovation: increase in competitiveness, increase in profitability, reduction in costs and increase in market share. For large firms innovation has the most significant impact on competitiveness, while for SMEs, innovation has the most significant impact on an increase in market share.

(*c*) Seventeen per cent of the large firms rank innovation as the top strategic priority and 75 per cent rank it among the top three priorities. All the large firms in our sample agree (of which 81 per cent strongly agree) that innovation has gained importance as being critical to growth and competitiveness since the start of economic liberalisation in India. All the large firms agree (of which nearly half strongly agree) that they cannot survive and grow without investment in innovation. An overwhelming 96 per cent of large firms in our sample see innovation spending increasing over the next three–five years.

(*d*) Breakthrough and incremental: 37.3 per cent of large firms have introduced breakthrough innovation, while 76.4 per cent have introduced incremental innovation, which may be an indication that large firms in India are still in the mindset of incremental innovation as opposed to breakthrough innovation.

Concluding Remarks

The evolution of the current structure of India's NSI explored in this chapter clearly demonstrates the important part played by the state and governing political leadership in laying foundations and chalking out a goal direction over the last six decades. State mediation through initiating public science, technology and innovation policies has been a determining factor in building a national science and technology system and creating national innovation capacities. The Indian case clearly demonstrates that these endowments and capacities take long periods of time to establish and require sustained state support and public legitimation from time to time. It is here that the role of governing political leadership comes in to play a crucial part. State mediation is very crucial for giving a goal direction but at the same time it is also important to draw relative autonomy in research policies and a space for an autonomous science and technology system. Indian NSI, throughout its evolution, was rather fortunate on both these counts. What is also of significance in the Indian case is the fact that in various sectors of the economy, the country was able to build a reasonable innovation system followed only by a strong base of a science and technology system. In other words, it is rather problematic to build innovation systems without a strong base in science and technology systems which create appropriate innovation capacities. The dynamic growth of reasonable sectoral systems of innovation such as in space, agriculture and food security (Green Revolution), pharmaceuticals, biotechnology, ICT software and telecommunications, are good examples.

The science and technology policies in India for almost five decades till the 1990s were in a large measure tilted in favour of strengthening the input or supply side rather than the demand side of innovation. This has resulted in building a large science and technology system as well as a reasonable R&D base across a range of sectors and fields both in 'big science' (space, defence and atomic energy) and high technology such as chemicals and pharmaceuticals, biotechnology, ICT software, among other areas.

As we are dealing with a relatively long historical period of three phases in the development of India's NSI, it is important to qualify the nature and character of state mediation in building national scientific and technological capacities in the Indian case. As dealt with in this chapter, the most central feature of the nature of state mediation has been sustaining the overarching goal of self-reliance over long periods of time after 1947. In fact this concept of self-reliance has its roots in India's freedom movement, drawing from politics into economic policies. Both economic and science and technology policies were governed by the concept of self-reliance and its associated strategy of import substitution from the 1940s to 1980s. As Sridharan (1995:184) argued, 'the import-substituting technology policy regime has created a state of growing technological backwardness over the past two decades and made Indian industry so uncompetitive that India was threatened . . . at the start of the 1990s'.

Such critiques are justified in their own right to an extent because of the lack of technological dynamism in various manufacturing sectors on account of such inward-looking policies.

However, what is generally seen in the literature in the Indian case is the glossing over or bypassing of the important factor of under-utilisation of scientific and technological capacities created as part of the strategies and perspectives followed in the decades around the 1970s and 1980s (Krishna 1997a). There is a need to make a distinction between becoming uncompetitive due to the lack of, or underdevelopment of, technological capabilities, and under-utilisation of existing scientific and technological capacities or potential. India was able to establish a good reservoir of these capacities in various sectors but the problems remained somewhere else on the demand side of the innovation spectrum. As Rosenberg (1990: 149) observed on reviewing various models of industrialisation:

> India represents what appears to be a case of low pay offs from a relatively well-developed and extensive scientific and technological infrastructure. Specifically, it is widely accepted that by comparison with her agriculture research, which enabled India to approach self-sufficiency in food grain production in the late 1970s and early 1980s, industrial research in India has been distinctly disappointing. I believe that this has a lot to do with the extremely tenuous links between the various public and private institutions that are involved in the process.

The disappointment which is expressed, in my view, is not so much due to lack of technological capabilities but on account of under-utilisation and lack of enabling innovation measures. Rosenberg was quite right in pointing towards the lack of enabling innovation policy measures which link science and technology capacities established with the growing industrial needs and demands. The turn to innovation in S&T policies and appropriate innovation policy measures which were introduced since the mid-1990s in the third phase as also the shift to decentralised S&T policies around the 1990s gave a new meaning to the policies. As India progressed from the 1990s into the new millennium, the results of long-standing policies of self-reliance in building a national science and technology system and innovation capacities became quite apparent as argued earlier based on the study of three sectors, namely ICT software, pharmaceuticals and biotechnology (Krishna 2007). For instance, in the case of pharmaceuticals, India's 1970 Patent Act led to varying degrees of technological capabilities in both public and private business enterprises throughout the 1980s and 1990s, and in the last decade (2000–2010), India began to progress from a phase of reverse engineering onto the drug discovery path. It is widely known that India produces over 75 per cent of essential drug requirements for the South Asian region.[34]

However, given the dominant proportion of R&D being performed in publicly funded national laboratories and universities, the problems of the supply side and the under-utilisation of the R&D capacity continue to persist. A major weakness of the current system is the lack of an innovation ecosystem with risk capital and intermediary mechanisms to foster and promote technology transfer and commercialisation of public R&D. It is only since the last few years that the government has begun to focus on the demand side of innovation and a serious attempt has been made to build an innovation ecosystem through a series of policy measures and programmes.

India has not yet articulated her national innovation policy or defined her NSI in the formal sense. Science, technology and innovation policies in the Indian context are to be understood in terms of decentralised sector-based (for instance, space, atomic energy, pharmaceuticals, ICT software, etc.) and problem-based (for instance, climate change, disaster management, drought and floods, etc.) policies. Hence the problem is that of innovation policies which are rather very fragmented in ministries and elite bodies such as the Planning Commission and the PMO, lacking coordination and networking with various actors and agencies in the system as a whole. The return of the Congress Party-led government with Dr Manmohan Singh as Prime Minister in May 2009 infused a renewed sense of optimism over science, technology and innovation policies for development and inclusive economic growth. However, a number of challenges and problems confront India's NSI.

One of the major problems for an economy the size of India, compared to other emerging nations and the international context is the very low level of gross expenditure on R&D. India is spending just over 1.13 per cent of GDP for R&D compared to 1.2 to 1.4 per cent for Brazil and China and around 2.2 per cent in the case of the Organisation for Economic Cooperation and Development (OECD) and EU countries. The government is committed to increase the current 1.13 per cent level to 2 per cent in the coming five years.

While both public R&D and business R&D are low compared to international standards, the rate of growth in their respective levels over the last five years has been positive. From almost a very low level of less than INR 6,919 million a decade back, currently India attracts over INR 1.03 billion for R&D every year through foreign firms setting up R&D laboratories and units in India. Currently by 2009, about 250 multinational firms had already set up R&D labs or units.

In higher education the major challenge still remains the big daunting task of increasing the enrolment ratio from the current 11 per cent to 15 per cent. India has set up over 400 universities and 18,000 colleges but the research intensity in these institutions of higher learning is quite weak. Only 25 per cent of this number is research based and the rest are teaching-based universities aspiring to achieve the 'Humboldtdian ideal' of teaching and research universities. In a large measure the innovation potential in the higher education sector in India is under-utilised for the lack of adoption of innovation policies by a large number of universities which foster university–industry partnerships and relations, with the possible exception of IITs and other leading universities. The major challenge is to infuse 'innovation culture' in academic institutions of higher learning. The same may be said of the industrial research system of CSIR-based laboratories. India has just articulated 'The Protection and Utilisation of Public Funded Intellectual Property Bill, 2008' — an Indian version of the US Bayh-Dole Act but it is yet to be implemented in 2012. There is a lot of expectation from this Bill for catalysing innovation and technology transfer from public research systems to industry and society.

The existing innovation policy measures routed through the Ministry of Science and Technology departments lack adequate personnel and professionals to monitor and make them more effective. The main problem is their limited sphere of influence and impact which needs at least a three- or fourfold increase in their operation compared to the present situation. For example, the Technology Development Board which is one of the major innovation agencies of the ministry gets hardly 10 to 15 per cent of the total budget collected by the government in the form of cess for import of technology. Similarly, the R&D tax incentive system operated by the S&T department lacks penal 'teeth' and legal provisions to effectively monitor the funds given to business enterprises to ensure whether they are in fact involved in quality control and analyses-related activities or R&D per se.

The government has committed a massive policy and budgetary provision to promote more than a dozen national programmes on inclusive development. India's innovation policies are still tilted in favour of high technology and global competition. What is needed is an appropriate institutional and governance structure which coordinates and networks the formal R&D structures and universities with the needs and demands of inclusive development programmes. What is also needed is a new framework and institutional networking structure on inclusive innovation, to which, these dozen development programmes are linked and connected. For instance, there is only one major institutional structure in the form of the National Innovation Foundation established by the DST, Ministry of S&T. Given the multiple challenges in health, urban renewal, employment guarantees to the poor, roads and infrastructure, among other programmes, all the major R&D agencies and laboratories and universities need to create institutional mechanisms and outreach research centres for impacting their 'near' and 'distant' neighbourhoods. In other words, these institutions must have an agenda for 'grass root innovations' along with high technology and global orientation in their research and innovation policies. India made an impressive mark in the world and is recognised for software services clusters in Bangalore, Hyderabad, Delhi, and Gurgaon and Chennai. This experience needs to be extended and replicated in the case of rural-based and district-based traditional industrial clusters. It is here that the knowledge institutions, universities and R&D agencies need to be linked to the needs and demands of half of India's population now being covered under inclusive development and growth through evolving effective inclusive innovation policy mechanisms.

Notes

1. This section is selectively drawn from Krishna (1997a).
2. Much of this discourse and concepts on nation building and self-reliance in science can be found in the various issues and pages of an important Indian journal in science and technology studies, *Science and Culture*, published from Calcutta, for the period 1938–1947. The journal was

edited by one of the eminent Indian physicists, Professor M. N. Saha, the founder of Saha Institute of Nuclear Physics and Member of Indian Parliament representing Calcutta constituency after 1947.

3. At that time in 1945 it was suggested to place all science and technology agencies under the control of Member, Planning and Development who operated under the government Department of Planning and Development.
4. Nehru inaugurated and spent a full day with the scientific community at the annual session of the Indian Science Congress from 1947 till his sad demise in the mid-1960s.
5. It was created in 1942 but was expanded rapidly during this phase under the leadership of S. S. Bhatnagar. It may also be pointed out that science organisations such as CSIR (India) which was based on the British Department of Scientific and Industrial Research (DSIR) model, created in the wake of World War I, were created in other former colonies such Australia, New Zealand, South Africa, and Canada.
6. See the website of the Department of Science and Technology, Government of India, http://www.dst.gov.in/stsysindia/spr1958.htm (accessed 2 December 2011).
7. Actually from the late 1990s China began to overtake India in science publications reaching more than double by 2005.
8. See Planning Commission (1980: xxi and 10).
9. http://www.dst.gov.in/stsysindia/sps1983.htm (accessed 2 December 2011).
10. See the website of the Department of Science and Technology, New Delhi, India for the full statement of Technology Policy Statement, 1983, http://www.dst.gov.in (accessed 8 January 2013).
11. Parts of this section are drawn from Krishna (2008).
12. See also Sridharan (1995).
13. This does not mean to suggest that there were no policy statements issued by different sectors in earlier phases. There were fewer policy statements issued by sectors compared to the current phase after 1991. Sectoral-based policies issued in the last decade basically articulated and formulated with the different stakeholders at the level of sectors in coordination with the government.
14. See http://dst.gov.in/stsysindia/stp2003.htm (accessed 2 December 2011), the website of the Department of Science and Technology, Government of India, New Delhi.
15. Parts of this section are drawn from Krishna (2008).
16. As noted earlier, NSI in the Indian context makes sense at the sectoral level of understanding rather than at the national level.
17. Different years are used for different sets of data as per their availability from reliable sources.

18. It may be noted that the figures being quoted are from the R&D statistics given by the Department of Science and Technology. However, the DST figures grossly underestimate the foreign R&D inflow that has come into India during the period ending 2005–2006. The estimates of a World Bank study (see Dutz 2007) show that total private R&D investment has risen from half a billion Euro in 2002 to 2.45 billion Euro in 2005.
19. India is attracting global auto manufacturers due to the country's large middle-class population, growing earning power, strong technological capability, and availability of trained manpower at competitive prices.
20. The launch of advance telecom services like 3G and IPTV will drive the future growth in India. The sector attracted $2,558 million FDI in the financial year 2009 as compared to the $1,261 million in financial year 2008. Telecommunications account for a 9.37 per cent share in total FDI inflow.
21. However, big foreign firms such as Microsoft, IBM, Cisco, Oracle, Intel, and Adobe witnessed only a marginal growth rate for the same period between 1 and 10 per cent. For instance, Microsoft which registered 26 per cent growth rate in 2007–8 declined to just 1 per cent in 2008–9 compared to the previous year; and Hewlett-Packard from 30 per cent to 2 per cent for the same periods.
22. However, as per the figures given by the DST, Government of India, based on their databases the total number of papers has increased from 59,315 in 2001 to 89,297 in 2005. These are non-SCI based publications which are covered in one or the other international database.
23. Some of the figures used here are taken from Herstaat et al. (2008) and compared with the data sets given by DST, Government of India. The figure of 14 million science graduates is from Farrel et al. (2005).
24. The first is the Draft National Innovation Act 2008, Department of Science and Technology, Ministry of S&T. It may be noted that this draft is being circulated only for soliciting views from interested public and intellectuals and not yet formalised; and the second is the 'The Protection and Utilisation of Public Funded Intellectual Property Bill, 2008', being circulated among government departments and public and pending ratification by the Parliament to enable it to come into operation.
25. The definition is taken from the Draft National Innovation Act 2008 document.
26. See the Prime Minister's and minister of science and technology's addresses at the 96th Indian Science Congress held at North Eastern Hill University, Shillong, Meghalaya during 3–7 January 2009. See also the Steering Committee Report on Science and Technology of the Planning Commission for the 11th Plan (2007–2012).

27. From the Prime Minister's address at the 96th Indian Science Congress held at North Eastern Hill University, Shillong, Meghalaya during 3–7 January 2009. See also http://www.dst.gov.in/scie_congrs/pmspeech09.htm (accessed 11 September 2012).
28. The government has announced the creation of 30 central universities; five new Indian Institutes of Technology; and 20 Indian Institutes of Information Technology. The government also established the Indian Institute of Space Science and Technology, Kerala; National Institute of Science Education and Research, Bhubaneswar, by the Department of Atomic Energy; Stem Cell Biology and Regenerative Medicine, Bangalore; Cancer Research Institute, Chennai; and Institute of Advanced Study in Science and Technology, Guwahati. See the Prime Minister's address at the 96th Indian Science Congress held at North Eastern Hill University, Shillong, Meghalaya during 3–7 January 2009.
29. See http://timesofindia.indiatimes.com/India/Cabinet_nod_for_bill_giving_scientists_share_in_IPRs/rssarticleshow/3659358.cms (accessed 2 December 2011).
30. See http://www.csir.res.in/csir/external/heads/collaborations/NM.pdf (accessed 2 December 2011).
31. It may be pointed out that India before 2005 WTO regulations opted for a unique Patent Policy which protected patents for seven years. This is not the case in other countries of Europe and North America which protected patents for 20 years. China came under the WTO regime only in 2005 and before that it did not have systematic patent regulation.
32. There are currently about 45 software technology parks spread all over the country. India's dynamic achievements in space research and launch of satellites helped communication and high speed connectivity to software technology parks. All these cities developed as educational and innovation hubs. Over the decades India's educational structure and system has produced a vast number of English-speaking graduates and educated professionals which is again related to the policies which led to the expansion of higher education. All these combined to infuse confidence among firms and entrepreneurs.
33. Research and innovation policies in space are enunciated by the Department of Space in coordination with the Indian Space Research Organisation (ISRO). Space R&D accounts for 22 per cent of total governmental R&D funding in 2007–2008. The main research focus in space is to accomplish high technology capabilities in designing, launching and commercialisation of satellites and manage complex system engineering and management in space technologies.
34. However, this holds good for certain sectors as noted earlier and not for the industrial spectrum across the board.

References

Department of Science and Technology (DST), 1975. *Research and Development Statistics 1973–74*. New Delhi: Department of Science and Technology, Ministry of Science and Technology, Government of India.

———, 1999. *Research and Development Statistics 1996–97*. New Delhi: Department of Science and Technology, Ministry of Science and Technology, Government of India.

———, 2002. *Research and Development Statistics 2000–01*. New Delhi: Department of Science and Technology, Ministry of Science and Technology, Government of India.

———, 2004. *Data Book*. New Delhi: Department of Science and Technology.

Dutz, M. A., 2007. *Unleashing India's Innovation: Toward Sustainable and Inclusive Growth*. Washington DC: World Bank.

Farrel, D., N. Kaka and S. Stürze, 2005. 'Ensuring India's Offshoring Future', *McKinsey Quarterly*, September.

Herstatt, C., R. Tiwari, D. Ernst, and S. Buse, 2008. 'India's National Innovation System: Key Elements and Corporate Perspectives', Working Paper no. 96, Economics Series, East-West Center, Honolulu, Hawai'i.

Jayaraman, K. S., 2008. 'India Creates Funding Council for Basic Science: Autonomous Agency Will Begin Operations in April', *Nature*, 456(7223): 685.

Kalam, A. P. J. Abdul and Y. S. Rajan, 2003. *India 2020 — Vision for the New Millennium*. New Delhi: Penguin Books.

Krishna, V. V., 1997a. 'A Portrait of the Scientific Community in India: Historical Growth and Contemporary Problems', in J. Gaillard, V. V. Krishna and R. Waast (eds), *Scientific Communities in the Developing World*. New Delhi: Sage Publications, 236–80.

———, 1997b. 'Science, Technology and Counter Hegemony: Some Reflections on the Contemporary Science Movements in India', in T. Shinn, J. Spaapen and V. V. Krishna (eds), *Science and Technology in a Developing World*. Dordrecht: Kluwer Academic Publishers, 375–411.

———, 2007. 'Dynamics in the Sectoral System of Innovation: Indian Experience in Software, Biotechnology and Pharmaceuticals', in T. Turpin and V. V. Krishna (eds), *Science, Technology Policy and the Diffusion of Knowledge: Understanding the Dynamics of Innovation Systems in the Asia-Pacific*. Cheltenham: Edward Elgar, 193–233.

———, 2008. 'INNO-Policy Trend Chart — Policy Trends and Appraisal Report: India', Report prepared for the European Union Network, http://www.proinno-europe.eu/extranet/upload/country reports/ Country_Report_India_2008.pdf (accessed 2 December 2011).

Ministry of Industry, 1991. *Annual Report.* New Delhi: Ministry of Industry, Government of India.

Mukherjee, R., 2009. 'The State, Economic Growth and Development in India', *India Review*, 8(1): 81–106.

National Knowledge Commission, 2007. *Innovation in India.* New Delhi: National Knowledge Commission, Government of India.

Planning Commission, 1961. *Third Five Year Plan 1961–66.* New Delhi: Planning Commission, Government of India.

———, 1970. *Fourth Five Year Plan 1969–74.* New Delhi: Planning Commission, Government of India.

———, 1980. *Sixth Five Year Plan 1980–85.* New Delhi: Planning Commission, Government of India.

Rahman, A., R. N. Bhargava, M. A. Qureshi, and S. Pruthi, 1973. *Science and Technology in India.* New Delhi: Indian Council of Cultural Relations.

Rosenberg, N., 1982. *Inside the Black Box: Technology and Economics.* Cambridge: Cambridge University Press.

———, 1990. 'Science and Technology Policy for the Asian NICs: Lessons from Economic History', in R. E. Evenson and G. Ranis (eds), *Science and Technology Lessons for Development Policy*. London: Intermediate Technology Publications, 149–50.

Sridharan, E., 1995. 'Liberalisation and Technology Policy: Redefining Self-Reliance', in T. V. Sathyamurthy (ed.), *Industry and Agriculture in India since Independence.* New Delhi: Oxford University Press, 150–88.

5

China

Lv Ping

The national system of innovation (NSI) conceptual framework has been playing a key role in enabling China to catch up and move forward to become an innovative country (Cassiolato and Vitorino 2009), as well as to build a prosperous society according to the 'Outline of National Medium and Long-Term Science and Technology Development Plan (2006–2020)' (State Council 1996). The idea of the NSI looks at the innovation process as an integrated and systemic (not linear) process. Hence, not only the enterprise, institutions and organisations, but also how they interact, is an important element of the NSI. Furthermore, history and context would affect the dynamics of the NSI, which requires us to investigate the relationship between the state and the NSI within a dynamic historical context.

This chapter deals with the role of the state in the evolution of China's NSI, and we consider the history that started with the 1978 reform and opening-up policy as the focus of this analysis. This chapter is structured as follows: the following four sections introduce the current context of China's NSI. The next section describes the evolution of the current form of state. We then analyse the institutions and policies of the state concerned with innovation. The fourth section discusses the specificities of the system of innovation in the country and its relationship with the state. The next section reviews China's explicit and implicit state policy towards science, technology and innovation (STI). We then analyse the outcomes of state policy and state institutions on the NSI. The last section summarises the main conclusions of this chapter.

China's Development Model

China has recently entered a historical phase where the established development model must be changed in order to attain the official macroeconomic objective of a growth in the GDP per capita from US$ 1,000 to US$ 3,000. In 2003, China's GDP per capita was $1,090, and reached $ 3,266 in 2008. International experiences indicate that this is a sensitive period which combines economic restructuring with accompanying changes in social formation. Corresponding with the above inevitable situation, two major changes have to take place: first, the marginal contribution rate that some key elements such as labour, resources, investment, and land have on economic growth will decrease, and the importance of knowledge and technological innovation will significantly increase; second, the official model of economic growth is in a critical stage of transition from a resource-based and extensive type into an intensive, high value added type. Therefore, only innovation can be a way to progress in accordance with these changes.

China has possessed the necessary conditions of the great-leap-forward development with the rapid economic growth of recent years. The Chinese economy is now the world's second largest in terms of its macroeconomic performance (*China Statistical Yearbook* 2010), and it has become a major destination for foreign direct investment (FDI) and a trading nation of global rank. Scientific output, in terms of publication of scientific research papers, grew at an annual rate of 8.9 per cent in 2009; and the number of granted patents increased at an annual rate of 41 per cent in 2009 (National Bureau of Statistics and Ministry of Science and Technology 2009). These conditions have laid a strong foundation for China to shift its development model into an innovation-based one.

The Constraints of the Traditional Development Model

China's industrialisation path was basically traditional relying mainly on natural resource endowments, and was developed on the basis of long-term intensive exploration and exploitation of natural resources and ecological environment. For example, China's consumption of coal, steel and fresh water accounts for 32 per cent,

27 per cent and 15 per cent of the total consumption of the world respectively (Chinese Academy of Sciences 2006). At present, China is suffering great pressure from resource constraints, environment damage and population growth.

In contrast with these factor inputs, however, China's innovation capability is relatively low, which has mainly manifested in a number of aspects. In the first place, the capability of technological invention is too low, with the number of annual authorised invention patents accounting for only 22.1 per cent of the total authorised patents, and 49.1 per cent of the intellectual property rights belonging to overseas inventors (*China Statistical Yearbook on Science and Technology* 2010). Second, most industries lack core technologies. Third, the enterprises' proclivity for technological innovation is weak. Fourth, technology is introduced repeatedly without digestion and absorption. Fifth, the key elements of innovation are isolated from each other, which makes it difficult to develop the country's comprehensive innovation capability, and the government, industry and research do not combine with each other effectively in innovation activities. In the development chain of science and technological innovation as well as enterprises' R&D activities, the allocation of innovation resources is unduly skewed, with the government putting too much emphasis on universities and colleges rather than on enterprises, especially innovative private enterprises.

In conclusion, these factors all indicate that China's economic development model has not broken off from the traditional one yet.

Regional Disparities in Economic and Social Development

As a big developing country with a large population and a vast land area, China has experienced a rapid and sustainable socio-economic growth as a result of the reforms in the past few decades. At the same time, the differences between urban and rural areas have been widening, and the regional development imbalance has become increasingly prominent. First there is the uneven distribution of income, mostly evident in the differences between urban and rural areas; second there is the uneven distribution of property; third is the employment and wages disparities, which means the differences of employment opportunities among workers in different regions (the imbalance of employment opportunities is an important factor for the widening gap of income and wealth distribution); fourth is the education disparities between urban and rural areas.

Regional Imbalances in Innovation Capability

The regional imbalance of innovation capability has experienced a historical evolution. Since 1949, when China was founded, the central government allocated a variety of resources in areas with better industrial basis, primarily in the north-east provinces, followed by eastern and northern China. In the 1960s, China shifted the strategic emphasis of industrial and science and technology layout, which improved the technological capability of western areas rapidly. However, the southern coastal areas with the exception of a few national-level investments, such as Fujian, Zhejiang, Guangdong, and other provinces, have only a few state-owned enterprises (SOEs), and their industrial infrastructure was weak and the development of science and technology lagged behind the rest of the country. Before China's reform and opening-up, the innovation capabilities of southern coastal areas generally lagged behind those of northern areas.

In 1978 a critical strategic decision leading to the reform of the political economy and the opening-up of the economy to global markets was made on the Third Plenum of the Eleventh Chinese Communist Party (CPC). Since then, China shifted its development emphasis into eastern coastal areas, by establishing special economic zones and opening the coastal port cities, and so on. The coastal areas became an important window for China to attract foreign capital as well as the most active centre for international technology transfer. In addition, this area attracted a large number of domestic skills to take part in innovation activities. Therefore, a significant change of China's regional innovation capability after the reforms and opening-up is the great improvement of innovation capability in southern and eastern coastal areas, while the development of innovation capability of the central and western areas was relatively slow, and the regional imbalance was reversed, that is to say, the differences of innovation capability between eastern and western areas have been widening.

The differences between urban and rural areas still exist. At present, China's development of rural science and technology innovation is very weak in general, and has become one of the weakest sections in China's science and technology programme. The problems include seriously insufficient inputs in rural areas, an inadequate scientific and technological innovation and service system, a relatively weak dissemination of science and technology, and the general inability of available technologies to meet the needs of peasants. The interaction between a poorly developed science and technology base and economic development may become a vicious circle. Compared with the urban areas, the rural areas lack effective policies and measures to attract and train scientific and technological personnel, so the phenomenon of skills loss is serious. In addition, a new scientific and technological service system which meets the economic market rules and requirements has not been established yet and the construction of an information-sharing platform is relatively slow.

At the 17th National Congress of the Chinese Communist Party in 2007, China put forward the ideology of 'Scientific Outlook of Development' as a strategic decision to develop and utilise indigenous innovation and build an innovative country.[1] This policy was adopted to enter the global economy with the rapid development of science and technology. China regards enhancing indigenous innovation capability as a development strategy of science and technology, and promotes an indigenous innovation path parallel to the great-leap-forward development of science and technology. In addition, China is establishing a new balanced NSI to attract more innovators and enterprises to join in, not only to promote innovation, but also to promote the construction of a harmonious society that more people may benefit from.

Evolution of the Current Form of State

The administration of China's innovation system consists of several major bodies: the Ministry of Education (MOE), formerly the State Education Committee; the Ministry of Science and Technology (MOST), formerly the State Science and Technology Committee (SSTC); the Chinese Academy of Sciences (CAS); Chinese Academy of Engineering (CAE); Chinese Academy of Social Sciences (CASS); and the National Science Foundation Committee (NSFC). These agencies cooperate with other industrial ministries, which also have their own research institutes and projects, including the Ministry of Industry and Information Technology (MIIT), and the National

Development and Reform Committee (NDRC). Together these administrative bodies formulate and implement national science and technology programmes and policies. Figure 5.1 provides the organisation form.

Figure 5.1: *Main Administrative Bodies of China's Innovation System*

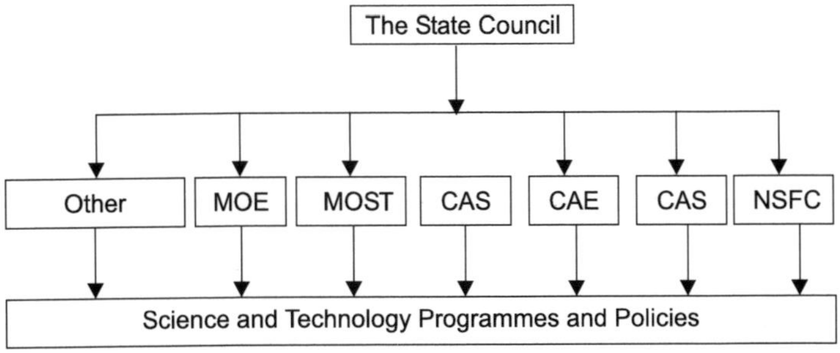

Source: Zhong and Yang (2007).

In this administrative framework of the NSI, the Chinese government's economic functions can be divided into two stages marked by the reform and opening-up.

The role of the state in a centrally planned economy prior to 1978

From 1949, the founding of the new China, to 1956, China almost completed the socialist transformation, which was a process wherein the state gradually extended into the private economic sector and eventually replaced the autonomy of the private sector in production and consumption. Since 1958, the state has at all levels completely dominated the entire economy, and controlled every aspect of the economy, including production planning as well as a coupons-based supply system for a variety of subsidiary food and manufactured goods for daily use.

The formation of the single public ownership and the planned economy resulted in the need to accelerate industrialisation, that is to say, at that time under the conditions of shortage of capital, China increased capital investment relying both on depressing domestic consumption and improving accumulation. In the 25 years from 1953 to 1978, China maintained a relatively high economic growth rate, and almost set up an autarkic industrial system, which was closely and inseparably related to such a high rate accumulation. In addition, the single public ownership and planned economic system has another function: to guarantee social security to all the people in China, to insure social stability during a period of high accumulation and deficiency in goods and materials, although this kind of social security is at low levels of income.

Originally, the planned economy was designed to reduce economic operating costs and to avoid inappropriate resource allocation and waste caused by business and individual production without government control. However, because the information for decision-making in the planned economy was insufficient, there were many uncertain factors and bureaucratic obstacles in the implementation process, which has led to a number of mistakes in allocation. Public ownership also did not play the expected function of arousing people's enthusiasm for production. In rural areas, the collective production and average income distribution in the People's Commune model have suppressed the farmers' enthusiasm for production. In urban areas, the phenomenon of 'workers eating from the same big pot of their enterprises, and enterprises eating from the same big pot of the country' also suppressed the enthusiasm of enterprises and workers.[2] Since in both, the single public ownership and the planned economic system, the desired economic performance and the goal of stimulating enthusiasm of all the people have not been achieved, the Chinese government has had to explore new ways and seek new approaches to improve the socialist economic management system.

The role of the state and the emerging mixed economy since 1978

After the Third Plenary Session of the 11th Party Central Committee in 1978, and with the deepening of the reforms and opening-up, China has gradually formed an economic framework in which a variety of economic sectors coexist, and the market mechanism plays a basic regulating role. Accordingly, the government's economic functions have consciously or unconsciously changed. This change can be roughly divided into two phases: the first phase was from 1979 to 1991, where the focus was to remove the old functions the government had, that was to narrow the government's economic management scope and power; the second phase was from 1992 to present, the focus of which was innovation and the re-establishment of the government's functions in accordance with the market economy.

In the first phase, the government's original economic function under the conditions of single public ownership and planned economy gradually cleared up on two fronts. The first was decentralisation, which allowed the existence and development of a non-public economy as well as the 'three capital' enterprises.[3] During this phase, the reform of rural areas was most prominent and made the greatest achievements. In urban areas, the reform of SOEs moved forward slowly, but from the implementation of reducing administrative power and decentralisation to the 'contract system', enterprises' autonomy and share of profits were increased significantly. This relaxation of government control on public economy and obtaining surplus has been one of the driving forces for China's rapid economic growth in the 1980s. During the reform of the public-owned economic system, the Chinese government also adopted the policy of opening up to the outside world, and encouraged urban and rural job-waiting persons to be self-employed or become 'specialised households' in order to let the market mechanism regulate. Thus, another highly vigorous economic sector has been established besides the existing public-owned system.

The second was the gradual relaxation of administrative control on the whole economy, which means that the government withdrew from some areas to allow the alternative regulation of market mechanism. In this aspect, the guiding ideology of the Chinese government shifted from a model of a 'planned economy-orientation with market regulation as a supplement' to the one that was 'combining planned management with market regulation', then to the top-down model of 'government adjusting market, and market guiding enterprise', and finally went back to an ambiguous formulation of 'combining planned economy with market regulation' in 1989. These changes in China's guidelines clearly show that the Chinese government has been giving increasing space to market regulation rather than direct state control. The obvious feature in this transition of the government's economic function was the reform and improvement of the economic system based on public-ownership and planned economy under the guidelines of 'emancipating the mind and seeking truth from facts' and China's 'four cardinal principles'.[5]

In the second phase, the market economy was commonly accepted as the goal of China's reform, and the measures taken by the Party and the government were to move towards this goal. The transition of the government's economic function took the initiation from 'feeling the way across the river' (Chen 1995: 279) in the 1980s, to establishing a basic market economy framework at the end of the 20th century, then to establishing a mature market economy in the first 20 years of the 21st century.

The reform of the government's economic function focused mainly on two aspects in this period. The first was the total adjustment and reform of the state-owned economy, which was the last bastion of the old system. The course of this reform was that in the first half of the 1990s, transforming operational mechanisms and establishing a modern enterprise system were emphasised; after 1996, the establishment of a modern enterprise system was combined with the policy of 'invigorating large enterprises while relaxing control over small ones' proposed in the document, 'A Number of Decisions on Major Issues about State-Owned Reform and Development by CPC Central Committee' in 1999 (The fifteenth Central Committee of the Chinese Communist Party, the Fourth Plenary Meeting 1999), as well as joint-stock transformation, during which the government transferred some state-owned economy, even totally withdrawing from some fields. Another is that the government constructed a management system in accordance with the market economy. In 1993 and 1998, two rounds of large-scale reforms of government institutions were conducted, which not only strengthened the government's macro-management functions, but also strengthened the government's regulating function on enterprises' behaviour and market order. In addition, a new social security system was included as a main duty of the government. At present, the government's economic functions have transformed from the overall direct control-type model before 1978 into the indirect adjustment–type model (Wu 2003).

Periodisation and Analysis of Institutions and Policies of the State Concerned with Innovation

Corresponding to the government's economic function, China had implemented a planned science and technology system before

1978, during which the enterprises, scientific research institutions, universities, and national defence research institutions were independent systems, in order to promote the science and technology projects and knowledge transfer (Fang and Liu 2004). In the situations of international blockade and extreme scarcity of domestic science and technology resources, this system has played a very important role in centralising limited resources, setting up an intact science and technology system and infrastructure. Over 20 years this science and technology system trained a large number of outstanding talents, solved a series of great scientific and technological problems in social, economic development and defence construction and greatly narrowed the gap between China and some advanced countries.

However, this planned science and technology system confronted some challenges at the end of the 1970s. At that time, the wave of new technological revolutions was surging and profound changes had taken place in almost all fields. Technological achievements were popularised and applied into production rapidly, which in turn brought tremendous changes in social productivity and accelerated global economic growth and industrial restructuring. In the meantime, the inherent structural defects of China's existing science and technology system appeared gradually. First of all, it was a closed system with vertical structure, with the result that the science and technology sector and the economy were separate. Second, there was little sense of intellectual property rights and there was no mechanism through which science and technology could be transferred with compensation in China, which hindered technology innovation and diffusion. Third, the government had intervened too much through administrative means on scientific research institutions, and the phenomenon of 'getting an equal share regardless of the work done' existed at that time, which was not conductive to arouse the initiative and enthusiasm of scientific research institutions. Therefore, the reform of the existing science and technology system was imperative.

Since that period until now, the Chinese government has made a great effort in policy making to push science and technology system reforms, which can be roughly divided into three phases according to the adjustment of reform objectives and focal points of the policy.

The first phase (1985–1992): The reform of the funding system and governance relaxation on scientific research institutions

In this phase, the main policy direction of science and technology was to give more flexibility to scientific research institutions, scientific and technological personnel. Policies in this period concentrated on the funding system, the technology market, organisational structures and the personnel system. During this period the reform of the science and technology sector proceeded on five levels.

The first thrust was on the reform of the funding system. According to the characteristics and division of science and technology activities, China divided national scientific research expenses into specific categories. For those scientific research institutions mainly engaged in technological development, the government would completely reduce the funding of their operating expenses over a five-year period. For those scientific research institutions mainly engaged in basic research, the government would implement a funding system which would subsidise a portion of their operating expenses. For those organisations engaged in social public welfare research and agricultural research, the government would still subsidise their operational expenses. The main purpose of this reform was to change the existing dependency relationship of scientific research institutions on their administrative departments, and in this manner to force scientific research institutions to serve economic development as well as to strive for multi-channel sources of funding. In this process the overall science and technology sector would be reoriented towards a market economy and overall investment on science and technology would be expanded in order to accelerate the commercialisation of scientific and technological achievements.

The second reform was to open the technology market. Technological achievements were acknowledged as a commodity in policy and legal system at that time, and a mechanism was established that technology transfer should be compensated in accordance with its value. In addition, the government promulgated the 'Patent Law', the 'Technology Contract Law' and some corresponding implementing regulations, which provided basic rules for technology transactions such as technology development, technology transfer, technology consultation, and technology service, and so on.

The third was the reform of the management model of scientific research institutions. The principles and direction of the reform was the separation of responsibilities between research divisions and administrative divisions in the departments of the State Council in order to decentralise the authority of scientific research institutions, to change the direct control model into the indirect management model that the Chinese government has as regards scientific research institutions. This reform was meant to expand the autonomy of scientific research institutions and to encourage the union among scientific research institutions, educational agencies, design units, and production units, as well as to strengthen the capability of enterprises in technology absorption and development.

The fourth thrust was to support and develop private scientific and technological enterprises. The government encouraged scientific and technological personnel to set up private scientific and technological firms engaged in technology development, technology transfer, technology consultation, and technology service in accordance with the business principles. These principles included self-financing, voluntary cooperation, making one's own management decisions, and taking full responsibility for their own profits and losses. This was meant to make these firms a vital force in the development of high-tech industries outside the existing system.

The fifth level of reform was to establish pilot high-tech industry zones. In May 1988, the State Council approved the establishment of the Beijing High-Tech Industry Pilot Zone and provided 18 preferential policies to it. By April of 2011, 86 national-level high-tech industry zones were established all over the country.

The second phase (1992–1998): China's support on basic research

In this phase, China carried out high-tech research and other projects that had long-term significance on economic construction, social development and national defence, and during which China has developed a growing body of science and technology personnel which is progressively placing it on the global market. In addition, China emancipated different kinds of R&D institutions which can directly serve China's economic construction and social development, as well as encouraged commercialisation and industrialisation activities of science and technology achievements in order to make them market-oriented. The main policies and measures taken are listed in the following paragraphs.

First, the government encouraged all kinds of scientific research institutions to implement the integration of technology, industry and trade, or to cooperate with firms in technology development, production and management. On the other hand, the government also encouraged scientific research institutions to adopt commercially oriented management models, with an emphasis on the relevant provisions of corporate finance such as independent accounting, and gradually achieved a balance of payments, economic self-reliance and assumed responsibility for its profits or losses. Second, the government granted managerial authority to some suitable scientific research institutions to operate state-owned assets, and encouraged them to invest in setting up scientific and technological enterprises or groups, merging and acquiring firms or being a shareholder of a firm in order to enjoy returns in accordance with the law. Third, the government provided support to eligible scientific research institutions in their cooperation with large and medium-sized enterprises or enterprise groups in various ways. Fourth, the government promoted social welfare organisations to become new legal entities. These organisations mainly relied on national policy-based input, social investment and income generation from their own scientific and technological business, and the Chinese government encouraged them to establish a mechanism of self-accumulation, self-operation and self-development with reference to foreign non-profit organisations. These organisations should be supervised and administrated by society, and conduct non-profit-oriented business activities and service for the society, which can be exempt from income tax and value-added tax. In this way the income of these organisations may be used to support their own development.

The third phase (since 1998): The policy of 'relying on science and technology to rejuvenate the nation' and building a national innovative system

In this phase, substantive adjustments were conducted to the science and technology development strategy and system, and 'Relying on Science and Technology to Rejuvenate the Nation', which was formulated in 'Decision on Accelerating Science and Technology Progress by the Central Committee of the Chinese Communist

Party and the State Council' in 1995 (Central Committee of the Chinese Communist Party and the State Council 1995), became a national-level strategy. Strengthening the NSI and speeding up industrialisation of scientific and technological achievements became a main policy direction of this period. Virtually all policies concentrated on restructuring scientific research institutions and improving the innovation capability of enterprises and industries, and so on.

With the accelerated pace of reform in government agencies, the State Council decided to conduct the administrative system reform of 242 scientific research institutions attached to 10 state-level bureaus managed by the State Economic and Trade Commission at the end of 1998, the means of which included transition into scientific and technological enterprises or technology intermediary service institutions, as well as mergers with enterprises in order to realise firm-based transformation (State Council 1999c). The goal of this reform was to reduce the number of independent state-level research institutions, encourage enterprises to set up their own applied research institutions and transform enterprises into the main actors of technology innovation. Thereafter, another 134 technological development scientific research institutions affiliated to the State Council had also carried out the transformation into enterprises (Ministry of Science and Technology 2000). At the same time, the government began to promote the transition of public welfare-based research institutions into non-profit organisations. These changes have transformed each of the main components of the NSI. The business sector has become the dominant R&D actor, now performing over two-thirds of total R&D, up from less than 40 per cent at the beginning of 1990. The share of public research institutions has declined from almost half of total R&D to less than one-quarter over the same period. The relative weight of higher education institutions (HEIs) has increased moderately, from 8.6 per cent to 9.9 per cent.

There has also been a vigorous promotion of the commercialisation of scientific and technological achievements. In May 1996, the Standing Committee of the National People's Congress approved 'China's Promotion Law of Commercialisation of Scientific and Technological Achievements' (Standing Committee of the National People's Congress 1996). In 1999, the General Office of the State Council transmitted the policy 'Some Provisions on Promotion of

Scientific and Technological Achievements' (Ministry of Science and Technology et al. 1999) from seven departments such as the Ministry of Science and Technology. The aforementioned policies established the following norms:

(*a*) If the high-tech achievements are regarded as assets invested to the limited liability company, the value of them can amount to 35 per cent of the total registered capital, except otherwise agreed by the parties.

(*b*) Scientific research institutions, colleges and universities should reward the author and related people when they want to commercialise the technology achievements, and the reward should be no less than 20 per cent of the net income of commercialisation, or no less than 5 per cent of the newly increasing profit that gained from new achievements for three–five years in succession. If a stock company wants to commercialise, it may also reward no less than 20 per cent of the value of technological achievements when they are regarded as share(s).

(*c*) Scientific research institutions, colleges and universities should reward the author(s) in form of donation of share or stock rights according to their contribution. The author(s) wouldn't pay personal income tax when obtaining these shares or capital ratio; but they would pay income tax if obtaining ratio of dividends or transferring investment shares.

(*d*) If the scientific and technological personnel have completed their assumed work in their own units, they can engage in R&D and commercialisation in other units.

A series of technological innovation policies was introduced, including: (*a*) 'Some Provisions on Mechanism of Venture Capital Construction' (State Council 1999b), which were used to boost the development of venture capital in China; (*b*) China established 'Innovation Funds for Small and Medium-sized Technology-based Firms' (1999), in order to promote the development of these firms; (*c*) the former State Economic and Trade Commission and the Ministry of Science and Technology have all proposed the 'Technology Innovation Project', in order to boost both enterprises' and regional innovation; (*d*) the government put forward some innovation policies to improve industries' innovation capability, the most important of which is 'Policies on Encouraging Development of Software Industry and IC Industry' (State Council 2000) issued by the State Council in 2000, which boosted the development of these two industries.

In January 2006, the National Science and Technology Conference was held in Beijing, where the 'Outline of National Medium and Long-Term Science and Technology Development Plan (2006–2020)' (State Council 1996) was issued. This policy marked that China's science and technology development strategy would transform from imitation-based innovation into indigenous innovation. This outline was based on the position of China in the global market and included a comprehensive plan and strategic proposal of China's science and technology development in the next 15 years. It aimed to enhance indigenous innovation as the main development strategy as well as setting innovation-oriented construction as a key national goal. This was a programmatic document to guide China's science and technology development in the new era.

Specificities of the System of Innovation in the Country and Its Relationship with the State

Since reform and opening-up in 1978, China's economic structure of primary industry, secondary industry and tertiary industry has changed a lot, which can be seen from Figure 5.2. During the past 32 years, the absolute value of these three industries has increased by 3328.32 per cent, 8932.71 per cent, and 16821.73 per cent respectively, which manifests the great economic achievements China has made. The proportion of primary industry decreased from 28.19 per cent in 1978 to 10.30 per cent by 2009, while the proportion of tertiary industry increased from 23.94 per cent in 1978 to 43.36 per cent by the same year, and the proportion of secondary industry has maintained the level of less than 50 per cent. Therefore, China has undergone a dramatic transition from an agriculture-based country into a manufactures-based country since reform and opening-up.

In the secondary industry, China's high-tech technology has also developed very fast. As Figure 5.3 shows, the percentage of China's added value of high-tech industries in the manufacturing sector has been increasing and by 2007, this percentage reached 12.7 per cent, which surpassed Italy, and the gap between China and other developed countries has been reduced significantly. Figure 5.4 shows China's

Figure 5.2: *Structural Evolution of China's Primary, Secondary and Tertiary Industries, 1978–2009 (percentage)*

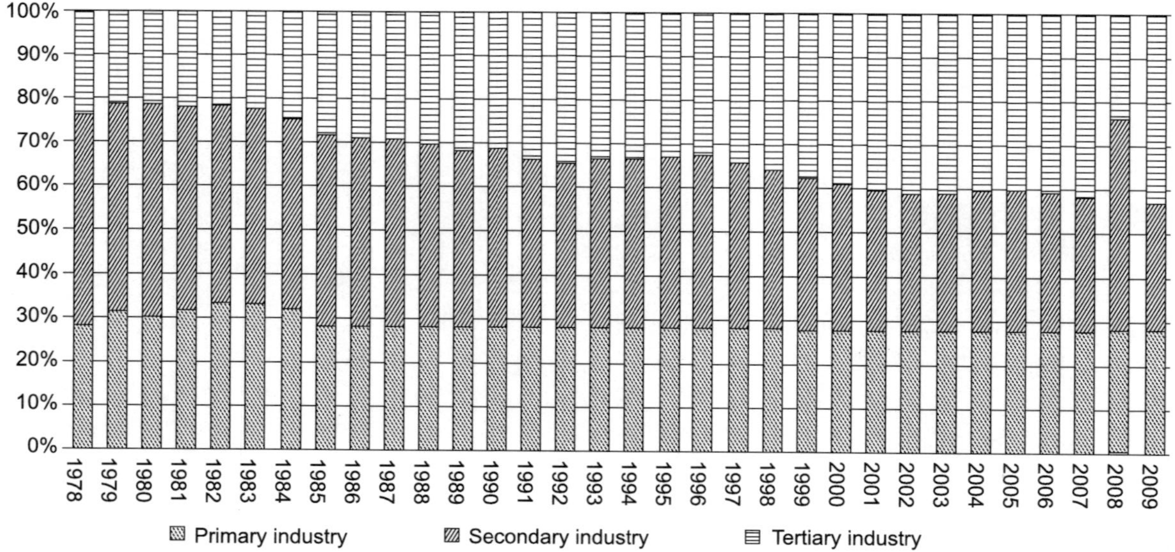

Source: *China Statistical Yearbook* (2010).

high-tech products exports and its percentage of total merchandise exports from 1992 to 2008, from which we can see that China's high-tech exports have increased from US$ 4 billion to US$ 416 billion, and its percentage of total merchandise exports has increased from 4.7 per cent to nearly 30 per cent.

Figure 5.3: *Value Added of High-tech Industries as a Percentage of Manufacturing in China and Selected Countries, 1995–2007*

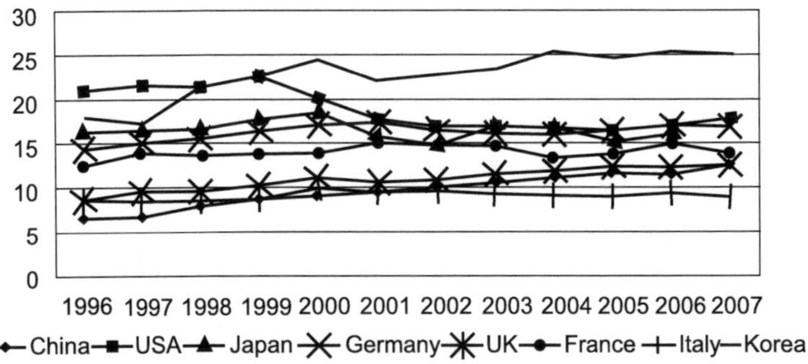

Source: China Statistical Yearbook on High Technology Industry (2004a, 2010).

Figure 5.4: *China's Exports of High-tech Products, 1992–2008*

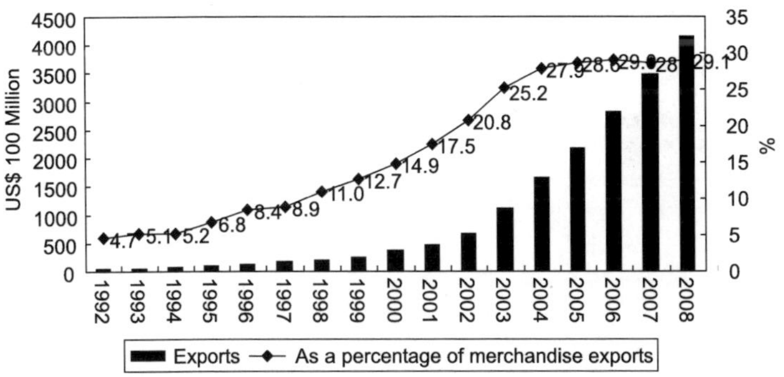

Source: China Statistical Yearbook on High Technology Industry (2004a, 2010).

China's NSI has developed with the transition from a planned economy into a market economy, as well as from an agriculture-based country into a manufactures-based country. China also has the potential to develop a NSI that will be a powerful engine for sustainable growth and facilitate the smooth integration of China's expanding economy into the global trading and knowledge system

(OECD 2008). China's NSI includes the following main actors: enterprises, universities and research institutions, government, intermediaries; their interaction is shown in Figure 5.5.

Figure 5.5: *China's NSI*

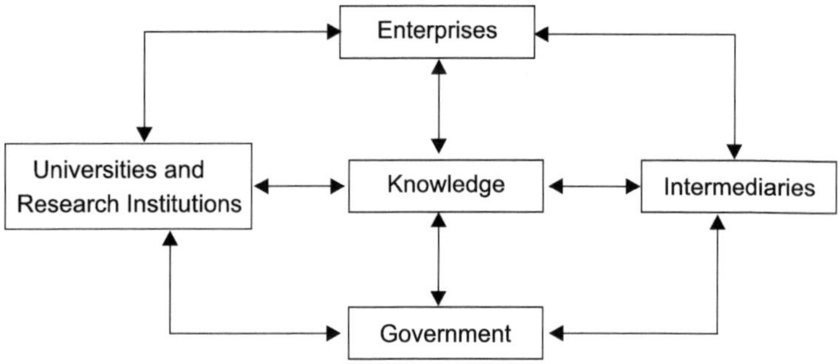

China's NSI has a number of unique characteristics, which have been emphasised by most scholars. In the first place, the Chinese government plays a critical role in the NSI and through the reform of the science and technology system has promoted the improvement of the NSI since China's reform and opening-up. Second, the establishment and implementation of national key science and technology programmes and projects has promoted the integration and cooperation among enterprises, scientific research institutions and universities, which became main actors of China's NSI. Third, Chinese enterprises are still lacking innovation capability, and the planned economic system developed in the past has been a serious impediment to the innovation of enterprises. It is therefore critical for China to establish a modern system and strengthen enterprises' innovation capability. Finally, the incentive system of innovation and the service system of intermediary organisation are imperfect, and all kinds of key elements have not developed an appropriate innovation structure and network.

The role of the state in the NSI depends on their own political system, on the nature of the economic system, and on the economic development stage of different countries, that is to say, governments play different roles in the national systems of innovation of different countries. As far as China is concerned, the functions that the government plays in the NSI can be summarised into five categories. It guides the allocation of innovation resources effectively; it facilitates and stimulates the interaction among all kinds of innovation elements; it creates a suitable mechanism and good environment for innovation activities; it intervenes where market failure exists; it monitors and assesses the implementation of the NSI.

Although the Chinese government has done a large amount of work in promoting and establishing the NSI, and the reform of the science and technology system has also made prominent progress, China's NSI still has some serious obstacles and weak segments from the perspectives of the current increasingly international competitive challenges and the requirements to carry out the policy of 'Scientific Concept of Development'. These obstacles and weaknesses still constrain the improvement of China's innovation capability.

The macro policy design and management system

There are a number of areas of weakness in macro policy-making and the management system in China. The macro policy-making system and mechanism for STI does not meet the needs of development since it lacks a national-level permanent agency engaged in consultation, assessment and supervision; there is still a large scope for the improvement of this function. The system of policy-making and implementation is also marked by fragmentation. Since the goals of each government department are different, there are disconnections in the innovation management process among them. As a result of the shortcomings inherited from the pre-reform planned economic system and the low national-level arrangement for the overall system, China's innovation chain was fractional and the problem of long-standing segmentation of the economic sector, science and technology sector, educational sector, and industrial sector could not be resolved fundamentally. Moreover, the allocation of scientific and technological strengths is irrational, and the regional allocation of innovation resources does not match with national-level economic and social development configuration. Most innovation resources were allocated in Beijing, Shanghai and other developed coastal areas, whose environment could attract talents and technological achievements from home and abroad. Therefore, the gap between developed eastern coastal areas and undeveloped central as well as western areas in China is wider than ever before.

The innovation capability of the main performers of innovation

Chinese enterprises do not, as yet, have strong indigenous innovation capability, and have not really developed a competitive technology innovation system. For a long time, Chinese enterprises have been attaching great importance to the introduction of technology and equipment with short-term efficiency while ignoring technology digestion, absorption and innovation. That is to say, the production capability of Chinese enterprises was maintained and upgraded mainly through technology imports, and enterprises spent more money on technology import than on their own R&D before 2000 (as shown in Table 5.1), which led to considerable difficulties in enhancing their innovation capability.

Table 5.1: *R&D Expenditure and Technology Import (US$ 100 million)*[6]

	Expenditure on R&D	*Share of Total Sales, %*	*Expenditure on Technology Import*	*Share of Total Sales, %*
1995	17.1	0.46	43.4	1.17
2000	42.7	0.71	29.6	0.49
2005	152.7	0.76	36.2	0.18
2009	470.0	0.96	57.8	0.12

Source: China Statistical Yearbook on Science and Technology (2004b, 2006, 2010).

As far as indigenous innovation capability is concerned, less than 1 per cent of all Chinese enterprises have applied for a patent, and only around 2,000 domestic enterprises, 0.03 per cent of the total, own their own intellectual property rights (*China Daily* 2005) despite the emergence of successful Chinese firms in the high-technology sector and in the international market. The innovation capability of Chinese enterprises is mostly focused on incremental innovation with little radical innovation, which can be observed from the patenting activities of the enterprises. Patents registered in China are classified into three categories: (*a*) invention, (*b*) utility model and (*c*) design (appearance). Design refers to new appearance and utility model refers to functionality modification or improvement without substantial technological contents. The invention patents are thus presumably more R&D intensive than the other two types of patents. Chinese enterprises have relatively high patenting activity in utility model and design, which accounts for the largest increase in the total number of patents, but is low in invention patents. However, since 2000, the number of invention patents granted has also increased more rapidly than before (see Table 5.2).

Table 5.2: *Patents Granted in China, by Type of Patents (in number)*

	1995	*2000*	*2005*	*2009*
Total number of patents granted	45064	105345	214003	581992
Share of invention patent (%)	7.5	12.0	24.9	22.1
Share of utility model patent (%)	67.6	52.0	27.1	35.0
Share of design patent (%)	24.9	36.0	38.0	42.9

Source: China Statistical Yearbook on Science and Technology (2004b, 2006, 2010).

Furthermore, the patenting activities differ significantly between domestic and foreign firms in China. For instance, even though both domestic and foreign firms have rapidly increased their patent applications, the largest increases in both invention patents applied and invention patents granted are from foreign firms.

Chinese scientific research institutions generally lack original innovation capability. China's conditions of scientific and technological support, resources integration and social sharing are insufficient, and the utilisation efficiency of resources as well as innovation efficiency is relatively low. In addition, the capability of China's social welfare research institutions is low. Because of inadequate awareness and deficient attention of the nature and value in research activities they are engaged in, investment has been insufficient to carry out many urgent scientific researches in China for a long time.

As an important base in personnel training and innovation, the potential of universities has not been brought into full play, and there are some defects in the system. Currently, applied research occupies the largest share of R&D activities in universities. For instance, in 2006, the shares of basic research expenditure, applied research expenditure, and experimental development expenditure in universities were 31.1 per cent, 53.4 per cent and 15.5 per cent respectively, and the shares of R&D personnel were 41.1 per cent, 51.3 per cent and 7.6 per cent respectively, which is contrary to that of developed countries (*China Statistical Yearbook on Science and Technology* 2010).

Finally, the strength of professional intermediaries is weak, which has a negative impact on the movement and integration of innovative elements, as well as the overall function of the innovation network. Intermediaries have developed gradually during China's transition from a planned economy into a market economy, so they have heavy government-run overtones and are not independent economic entities, and could not play a full role in optimising the combination of scientific and technological elements.

The innovation mechanism

Elements involved in the innovation activities are disconnected, separate from each other, and lack cooperation. In addition, the exchange of knowledge and information is not smooth. The interaction mechanism of production, teaching and research is imperfect since the connections, cooperation and exchanges among firms, scientific research institutions and universities are weak. Universities and scientific research institutions are unable to participate in the processes of technology introduction, digestion, absorption, and innovation in enterprises. On the contrary, enterprises also cannot participate in the national scientific research tasks undertaken by scientific research institutions and universities.

The investment mechanism of science and technology is still insufficiently developed to meet the requirements of innovation. In recent years, although the total amount of state financial investment in science and technology has increased, its proportion in all financial expenditure for the same period did not simultaneously increase, and there is little monitoring of the expenditure of national scientific and technological funds in the entire process. In addition, there is no well-formed mechanism to guide and encourage investment by a variety of social resources.

There are also still deficiencies in the incentive mechanism, which should reflect the principle of a 'people-oriented' concept, promote scientific and technological innovation, as well as accelerate the transfer of scientific and technological achievements. The role of the market mechanism to guide and promote innovation has not been fully played out. Finally, the planned management system does not keep pace with the country's development. Innovative activities should be totally different in scientific research organisations for they have different laws. The existing single innovation mechanism does not meet the diversity of the legislation on innovation.

Constraints in the innovation environment

The legal system governing innovation and the relevant policy environment still need to be improved on a number of levels. Legislation has not evolved fast enough to accommodate the requirements of scientific and technological development. The construction of the infrastructural platform for science and technology is relatively lagging behind. The infrastructure for science and technology is still relatively weak, and the limited resources could not be used reasonably, which constrains the serious development of many important research and development fields; it is difficult to provide basic guarantees to increase national-level innovation capabilities. The basic role of the market mechanism is still to be put to full use in innovation. During the process of promoting scientific and technological innovation, and with the withdrawal of the previous strong direct participation of the state, the fundamental role that the market mechanism plays still needs to be further strengthened. The existing pool of scientific and technological innovation talents is still insufficient to meet the needs of development. While this pool is large, its composition is ill-suited to the development needs of the NSI and the overall innovation capability is not high. In addition, qualified R&D personnel have still not been given full play in scientific and technological innovation, and their enthusiasm has not been fully aroused.

The culture of innovation

A number of aspects of the current culture of innovation do not meet the development requirements of the NSI. In the first place, academic democracy has not been given full play and some academic agencies and scientific research institutions tend to be overly administrative. Second, the cooperative spirit is insufficient, and the phenomenon of partition exists as a serious problem, which hinders the interaction and communication among all innovative mainstays and increases the obstacles to innovation. Third, there is evidently an over-emphasis on short-term quick success and instant benefits to the detriment of long-term development. Finally, the spirit of competition and innovation needs to be strengthened. Both the long-term impact of the planned economic system, as well as the corresponding imperfection of the scientific research system and incentive mechanism lead to the weak driving forces of competition and the low competitiveness of researchers, as well as an insufficient level of entrepreneurship.

Since the government includes both the central-level and regional-level tiers of administrative influence, the NSI can also be analysed from these two levels. In the NSI, the central government always tries to achieve sustained, stable development in accordance with international competitive norms through good policies, legal guarantees and infrastructure for innovation activities, organising important innovation programmes and projects, as well as promoting the cooperation between industry and research from an overall perspective of the national economic development situation. In a regional innovation system, the local government always develops local innovation and development policies in accordance with national guidelines and related policies, in order to promote industrial upgrading and high-quality economic growth. Thus, the local government is to create a regional innovation environment, while the national innovation environment is largely created by the central government. Moreover, the local government generally needs to specify and combine the innovation policies and rules made by the central government into their local policy making and economic operation, which can reflect local characteristics and have a direct effect on local economic development.

Therefore, the local government plays an important role in the construction of a regional innovation system and the NSI. The local government is familiar with regional situation, such as the resources, market demands, talents, technology, and management of local firms, which can reduce the cost of innovation system construction. The fact that China's market system is still in a transition phase requires intervention by local government in the innovation system. On the one hand, the regional policies which are intended to encourage innovation are always more specific and operational; on the other hand, many factors which maintain the market system, such as property rights and provision of public goods, need to be improved by the local government.

Explicit and Implicit State Policy towards Science, Technology and Innovation

Over the past three decades since reform and opening-up, China's science and technology system has transformed from a planned one based only on planning into a market-based system built on both planning and policy, during which the science and technology policies and regulations have played an increasingly important role, which is not only a parallel process with China's transition from a planned economy to a socialist market economy, but is also a formation process of science and technology policies and a legal system with Chinese characteristics. Before reform and opening-up, the Chinese government played a dominant role in the allocation of science and technology resources. In China's transition from a planned economy to a market economy, the intervention of the Chinese government in scientific and technological activities has diminished gradually, but did not disappear. The government has always been a provider of science and technology policies, so guiding and regulating scientific and technological activities through relevant policies in order to compensate for market failure is an important function the government should assume in the field of science and technology.

Science and technology policies in the 1980s

From the perspective of science and technology policy supply, purely science policies were relatively few in the 1980s, and the science and technology policies were much inclined to the technology side, which is consistent with the general direction of the science and technology development strategy of China at that time, that was emphasising high-tech industries, in line with the strategy that 'economic construction must rely on science and technology, and science and technology must work for economic development'. In this phase, the science and technology policies focused on the following areas:

(a) High-Tech Development and Construction of Key Laboratories

At that time, the State Economic and Trade Commission, the State Planning Commission, the National Science and Technology Commission, and other departments successively promulgated a number of science and technology policies, most of which focused on high-tech development and the construction of key industrial laboratories, while few focused on basic research. For example, the State Economic and Trade Commission issued the 'National Key Scientific and Technological Planning' in 1982 (State Economic and Trade Commission 1982a), which consisted of 38 key research projects. This was the first national-level science and technology plan in China in order to resolve key scientific and technological problems in national economic construction and social development. Later, the 'Planning of State Key Laboratory Construction' (State Economic and Trade Commission 1984a) and the 'National Key Industrial Pilot Projects' (State Economic and Trade Commission 1984b) were introduced in 1984. Other examples such as the 'National Key Technology Development Plan' (State Economic and Trade Commission 1980) and the 'National Technology Upgrading Plan' (State Economic and Trade Commission 1982b) introduced by the State Economic and Trade Commission in the early 1980s and 1982 respectively, all reflected that China attached great importance to technology development at that time.

(b) Development of Technology Market

China had a good-sized technology market at that time. The development of the technology market experienced three stages in general: (*i*) the stage of technology market cultivation, which can be characterised by the voluntary cooperation between scientific research units and production units in jointly launching key projects, when scientific research units began to get compensation from production units for their technology transfer, consultant service and technology problems solving; (*ii*) the stage of technology market formation. At the National Science and Technology Awards Conference held in 1982, the CPC Central Committee and the State Council put forward the strategic approach of 'economic construction must rely on science and technology, and science and technology must work for economic development', which facilitated China's comprehensive development in science, technology, economy, and society, as well as accelerating the formation of the technology market; (*iii*) the stage of technology market development. In January 1985, the State Council proposed the 'Provisional Regulations on Technology Transfer' (State Council 1985a), and in March pointed out that the 'technology market is an important component of socialist commodity market' in the 'Decision Made by the Central Committee of the Chinese Communist Party on Reform of Science and Technology' (State Council 1985b). So the status and role of the technology market in China was affirmed, and China made a breakthrough in some principle problems of commercialisation of technology achievements.

The overall development of the technology market can be measured by the total number and total value of technology transactions. In 2009, the size of China's technology market (contract value) was estimated at US$ 44.5 billion, nearly five times its size in 2000 (*China Statistical Yearbook on Science and Technology* 2010).[7]

(c) Establishment of China's National Nature Science Foundation (NNSF)

In February 1986, the State Council approved the establishment of the National Natural Science Foundation in order to support basic research, which developed into two blocks: project funding system and talent funding system. In addition, this foundation established a support pattern consisting of three levels: common project fund, key project fund and grand project fund, as well as a series of special funds. It has also developed an integrated personnel training and support system mainly consisting of the National Basic Science Talent Fund, Youth Science Fund, National Outstanding Youth Science Fund, and Innovation Research Group Fund through the implementation of a strategy of attracting and training excellent young scientific talents.

(d) Technology Policies

After 1986, China has changed the former policy-making pattern that combined science policy with technology policy, and formed a new separate technology policy-making system. Technology policy is an important basis to introduce the science and technology development planning, economic and social development planning, as well as guiding scientific research, technological innovation and introduction, industrial structure adjustment and development. Technology policy generally includes development objectives, industrial structure, technology options and ways to promote technology progress. At that time, China's technology policy made progress in the following areas: In 1986, the State Council issued the technology policy outlines in the 12 fields of energy, transportation, communication, agriculture, consumer goods industry, machine building, materials, building materials, urban construction, rural construction, urban and rural housing construction, and environmental protection. In this case, a number of national-level technology policies were developed, which also accelerated the research on technology policy and encouraged various sectors and regions to build up their own development policies.

(e) All Kinds of Science and Technology Plans

In high-tech areas, the Ministry of Science and Technology has developed the 'Spark Programme', '863 Programme', 'Torch Programme', as well as opening up the technology market and strengthening intellectual property rights protection by establishing high-tech zones, incubators, and so on. For programmes to support the commercialisation of research, such as the Torch Programme and the Spark Programme, the government accounts for no more than 2 per cent to 5 per cent of total funding, while local governments and enterprises typically provide large shares of funding for programmes related to innovation and dissemination of technologies.

Early in 1986, the Chinese government approved the implementation of the 'Spark Programme', the purpose of which was to introduce advanced and applicable technology to rural areas, guide hundreds of millions of farmers to develop a rural economy relying on science and technology, improve the overall quality of rural labour, as well as promote the sustainable, rapid and healthy development of agriculture and rural economy in China.

The '863 Programme' upheld the mission of 'focusing on the key fields with limited objectives', which conformed to the world-wide high-tech development trends and China's reality and demands. Seven fields were selected as keystones of China's high-tech research and development. These were bio-technology, space technology, information technology, laser technology, automation technology, energy technology, and new material technology (marine technology was included in 1996). The purpose of the '863 Programme' was to focus on a small number of elite forces, aiming at the forefront of the world in selected fields, thus narrowing the gap with developed countries, stimulating the achievements of science and technology in related fields, cultivating a number of high-level technical talents, as well as preparing for the development of high-tech industries in the future.

The Torch Programme was introduced in 1988, the purpose of which was to make good use of China's scientific and technological strengths and potential, to be market-oriented to facilitate the commercialisation, industrialisation and internationalisation of high-tech achievements. The Torch Programme encouraged researchers in universities and research institutes as well as technical entrepreneurship to go into business and start up high-tech firms. Since the State Council approved the establishment of the Beijing High-Tech Development Pilot Zone in 1988, China has established 86 state-level high-tech industrial development zones.

The main strengths of these programmes lie in their power to allocate public resources to the national priorities identified by the government (OECD 2008). It is widely recognised that these programmes have played a significant role in advancing science and technology in China by introducing the new funding mechanisms needed to move from the old science and technology system to the new market-based one, feeding economic development with science and technology inputs.

(f) Science and Technology Laws and Regulations

The development of the legislative framework of China's science and technology sector can be divided into two aspects. The first is that the effective implementation of science and technology legislative work has provided a better legal ground for administrative decision-makers. Since China's reform and opening-up, a series of legal documents have been issued, which improved the science and technology legal system further. Second, the technology law, regulations, as well as technology policies have constituted the initial legal framework of China's science and technology system.

In China, the first law for technology was about introducing technology in the field of cooperating with foreign firms or government. At the beginning of reform and opening-up, China introduced the 'Provisional Regulations on Technology Introduction and Equipment Import' (State Council 1981) and the 'Regulations on Technology Introduction Contracts' (State Council 1985c) in 1981 and 1985 respectively, in order to make technology introduction more normative.

The second important law was the 'Decision on Science and Technology Reform by the Central Committee of the Chinese Communist Party' issued in 1984, which began a prelude to China's reform of science and technology, and especially introduced a competition mechanism to encourage scientific research institutions to involve themselves in economic activities in various ways. Since then, China has developed a series of policies and programmes to promote changes in the science and technology system and to shape a new system combining science and technology with economic development.

The third far-reaching law was related to the high-tech development zones and technological start-ups. In 1988, the 'Provisional Regulations of Beijing High-Tech Development Pilot Zone' (State Council 1988) was introduced, which was the first approved set of regulations supporting new technology and high-tech technology by the State Council. Firms in pilot zones can enjoy a series of business concessions, such as tax reduction, export subsidy and loan, and so on. In order to stimulate the enthusiasm of different regions, besides Beijing, many cities such as Shanghai, Tianjin and Harbin, all developed local laws and regulations for the development of new technology and high-tech industries.

The fourth important law was the 'Patent Law of China' formally promulgated in 1984. In the era of planned economy, China lacked such a law, which severely limited the incentive for Chinese firms and individuals to engage in innovation. Consequently the introduction of this law has laid a far-reaching foundation to promote technology innovation and attract foreign direct investment (FDI). Without this law, China could not make today's scientific and technological progress, and would find it impossible to become the developing country attracting the most FDI.

Therefore, the laws and regulations framework at the beginning of China's reform and opening-up was very limited; all relevant laws and regulations were introduced in time in some important scientific and technological fields later.

Science and technology policies in the 1990s

The development of China's science and technology system entered a new phase marked by the holding of the 14th National Congress. In 1992, China established the development direction the construction of a socialist market economic system, and required that the science and technology policy should be adjusted around the development of the market economy. In the same year, the State Council issued the 'Key Points on Acclimatize Development to the Socialist Market Economy, and Deepen the Implementation of Science and Technology System Reform' (State Council 1992). In 1999, the National Innovation Conference was held, at which the 'Decision on Strengthening Technology Innovation, Developing High Technology, and Realizing Industrialization' (State Council 1999a) was issued. These policies stimulated further reform of the science and technology system in China.

(a) 'Relying on Science and Education to Rejuvenate the Nation' became a new science and technology development strategy

In May 1995, the 'Decision on Accelerating Science and Technology Progress by the Central Committee of the Chinese Communist Party and the State Council' (Central Committee of the Chinese Communist Party and the State Council 1995) was formally promulgated, which made clear that China would boost the economic and social development relying on science, technology and education, and also pointed out that science and technology are primary productive forces, and scientific and technological progress is a decisive factor on economic development. China should develop medium and long-term scientific development planning according to the national long-term needs, strengthen basic research and high-tech research, and accelerate the industrialization of high technology.

With the holding of the National Science and Technology Conference, 'Relying on Science and Education to Rejuvenate the Nation' has become an important development strategy in China.

(b) Establishing National Knowledge Innovation System and Attaching Importance to Sustainable Development

In June 1998, the first meeting of the National Science, Technology & Education Leading Group was held, at which 'the Report Outline on Pilot Implementation of Knowledge Innovation Programme' was discussed and passed, and it was determined that the Chinese Academy of Sciences would first initiate the 'Knowledge Innovation Programme' as a pilot base in establishing the NSI. In order to implement this important thinking, in August 1999, the Central Committee of the Chinese Communist Party and the State Council made the 'Decision on Strengthening Technology Innovation, Developing High Technology and Realizing Industrialization', and pointed out that 'strengthening technology innovation, developing high technology and realizing industrialization' is not only a solution to the deep-rooted problems faced by China's national economic development, but also a strategic choice for China to deal with international competition.

(c) Putting Forward and Implementing the Three Strategies of 'Talents, Patents and Technology Standards'

During the 'Tenth Five-Year' period (2001–2005), the Ministry of Science and Technology put forward the three strategies of

'Talents, Patents and Technology Standards', and for the first time integrated technology standards into the practice of science and technology.[8] In 2002, after the approval of the National Science, Technology & Education Leading Group, 12 important science and technology programmes including 'A Study on Important Technology Standards' (National Science, Technology & Education Leading Group 2002) were formally started. The first strategy was a human resources strategy, which was used to stimulate the participation in a scramble for international talents. The second was patent strategy, which was used to strengthen intellectual property rights management. The third was a technology standards strategy, which was used to establish and improve the system of technology standards in China. China is striving to promote its own technology standards and to comply with international standard settings. China's size, the dynamism of its domestic market and its rapidly evolving technological capabilities give it unique opportunities. It is now a strategy for China to use the standards regime to foster innovation.

(d) Issuing Financial and Taxation Policies Closely Related to Science and Technology

In 1996 and 1997, the Ministry of Finance in conjunction with other relevant departments developed the 'Management Rules of Three Items of Expenditure on Science and Technology' (Ministry of Finance 1996c), 'Notification on Finance and Taxation to Promote Technology Progress' (Ministry of Finance 1996e), 'Management Approach on Science and Technology Working Capital' (Ministry of Finance 1996a), 'Grant Funds Management Approach on National Key New Products' (Ministry of Finance 1996b), 'Loan and Discount Management Approach on Innovation Development of Large Equipment-Made Project' (Ministry of Finance 1997a), 'Loan and Discount Management Approach on Application of Electronic Information' (Ministry of Finance 1997b), 'Loan and Discount Management Approach on Special Technology Renovation Project' (Ministry of Finance 1997c), and so on. The promulgation of the above policies beneficially promoted the implementation of technology policies.

Many fiscal and taxation policies promulgated during this period were closely related to the development of science and technology at that time. The introduction and implementation of these policies have promoted the rapid development of science and technology to some different degrees. Moreover, with the gradual establishment of China's market economic system, the financial and taxation measures have increasingly accounted for a large proportion of all measures in promoting science and technology development, which were also much better than those measures simply relying on administrative allocation in the period of the planned economy.

There are three very important financial policies that closely related to science and technology. The first is the 'Rules on the Implementation of the Budget Law of People's Republic of China' (State Council 1995) promulgated by the State Council in 1995. The second is the 'Management Rules of Three Items of Expenditure on Science and Technology' (Ministry of Finance 1996c) issued by the Ministry of Finance in 1996, in which the three items of expenditure on science and technology refer to expenses for trial manufacture of new products, expenses for intermediate experiments, and subsidies for major scientific research projects established by the government to support science and technology development. The third is the 'Notice on Financial and Taxation Issues in Promoting Enterprises' Technological Progress' (Ministry of Finance 1996d) also issued by the Ministry of Finance in 1996, which encouraged enterprises to increase their technology development input and undertake more joint development with institutions, such as research institutes and universities, which also aimed to accelerate the industrialisation and commercialisation of technology achievements from enterprises, as well as promoted the upgrading of their machines and equipments.

Enactment of some taxation policies has had a more obvious effect on science and technology development. For example, the State Council and the General Administration of Customs promulgated the 'Provisional Rules on Scientific Research and Teaching Equipments Exempt from Import Taxation' in 1997 (State Council and the General Administration of Customs 1997), which pointed out that a certain number of scientific research and teaching equipments imported by non-profit scientific research institutes and universities used for scientific research and teaching directly could be exempted from both value-added tax (VAT) and consumption tax. In 1999, the Ministry of Finance and State Administration of Taxation issued the 'Notice on Taxation Policies to Accelerate the Commercialization of Science and Technology Achievements' (Ministry of Finance and State Administration of Taxation 1999), which proposed that scientific research institutes and universities' income from technology transfer could be exempt from turnover tax.

(e) Implementation of the 'Decision on Strengthening Technology Innovation, Developing High-Tech and Realizing Industrialization by the Central Committee of the Chinese Communist Party and the State Council'

In August 1999, the Central Committee of the Chinese Communist Party and the State Council held a meeting in Beijing, at which the 'Decision on Strengthening Technology Innovation, Developing High-Tech and Realizing Industrialization by the Central Committee of the Chinese Communist Party and the State Council' was issued. This was a decision made by the CPC in line with the actual situation of world economy and technology development trends, as well as the development of domestic economy, science and technology. This policy was a typical top-down policy-making model, which aimed to emphasise innovation and industrialisation of high and new technology. Therefore, the introduction of this policy has far-reaching effects on China's technological innovation.

The Science Conference held in 1978, the National Science and Technology Conference held in 1995 and the National Innovation Conference held in 1999 all reflected the new demands of the evolution of science and technology policies and economic development on science and technology development strategy. Corresponding with the National Innovation Conference, the Central Committee of the Chinese Communist Party issued many new policies in this period, such as the policies on promoting the transfer of scientific and technological achievements. In February 1999, the General Office of the State Council transmitted the 'Suggestion on Reform of Scientific Research Institutions Affiliated to 10 State-Level Bureaus and Managed by the State Economic and Trade Commission' (Ministry of Science and Technology et al. 1999) made by six departments including the Ministry of Science and Technology and the State Economic and Trade Commission. In addition, the State Council issued 'Policies on Encouraging Development of Software Industry and IC Industry' (State Council 2000). Therefore, a surge of policies promoting technology innovation and developing high-tech emerged around 1999.

(*f*) *Science and Technology Laws and Regulations in the 1990s*

Most of China's science and technology laws and regulations were introduced in the 1990s. In July 1993, the Standing Committee of the National People's Congress discussed and passed the 'Science and Technology Progress Law of People's Republic of China' (Standing Committee of the National People's Congress 1993), which came into operation on 1 October, 1993. This science and technology law was a basic one to guide and promote the development of science and technology in the new era, which was not only a fundamental norm to promote science and technology progress, but also the foundation to develop a set of corresponding laws and regulations. At present, most local governments formulate the 'Regulations on Science and Technology Progress' (National People's Congress 1993b) in accordance with this. Overall, the 'Law on Science and Technology Progress of People's Republic of China' (National People's Congress 1993c) combined the basic strategy of governing the country by law with the development strategy of 'Relying on Science and Education to Rejuvenate the Nation', and played a very important role in promoting, guiding, regulating, and safeguarding China's science and technology progress and innovation.

The mission of science and technology development in the 1990s was to promote the commercialisation of scientific and technological achievements. On the one hand, this was due to the acceleration of the international scientific and technological revolution, especially the push of knowledge-based economy from US; on the other hand, the high rate of domestic economic development needed the contribution from the science and technology sector.

In July 1993, the National People's Congress passed the 'Agricultural Popularization Law of People's Republic of China' (National People's Congress 1993a), which was to strengthen the popularisation of agricultural technology, promote the application of agricultural scientific and technological achievements into agricultural practice as soon as possible, as well as ensure the development of agriculture and realise the modernisation of agriculture.

In August 1999, the Central Committee of the Chinese Communist Party and the State Council promulgated the 'Decision on Strengthening Technology Innovation, Developing High Technology and Realizing Industrialization', which was an important decision for China to deal with world-wide scientific and technological revolution. Before this decision, the Chinese government has issued seven supporting policy documents. In March 1999, the 'Provisions on Promotion of Commercialization of Scientific and Technological Achievements' (Central Committee of the Chinese Communist Party and the State Council 1999b) was introduced, and in May 1999, the 'Regulations on Science and Technology Progress Award' (Central Committee of the Chinese Communist Party and the State Council 1999d) was issued, and in December, the 'Implementing Rules of Science and Technology Progress Award' (Central Committee of the Chinese Communist Party and the State Council 1999a) was launched; other dozens of laws and regulations were also issued such as the 'Regulations of Natural Sciences Award' (Central Committee of the Chinese Communist Party and the State Council 1999c).

(g) Knowledge Innovation Project

In June 1998, the National Science, Technology & Education Leading Group discussed and approved the 'Report Outlines on Pilot Implementation of Knowledge Innovation Project' by the Chinese Academy of Sciences, with which the Chinese Academy of Sciences started to implement the science and technology system reform and innovation. The basic tasks of the Knowledge Innovation Project were the following:

First, developing and maintaining a strong national-level knowledge innovation capability. The Knowledge Innovation Project was to engage in basic research and strategic research to resolve the basic, strategic, comprehensive, forward-looking, and critical scientific and technological issues in China's industrialisation construction, by aiming at national strategic targets and the frontier of world-wide science and technology.

Second, speeding up the dissemination of the latest scientific and technological knowledge. On the one hand, the Knowledge Innovation Project was to train and continuously provide a large number of high-quality scientific technological personnel with a stream of information on cutting edge innovation during the process of scientific research. On the other hand, the Knowledge Innovation Project was to enhance the popularisation of science and technology, and make a contribution to improve people's scientific and technological capabilities.

Third, promoting knowledge and technology transfer comprehensively. The Knowledge Innovation Project was to promote the development of China's high technology sectors such as information, new material, biotechnology, as well as the technology upgrading of traditional industries. In addition, it was to provide a solid foundation and knowledge sources to enhancing China's innovation capability.

Fourth, providing technological and scientific advice to national macroeconomic policy-making. The Knowledge Innovation Project was to strength the Chinese Academy of Sciences and the strategic development research of national science and technology, education, economy, and safety, in order to provide advice and basis, as well as make recommendations and conduct a scientific evaluation of China's macro policy-making.

Fifth, training and fostering a contingent of world-class professionals with a good mastery of advanced science and technology through the principles of open and fair competition on the basis of merits.

Sixth, strengthening the construction of national knowledge innovation bases continuously. The Knowledge Innovation Project was to deepen the reform of the science and technology system, gradually improve and establish a new modern national research agency system in conformity with the international practice and domestic actual situation, focus on building and supporting those world-class national knowledge innovation bases among which a number of bases should strive to become one of the acknowledged international research centres in the world or an important part of international research centres.

Taking various factors into account, the central government developed additional pilot special funds for the Knowledge Innovation Project during 1998–2002.

(b) Enterprise-based Reforms in Applied Science Research Institutions

With the accelerating pace of reform of government agencies, the State Council decided to start the management system reform of 242 institutes affiliated to 10 state-level bureaus, which were managed by the National Economic and Trade Committee at the end of 1998, through which these institutions turned themselves into scientific and technological enterprises or intermediary services. The purpose of this reform was to reduce the number of independent state-level applied research institutions, encourage enterprises to establish their own applied research institutions and become a mainstay of technological innovation. In order to promote the implementation of this science and technology system reform smoothly, the relevant national ministries issued numerous complementary policies, including taxation policies, industrial and technology policies, and so on.

Science and technology policies in the 21st century

The strategic significance of indigenous innovation was formally established at the National Science and Technology Conference held in 2006, and the 'Outline of National Medium- and Long-Term Strategic Plan for the Development of Science and Technology (2006–2020)' (State Council 2006a) was also issued at this conference, which marked and indicated a significant transition and readjustment of China's science and technology development strategy from imitation-based innovation to indigenous innovation. Based on the actual local and global conditions, regarding the enhancement of indigenous innovation capability as a core strategy, constructing an innovation-based country as a goal, this plan made an overall scheme and deployment plan for China's science and technology development in the next 15 years, and was a programmatic document in guiding the new era. This plan pointed out that the guideline of China's science and technology development in the new era was to build an innovation-based economy by fostering indigenous innovation capabilities, to foster an enterprise-centred technology innovation system and enhance the innovation capabilities of Chinese firms, to achieve major breakthroughs in the targeted strategic areas of technological development and basic research.

To this end, the State Council announced late in 2006 a new policy package covering nine broad categories:

(a) Protecting Intellectual Property Rights, and Improving Intellectual Property Rights System

In view of the current status that intellectual property rights have not yet played a significant role in supporting China's indigenous innovation strategy, the State Council issued the 'Several Related Policies of the Outline of National Medium- and Long-Term Strategic Plan for the Development of Science and Technology (2006–2020)' (State Council 2006b), which pointed out that the introduction of five policies by the Chinese government would protect intellectual property rights, further improve China's intellectual property rights system and create a legal environment respecting and protecting intellectual property rights. The contents of these policies covered the property rights of key technologies and products of indigenous innovation, the establishment of international standards, the reinforcement of an intellectual property rights system, stronger control on intellectual property rights protection, shortening the patent review cycle, and a preferential treatment in government procurement for new products.

(b) Giving Full Support to Talented Personnel

There are about 14 policies on supporting talented personnel, which have developed detailed and operational rules mainly for post-doctoral, high-level overseas talents, innovative talents cultivation, scarce talents in key areas, and continuous education for professional and technical personnel.

In order to further improve the post-doctoral system and give it full play to strengthen high-level professional and technical talents team construction, the Ministry of Personnel promulgated the 'Eleventh Five-Year Plan on Post-Doctoral System' (Ministry of Human Resources and Social Security 2006) in October 2006, which set the main objective, stressed the necessity to increase investment and implement the Special Assistance Scheme. Moreover, this plan required that the annual subsidiary standard for each post-doctoral should increase 67 per cent after 2006, more attention should be paid to the construction of post-doctoral workstations, and the international exchanges and cooperation for them should be expanded.

There are several programmes on nurturing outstanding scientific talents in China now, such as the Yangtze River Scholar Programme, the Chinese Academy of Sciences (CAS) Hundred Talents Programme, the Truth Award, the Special Research Fund for University Doctorate-Awarding Units, the Fund for Overseas Chinese Scholars, and so on.

Four departments including the Ministry of Finance issued the 'Guidelines on Implementation of Incentive Distribution System of Indigenous Innovation in Enterprises' (Ministry of Finance 2006a) in October 2006, the core requirements of which were that high-tech enterprises can reward critical R&D staff by equity (shares) or by a certain coefficient of income from the sales price (shares) during the implementation of corporate capital transformation into share capital. The Ministry of Science and Technology issued the 'Interim Procedures of Strengthening Innovative Talents Training in the Implementation of Major Projects' (Ministry of Science and Technology 2006b), which emphasised that the proportion of young researchers (no more than 45 years old) in a team should be no less than 60 per cent in principle; the proportion of young leaders in a major project (no more than 45 years old) among all project leaders should be no less than 60 per cent in principle.

(c) Increasing Science and Technology Investment

There are about seven policies relevant to science and technology investment, which introduced a number of management regulations mainly targeting the 973 Special Programme, 863 Special Programme, National Science and Technology Support Programme, Public Welfare Special Programme. They focused on standardising and strengthening national management of these special programmes so as to improve the capital efficiency. On 30 September 2006, the Ministry of Finance and the Ministry of Science and Technology issued the 'Management Measures of Special Funds in National Key Basic Research Development Programme' (Ministry of Finance and the Ministry of Science and Technology 2006a), which clearly notified that the expenditure of the 973 Special Programme should include 11 items, and also provided a very detailed rule of management fee; on the same day, these two ministries also issued 'Management Measures of Special Funds of National Science and Technology Support Programme' (Ministry of Finance and the Ministry of Science and Technology 2006b), which clearly distinguished the fund free of charge and the loan-funded financial support, encouraged the exploration of other sources of funding, and guided the social capital to enter fields of science and technology.

(d) Strengthening the Construction of Science and Technology Innovation Bases and Platforms

There are about 11 policies to support the construction of science and technology innovation bases and platforms, which are mainly for the National Engineering Laboratory, science and technology parks in universities, technological business incubator, National Engineering Centre, firms' technology centre, State Key Laboratory, and so on.

In July 2006, the National Development and Reform Commission promulgated the 'Guideline on Construction of National Engineering Laboratory'. In November 2006, the Ministry of Science and Technology and the Ministry of Education jointly issued the 'Identification and Management Rules of National University Science and Technology Park (USTP)' (Ministry of Science and

Technology and the Ministry of Education 2006b), which gave a detailed illustration of the identification and management of university science and technology parks, and especially highlighted a number of conditions of the application of national university science and technology parks. For example, more than 50 per cent of enterprises in university science and technology parks should have a strong relationship with universities in technology achievements and talented personnel; more than 85 per cent administrative managers should have a bachelor's degree or above; the number of enterprises in the incubator should be more than 50. In addition, the 'Suggestions on Further Promoting Research Bases and Its Facilities Open to Enterprises and Community' (Ministry of Science and Technology and the Ministry of Education. 2006a), the 'Guideline on Construction of National Key Laboratory Relying on Transformed Institutions and Enterprises' (Ministry of Science and Technology and the Ministry of Education. 2006c) and other policies were issued.

(e) Enhancing the Development of Education and Science Popularisation

There are about seven policies to support education and science popularisation, which include some guidelines, notifications and management rules mainly for the construction of national key disciplines, national-level programmes for sending people to study abroad, carrying out science popularisation activities, and enhancing the innovation capability of universities. For example, in October 2006, the Ministry of Education issued the 'Guidelines on Strengthening the Construction of National Key Disciplines' (Ministry of Education 2006a), which emphasised the importance of establishing multiple input mechanisms for the construction of national key disciplines, integrating resources to speed up the development of national key disciplines, as well as giving full play to the role of national key disciplines as backbone and model. At the same time, the Ministry of Education also issued the 'Provisional Measures on Construction and Management of National Key Disciplines' (Ministry of Education 2006b), which clarified identification and evaluation issues. In order to carry out the task of science popularisation, in November 2006, seven departments including the Ministry of Science and Technology, the Ministry of Education, and the Propaganda Department of the Central Committee of the Chinese Communist Party jointly issued the 'Guidelines on Carrying Out

Science Popularity Activities by Scientific Research Institutions and Universities to the Society' (Ministry of Science and Technology et al. 2006), which required that the participation units should create good conditions and gradually increase the opening hours of science popularity activities, so that by the end of 'Eleventh Five-Year' Plan, the annual opening hours of science popularity activities should be no less than 15 days in general. Moreover, seven departments including the Ministry of Science and Technology jointly issued the 'Guidelines on Strengthening Capability of National Science Popularization' in January 2007 in order to promote the capability of science popularisation through a number of measures.

(f) Venture Capital and Financial Policies

There are about nine policies on financial support, which are mainly for the credit guarantee system for small and mid-sized enterprises, high-tech enterprise insurance services, establishing and improving intellectual property trade market, funds on guiding venture capital for technological small and medium-sized enterprises, and so on. In order to resolve the problems in the construction of a credit guarantee system for small and mid-sized enterprises, in November 2006, the General Office of the State Council issued the 'Notification on Strengthening the Construction of Credit Guarantee System for Small and Medium-Sized Enterprises' (State Council 2006a), which emphasised the necessity to establish and improve the risk compensation mechanism and the tax preference policies in security agencies, as well as promote the mutual beneficial cooperation between the security agencies and financial institutions, and so on. In December 2006, the China Banking Regulatory Commission issued the 'Guidelines on the Reform of Commercial Bank and the Enforcement of Financial Services for High-Tech Enterprises' (China Banking Regulatory Commission 2006a) and developed 18 detailed guiding rules, in order to create a better financial environment to support and encourage indigenous innovation. At the same time, another policy of 'Implementing Regulations of Financial Policies to Support National Key Science and Technology Programmes' (China Banking Regulatory Commission 2006b) was issued, which proposed some requirements from the perspectives of supporting areas, conditions, risk prevention and control, and so on.

(g) Tax Incentives for Innovation in the Business Sector

There are about nine policies relating to tax incentives, which are mainly for income tax preferential policies on enterprises' technological innovation, provisional regulations tax exempting scientific and technological development equipment imports, taxation policy on national university science and technology parks as well as scientific and technological incubators, and regulations of exempting scientific research and educational equipment imports from tax, and so on.

In December 2006, the Ministry of Finance and the State Administration of Taxation jointly issued the 'Notification on Income Tax Preferential Policies for Enterprises' Technological Innovation' (Ministry of Finance and the State Administration of Taxation 2006b), which clearly required that after 1 January 2006, the new high-tech enterprises setting up in the National High-Tech Development Zones can enjoy income tax exemption within the two years after they show profit, and enjoy the 15 per cent annual income tax after the first two years. At the same time, another policy, the 'Notification on Adjustment of Pre-Tax Deduction Policy of Income Tax' (Ministry of Finance and the State Administration of Taxation 2006a) was also issued.

(h) Public Procurement Policies

Public procurement can help promote innovation and accelerate the diffusion of innovative products and services. Public procurement should give priority to products developed by domestic firms through indigenous innovation. The Chinese government has recognised this point and began to implement it. There are about six policies relating to public procurement, which are mainly for identification of national indigenous innovation products, budget management of government procurement, evaluation rules, contract management rules, import and export management regulations, order management regulations, and so on.

On 26 December 2006, the Ministry of Science and Technology, the National Development and Reform Commission, and the Ministry of Finance jointly issued the 'Management Regulations on Identification of National Indigenous Innovation Products (For Trial Implementation)' (Ministry of Science and Technology et al. 2006), which was to develop rules on identification of indigenous innovation products. Subsequently, the Ministry of Finance successively issued a series of policies, such as the 'Management Rules on Government Procurement Budget of Indigenous Innovation Products' (Ministry of Finance 2006), 'Regulations on Government Procurement Evaluation of Indigenous Innovation Products' (Ministry of Finance 2006c), 'Management Rules on Government Procurement Contract of Indigenous Innovation Products' (Ministry of Finance 2006d), and so on, which were conducted to promote China's indigenous innovation and improve the competitiveness of indigenous innovation products.

(i) Science and Technology Legislation

The science and technology policy in China affects all public policies. Many of these science and technology policies were established to match with the reform and development of the national science and technology strategy and system. From the 21st century, with the setting of the development of indigenous innovation as China's national strategy, a number of new science and technology policies were issued. With the release of the 'Outline of National Medium- and Long-Term Science and Technology Development Planning' in January 2006, a development guideline was proposed as 'indigenous innovation, achieving a leap-frog development in key fields, sustainable development and guiding the future', and the goal was set as 'improving the capability of indigenous innovation and constructing an innovation-oriented society'. With the gradual improvement of the socialist market economic system and implementation of national medium- and long-term science and technology planning, China's science and technology innovation policies and relevant economic supporting policies should be readjusted in keeping with the new context, which proposes new requirements to improve national science and technology legislation further, and especially, the science and technology legislation should keep pace with the development of science and technology innovation. The highlights of the major amendments of the 'Science and Technology Progress Law' on 1 July 2008, were that indigenous innovation and construction of an innovation-oriented society were included in this law. The view that enterprises should become the main actors of scientific and technological innovation was also included in this law, and establishing modern scientific research institutions was clearly proposed.

Outcomes of State Policy and State Institutions on the NSI

Since the 1980s, the Chinese government at all levels has taken a variety of measures, such as policies promulgation, implementation of science and technology planning, direct financial investment or subsidies, tax incentives, financial leverage regulation, public procurement, implementation of science and technology awards, as well as involvement of technology management elements in resource allocation, in order to promote science and technology progress and innovation. The policy portfolio includes direct means, as well as indirect means, and targeted as well as neutral intervention. In the key fields of science and technology development, the reform of the science and technology system, conditions and basic platform of scientific research, industrialisation, science and technology intermediary service system, flow of scientific and technological talents, as well as international cooperation, the Chinese government has developed and implemented a large number of normative policy documents and created a good environment for science and technology progress and innovation. These policies have played a very important role in the development of China's science, technology, economy, and society, which are mainly represented as the following areas:

First, they greatly enhanced the awareness of scientific and technological innovation as well as competition, and the adaptive changes of these minds are an important foundation to the development of innovation activities. For example, the R&D intensity — the ratio of gross domestic expenditure on research and development (GERD) to gross domestic product (GDP) — of China's economy has increased spectacularly. It reached 1.47 per cent of GDP in 2008, up from 0.6 per cent in 1995 (Figure 5.6). In addition, China has developed a huge pool of human resources for science and technology. With 1.64 million full-time equivalent (FTE) researchers in 2008, China has ranked second in the world since 2000, after the United States (Figure 5.7).

Figure 5.6: *China's R&D Intensity, 1994–2008 (GERD as a Percentage of GDP)*

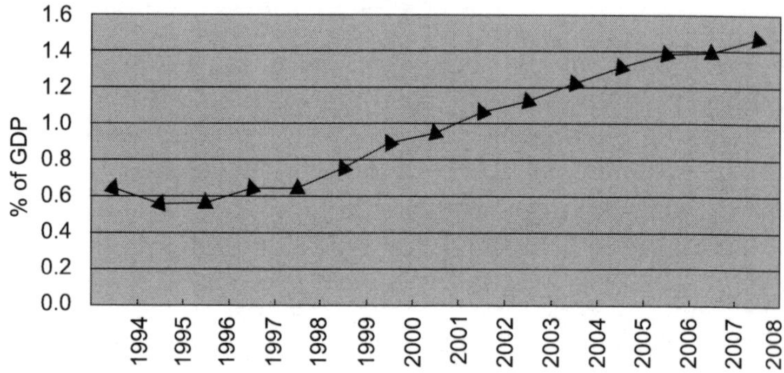

Source: *China Statistical Yearbook on Science and Technology* (1996–2010).

Figure 5.7: *The Number of Researchers in China, 1995–2009: Total Researchers (FTE)*

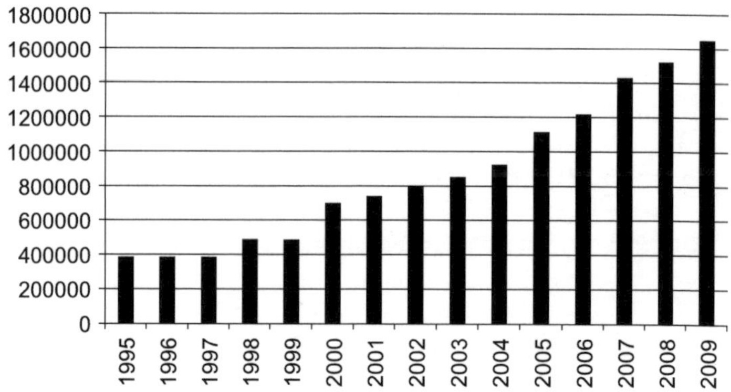

Source: *China Statistical Yearbook on Science and Technology* (1996–2010).

Second, they promoted the combination of science, technology and economy. The role that science and technology plays has increasingly influenced economic restructuring, the transformation of traditional industries, as well as the development of high technology. Many scientific research institutions further defined the development direction of scientific and technological innovation in accordance with the industrial or regional economic development strategy and market demand after their transformation. In addition, these scientific research institutions also participated in the major national or local scientific and technological projects jointly with other enterprises, carried out the R&D and application of major common technology, developed high technology, and drove the upgrading of traditional industries, which made the support power of science and technology on economic and social development increase gradually.

Third, the transformation of technology development–based research institutions into enterprises promoted the process during which enterprises have become innovation subjects. Since 1985, China has made great efforts in promoting the market-oriented reform of the science and technology system, which sped up the transformation of application-oriented research institutions into enterprises, promoted the enterprises to become innovation subjects, as well as cultivated a large number of scientific and technological enterprises. The percentage of enterprises' R&D expenditure in total social R&D expenditure increased from 59.95 per cent in 2000 to 72.28 per cent in 2007 (see Table 5.3).

Table 5.3: *R&D Expenditure by Performer in China, 2000–2007 (percentage)*

Year	*Enterprises*	*Research Institutions*	*Higher Education*	*Others*
2000	59.95	28.80	8.56	2.68
2001	60.43	27.67	9.82	2.07
2002	61.18	27.28	10.14	1.40
2003	62.37	25.92	10.54	1.18
2004	66.83	21.95	10.22	1.00
2005	68.32	20.94	9.89	0.85
2006	71.08	18.89	9.22	0.82
2007	72.28	18.54	8.48	0.69

Source: *China Statistical Yearbook on Science and Technology* (2001–2008).

Fourth, the scientific and technological business incubators, productivity promotion centres, science and technology advice and evaluation agencies developed fast, which gradually constitutes a scientific and technological service system. By 2007, China had more than 1,000 productivity promotion centres, more than 500 scientific and technological business incubators, more than 400 venture capital institutions, more than 400 science and technology information and intelligence agencies, as well as more than 2,300 various kinds of scientific and technological advice and evaluation agencies, which all promoted the science and technology innovation and industrial development. A large number of independent intellectual property rights accumulated by colleges, universities and scientific research institutions have been commercialised into practical productivity rapidly, during which a number of forces engaged in commercialisation of scientific and technological achievements are developed. For example, Tsinghua University, Peking University and Shanghai Jiao Tong University all have their own listed companies. By the end of 2005, the number of national private technological companies had reached 143,991, the total revenue of which was 6.1218 trillion Yuan. Among these enterprises, the revenue of 8,168 was more than 0.1 billion Yuan, the revenue of 874 was more than 1 billion Yuan (Ministry of Science and Technology 2006a). In addition, many high-tech enterprises with considerable international competitiveness have emerged, such as ZTE, Huawei, and so on.

Fifth, they promoted the development of high-tech industries. Since the 1980s, China has promoted the development of high-tech industries through the establishment of high-tech industrial development pilot zones. In May 1988, the State Council approved the establishment of the Beijing New Technology Industry Development Pilot Zone and granted 18 preferential policies to it. In August of the same year, the implementation of the 'Torch Programme' was started. At present, China has established 54 National High-Tech Industrial Development Zones all over the country. In 2006, 30,403 enterprises were identified as high-tech in these zones, the new product sales revenue of which was 811.98 billion Yuan, and the new product sales revenue accounted for 22.5 per cent of total product sales revenue (Ministry of Science and Technology 2008).

Sixth, the promotion of industrialisation of scientific and technological achievements enhanced the industrial core competitiveness. Through the implementation of relevant national industrialisation plans, China has made major breakthroughs in the information industry, bio-industry, new material industry, new energy industry, manufacturing industry, and so on, which made a great contribution to promote the upgrading of industrial structure, enhance the industrial core competitiveness and promote China's economic and social development.

China has made great achievements in the development of science, technology, economy, and society due to the introduction of all these policies, but a wide gap still exists between these achievements and the demands of China's economic and social development, and a number of obstacles and problems in China's scientific and technological innovation and development need to be resolved. Chinese enterprises have not really become as active as they could be in the commercialisation of scientific and technological achievements. As most Chinese enterprises are lacking in technological capabilities and participate in market competition relying mainly on cost advantages both at home and abroad, they usually do not have enough capability of transforming new technology into innovation. They also tend to be risk averse and suffer from a low level of financing capability. A corresponding fact to this is that universities and scientific research institutions have become the performers of technological innovation. As a large number of scientific and technological achievements come directly from science and technology projects supported by the national level rather than the market players with demands of commercialisation, many of them do not have high technical practicality and only stay at the laboratory stage, so that it is difficult for them to meet the actual needs of enterprises. For example, in all national-level science and technology programmes, the projects assumed by universities and scientific research institutions account for 90 per cent, and the technical and economic practicality of achievements of these projects is not high and cannot meet the actual needs of enterprises.

The environmental factors for commercialisation of scientific and technological achievements need to be improved. At present, there are many imperfections in the state support for the industrialisation of indigenous innovation achievements. The law and regulations on promoting industrialisation of scientific and technological achievements still need extensive refinement. Intellectual property rights protection is weak and the problem of infringement of intellectual property rights is still serious, which leads to the fact that it is difficult for enterprises to appropriate the returns on their investments in indigenous innovation. The financial system to support the industrialisation of scientific and technological achievements in China is still weak. The support and incubation services for start-up enterprises are weak and the implementation of government procurement measures is still ineffective. Because of these factors, the state is still not providing enough support on indigenous innovation achievements.

It is still very difficult for talents to flow between research institutions and enterprises. Since enterprises on their own cannot provide a stable research environment and there is a gap between research institutions and enterprises in research conditions, it is difficult for talents to flow between enterprises and research institutions. At present, there are tens of thousands of engineering Ph.D. graduates every year in China, most of whom enter into universities and scientific research institutions, leaving only a small portion to enter into enterprises.

Conclusion

In the past three decades since the reform and opening-up, China's NSI has experienced deep structural changes. First, the core of the NSI has transformed from the scientific research institutions into enterprises. Second, the base of the NSI has transformed from a dependence on imported innovation to an increasing reliance on indigenous innovation. Third, the composition of innovators has been transformed from only state-owned enterprises into a mix of public and private sector enterprises. Fourth, the NSI has transformed from a close innovation model into a global innovation model. Fifth, the NSI has transformed from the one led by cost advantage into that led by innovation. These five aspects have greatly changed China's innovation pattern. During the transition, as an initiator of the NSI, the government has been playing an irreplaceable role.

In spite of its significant and remarkable achievements, China still has a long way to go to build a modern, enterprise-centred and efficient NSI. To achieve this goal, it will have to maintain a high level of investment in R&D, innovation and education and overcome the remaining institutional and structural weaknesses of its current innovation system.

The near future is a critical period for China to implement the strategy of indigenous innovation. In order to promote the construction of the NSI in the new era, the Chinese government must play a leading role in the establishment and improvement of the science and technology system in the basic framework of a socialist market economic system. In addition, the relationship between the market mechanism and the state should be more fully addressed. The guiding, planning and encouraging role of the national science and technology policies as well as macro science and technology management rules must be given full play, and the market mechanism should play a basic role in the allocation of scientific and technological resources. China's allocation and integration of scientific and technological resources must be implemented from the perspective of a national strategy in order to improve the capability of science and technology innovation and comprehensive competitiveness in essence on a national level.

China should continue to deepen the reform of science and technology system, and construct an institutional framework of the NSI. Two tasks in the reform of the science and technology system are essential to the construction of the NSI. One is to deepen the reform of scientific research institutions, and the other is to change the role of the state. The core elements of the NSI are enterprises, scientific research institutions and government agencies, which correspond to the technological innovation, knowledge innovation and institutional innovation respectively, and are the backbone of the NSI. The reform of science and technology policy is designed to put all performers of innovation in the right positions and make them perform their respective duties. The government should play a role in the three aspects. It should construct an institutional and policy environment conducive to innovation, including a venture capital management system and an intellectual property system, which are necessary both to increase the propensity of domestic firms to innovate and to maintain China's attractiveness for knowledge-intensive foreign direct investment. It should play a leading role in the areas marked by a prevalence of market and systemic failures through direct involvement in technology innovation activities and the provision of public goods and common basic technology. Finally, it should guide the science and technology development of some specific industries following the principle of 'to be aware that there are things must be done and things must not be done', as well as make the innovation resources in line with the interests of specific industries through making good use of various financial means.

China should continue to improve the organising mechanism for science and technology programmes and major science and technology projects and straighten out the relationships among all kinds of innovation subjects in order to improve the efficiency of the NSI. Various kinds of science and technology programmes and major special projects are the most important innovation activities, and the government usually invests and allocates innovation resources through the organisation of these innovation activities, so they can be regarded as a lubricant for the NSI. The successful organisation of these major innovation activities, to a large extent, can improve the NSI and its efficiency. During the process of organisation of major science and technology innovation, initiating the full mobilisation of various innovation subjects in the NSI should be considered. Meanwhile, an innovation aggregation should be established, which regards enterprises as a core element and forms a close relationship among the government, industry and learning. The application of science and technology projects should require not only the participation of enterprises, but also the support and incubation of innovation activities of enterprises, and the conditions created for enterprises' technological innovation through various financial means. Led by the national science and technology programmes, all performers of innovation in the NSI should interact with each other frequently, so that the mutual cooperation can be realised as well as their complementary advantages can be finally developed.

China should explore diversified scientific and technological investment and financing means, and guide the development of the NSI in line with the interests of the country. The government guidance on the NSI refers to the innovation resources allocation that the government implements through the means of science and technology investment, personnel training, policy-making, and so on, which make the development of the NSI in line with the national interests and development strategy. How to use the science and technology investment policy to guide the efficient allocation of science and technology resources in the NSI is a challenging task that the Chinese government is facing. Only a wide range of science and technology investment and financing methods are explored actively but China can achieve the purpose of allocating resources through science and technology investment and making the resources from all aspects of society flow and participate in science and technology innovation activities. The Chinese government should utilise its capability of mobilising and allocating the scientific and technological resources of the whole society through direct financial investment, tax incentives and other means. The state financial input is mainly used to support public science and technology activities, such as basic research, cutting-edge high-tech research, social welfare research, and major common technology, which the market mechanism cannot resolve effectively. For those projects with high degree of market-orientation and good market prospects, enterprises should be guided actively to become the main investment agents.

Finally, a systematic science and technology evaluation and monitoring mechanism should be established, which is used to monitor and evaluate the efficiency of the NSI. The evaluation and monitoring of the NSI refers mainly to scientific and technological projects and investment. In developed countries, they have already established relatively efficient systems for science and technology evaluation and monitoring. Compared with the year-on-year increase of scientific and technological investment and the improvement of scientific and technological system, the construction of China's science and technology evaluation and monitoring system lags behind. The existing science and technology evaluation and monitoring is still at the project level without top-level design. A systematic scientific and technological evaluation and monitoring mechanism as well as the relevant laws and regulations should be established urgently, and which also should be implemented into practice in order to adjust the allocation of science and technology resources and improve the efficiency in using these resources.

Notes

1. 'Scientific Outlook of Development' was proposed by President Hu Jintao in the speech 'Hold Highly the Great Banner of Socialism with Chinese Characteristics, and Strive for New Victories in Building a Moderately Prosperous Society' at the 17th National Congress of Chinese Communist Party on 15 October 2007.
2. This was a popular metaphor to describe the egalitarian phenomenon during China's planned economy.
3. 'Three capital' refers to three types of foreign-funded enterprises: foreign joint ventures, Sino-foreign cooperative enterprises and wholly foreign-owned enterprises.
4. 'Emancipating the Mind and Seeking Truth from Facts' was proposed by Mr Deng Xiaoping in the speech 'Emancipating the Mind, Seeking Truth from Facts, Look Forward as a United One' at the closing ceremony of CPC Central Committee Working Conference on 13 December 1978.
5. 'Four Cardinal Principles' was generalised by Mr Deng Xiaoping in the speech 'Uphold the Four Cardinal Principles' at a CPC theory-discussing meeting on 30 March 1979.

6. The nominal values of R&D expenditure and technology import in RMB were converted to US$ using the annual average exchange rates in 1995 (1US$ = 8.31 RMB), 2000 (1 US$=8.28 RMB) and 2005 (1 US$= 8.19 RMB).
7. The nominal values of R&D expenditure and technology import in RMB were converted to US$ using the annual average exchange rates in 1995 (1US$ = 8.31 RMB) and 2005 (1 US$= 8.19 RMB).
8. These three strategies were proposed by Xu Guanhua, minister of science and technology, in the speech 'Making Overall Arrangements, Emphasizing Key Points, and Making Earnest Efforts to Do Science and Technology Work Well in 2002' at the National Science and Technology Work Conference on 9–10 January 2002.

References

Cassiolato, J. E. and V. Vitorino, 2009. *BRICS and Development Alternatives: Innovation Systems and Policies*. London: Anthem Press.

Central Committee of the Chinese Communist Party and the State Council, 1995. 'Decision on Accelerating Science and Technology Progress by the Central Committee of the Chinese Communist Party and the State Council', Government of the People's Republic of China.

Chen, Y., 1995. *Selected Works of Chen Yun*. Beijing: People's Publishing House.

China Banking Regulatory Commission, 2006a. 'Guidelines on the Reform of Commercial Bank and the Enforcement of Financial Services for High-Tech Enterprises', China Banking Regulatory Commission, Beijing.

———, 2006b. 'Implementing Regulations of Financial Policies to Support National Key Science and Technology Programmes', China Banking Regulatory Commission, Beijing.

China Daily, 2005. 'High Tide', http://www.chinadaily.com.cn/english/doc/2005-12/12/content_502577.htm (accessed 12 December 2005).

Communist Party of China, 1999. 'A Number of Decisions on Major Issues about State-Owned Reform and Development by CPC Central Committee', 15th Central Committee of the Chinese Communist Party — Fourth Plenary Meeting.

Chinese Academy of Sciences, 2006. 'China Sustainable Development Strategy Report', Chinese Academy of Sciences, Beijing.

Fang, X. and X. L. Liu, 2004. 'Review and Outlook of China's Science and Technology System Reform', *Qiushi*, 5: 43–45.

Ministry of Education, 2006a. 'Guidelines on Strengthening the Construction of National Key Disciplines', Ministry of Education of the People's Republic of China.

Ministry of Education, 2006b. 'Provisional Measures on Construction and Management of National Key Disciplines', Ministry of Education of the People's Republic of China.

Ministry of Finance, 1996a. 'Management Approach on Science and Technology Working Capital', Ministry of Finance of the People's Republic of China.

———, 1996b. 'Grant Funds Management Approach on National Key New Products', Ministry of Finance of the People's Republic of China.

———, 1996c. 'Management Rules of Three Items of Expenditure on Science and Technology', Ministry of Finance of the People's Republic of China.

———, 1996d. 'Notice on Financial and Taxation Issues in Promoting Enterprises' Technological Progress', Ministry of Finance of the People's Republic of China.

———, 1996e. 'Notification on Finance and Taxation to Promote Technology Progress', Ministry of Finance of the People's Republic of China.

———, 1997a. 'Loan and Discount Management Approach on Innovation Development of Large Equipment-Made Project', Ministry of Finance of the People's Republic of China.

———, 1997b. 'Loan and Discount Management Approach on Application of Electronic Information', Ministry of Finance of the People's Republic of China.

———, 1997c. 'Loan and Discount Management Approach on Special Technology Renovation Project', Ministry of Finance of the People's Republic of China.

———, 2006a. 'Guidelines on Implementation of Incentive Distribution System of Indigenous Innovation in Enterprises', Ministry of Finance of the People's Republic of China.

———, 2006b. 'Management Rules on Government Procurement Budget of Indigenous Innovation Products', Ministry of Finance of the People's Republic of China.

———, 2006c. 'Regulations on Government Procurement Evaluation of Indigenous Innovation Products', Ministry of Finance of the People's Republic of China.

———, 2006d. 'Management Rules on Government Procurement Contract of Indigenous Innovation Products', Ministry of Finance of the People's Republic of China.

Ministry of Finance and Ministry of Science and Technology, 2006a. 'Management Measures of Special Funds in National Key Basic Research Development Programme', Government of the People's Republic of China.

———, 2006b. 'Management Measures of Special Funds of National Science and Technology Support Programme', Government of the People's Republic of China.

Ministry of Finance and State Administration of Taxation, 1999. 'Notice on Taxation Policies to Accelerate the Commercialization of Science and Technology Achievements', Government of the People's Republic of China.

———, 2006a. 'Notification on Adjustment of Pre-Tax Deduction Policy of Income Tax', Government of the People's Republic of China.

———, 2006b. 'Notification on Income Tax Preferential Policies for Enterprises' Technological Innovation', Government of the People's Republic of China.

Ministry of Human Resources and Social Security, 2006. 'Eleventh Five-Year Plan on Post-Doctoral System', Government of the People's Republic of China.

Ministry of Science and Technology, 2000. 'The Notification on Transformation of 134 Scientific Research Institutions affiliated to 11 Departments including the Ministry of Construction', Government of the People's Republic of China.

———, 2006a. 'China's Private Science and Technology Enterprises Statistics Report in 2005', Government of the People's Republic of China.

———, 2006b. 'Interim Procedures of Strengthening Innovative Talents Training in the Implementation of Major Projects', Government of the People's Republic of China.

———, 2008. 'China's Science and Technology Development Report in 2006', Government of the People's Republic of China.

Ministry of Science and Technology and Ministry of Education, 2006a. 'Suggestions on Further Promoting Research Bases and Its Facilities Open to Enterprises and Community', Government of the People's Republic of China.

———, 2006b. 'Identification and Management Rules of National University Science and Technology Park (USTP)', Government of the People's Republic of China.

———, 2006c. 'Guideline on Construction of National Key Laboratory Relying on Transformed Institutions and Enterprises', Government of the People's Republic of China.

Ministry of Science and Technology, Ministry of Education, Ministry of Personnel, Ministry of Finance, People's Bank of China, State Administration of Taxation, and State Administration for Industry and Commerce, 1999. 'Some Provisions on Promotion of Scientific and Technological Achievements', Government of the People's Republic of China.

Ministry of Science and Technology, National Development and Reform Committee and Ministry of Finance, 2006. 'Management Regulations on Identification of National Indigenous Innovation Products (For Trial Implementation)', Government of the People's Republic of China.

Ministry of Science and Technology, Propaganda Department of the Central Committee of the Communist Party of China, National Development and Reform Committee, Ministry of Education, Commission of Science, Technology and Industry for National Defence, Ministry of Finance, China Association for Science and Technology, and Chinese Academy of Sciences, 2007. 'Guidelines on Strengthening Capability of National Science Popularization', Government of the People's Republic of China.

Ministry of Science and Technology, Propaganda Department of the Central Committee of the Communist Party of China, National Development and Reform Committee, Ministry of Education, Ministry of Finance, China Association for Science and Technology, and Chinese Academy of Sciences, 2006. 'Guidelines on Carrying Out Science Popularity Activities by Scientific Research Institutions and Universities to the Society', Government of the People's Republic of China.

Ministry of Science and Technology, State Economic and Trade Commission, State Committee of Planning, Ministry of Finance, and State Administration of Taxation, 1999. 'Suggestion on Reform of Scientific Research Institutions Affiliated to 10 State-Level Bureaus and Managed by the State Economic and Trade Commission', Government of the People's Republic of China.

National Bureau of Statistics (NBS) of China, 2004a. *China Statistical Yearbook on High Technology Industry 2004*. Beijing: China Statistics Press.

———, 2004b. *China Statistical Yearbook on Science and Technology 2004*. Beijing: China Statistics Press.

———, 2006. *China Statistical Yearbook on Science and Technology 2006*. Beijing: China Statistics Press.

———, 2009. *China Statistical Yearbook on Science and Technology 20096*. Beijing: China Statistics Press.

———, 2010. *China Statistical Yearbook 2010*. Beijing: China Statistics Press.

National Development and Reform Commission (NDRC), 2006. 'Guidelines on Construction of National Engineering Laboratory', National Development and Reform Commission, People's Republic of China.

National People's Congress, 1993a. 'Agricultural Popularization Law of People's Republic of China', National People's Congress of the People's Republic of China.

———, 1993b. 'Regulations on Science and Technology Progress', National People's Congress of the People's Republic of China.

———, 1993c. 'Law on Science and Technology Progress of People's Republic of China', National People's Congress of the People's Republic of China.

National Science, Technology and Education Leading Group, 1998. 'The Report Outline on Pilot Implementation of Knowledge Innovation Programme', State Council of the People's Republic of China.

———, 2002. 'A Study on Important Technology Standards', State Council of the People's Republic of China.

Organisation for Economic Co-operation and Development (OECD), 2008. *OECD Reviews of Innovation Policy: China*, Paris: Organisation for Economic Co-operation and Development.

Standing Committee of the National People's Congress, 1993. 'Science and Technology Progress Law of People's Republic of China', National People's Congress, People's Republic of China.

———, 1996. 'China's Promotion Law of Commercialisation of Scientific and Technological Achievements', National People's Congress, People's Republic of China.

State Council, 1981. 'Provisional Regulations on Technology Introduction and Equipment Import', State Council of the People's Republic of China.

———, 1985a. 'Provisional Regulations on Technology Transfer', State Council of the People's Republic of China.

———, 1985b. 'Decision Made by the Central Committee of the Chinese Communist Party on Reform of Science and Technology', State Council of the People's Republic of China.

———, 1985c. 'Regulations on Technology Introduction Contracts', State Council of the People's Republic of China.

———, 1988. 'Provisional Regulations of Beijing High-Tech Development Pilot Zone', State Council of the People's Republic of China.

———, 1992. 'Key Points on Acclimatize Development to the Socialist Market Economy, and Deepen the Implementation of Science and Technology System Reform', State Council of the People's Republic of China.

———, 1995. 'Rules on the Implementation of the Budget Law of People's Republic of China', State Council of the People's Republic of China.

———, 1996. 'Outline of National Medium and Long-Term Science and Technology Development Plan (2006–2020)', State Council of the People's Republic of China.

———, 1999a. 'Decision on Strengthening Technology Innovation, Developing High Technology, and Realizing Industrialization', State Council of the People's Republic of China.

———, 1999b. 'Some Provisions on Mechanism of Venture Capital Construction', State Council of the People's Republic of China.

———, 1999c. 'Suggestions on Reform of Scientific Research Institutions Affiliated to 10 State-Level Bureaus Managed by the State Economic and Trade Commission by departments including the Ministry of Science and Technology Transmitted by the State Council', State Council of the People's Republic of China.

State Council, 2000. 'Policies on Encouraging Development of Software Industry and IC Industry', State Council of the People's Republic of China.

———, 2006a. 'Notification on Strengthening the Construction of Credit Guarantee System for Small and Medium-Sized Enterprises', State Council of the People's Republic of China.

———, 2006b. 'Outline of National Medium- and Long-Term Strategic Plan for the Development of Science and Technology (2006–2020)', State Council of the People's Republic of China.

———, 2006c. 'Several Related Policies of the Outline of National Medium- and Long-Term Strategic Plan for the Development of Science and Technology (2006–2020)', State Council of the People's Republic of China.

State Council and the General Administration of Customs, 1997. 'Interim Provisions Concerning the Exemption of Import Duties on the Articles used for Scientific Research and Teaching as Approved by the State Council on 22 January 1997 and promulgated by Decree No. 61 of the General Administration of Customs on 10 April 1997', People's Republic of China.

State Economic and Trade Commission, 1980. 'National Key Technology Development Plan', State Economic and Trade Commission of the People's Republic of China.

———, 1982a. 'National Key Scientific and Technological Planning', State Economic and Trade Commission of the People's Republic of China.

———, 1982b. 'National Technology Upgrading Plan', State Economic and Trade Commission of the People's Republic of China.

———, 1984a. 'Planning of State Key Laboratory Construction', State Economic and Trade Commission of the People's Republic of China.

———, 1984b. 'National Key Industrial Pilot Project', State Economic and Trade Commission of the People's Republic of China.

Wu, L., 2003. 'Review of Evolution of Chinese Government's Economic Functions 1949–2002', *Researches in Chinese Economic History*, 4: 144–52.

Zhong, X. W. and X. D. Yang, 2007. 'Science and Technology Policy Reform and its Impact on China's National Innovation System', *Technology in Society*, 29(3): 317–25.

6

South Africa

Mario Scerri

This chapter deals with the current role of the state in the evolution of the South African system of innovation. However, a 'snapshot' would not be adequate since we are dealing with dynamic systems in a constant state of flux. Hence there is a need to place the current relationship between state and innovation system within a historical context. In this chapter, the history covered starts with the 1996 White Paper on Science and Technology policy (hereafter referred to as the 'White Paper') as the focus of this analysis. This is done in full cognisance of the fact that the context for state policy and the forming of the post-apartheid system of innovation was strongly affected by the prior evolution of the South African national system of innovation (NSI) during the preceding periods of segregation and apartheid.

Although the broad definition of the NSI is adopted as the conceptual framework for this chapter, the length constraints impose a choice of the policies which will be specifically discussed. This choice is informed by a wider filter than just basic science and technology policies but it excludes the amalgamation of the broader human capital development policy arena which would include housing, health, social benefits, and other areas of basic needs provision.

Evolution of the Current Form of State

This section serves to set the historical context of the post-apartheid history of science, technology and innovation (STI), specifically focusing on the history of the relationship between state and market during the 20th century as the precursor of the changing relationship in the post-apartheid era. This then helps the understanding of the nature of ruptures and continuities in the evolution of the South African NSI in the transition from apartheid to democracy.

The pre-democracy period

The role of the state in the evolution of the South African NSI since the turn of the 20th century and before the coming of democracy was, until the 1980s, marked by a strong element of intervention aimed at re-shaping the structure of most aspects of the South African economy. Briefly, this period can be divided into the pre-apartheid period of segregation and the apartheid era. Politically, the start of the 20th century was marked by the Anglo-Boer war and the formation of the Union of South Africa in 1910. The economy was based on the mining sector, most of which was British-owned, and the state intervened directly to ensure that the requirements of the mining sector, especially the supply of cheap black labour, were assured. The landmark piece of legislation in this regard was the 1913 Lands Act which expropriated over 90 per cent of African-owned agricultural land. This was partially due to the acknowledged fact that African peasantry was more productive than Afrikaner farmers with the consequence that African farmers were generating surpluses which were used to buy up white-owned farms. The other, less overt, reason for the Act was to ensure a supply of mine workers by displacing the larger portion of the rural black population from their primary source of income (see Bundy 1988).

After World War I, the state set up the Iron and Steel Corporation of South Africa (ISCOM) to address the openly recognised failure of the market to take up the incentive for the beneficiation of pig iron provided by plentiful supplies of ore on the one hand and the assured demand by the rapidly expanding rail system on the other. Through this and other initiatives, including the Electricity Supply Commission (ESKOM) and the Industrial Development Corporation (IDC), the state was instrumental in ushering in the manufacturing sector and the industrial diversification of the South African economy (Scerri 2009: chapter 3). These developments occurred within the context of a racially defined political economy which in this aspect was not markedly different from other colonised countries within the empire. Its distinguishing feature was rather the intra-white ethnic conflict with the polarisation between an Afrikaner government and a largely English-speaking capitalist class.

The establishment of apartheid, shortly after World War II marked the start of a programme of political, social and economic engineering that was to shunt the evolution of the South African system of innovation on to a path which became progressively regressive and, in its growing dissonance with the evolution of other systems in the post-colonial era, progressively anti-modern. The final entrenchment of the 'separate development' model of apartheid, wherein the black population was effectively excluded from the country's citizenry, had long-term devastating consequences on broad-based human capital formation which still poses the major constraint on the development of the post-apartheid system of innovation.[1] Ironically, however, the increasing political and economic isolation of South Africa during apartheid provided a strong incentive for the establishment of a strong military–industrial complex and the consequent development of a relatively formidable system of science and technology. The economic interventions of the state operated on three main fronts, all driven by the apartheid agenda.

The first was the creation of *bantustans* and homelands with separate administrative structures with varying degrees of autonomy. The model of 'separate development' required the development of employment bases in these homelands and extensive industrial incentive schemes, mostly in the form of employment subsidies which were established to promote industrial development in these *ersatz* political creations. Given the economic geography of apartheid, the *bantustans* and homelands could never have been economically viable and their industrial bases necessarily remained artificial economies, always dependent on transfers from the apartheid state.

The second intervention was driven by the need to integrate the capitalist sector and to 'de-ethnicise' white-owned capital. This required the inter-penetration of Afrikaner and English-speaking capital and was achieved through establishments, mergers and acquisitions.[2] This policy significantly reduced the (intra-white) ethnicity of capital and hence the state/market conflict which had been consistently evident during the segregationist period. While the patterns of concentration were changed, the degree of concentration of ownership and control was not, but this was not a major concern of the state.

The third major front of state intervention was in the form of price controls, supported by subsidies, particularly in staple foods and transport. The economies of the *bantustans* and homelands would never be able to absorb the populations allotted to them under apartheid and the majority of the oppressed lived as transient foreigners in 'white' South Africa, providing the bulk of the labour force. Apartheid economic geography placed this semi-permanent labour force in townships, denied residential rights in the urban centres and necessitated commuting long distances every day to work there. The main concern of the apartheid regime regarding this unique labour market system was that the inevitable political and civil unrest should not turn into outright revolution. There was a clear awareness that the supply of labour had to be assured through the price stability of the basic cost of living and the cost of transport required to bring workers to their places of employment and ferry them back to what essentially amounted to 'workers' dormitories'. During the 1980s, effectively the last decade of apartheid, the inherent wastefulness of the apartheid economy led to a widespread programme of privatisation of state organs which had formed the economic pillars of the system.

The post-apartheid era

Periodisation is necessarily arbitrary to some extent. This is especially true when the period under consideration is relatively short. The post-apartheid era effectively, though not constitutionally, started with the unbanning of the African National Congress (ANC) in 1990 and the start of negotiations towards a democratic state. The first democratic elections took place in 1994 and the first post-apartheid STI policy document was passed by Parliament in 1996. This chapter looks at the period of time since 1996 and the relation between state and market over this time span is roughly divided into three periods.

The first period started with the launch of the Growth, Employment and Redistribution: A Macroeconomic Strategy (GEAR) in 1996 (RSA 1996a) and lasted until the first review of the programme in 2001. South Africa's first democratic government had come into being in 1994, during the pinnacle of the hegemony of the Washington Consensus, a period during which market liberalisation was the only acceptable economic policy prescription worldwide. In the last few years of apartheid there had been a progressive adoption of this economic ideology and the legitimacy of the new South Africa government and its consequent sudden entry into the global economy intensified this shift which was formalised as policy in GEAR. GEAR was an explicitly neoliberal macroeconomic programme which advocated liberalisation of markets in expectation of a 'trickle down' effect which would address the inherited inequalities of income, wealth and opportunities.[3] The role of the state was confined to the provision of basic needs, the maintenance of infrastructure and other aspects of the public goods provision function. The basis of this approach was that apartheid had been an allocative distortion which would not have been tolerated by a free market and that it therefore required the freeing up of market forces to correct for the 'distortion'.

The second period emerged with the review of GEAR and the growing sense of disillusionment with the performance of the programme and its capability to stimulate the structural transformation that was required for the development of the South African economy. The official review of the first four years of GEAR in 2001 found that, while macroeconomic stability, in terms of fiscal discipline, had been achieved, economic growth, investment and savings still fell below the GEAR targets. Moreover, net foreign direct investment had been consistently negative, education was falling behind the country's skills requirements, and unemployment and poverty had not been significantly addressed.

It was widely recognised that the persistent levels of unemployment were largely due to the failure to address the inherited shortage of human capital, within the context of an economic structure which has little absorptive capacity for low-skilled and unskilled labour.[4] The two complementary challenges were now to increase the employment of the low-skilled and the unskilled portion of the labour force while simultaneously increasing the overall skills level of the labour force. The recognition of the failure of GEAR in this area led to a series of initiatives, culminating in the Accelerated and Shared Growth Initiative for South Africa (AsgiSA) (RSA 2004) programme, which arose from the recognition of the need for an integrated state intervention on a number of complementary fronts in order to address the development challenges of the country. It was recognised that the shortage of skills was one of the major constraints to growth and this led to the launch of the Joint Initiative on Priority

Skills Acquisition (JIPSA) (RSA 2006b), which was formulated specifically to strengthen and coordinate a number of strategies designed to address the shortage of skills. However, although GEAR was revised in light of its failure to address the enduring high rate of unemployment, the remedial attempts were still marked by a high degree of fragmentation and a lack of coordination. This was due to the absence of an alternative comprehensive planning paradigm.

A possible third stage in the relationship between the state and market has its origin in the radical shift in the power base of the governing party that started with the election of its new national executive council at the end of 2007. This change ushered in the main labour union confederation and the South African Communist Party to the centre of the ideological base of the party, ostensibly displacing the market-friendly neoliberal ideology that had governed policy since 1994. The possibilities for this shift were further reinforced by the global financial crisis that led to a worldwide disillusionment with unregulated markets and again brought to the fore the central role of governments in the economic destinies of nation states. In 2010 the state issued the New Growth Path (NGP) policy document (RSA 2009) with the explicit opening statement that 'creating decent work, reducing inequality and defeating poverty can only happen through a new growth path founded on a restructuring of the South African economy to improve its performance in terms of labour absorption as well as the composition and rate of growth' (RSA 2009: 1).[5] However, in the intervening period since 2008 the rift between labour organisations and movements and the state has re-emerged with a growing perception that economic policy formulation is still caught up in the language of GEAR and that the financial crisis, with the strain that it is already imposing on the fiscus, may reinforce the original 'pragmatic' justification for fiscal caution with the consequent restraints on a state-led development programme. This period is now one of an open ideological contestation over the appropriate relationship between state and market in South Africa. The 2012 report of the Department of Science and Technology (DST) ministerial review committee (RSA 2012) was dismissive about the capacity of the approach adopted by the NGP document to address the developmental requirements of the South African NSI.[6]

Periodisation and Analysis of Institutions and Policies of the State Concerned with Innovation

The role of the state in the planning of the evolution of the South African NSI since the end of apartheid is marked by two divergent trends, both of which emerge from policy positions that were ratified by Parliament in 1996. In the case of the national science, technology and innovation policy there was a significant break with the old policy regime with the introduction of the 1996 White Paper on Science and Technology: Preparing for the 21st Century (RSA 1996b).[7] This marked the start of national STI policy formulation and implementation in the post-apartheid era. The White Paper was explicit in its adoption of the NSI concept as the informing planning framework for STI policy. The other trend was that of overall economic policy which affected the broadly defined national system of innovation. In this case there was a marked continuity with the shift towards neoliberalism during the late years of apartheid. There was therefore an essential disjuncture between an STI plan which effectively implied an interventionist approach and an overall economic planning context which required a reduction of state intervention. The result was a divergence between the two policy environments with a general isolation of STI planning from most of the other aspects of economic planning. This isolation of STI from other aspects of economic and social planning essentially reduced it to an exercise in the rationalisation of the various organs of an inefficient and wasteful public S&T apparatus that had been inherited from apartheid.

The state agency that was initially charged with designing and implementing the post-apartheid STI planning was the Department of Arts, Culture, Science and Technology (DACST), which was established in 1994. The initial placement of STI planning within a ministry which also included arts and culture at the inception of the new political economy provides some indication of the low priority assigned to STI planning at the time.

The democratic government's foundation document on STI planning was passed simultaneously with GEAR but was based in a radically different economic paradigm. When South Africa's 1996 White Paper on science and technology (S&T) policy was being drafted, shortly after the end of apartheid, the national system of innovation was widely recognised to be disintegrating.[8] R&D expenditure was low by international standards and had been steadily decreasing over the previous seven years as the military–industrial complex of the apartheid regime was dismantled and the associated public R&D spending declined. South Africa exported manufactured goods which were intensive in physical capital and unskilled labour, and imported commodities which were intensive in technology and human capital (Scerri 1990, 2003). This was inevitable in an economy where the capacity for adding value to the abundant natural resources was fundamentally constrained by the human capital development consequences of the apartheid political economy. Moreover, the tariff system under apartheid had further served to reinforce these trade patterns.[9] By most definitions, the country's system of innovation was peripheral within the global framework.

The prime task of the White Paper was to define and establish national STI policy in line with the requirements of the newly democratic political economic system. The starting point of the White Paper was to a large extent based on the review of South Africa's NSI undertaken by the International Development Research Centre (IDRC) in 1993. The IDRC report concluded that not only had the science and technology policy been determined by the exigencies of apartheid but that it had also been badly coordinated.[10] These were therefore the two factors which needed to be addressed urgently — the reorientation of the national system of innovation to the requirements of the new political economy and the design of a coordinated national STI planning framework. However, even though the White Paper clearly envisaged STI planning as an integral part of national economic planning, the scope and the level at which DACST should have coordinating powers was determined by the overall economic planning context.[11]

The initial draft of the Reconstruction and Development Programme (RDP) (ANC 1994) preceding GEAR was a Keynesian economic plan, which placed the radical alteration of the living conditions of the majority of the population towards the top of its agenda. This was seen as the essential pre-requisite to provide the required preconditions to the long-term structural transformation of the South African economy. This transformation would be driven simultaneously on the demand side by the conventional income multiplier effects of the enhanced quality of life of the broad population base, and on the supply side through the deepening and broadening of the technological capabilities pool, arising from an overall rapid improvement in the conditions of life of the population as a whole. However, in the three-year gap between the publication of the IDRC report and the submission of the White Paper, national economic planning shifted from the relatively interventionist position of the RDP to the neoliberal GEAR programme, which restricted the state to the role of a facilitator for market forces. Strategic intervention in the identification and promotion of potential growth sectors was largely abandoned and the market was placed at the centre of the economic coordinating mechanism. The consequence of this shift was the restriction of the coordinating role of DACST within the STI sector to a bureaucratic realignment of existing public sector STI specific institutions.

Within the context of the GEAR programme, STI policy could not interface with industrial, trade and labour policies, as well as education policy outside of the higher education sector both because of the restricted vision of the NSI and the generally neutral stance of the state towards the market.[12] Thus, for example, trade policy aimed at accelerating trade liberalisation (at a faster rate than the one proposed by the WTO) instead of trying to reverse the existing trade patterns, in spite of evidence against the wisdom of such a policy approach.[13] The White Paper had argued for a policy which maintained 'an appropriate balance between opening up the economy to global competitiveness and nurturing local initiatives' (RSA 1996b: 5), but the established neoliberal position drastically restricted the ability to pursue the 'nurturing local initiatives' side of the balance, and very rapidly exposed the national system of innovation inherited from apartheid, with its recognised structural weaknesses, to global competition without any provision for a transition period. The poverty of industrial policy was especially detrimental to the ability to design STI demand-side policies and this spilled over to most other areas of public sector programmes. So, for example, the innovation potential of housing programmes was totally excluded, thus foregoing a significant incentive for the development of indigenous technologies suited to the South African physical, social and economic environments.

Supply-side STI policy was also restricted to direct R&D subsidies, in spite of the explicit acknowledgement in the White

Paper of the extensive use of fiscal incentives for R&D activities in industrialised economies, including high tax incentives. In the case of South Africa the only fiscal tool was to be direct subsidies on a matching grant basis. Consequently, within this constrained policy environment the recommendations in the White Paper were restricted to improving intra-governmental information flows, as well as improving links with the private sector. Moreover, the authority to coordinate S&T policy across the broad spectrum of the public service was allocated to the Ministers' Committee on Science and Technology which comprised all those ministers whose portfolios contained a significant S&T component. This was a weak coordinating mechanism and as a consequence STI initiatives have to a large extent been marked by a 'silo' mentality with each ministry and government department pursuing its own goals without much reference to an overall STI planning framework.

The White Paper also contained a specific proposal to develop an indigenous technology initiative, in collaboration with the Department of Trade and Industry, by addressing the technology requirements of small-, medium- and micro-scale enterprises. The state procurement policy was also intended to provide a demand-side stimulus to technology-intensive industries. This was an improvement on the previous promotion of all local industries regardless of their technological capabilities content.

The White Paper proposed a new coordinating mechanism for all government science, engineering and technology institutions which would be grouped as science councils and department-based institutes. Science Councils had been established in the 1980s to move public sector R&D institutions progressively towards private sector funding through contract work in order to increase funding beyond the state baseline funding scheme. However, the disadvantages of this system were the gaps between the R&D policies of individual councils and national development priorities and the tendency to crowd out private sector R&D performers through costing practices which did not cover full cost. The White Paper proposed that the fragmentation of research programmes could be reduced if Science Councils as well as department-based institutes would operate within a national goal framework with an increased level of coordination. The White Paper further proposed that department-based institutes should progressively shift to the Science Council category in order to escape the budget constraint of public funding, primarily in order to allow the recruitment of qualified research personnel at competitive remuneration rates. While an institutional review process charged with the alignment of state R&D programmes with national objectives was established as the joint responsibility of DACST and the line department governing particular institutes, it was not going to be easy to enforce national priorities while increasing the dependence on private sector funding. Research and Technology Foresight Exercises were established to provide the guidelines for the investment of public S&T funds, specifically to identify 'potential technological trends and trajectories of significance to the social and economic development of South Africa' (IDRC 1993: 21). However, given the absence of fiscal R&D incentives and incentives emerging from related policy areas, the ability of the state to affect private R&D investment patterns was quite restricted.

The National Research Foundation (NRF) explicitly recognised the crucial role of human capital in the development process and it extended the definition of human capital to incorporate all aspects of human resource development, rather than restricting it to scientists and engineers. It set DACST with the task of introducing an S&T perspective into education programmes.[14] Quality control over the education sector was assured by the establishment of a National Qualifications Framework as the accreditation mechanism across the country. The role allotted to DACST was to develop curricula for pre-tertiary education levels and for adult training programmes. The NRF was set up to coordinate research funding in the tertiary education sector and to operate through four agency divisions — natural sciences and engineering, social sciences and humanities, health sciences, agricultural and environmental sciences. The NRF would also administer the National Facilities for Research.

The National Advisory Council on Innovation (NACI), a council of experts from diverse fields and sectors, representing various stakeholder bodies, was established as an advisory body for DACST. This council was designed to address some of the deficiencies of the previous Scientific Advisory Council identified in the IDRC report (IDRC 1993: 25–27) and, in contrast with the period of apartheid, the terms of reference and the areas covered by NACI were to be public knowledge.

The NRF supplanted the Foundation for Research Development as the national agency responsible for promoting and supporting basic and applied research as well as innovation. It funds knowledge generation, the development of researchers, products and infrastructure. The NRF provides services and grants to support research and postgraduate research training. Funding from the NRF is largely directed towards academic research, the development of high-level human capital, and the national research facilities. The terms of reference of the NRF extend to all fields of the humanities, social and natural sciences, engineering, indigenous knowledge and technology. It has forged local and international strategic partnerships to promote research capacity development. The latest dramatic intervention in the shaping of the development of the higher end of the human capital chain is the South African Research Chairs Initiative (SARChI). This targeted approach towards human capital development has been designed as a medium- to long-term measure to enhance research capacity and its long-term reproduction in the higher education sector by drawing foreign expertise into South African universities with sufficient complementary funding to build lasting areas of excellence.

The main institutional instrument for the financing and control of specific R&D projects was the Innovation Fund, whose budget would derive from the reallocation of science funding across government ministries and departments. DACST would cooperate with the Department of Trade and Industry which administered the Support Programme for Industrial Innovation. The choice of projects to support was guided by the following three governing criteria:

- the needs of the previously disadvantaged (initially half of the funding was to be directed at such projects);
- large, long-term projects, in order to reverse the trend towards short planning horizons;
- strong links between innovation, diffusion and use, thus reducing endemic fragmentation and delivery bottlenecks.

While these priorities have remained reasonably constant since 1996, the capacity of S&T planning to address these priorities has improved since then.

In the case of the humanities, the Human Sciences Research Council (HSRC), which was established by the Human Sciences Research Act, No. 23 of 1968 is specifically charged with performing, coordinating and promoting research in social and human sciences. The HSRC has aligned its research structures and activities to major development priorities and its current structure reflects this. Its main areas of activity are divided into cross-cutting units, research programmes and centres.

One of the cross-cutting units, 'Knowledge Systems', is charged with undertaking R&D and innovation surveys. The other focuses on policy analysis, capacity development and gender. The research programmes cover social development, focusing on the family, political structures, education, and health. The three centres cover: (*a*) poverty, employment and growth, (*b*) service delivery, and (*c*) education quality improvement.

On the whole, the strictures of the macroeconomic planning framework prevented the White Paper from addressing the fragmentation of the S&T planning framework. The definition of the perimeters of S&T planning was therefore not altered substantially from that during apartheid. What occurred was rather a refinement of the inherited structure within a democratic context. Effectively, the macroeconomic planning context restricted STI policy to managing the system of science and technology. Within this constraint the White Paper provided a sound plan for the overhaul of the institutional basis for the development of a sound S&T base. However, the lack of coordination with complementary policy contexts prevented the S&T policy from extending to an innovation policy that would radically alter the national system of innovation.

The second period of the post-apartheid era emerged in 2002 during the revisiting of the country's macroeconomic planning framework. The priority assigned to STI policy was significantly upgraded when DACST was split into two departments with a separate minister of science and technology and the Department of Science and Technology (DST) as the new agency for STI planning. This development came at a time when disillusionment with the performance of the GEAR programme led to a series of targeted initiatives towards the structural transformation of the South African economy.

The new policy statement on STI policy (RSA 2002a) allocated a significantly extended coordinating role over various aspects of STI for the DST. Several STI functions which were located in other ministries and departments have since then been located within the DST. The most notable was the transfer of the Council for Scientific and Industrial Research (CSIR) from the Department of Trade and Industry to the DST in 2005. However, the planning context of the DST is still largely limited to science and technology planning, to the exclusion of some of the more crucial determinants of innovation. Thus, for example, human resource development was largely the domain of the Department of Education (DoE) which, in 2009, was split into the Department of Higher Education and Training (DHET) and the Department of Basic Education. The influence of the DST over the funding of higher education has grown considerably over the past few years. However, the splitting up of the DoE has introduced a possible disjuncture in the national stream of human capital development. The DST and the DHET now collaborate to an unprecedented degree that marks a significant shift in human resource development policy. However, the influence of DST over primary and secondary education policy formulation and implementation, or in overall skills development, is still limited, apart from the relationship between the DST and the Department of Labour (DoL) which was established through the National Skills Development Strategy which commenced in 2001. Overall, the role of the DST is still defined by the generally neutral intervention stance of the implicitly neoliberal economic policy environment that still dominates development planning in South Africa. In this role it acts as a facilitator for the mobilisation of R&D resources but was, until the publication of its 10-year plan in 2007, prevented from designing and implementing strategic intervention initiatives and 'picking winners'. Again, this vague policy mission of the DST reflected the still hesitant and fragmented state of economic planning following the implicit loss of faith in GEAR.

Innovation policy and the development of structures for its implementation have developed rapidly since 1996. In the first five years after the White Paper the disjuncture between the conceptual framework of STI policy and the neoliberal grounding of the overall macroeconomic plan severely inhibited the ambit of the innovation policy. Since 2002 and the reassessment of GEAR there has been a progressive narrowing of the gap between innovation policy and economic policy, and this has generated a rapid institutional development that goes substantially beyond the science and technology sphere.

Specificities of the System of Innovation in South Africa and Its Relationship with the State

Using a biological metaphor, national systems of innovation may be usefully identified on the basis of their viability, defined in terms of their capacity for reproduction, growth and evolution (Scerri 2009: 37). The ability to reproduce a given system is seen as the minimum requirement for the survival of the system, but long-term viability also requires that systems are capable of growing along their current trajectories and, even more importantly, evolve either to adapt to changing environmental conditions or to lead changes in the knowledge environment. The three aspects are of course strongly interrelated, especially when different time horizons are considered.

We can assess the viability of a system of innovation at various levels of inclusion or aggregation, depending on the particular definition that is adopted. The two definitions that we will look at are the system of science and technology and the broader system of innovation. This distinction is important because we may obtain significantly different assessments at the two levels. A healthy and viable system of innovation does not necessarily require a sophisticated system of science and technology for its long-term survival. On the other hand there are numerous examples of strong systems of science and technology which are set against a backdrop of a severely underdeveloped national system of innovation. In such cases the national system of innovation resembles the enclave economy model, with pockets of excellence in a sea of poverty. Such systems are more sustainable than ever due to the integration of markets with globalisation. In such cases the links between the local high technology enclaves and the global market are closer than those with the rest of the NSI. There is, however, always a latent instability in this type of NSI with its enduring inequalities of incomes and life chances. In the broader version of the concept, the NSI which evolved under apartheid constituted such a system and it is its enduring legacy which forms the formidable obstacle to the needed developmental transition in the current South African economy.

Major features of the national, regional and local production and innovation structures

The economic history of South Africa is intimately tied to its rich endowments of a wide range of mineral resources and in most aspects the development of secondary and tertiary sectors can best be understood within the analytical framework of the minerals–energy complex. Even with the increasing diversification of the South African economy away from the primary sector it can still be shown (Fine and Rustomjee 1996) that the South African economy can be seen as resource-based, even if several times removed. The performance of the South African economy since democracy has not fulfilled the set of objectives set out in the first macroeconomic plan.

Macroeconomic indicators for South Africa are presented in Annexure A to this chapter. The annual growth rate of real GDP in South Africa moved along an upward trend between 1999 and 2007. However, as can be seen from Figure A6.1, this growth rate dipped considerably after 2007, in line with global economic changes, becoming negative in 2009, though it showed a sharp recovery in 2010. GDP per capita shows a similar trend over the same period, as can be seen from Figure A6.2. However, the significance of this growth rate for economic development or the transformation of the South African system of innovation has to be qualified by two important provisos. In the first place, unemployment has not been significantly addressed and remains extremely high. Figure A6.3 in Annexure A, shows that the rate of unemployment, estimated to include discouraged job seekers who no longer register with the DoL was running at slightly below 40 per cent by 2006. Second, the enduring income and wealth inequalities means that the relative material conditions of life and the life prospects of a significant portion of the South African population have not improved over time. This is reflected in the Gini-coefficient depicted in Figure A6.4. These two variables provide an indication of the lack of fundamental transformation in the South African economy in the enduring phenomenon of jobless growth. This concern with enduring structural unemployment is the current overwhelming focus of macroeconomic planning in South Africa.

The sectoral structure of the South African economy is shown in Table A6.1, in terms of the composition of GDP. Again, we need to note that while the economy has diversified considerably over its history of industrialisation since the inter-war period, with the secondary and tertiary sectors attaining increasing prominence, the linkages to the primary sector are still a defining feature of the South African system of innovation. This can be seen through a look at the composition of South African exports as depicted in Figure A6.5.

The other salient feature of the South African economy, which is discussed in more detail in a subsequent section, is the high degree of regional unevenness of economic performance. As argued further on, this is to a large extent the heritage of apartheid economic geography and the failure to redress its effects significantly in the post-apartheid era.[15] Table A6.2 in the annexure provides a snapshot of the divergence in the economic structures of the nine provincial economies which were established after apartheid. The composition of these nine provinces varies substantially in terms of the inclusion of the former four 'white' provinces established under apartheid and the various *bantustans* and homelands.[16] The previous 'white' provinces had grown organically on the basis of comparative, and the emerging competitive, advantage. The *bantustans* and homelands, on the other hand, were *ersatz* creations designed to justify the apartheid model of equitable separate development. None of these had an inherent rationale for autonomous economic integrity and survived as supposedly independent administrative structures on the basis of streams of transfers from the apartheid state.

We can briefly note at this stage that those provinces which are economically sound are the ones which are the least reliant on the primary sector. This is especially notable in the case of Gauteng, where, in spite of its rich mineral resources and a well-established mining sector, the primary sector contributes a negligible proportion to its Gross Geographic Product. On the other hand, those provinces whose economic performance on several fronts is well below the national average are heavily reliant on the primary sector. In general there is a strong correspondence between the inclusion of those provinces defined as 'white' under apartheid and economic performance.

System of science and technology

The South African system of science and technology has been substantially reformed since 1994 and the role of the state in this reform is quite evident. The three main indicators that are used to assess this are: (*a*) R&D expenditure and activity, (*b*) R&D human capital development, and (*c*) the convergence patterns of public R&D spending.

R&D Activity

Table 6.1 summarises the basic R&D indicators for South Africa over an 18-year period. It shows that R&D intensity (as a percentage of GDP) grew steadily between 2001 and 2007 but dropped slightly every year since then. R&D intensity had dropped to a low of 0.69 per cent of GDP in 1997–1998 due to the vacuum caused by the drop in defence-related research since the demise of apartheid, but has picked up steadily since. If we decompose national R&D expenditure, some interesting patterns and trends emerge.

Figure 6.1 shows that the share of government R&D financing (government plus science councils) remained stable at approximately 20 per cent over the period. In fact most of the increase in R&D intensity was due to public financing. The proportion of financing contributed by business dropped correspondingly for 2005. The one worrying trend is the downward trend in the share of R&D performed in the higher education sector, which dropped from 25 per cent to 19 per cent from 2001 to 2009.

Figure 6.1: *Expenditure Breakdown of GERD by Sector, 1997–2009 (percentage)*

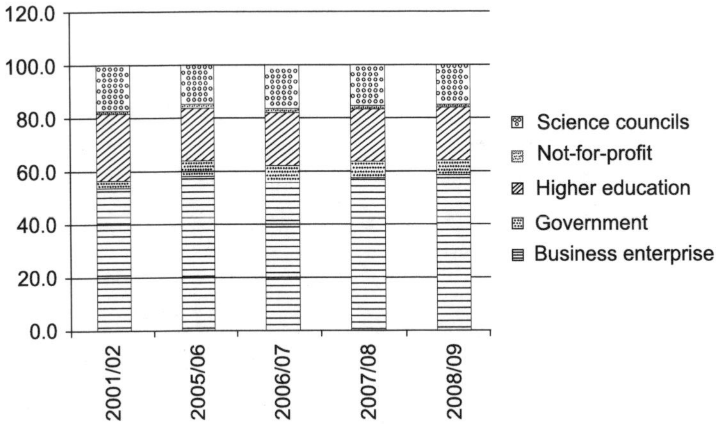

Source: Calculated from RSA (2012: 196, Table 1).

In the 2008–2009 National Survey of Research and Experimental Development (RSA 2011) it emerged that the largest component (87.4 per cent) of government R&D expenditure (government and Science Councils) was spent in natural sciences, technology and

Table 6.1: *Summary of NSI Indicators*

	1991/92	1993/94	1997/98	2002/02	2003/04	2004/05	2005/06	2006/07	2007/08	2008/09
Gross Domestic Expenditure on R&D (GERD) (Rand Billions)	3	3	4	8	10	12	14	17	19	21
% GERD*	1.04	0.75	0.69	0.76	0.81	0.87	0.92	0.95	0.93	0.92
Total R&D Personnel (FTE) (1000s)				34	25	30	29	31	31	31
Total Researchers (FTE) (1000s)				9	14	18	17	19	19	19
Total Researchers per 1,000 Total Employment (FTE)				1.9	1.2	1.6	1.5	1.5	1.5	1.4
Total R&D Personnel per 1,000 Total Employment (FTE)				7.3	2.2	2.6	2.4	2.5	2.4	2.2
% Civil GERD**				0.7	0.7	0.8	0.9	0.9	0.9	0.9
Total Researchers*** (1000s)				19	31	37	39	40	40	40
% Women Researchers****				35	38	38	39	40	40	40

Source: Maharajh (2011: 244).
Note: All figures have been rounded off to the nearest positive integer level to show the trends in stark contrast.
* As a percentage of GDP.
** As a percentage of GERD.
*** Headcount.
**** Expressed as a percentage of Total Researchers.

engineering compared to 86.4 per cent in the 2003–2004 survey (RSA 2005b). The major recipients of government R&D for 2008–2009 were agricultural sciences (17.6 per cent), medical and health sciences (15.8 per cent), and earth sciences (14.3 per cent). In the case of Science Councils the main recipients were engineering sciences (27.5 per cent), medical and health sciences (14.3 per cent) and agricultural sciences (14.1 per cent).

The spread of R&D expenditure among national departments, provincial departments, government research institutes and museums changed dramatically over the period 2003–2004 to 2008–2009, as can be seen in Table 6.2.

Table 6.2: *Breakdown of Government R&D Expenditure (percentage)*

Performer	*Year*	
	2003/2004	2008/2009
National Departments	40.8	25.2
Provincial Departments	18.7	20.4
Research Institutes	33.3	50.8
Museums	7.2	3.6

Source: RSA (2005b, 2011).

The public sector's share of total R&D expenditure is also evident in state-owned enterprises which account for 20 per cent of business enterprise R&D (RSA 2012: 203). Taking this into account, the share of the public sector in total R&D amounts to around 32 per cent as compared with an almost 47 per cent share by the private business sector. For 2008–2009, approximately 6 per cent of all R&D personnel were employed in the government sector, as compared with 44 per cent and 37 per cent for the higher education and the business sectors, respectively (RSA 2012: 35).

The other two aspects of the NSI which are strongly related to the system of science and technology are the production of the higher end researchers, in the form of scientists, engineers and technologists, and the regional convergence in S&T development.

Human R&D Capital Development

The human capital constraint inherited from apartheid was clearly identified in the National Research and Development Strategy:

> Our human resources in science and technology are not being adequately developed and renewed; we have an aging and shrinking scientific population. The key indicators show that black and women scientists, technologists and engineers are not entering the academic ranks and that the key research infrastructure is composed of people who will soon retire. In 1990, the percentage of scientific publications produced by researchers 50 years of age and older was 18% (one in five), but by 1998 this figure had increased, alarmingly, to 45% (one in two). Over the same period the percentage of publications by black scientists rose only very slightly, from 3.5% to 8% (less than one in ten). Participation by women has not changed over the 1990s, with publication output being about 10% of the total. Currently, there is less than one researcher for every thousand members of the workforce, as compared with five in Australia and ten in Japan. Given that 'technology walks on two legs', the 'frozen demographics' prevalent in our National System of Innovation represents a critical state of affairs (RSA 2002a: 21).

However, this statement refers solely to the S&T population in South Africa, thus implicitly restricting the focus of STI strategy to the system of science and technology. In this area South African statistics paint a poor picture of the country's STI capacity, as may be seen in the following two figures.

Figure 6.2 compares Ph.D. production rates across selected developed and developing economies. Compared to developing countries such as Taiwan, Brazil, China, and India, South Africa's production rates are not all that poor. The 10-year innovation plan estimates that 'to build a knowledge-based economy positioned between developed and developing countries, South Africa will need to increase its PhD production rate by a factor of about five over the next 10–20 years' (RSA 2007b: 34) which has formidable implications for re-building a tertiary education system that while growing, is not nearly growing fast enough to make the attainment of the stated requirement feasible.

Figure 6.3 compares the number of Ph.D.s relative to the population in South Africa with those of selected developed economies. As the figure shows, the South African production of Ph.D.s per 1,000, is far below that of leading knowledge economies.

Figure 6.2: *International Comparisons of Ph.D. Production Rates*

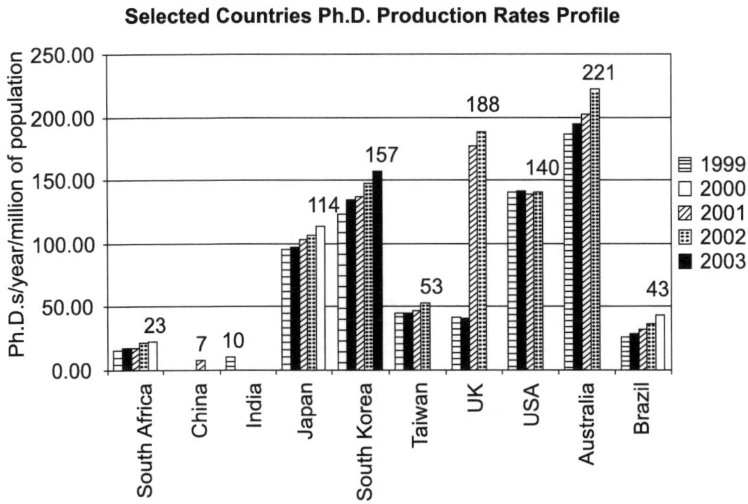

Source: RSA (2007b).

Figure 6.3: *Number of Ph.D.s per 1,000 of the Population*

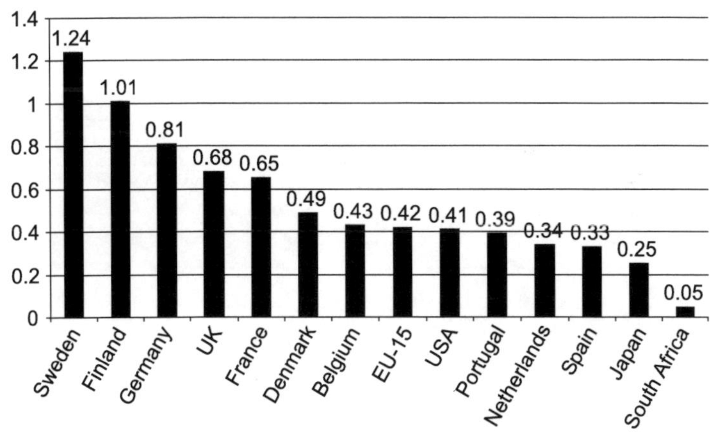

Source: RSA (2007b).

The human capital requirements of the South African national system of innovation, at least at the higher end of the human capital spectrum are well-recognised by the government in its stated goals in the DST's 10-year innovation plan. These goals are listed in Table 6.3.

Table 6.3: *Human Capital and Knowledge Generation*

	By 2018 South Africa will have:
Human Capital Development Actions and Outcomes	➢ 210 research chairs at universities and research institutions across the country by 2010 and 500 by 2018 (58 were in place in 2006) ➢ About 6,000 Ph.D.s produced per year in all SET disciplines by 2018 ➢ About 3 000 SET Ph.D.s/doctorates produced per year by 2018 ➢ An optimal ratio of technicians to researchers ➢ A 2.5 per cent global share of research publications (2006: 0.5 per cent) ➢ 2,100 Patent Cooperation Treaty international applications originating in South Africa (2004: 418) ➢ About 24,000 patent applications at the South African Patent Office (2002: 4721).

Source: Ten-year innovation plan (RSA 2007b).

However, the challenge to achieve the stated higher education targets is quite formidable. The DST document talks about a 'human capital pipeline' from postgraduate students to recognised researchers. In the case of scientists, engineers and technologists the output of Ph.D.s would have to increase fivefold from the 2005 base in order to achieve the set target. The reforms that are planned to try to achieve this target mainly have to do with improving the incentives mechanism for academic careers. However, the sphere of influence of the DST is limited to higher education while the bottleneck in the production of accredited researchers is most stringent at the primary and secondary school levels. This is a much greater challenge, given that the matriculation pass rate has been declining since 2003 and is less than that of 2002. When combined with the quality of the education of South African pupils as indicated in their performance on internationally comparable tests (see Annexure D), this indicates a severe inter-generational constraint on the achievement of the targets set in the DST 10-year innovation plan.

The difficulty in the way of achieving these goals is easily evident in the demographics of the R&D community, as depicted in Annexure B. This is further reinforced when looking at the trends in HEI enrolments as presented in Annexure C. These indicate that enrolments have reached a plateau which is significantly lower than the requirements for the South African NSI.

This bottleneck in the production of researchers is due to reasons which are both supply side and demand side. In terms of the supply into the university system the poor quality of the South African school system (see Figure D6.1 in Annexure D to this chapter) has had a knock on effect on universities in the form of dropout rates of up to 50 per cent and a reduction in the number of undergraduates with sufficiently high exit scores to enter graduate programmes. On the demand side, there is little perceived incentive for students to enter into doctoral programmes. On the one hand, the total opportunity costs of a doctorate are generally seen as much too high, given the private sector labour market conditions for the masters qualification level. On the other hand, the returns from a university career both in terms of remuneration and of the conditions of work, are not seen as being sufficiently high to warrant the cost of a Ph.D.

The national systems of innovation

The core determinants of the three aspects of the long-term viability are human capital development, regional convergence processes and an equitable distribution of income, wealth and life chances. Human capital is the *sine qua non* pre-requisite for the indigenous technological capabilities of an innovation system. Given the appropriate institutional context, it defines the main source of the wealth of nations in the global knowledge and learning economy. When we approach the analysis of NSIs from the broader perspective we need to be circumspect in the easy adoption of the concept of human capital. Its orthodox definition is firmly set within a neoclassical theoretical context which places it alongside other types of capital as primarily instrumental in production and as a source of returns for its owner. Within the broad definition of the NSI, this usage is inappropriate in its limitations and ideological implications (see Bowles and Gintis 1975). In this chapter human capital is rather defined along the lines of human capability, *a la* Sen's (1999) definition.

The other essential pre-requisite for the formation of a viable national system of innovation is a stable (multi)nation state where all parts of the economy are seen to be developing. Enduring regional imbalances in economic performance threaten the stability of the political economy and the integrity of the NSI. Finally, extreme inequalities in income, wealth and life prospects, with their implications for human capital development and social and political stability, can have dire consequences for the long-term viability of the NSI.

In the case of South Africa, the analysis of these three sets of determinants indicates that there is still an urgent need to address the fundamental flaws of the apartheid national system of innovation. Simultaneously, they indicate those areas which would, if addressed in a coherent integrated fashion, go a long way towards creating the required rupture with history that should have marked the dawn of the new democratic political economy of South Africa. These are now areas that are recognised by the state as of major concern.

Human Capital

The performance of South African pupils in standard literacy and numeracy tests compared with a range of developed and developing economies is extremely poor (see Figure D6.1 in Annexure D). This is of greater concern than the output of the higher education sector, because of the inter-generational implications for the future human capital base in South Africa. In terms of education and training the indications are that South Africa is struggling to reproduce its human capital base.

From a systems perspective we need to extend the concept of human capital beyond training and education. Human capital formation occurs in a broader context than that of schools, technical colleges and universities. From a broad economic perspective human capital is a public good whose availability is crucial to the economic well-being and development prospects of the nation. In this sense it has large externalities in that the returns on it cannot be entirely appropriated by any single agency but only by the whole of society. Moreover, human capital formation is a fundamentally dynamic process, subject to accelerating obsolescence rates, and if its rate falls below specific thresholds it will be impossible to achieve its sustainable reproduction and development, with the returns on it mainly being private with little or no spillovers to the economy at large.

Within systems of innovation, human capital is probably the single most important factor for success. Hence it constitutes the crucial channel for an economy's investment efforts. It is, however, a particularly long-term investment with an average of 18 to 22 years from birth to the 'production' of a skilled participant in the economy. This factor, when combined with the heavy externalities content, automatically implies that the main responsibility for human capital development lies with the state. It also implies that the family unit, however that is defined, which provides the basic framework for human capital development, has to be protected from instability in order to ensure an uninterrupted stream of investment.

In the case of South Africa the impact of apartheid, and the long pre-democratic history before that, on the family unit was prolonged and devastating, with forced removals, institutionalised and widespread migrant labour, job reservation and separate education effectively degrading the country's broad-based stock of human capital. In South Africa the family is generally extended, often trans-generationally and increasingly impoverished of parents due to the HIV/AIDS pandemic. It is marked by an inherited and now structurally entrenched system of migrant labour with absent men, fathers and husbands as well as absent women, wives and mothers. In the rural areas extended families are often headed by grandparents. In urban areas the prevalence of single-parent families is increasing and, against the backdrop of abject poverty, this is seriously prejudicial to human capital development. Moreover, the average family unit is much too vulnerable to a volatile employment environment to allow for long-term planning. In these conditions the loss of employment has disastrous effects on human capital formation, often interrupting or delaying education streams. Third, a family structure that is typically constantly under attack by the conditions of endemic poverty is always threatened with disintegration. The impermanence of the family structure has a highly adverse effect on the socialisation of children and on the proper internalisation of a society's values which is the ground in which formal education takes root. While it forms the foundation of the human capital formation process which is required for sustainable development, it is also the most vulnerable component of human capital. The brunt of the responsibility for a country's human capital formation thus lies fundamentally with the state. In the post-apartheid South Africa business operates within the context of a labour market that is still very much an apartheid construct, with a widespread scarcity of skills among the labour force and a poor institutional infrastructure for human capital formation. In this regard it is the family, as the bedrock institution, that is the damaged link in the human capital formation chain. Hence the focus of national policy should be on the redressing of past institutionalised generalised disintegration of the family's ability to fulfil its human capital formation function.

The main policy implication of these arguments is the fusion of policy ends and means. The increasing well-being of the family unit is both a robust measure of the objective of development policy and the main mechanism towards the achievement of the objective. The acceptance of this proposition will require a fundamental re-prioritisation of the various development policy measures. It will also enable the development of an integrated policy framework in that various sectoral policies will be assessed in terms of their estimated contribution towards the establishment of a programme of human capital investment that is sound, broad-based and sustainable.

On a broad-based level, a sustained programme of human capital formation will have two effects on the system of innovation. In the first place, there is the supply-side push in terms of enhanced inputs into the system of innovation which expands the ability of a nation to absorb, adapt and create new knowledge. Second, a broad-based enhancement of human capital implies an expansion of the internal market, with the consequent income multiplier effects especially on those goods which have higher technology content, since these usually exhibit high income elasticities of demand.

Poverty and Income Inequality

Broad-based human capital development can be severely constrained by endemic high levels of poverty and income inequality. The two are strongly related since income inequality over inter-generational periods leads to persistent poverty traps which translate into a class-determined divergence of streams of human capital formation.

Income inequality in South Africa, as measured by the Gini-coefficient, has remained persistently high in South Africa (see Figure A6.4 in Annexure A).

Inequality between races has declined, while inequality within race groups has grown. In 1993, 61 per cent of inequality was between race groups; however, by 2006 inequality between race groups had declined to 40 per cent. Over the same period, inequality within race groups has become much more prominent (RSA 2007a: 22). These trends continued through to 2008 (RSA 2010).

These divergent trends indicate that the South African economy may be slowly moving from one where the basis of inequality is defined by race to one defined by class. Be that as it may, poverty remains endemic in South Africa. An indicator of the trend of poverty is the behaviour of the Human Development Index over time, depicted in Figure A6.5 in Annexure A. South Africa's HDI is 0.597, which gives the country a rank of 110 out of 169 countries. This is above the average of sub-Saharan Africa which stands at 0.389 but below the world average of 0.624 (UNDP 2011). Although there is a shallow upward trend in the HDI between 2005 and 2010, its consistent low level is a worrying indicator of enduring poverty, which when combined with growing income inequality holds out poor prospects for human capital development in South Africa. The mitigating factors making for a degree of poverty since 2005 are provided by the alleviation in incomes from increased transfers such as social grants and employment in expanded public works programmes. On the other hand, the increasing loss of jobs in the wake of the financial crisis will dampen, if not reverse, the possible redress of poverty and inequality. The other factor that may change the trend of the Human Development Index is the reform in the public health sector, with an invigorated HIV/AIDS strategy that will significantly alter the impact of the pandemic on the life expectancy component of the Human Development Index.

Both the poverty levels and the unequal income distribution have been alleviated somewhat in recent years through increasing social grants (old age pensions, disability compensation and child support) and expanded public works programmes. These are not sufficient, however, to alter the structure of an economy that is still tied into the generally low-skilled factor market. Low labour productivity forms the basis for the claim that South African wages are uncompetitive and the only way out of this bind is the enhancement of the human capital base. Allowing market forces to bring wage levels down would be fundamentally counterproductive and force the economy permanently into a low skills trap.

Regional Convergence

The economic geography of apartheid has not been adequately addressed by the post-apartheid re-drawing of provinces and municipalities (see Scerri 2010). In fact, the post-apartheid economic geography is one which is characterised by enduring, and sometimes increasingly divergent, development paths across the country.

Indicators of the quality of human capital in the provinces, as an indication of the capacity of the system of innovation again show large disparities across provinces. There are marked disparities in the Human Development Index across the nine provinces (Scerri 2010).

Provincial disparities are also starkly evident in the area of education (ibid.), with two provinces (Gauteng and the Western Cape) showing significantly higher achievements than national averages in terms of the percentage of their populations with some secondary education, matriculation level and tertiary education. In the absence of effective intervention, these trends have become cumulative and path dependent. Vast regional disparities in terms of most of the indicators of a healthy innovation system have thus emerged. If we were to apply the concept of the local system of innovation, we would then have to ask which provinces actually do constitute a provincial system of innovation. The answer is strongly correlated with the original constitution of the provinces. Where a specific post-apartheid province most closely corresponds to the industrial heartland of one of the four 'white' provinces under apartheid, there are strong indications of a healthy and viable provincial system of innovation. In the case of those provinces which contain a large component of the homelands and *bantustans* created under apartheid, the indications are strong that the statutory definition of a province does not correspond to a provincial system of innovation.

This divergence is further reinforced by the internal migration patterns among provinces (ibid.), with only two provinces (Gauteng and the Western Cape) showing net immigration in 2001. Moreover, the comparison between 1996 and 2001 shows an increased reinforcement of this pattern as the North West province and Mpumalanga moved from positive to negative net migration figures and even the Western Cape showing a drop in its (positive) net migration. These net migration patterns tend to reinforce regional divergence because of the effect on human capital. We usually assume that those who migrate in search of a better life tend to be the more skilled and enterprising members of communities. If this assumption holds, the shift in human capital from poor to richer provinces would be more than proportional vis-à-vis the simple migration figures.

Unlike national systems of innovation, provincial systems do not exist simply by virtue of their legal definition. Intra-state legal entities are not sovereign polities and their status is subject to legal redefinitions. Simultaneously, from our perspective the rationale for the existence of sub-national legal/economic constructs, such as provinces, should be assessed on the basis of whether specific provinces actually constitute provincial systems of innovation. The information which has been provided in this section indicates that a number of provinces in South Africa do not constitute, and possibly cannot constitute, provincial systems of innovation.

Generally those provinces which are made up of the economic heartlands of the previous 'white' provinces under apartheid do constitute viable sub-national systems of innovation. These systems evolved on the basis of comparative advantage and on that basis developed formidable sets of competitive advantage with the ongoing support of the state. Path dependency ensured that their viability tended to be reinforced over time. These provinces are Gauteng, the Western Cape, Kwa-Zulu Natal, and the Free State.

The composition of the other five provinces is more closely aligned with the artificial economies created under apartheid to lend some semblance of legitimacy to the grand model of separate development. These various *bantustans* and homelands were never, and could never, be economically viable without extensive, complex and enduring transfers from the apartheid government. In the post-apartheid era, it is difficult to imagine that they could ever be viable given their history. Their formation was the result of an essentially flawed process of negotiation in the short negotiation period before the country's first democratic elections and there is sufficient argument that the provincial map of South Africa should be revisited.

Explicit and Implicit State Policy Towards Science, Technology and Innovation

Explicit state policy regarding science, technology and innovation covers those policies which directly refer to the system of science and technology and define the role of the state in this regard. In the case of post-apartheid South Africa, there are three core documents which are landmarks in the evolution of state STI policy. These are the 1996 White Paper on Science and Technology, the 2002 National Research and Development Strategy and the 2007 Ten Year Innovation Plan. All these policies were the product of the government agency in charge of STI planning (first DACST and then DST).

The second set of policies, which we have termed implicit, are those which are not officially seen to belong in the sphere of STI planning but which nevertheless have an impact on the evolution of the NSI, as defined in the broader sense. The implicit policies that have been considered more relevant are those that refer to industrial policy, education and local development. The link between industrial and STI policy should be obvious, but in the case of South Africa this development and the cementing of this link really began with the review of GEAR in 2001. The rationale for the inclusion of education policy is obvious because of its impact on human capital development. This is dealt with in the section on policies affecting human capital development, further on. In the case of local development, we have seen that the high degree of unevenness is threatening the integrity and durability of the South African system of innovation in all but the legal definition. Given the divergence in regional rates of development and growth within the country, we could well end up with permanently entrenched enclave economies with two provinces on a high growth path, two others on a faltering growth trajectory and the remaining five progressively denuded of their development potential. Policies on local development are addressed further on in this section of the chapter.

STI specific policies

The White Paper

The 1996 White Paper was caught in a policy contradiction that arose from the incompatibility between its explicit choice of the NSI approach as its conceptual framework and the imperative to align its policy prescriptions with the broader neoliberal macroeconomic policy framework. The outcome of this conflict was a compromise between a broad coordinating vision for STI policy and the effective limitation of STI policy to science and technology initiatives. The specific terms of reference for DACST as set out in the White Paper were as follows (RSA 1996b: 33):

- to promote coherence and consistency in the government's approach to stimulating South Africa's national system of innovation in general, and in its commitment to the support of science, engineering and technology development in particular;
- to promote and coordinate interdepartmental and government-wide initiatives relating to the support of innovation and technology diffusion;
- to direct the preparation of a government-wide Science Budget, in order to permit ministers to assess relative spending

priorities on a multi-year basis, across the full spectrum of government's activities in support of innovation;

- to design and present to ministers a comprehensive system for the management of government science, engineering and technology institutions, in order to ensure that their roles within the national system of innovation are clearly defined, that they have clearly defined and understood objectives, and that they undertake their mandate with efficiency, economy and effectiveness;
- to ensure that the management system referred to above includes adequate arrangements for evaluation of performance against international best practice, and that output measures are in place to indicate the nature of the contribution being made by government SETIs (science, engineering, technology, and innovation organisations) to South Africa's development;
- to manage the process of evaluation and review created within the management system described here and to recommend to ministers any actions necessary as a result of assessments carried out;
- to represent the government in formal international, inter-governmental negotiations dealing with science, engineering and technology and with the promotion of innovation;
- to provide a link between government and the activities of the National Advisory Council on Innovation;
- to commission or conduct any policy research necessary to the fulfilment of the responsibilities set out above.

Apart from the first item on this list, the White Paper focused entirely on science and technology policy. This is quite common in ministries or departments of science and technologies across most countries. However, it is the broader policy context within which such functions are set that determines whether S&T policy translates into STI policy. The neoliberal policy framework of GEAR grievously impeded this transformation.

The National Research and Development Strategy (NRDS)

The 2002 National Research and Development Strategy (NRDS) document, which was drafted around the time of the review of the GEAR macroeconomic plan, identified some key systemic fault lines within the national system of innovation that needed to be addressed. It is worth quoting the listing of the text in full:

1. *The termination of key technology missions (such as military dominance in the subcontinent and energy self-sufficiency) by the previous government between 1990 and 1994.* This resulted in a drop in national R&D spending from 1.1 per cent in 1990 to 0.7 per cent of Gross Domestic Product (GDP) in 1994.[17] This reduction happened at a time when the National System of Innovation needed to expand to cope with the needs of 40 million people as opposed to a mere 5–6 million.
2. *Strategic considerations, from human, economic and security perspectives.* Adequate responses to new diseases and to old forms of new diseases, whether these diseases affect humans or animals, need to be informed by local research programmes. From a security perspective, even being a smart buyer of rapidly developing technology rather than a developer requires a critical mass of local scientists doing research in relevant areas. The S&T capacity of the country is running as fast as it can, but is still losing ground.
3. *Human resources.* Our human resources for science and technology are not being adequately renewed. An overwhelmingly white, male and aging scientific population is not being replaced by younger groupings more representative of our demographics.
4. *A complex set of factors driven largely by globalisation has resulted in reduced levels of both investment and performance by the South African private sector in R&D.* This could result in a loss of local control of the developing knowledge base that underpins the success of our most competitive companies.
5. *Inadequate intellectual property legislation and infrastructure.* New developments in biotechnology have increased our vulnerability with respect to the exploitation of our biodiversity, and inventions and innovations from publicly financed research is not effectively protected and managed.
6. *Fragmented governance structures* (RSA 2002a: 15–16, numbering added). Although research institutions have been reviewed and key performance indicators put in place, the roles of different departments in governance and in setting output targets for government research institutions is [sic] not clear or synergistic. From a budget perspective there is no holistic view of science and technology spending by government.

The key to this analysis lies in point 6, the fragmentation of relevant government structures, and the ensuing policy direction was driven by the recognised need to address the coordination failure. Since 2003 the DST has dramatically increased its funding for the biotechnology sectors, marking a shift to a strategic 'picking winners' intervention. Enhanced tax incentives for R&D expenditure were introduced in 2006. Overall, S&T policy has now acquired a sustained focus and direction that are supported by an increased budget and human resource complement. Its coordination role was redefined and has been significantly enhanced since 2002 (Kahn 2008). The NRDS (RSA 2002a) set itself the following three main objectives:

(a) Measures to enhance innovation

- † The need to address the 'innovation chasm', i.e., the gap between innovation and diffusion: to this end the Foundation for Technological (FTI) was planned to create technology missions and to address the innovation chasm.
- † A specific recognition of the need to develop social sciences to understand the workings of the South African NSI.
- † A review and coordination of innovation funding instruments.
- † The current formulation of missions is:
    - Poverty reduction (focus on demonstration and diffusion of technologies to impact quality of life and enhance delivery)
    - Key technology platforms (focus on knowledge-intensive new industries):
        - National Biotechnology Strategy
        - ICT
    - Advanced Manufacturing with linkages to the Integrated Manufacturing Strategy (see RSA 2002b)
    - Leveraging resource-based industries and developing new knowledge-based industries from them (mobilising the power of existing sectors). This amounts to the 'knowledge beneficiation' of a historically resource-based economy
- † Science and technology for poverty reduction oriented towards enhancing basic skills provision: this recognises the critical role of broad-based pre-university education in the development of the human capital base of the NSI.
- † Two technology platforms, ICT and biotechnology, are assigned a development priority.

- Access to technology for SMMEs (small, medium and micro enterprises) and BBEE (Broad Based Economic Empowerment) enterprises; again this is linked to the Integrated Manufacturing Strategy.
- An integrated approach to the development of the agricultural sector with respect to areas of R&D (indigenous knowledge, biotechnology, earth observation, and aspects like logistics) and between national and provincial R&D programmes.

(b) SET human resources and transformation

The document identifies potential and actual areas where South Africa has a scientific competitive strength. Astronomy, human palaeontology, biodiversity, Antarctic research, geology, geomagnetism, and space science are areas of competence which arose from geographic attributes. Other areas of evident knowledge advantage include indigenous knowledge, deep mining technology, medical research, microsatellite engineering, encryption technology, and fluorine technology.

However, the main concern is the faltering education system which has been unable to provide the required flow of qualified students for higher education, especially in SET areas. The NRDS advocates programmes aimed at raising matriculation pass rates and the number of pupils taking science and mathematics.[18]

(c) An effective government science and technology system and infrastructure

The NRDS identified the excessive fragmentation of R&D activity, spread across state-owned corporations, Science Councils (performers and funding agencies), universities and domain-specific research organisations/capacities within the public sector with separate budgets and reporting systems as a major impediment to building a coherent S&T planning framework. The NRDS states categorically that '(t)he size, shape and content of the system of government-owned and funded science and technology institutions and programmes must be aligned with the economic and social development strategies of government' (RSA 2002a: 62).

(d) Private sector interventions

A number of new incentive and restructuring schemes were introduced by the NRDS to stimulate and facilitate private sector

R&D. These included:

- Tax incentives for R&D
- Provincial innovation initiatives, such as incubators to be run by the proposed Foundation for Technological Innovation
- Dedicated funding for global technology sourcing aimed at small and medium firms complemented by information drives to expose local firms to new sources of technology
- Venture capital in the form of seed and early-stage venture capital for high-technology businesses, in conjunction with the DTI

The Ten-Year Innovation Plan

The most recent statement on the shape and direction of S&T policy was laid out in the DST's 10-year plan (RSA 2007b). This plan articulates a firm commitment to move S&T planning more specifically towards innovation and to shift the base of the economy from natural resources to the knowledge economy. It specifically defines an 'innovation chasm' in the national system of innovation, i.e., a failure of R&D, especially state-sponsored R&D, to translate into outcomes which have a significant economic return. The main constraints on the path to the knowledge-based system of innovation are identified as:

- human capital development
- low R&D levels and intensities
- a poor knowledge infrastructure, and
- sub-optimal levels of ancillary functions, such as finance, that impede the flow from R&D to innovation.

The plan provides for priority areas for R&D support on the basis of the contribution of these areas to the transformation and development of the national system of innovation. The explicit vision for the South African National System of Innovation by 2018 includes:

- Being among the global top 10 in terms of the pharmaceutical, nutraceutical, flavour, fragrance, and bio-pesticide industries
- Deploying satellites that provide a range of scientific, security and specialised services for the government, the public and the private sector
- Achieving a 25 per cent share of the global fuel cell market with novel platinum group metal (PGM) catalysts
- Development of a fuel cell programme for transport and domestic use

- Initial capability in the production of hydrogen by water splitting
- Being a world leader in climate science and the response to climate change
- Having met the 2014 Millennium Development Goals to halve poverty

(RSA 2007b: 5)

This represents a decisive shift away from neutral intervention towards the type of strategic role of what Kahn (2008: 153) calls 'the mission-oriented push of the three decades of the apartheid wars in Angola, Mozambique and the then Rhodesia'. Within the context of the post-apartheid innovation system this strategic intervention should, if sustained, provide the required transformation of the system of science and technology into a system of innovation. This shift to 'picking winners' also takes cognisance of the main requirements for the success of state-supported R&D projects. These are:

- the need to achieve critical R&D mass (lumpiness of R&D capital),
- a systems approach with due regard for the required complementarities with skills development, physical capital investment and services, and
- the long-term nature of such R&D programmes which takes into account the depreciation of knowledge.

The 10-year plan identifies five 'great challenges' which demand a multi-disciplinary approach for their attainment and which 'are designed to stimulate multidisciplinary thinking and to challenge our country's researchers to tackle existing questions, create new disciplines and develop new technologies'. The grand challenges, listed here, provide a clear indication of the envisaged expertise requirements:

- The *Farmer to Pharma* value chain to strengthen the bio-economy
- Space science and technology
- Energy security
- Global change science with a focus on climate change
- Human and social dynamics

Human capital at the high end of the spectrum, and the institutions that are directly charged with its production, form the core foundations, or enablers. Progress in all these areas is seen as based on the three foundations of innovation, human capital and knowledge infrastructure. Figure 6.4 illustrates the interconnections between these foundations and the grand challenge programmes. There is also an acceptance that international collaboration in innovation needs to be promoted.

Figure 6.4: *Grand Challenges and Enablers of the Ten-year Plan*

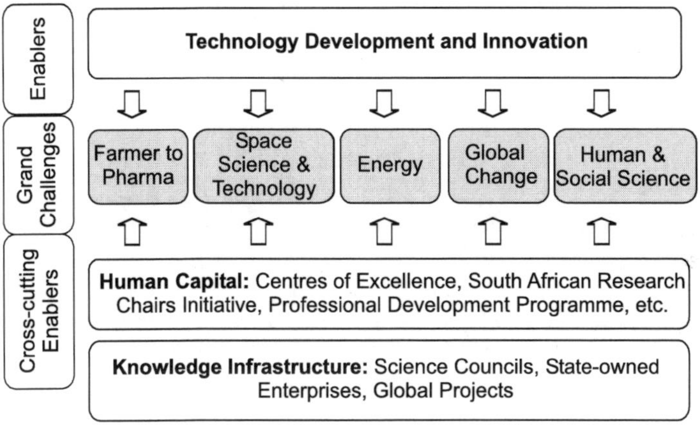

Source: RSA (2007b: 11).

The 10-year plan also seeks to address the fragmentation of funding mechanisms for STI by forming a separate entity, the Technology Innovation Agency (TIA) as a specialised agency which incorporates, among others, the Innovation Fund and the Biotechnology Regional Innovation Centres. The TIA was established in 2008 (RSA 2008a) and its main brief is to enhance market opportunities in partnership with industry and state research institutions. The TIA's broad objectives are listed as follows (RSA 2007b: 32):

- Act as a technological agency that will provide funding and complementary services to bridge the gap between the formal knowledge base and the real economy
- Stimulate development of technology-based services and products
- Support development of technology-based enterprises — both public and private
- Provide an intellectual property support platform

- Stimulate investment (venture capital, foreign direct investment, etc.). Facilitate the development of human capital for innovation.

This new public entity is specifically designed to stimulate and intensify innovation in order to develop technological innovations and interventions and create the appropriate environment for commercialisation. The TIA is expected to serve the development of technology-based products and services, by the public and private sector technology-based enterprises. The conceptualisation of TIA has been criticised from a number of perspectives (see Masilela [2008] for a comprehensive assessment of the TIA bill). Van Zyl (2011) is unambiguous about the implementation failure of the TIA to date.[19]

The 10-year plan marks a decisive shift in the policy stance towards the development of the South African system of innovation. While there is still a degree of disjuncture between STI planning and other policy areas, shifts in related policies also indicate a broad-based move towards a programme of targeted state intervention in the development process. However, there is still an evident gap between intent and implementation, as obvious in the case of the TIA.

Broader policy framework

As discussed earlier, the overall policy framework in which the new democratic South African system of innovation was born was the neoliberal programme contained in the GEAR document. This is still the overall policy document and even though there is a widespread loss of confidence in the validity of the underlying paradigm, it still sets the policy language. Any initiatives to address specific problems on any front through direct intervention are isolated and fragmented, and lack the required alternative paradigmatic context. Within the GEAR framework, performance shortcomings are seen purely as delivery failures due to an under-qualified and inept civil service at the provincial and municipal levels. While this is true, a neoliberal approach to planning will still be inappropriate to address the structural transformation which is needed to alter the evolutionary path of the NSI to one which is more appropriate to the requirements of a democratic political economy.

However, as mentioned earlier, there is now a widespread shift towards a more interventionist approach. This is reflected in a number of areas and we briefly outline relevant policies in industrial policy, before proceeding to policies affecting human capital development and local development further on in this section.

Industrial Policy

The Microeconomic Reform Strategy and the Integrated Manufacturing Strategy (RSA 2002b) are explicit in their recognition of the failure of the state to engineer the required structural transformation of the South African economy:

> The Microeconomic Reform Strategy seeks to affect positively six key performance areas, namely, growth, competitiveness, employment, small business development, black economic empowerment, and geographic spread of economic activity. Government has recognised that weaknesses in addressing these issues arise, in part, from a failure to integrate government policies and programmes adequately (RSA 2002b: 27).

The main initiatives which were adopted in the strategy addressed the promotion of Black Economic Empowerment (later changed to Broad-Based Black Economic Empowerment), small business development, an alignment of policies and strategies towards employment creation and the integration of the various levels of national and local government to foster a more evenly spread growth and development process.

The Accelerated and Shared Growth Initiative for South Africa (RSA 2004) programme set out the following overarching objectives:

- Reduce the unemployment rate from 30 per cent to 15 per cent by 2014.
- Reduce poverty from one-third to one-sixth of the population by 2014.
- Increase the annual GDP growth rate from the then average of 3 per cent to 4.5 per cent per year for the period 2005 to 2009 and to 6 per cent for the period 2010 to 2014. This target should create a sustainable annual growth rate of 6 per cent.

The binding constraints to the achievement of the growth rate required to reduce poverty significantly were identified as:

- currency volatility,
- an inefficient national logistics system whose infrastructure lacked the required capacity for growth,

- the shortage of skilled labour,
- market concentration, monopoly power and barriers to entry,
- limited new investment opportunities,
- a regulatory environment which was not appropriate for the SME sector; labour law was identified as one of the constraints,
- shortcomings in state organisation, capacity and management.

In order to address goals in light of the constraints broad policies were developed with regard to macroeconomic management, the development of infrastructure, sectoral and industrial strategies, skills and education, the Second Economy (referring to the economy 'inhabited' by the majority of the population which bore all the symptoms of severe underdevelopment), and public administration.

National Integration of the NSI

The landmark policy document on local development is the 2006 National Framework on Local Economic Development. This policy statement is unusual in that it explicitly specifies its underlying theoretical foundation. This is identified as 'new institutionalism' which is defined as follows:

> New Institutionalism breaks down the distinction between economy and society, showing how economic decision-making and action is shaped by the shared values, norms, beliefs, meanings, and rules and procedures, of the formal and informal institutions of society. The normative agenda of the New Institutionalism is to develop shared meaning and values, and to strengthen the networks of social interaction. This has also been variously described as building *social capital* or developing *social cohesion* (RSA 2006a: 7).

The various characteristics that are identified as the indicators of successful and sustainable local development include a combination of causes and effects. They can be grouped into the following broad categories (Scerri 2009):

- **Human capital** which is defined in terms of a population that is skilled, problem solving and innovative. The long-term development of human capital is set in a context of guaranteed safety nets. This is further reinforced by a sound environmental policy which provides for the aesthetic component of social life.

- **Institutional networks** which include sound governance in terms of innovative, transparent and fully accountable local authorities, and complex sets of private sector relationships which lead to an optimal utilisation of local assets. Assets in this case are defined to include the natural, physical, financial, human, and social capital of local economies. The availability of a sound physical and social infrastructure significantly lowers the incidence of transactions cost in the local economy. This lowering of transaction costs is further enhanced by sound institutional networks. One of the effects of a vibrant provincial system of innovation would be a complex economic structure with a wide diversity of production sectors. In such a context the larger portion of the income earned by the provincial population would be spent in the province. This would feed into the virtuous cycle of tax revenue generation, leading to better infrastructure with feedback effects to local consumption.
- **Linkages across municipal, provincial, national, continental, and global systems** provide an immediate access to the population and the economy to cutting edge information and global finance. These linkages also reinforce the competitive advantage of local economies and their ability to access the full set of development incentives offered by the national government and global institutions.

The main constraints on the achievement of an even process of local development are the familiar ones of low levels of human capital, inefficient and corrupt local public management, and the poor quality of infrastructure. On top of that there is the low level of integration resulting in weak links to other local systems of innovation. The corresponding strategy areas are governance and delivery, the proper assessment of local comparative and competitive advantage in order to target intervention with support schemes for business and business infrastructure development, and the development of community investment programmes.

Human Capital Development

In line with the discussion throughout this chapter, the broad definition of human capital is adopted in this document. This covers more than education; it also includes those aspects which determine the conditions for the long-term nature of human capital development. While human capital development is a supply-side policy, in the sense that it enhances the technological capabilities of the NSI, it also has demand-side effects in that a generally improving quality of life implies an increasing demand for the products of innovation.

The review of the performance of the South African economy during the first five years of GEAR brought in an urgent drive to address human capital development in a comprehensive manner. This drive was articulated in the 2001 Human Resource Development Strategy for South Africa (RSA 2001) document which addressed the crippling shortfall of human capital in a holistic manner. The document which focuses primarily on education and training is remarkable in that it lays the foundation for the proposed initiatives in the broader terms of human development. The goals (RSA 2001: 10) are specified as:

- To improve the Human Development Index: an improved basic social infrastructure is critical for a productive workforce and a successful economy
- To reduce disparities in wealth and poverty and develop a more inclusive society (measured by the Gini-coefficient)
- To improve international confidence and investor perceptions of the economy (measured by South Africa's position in the international Competitiveness League)

Although there is a conflation of causes and effects in the grouping together of these three goals, this statement of intent signals a decisive shift in the placing of human development as a strategy for development as well as the objective of development. The strategic objectives of human resource development were listed as:

- a solid basic foundation, consisting of early childhood development, general education at school, and adult education and training;
- securing a supply of skills, especially scarce skills, within the Further and Higher Education and training bands of the National Qualifications Framework (NQF), which anticipate and respond to specific skill needs in society, through state and private sector participation in lifelong learning;
- an articulated demand for skills, generated by the needs of the public and private sectors, including those required for social development opportunities, and the development of small business and;

- a vibrant research and innovation sector which supports industrial and employment growth policies. (RSA 2001: 11)

The 2004 AsgiSA document identified a number of medium- and long-term interventions to address the skills shortage. These covered the improvement of public schooling, especially in mathematics and science, investment in priority areas in tertiary education and the development of work-based training programmes and scarce skills initiatives. This led to the establishment of a joint council in government to strengthen and coordinate the activities to address the skills shortage. The urgent need for skills, which are a necessary input for AsgiSA programmes, led to the idea of creating a short- to medium-term troubleshooting approach towards skills challenges. This gave rise to the Joint Initiative on Priority Skills Acquisition (RSA 2006b), which was designed to address the acquisition of scarce and priority skills. JIPSA adopted a three-point strategy:

1. Five high-profile priority skills areas were identified for immediate attention:
    a. high-level, world-class engineering and planning skills for the 'network industries' — transport, communications, water, energy
    b. city, urban and regional planning and engineering skills
    c. artisanal and technical skills, with priority attention to infrastructure development, housing and energy, and in other areas identified as being in strong demand in the labour market
    d. management and planning skills in education and health
    e. Mathematics, Science and language competence in public schooling.
2. JIPSA launched a systematic process of discussion with key 'project owners' and role-players regarding the skills required to underpin AsgiSA projects and to increase labour absorption. This led to concrete proposals for priority skills initiatives in the fields of tourism, ICT, BPO, and biofuels. During the reporting period, JIPSA focused on engaging the project owners in the tourism, ICT and BPO sectors.
3. A limited number of focused analyses and consultations were initiated to address perceived constraints and inefficiencies in the current frameworks and institutional arrangements

for skills delivery. The following issues are receiving priority attention:

a. analysis of the problem of unemployed graduates
b. strengthening of the labour market and skills information system
c. the National Qualifications Framework Review and quality assurance mechanisms
d. analysis of artisan training capacity.

Inter-NSI Integration (Scale Issues)

It is widely agreed (see Muchie et al. 2003) that the development of the South African NSI cannot be considered in isolation from the rest of Africa. In the new world economic order of economic blocs, there is a dire need to create an African (or a sub-Saharan African) system of innovation. A number of customs unions exist in Africa and the one that is immediately relevant to South Africa is the Southern African Development Community (SADC).

The 2007 SADC Protocol on Science Technology and Innovation is a legally binding document aimed at regulating collaborative initiatives within the framework of the SADC Regional Indicative Strategic Development Plan (RISDP) and Africa's Science and Technology Consolidated Plan of Action. The overall aims of the protocol are to:

- Establish institutional mechanisms in order to strengthen regional cooperation on and coordination of science, technology and innovation,
- Institute management and coordination structures, with clearly defined functions, which will facilitate the implementation of regional STI programmes,
- Promote the development and harmonisation of science, technology and innovation policies in the region,
- Pool resources for scientific research, technological development within the region,
- Demystify science, technology and innovation by promoting public understanding and awareness of and meaningful participation in these disciplines, and
- Work towards the elimination of restrictions that restrict the free movement of scientists, technologist and engineers for the purposes of education, research and participation in joint STI programmes.[20]

This agreement is set within the broader 2003 NEPAD (New Partnership for African Development) STI cooperation framework. The structure of the NEPAD Science and Technology programme covers governance structures, priority S&T areas with key outputs in each area, business and implementation plans and human capital development.[21] The governance structure is composed of a ministerial council, a steering committee of relevant director general-level officials, the NEPAD secretariat, as well as regional coordinators. The priority S&T areas have been grouped into the following programme clusters:

- biodiversity, biotechnology and indigenous knowledge
- energy, water and desertification
- material sciences, manufacturing, laser, and post-harvest technologies
- ICT and space science and technology
- mathematical sciences

The key outputs in each area are specified as:

- Research outputs targeted at addressing social and economic problems in Africa
- Technology hubs/incubators to nurture new innovations
- Human resource development
- Stemming of the brain drain
- Strengthening of institutional capacity

The programme of action requires that business plans be formulated in each NEPAD region for each cluster, which is to be consolidated into a single overall consolidated plan. The implementation mechanism includes the establishment of centres of excellence in each region for each programme and the development of continent-wide networks to maximise economies of scale and scope in R&D programmes.

Regional integration across sub-Saharan Africa is relevant at yet another level. The entry of South Africa in the BRICS grouping is at first sight odd, given the small size of its economy, in terms of population, GDP and all other macroeconomic variables, relative to those of the other countries in the group. Its presence alongside considerably larger economies can only be understood in terms of its being an African economy with the most diversified and complex NSI in the sub-Saharan region. Implicitly, South Africa brings the rest of the region into the BRICS grouping. This proposition, however, can only be valid if premised on an evident degree of regional economic integration. Alternatively, South Africa's continued effective 'membership' in BRICS can only be sustainable on the basis of a progressive transition from a national to a regional system of innovation across sub-Saharan Africa.

Outcomes of State Policy and State Institutions on the NSI

The assessment of any single policy is not easy given the large amount of determinants which may influence outcomes. These determinants consist of other state policies and state performance, as well as factors exogenous to the state planning arena, whether local, or global. Thus the identification of clear lines of causality is rarely simple. In the case of the South African system of innovation, the search for causalities is further complicated by the short time span of the relevant period. The South African political economy changed fundamentally in 1994, but most of the policies which are relevant today originated in 2002. This is far too short a time to assess the effects of policies which have been, or should have been, designed to fundamentally alter the structure of the NSI in its broadest sense.

Within the confines of S&T policy design and implementation, the DST has certainly extended its coordinating role considerably since its transformation from DACST in 2002. In the short span of time since then it has moved much closer to placing its activities within the NSI conceptual framework, as articulated in the 1996 White Paper. The 2007 10-year innovation plan following on the 2002 National R&D Strategy document sets out the agenda for the next stage in the strategic path of the DST. While it is much too soon to discern any results, the restructuring of the Ministry of Science and Technology is already following the recommendations of the 2007 plan.

On the broader canvas, the most worrisome failure of policy is on the education and training front. It is widely acknowledged that the performance of public education from primary schooling to the tertiary education level has failed to produce the sufficiently educated labour force that is required for the country's development process. It is also widely acknowledged that the National Skills Development Strategy and the Human Resources Development Strategy working through the Sector Education and Training Authorities have also generally failed to increase at any significant level the skills base of the economy. The AsgiSA and JIPSA programmes, drafted largely as another response to the continuing failure to address the country's human capital constraints are still too young to enable an assessment of their effects. The DST has been actively trying to redress the lack of research capacity in universities and the SARChI programme, has, in its short lifetime, been a highly successful means for addressing the low reproduction rates of researchers.

In the case of local development, the 2006 National Framework for Local Economic Development document (RSA 2006a) marks a decided break in the approach to regional imbalances in the development process. It is obviously much too soon to assess the impact of this policy initiative on the highly distorted economic geography of South Africa. However, the current provincial map will continue to place a severe constraint on the roll out of the new local economic development policy framework.

Most of the STI cooperation initiatives within the context of the SADC and NEPAD are still bogged down by bureaucratic inefficiencies in a structure which is top heavy and wasteful of funds. There is little beyond statements of intent specifying areas of cooperation in STI among member countries of the AU (as articulated in NEPAD 2006) and the SADC. One of the more promising initiatives within NEPAD is the development of common STI indicators for the region which would allow intra-Africa comparability.

Conclusions and Recommendations Targeting Improvements in the NSI with Specific Emphasis on the Role of the State

The South African system of innovation which forms the object of this study can be seen as a very young one. The advent of democracy in 1994 marked a decisive shift in the legal underpinnings of the system. There are, however, strong reservations as to whether political change was sufficient to engender a corresponding transformation of the NSI. There are strong arguments, which have been briefly outlined in this chapter, that the fact that the first macroeconomic plan for the new democracy was a neoliberal one meant that there was a continuation, and indeed an unprecedented legitimacy, of the economic structure which developed under apartheid. The review of the performance of the South African economy led to a revision, albeit a fragmented one, of the role of the state in the structural transformation of the South African economy. From this perspective, therefore, the origin of the post-apartheid system of innovation, in terms of state policy aimed at engineering the required break from the economic structure carried over from apartheid, should be defined as from the earlier part of the 21st century. This makes the new South African system of innovation quite young.

There are two main constraints on the development of the post-apartheid NSI that were carried over from the apartheid economy. They are the depletion of broad-based human capital and the regional unevenness that grew from the economic geography of apartheid. State policy within the framework of the GEAR macroeconomic plan was severely restricted to a market facilitation role and the provision of public goods, including education. The expectation was that the liberalisation of markets would stimulate a burst of growth whose benefits would trickle down to the general public and progressively raise the quality of life. It was never clear how this policy would redress the degeneration of the human capital base under apartheid and the review of the first five years of GEAR made it clear that unemployment, poverty, income inequality and education and training had not improved. It was also acknowledged that the enduring levels of market concentration and the associated barriers to entry had proved to be an insurmountable obstacle to the redistribution of wealth through Broad-Based Black Economic Empowerment. The negotiated settlement on the definition of provinces also tied in the economy to one of the more debilitating aspects of apartheid. The high level of the unevenness of development among provinces has become highly path dependent and has formed the basis for a distorted NSI.

It is now clear that the South African state has taken upon itself the role of the leader of the reshaping of the NSI, even though it may not be stating it in quite those terms. Certainly, the DST has shifted to a targeted intervention policy and has adopted the role of a leader in R&D financing and activity. There are a number of recommendations which would enhance the effects of state policy on the development of the South African system of innovation that we list here:

1. The coordinating role of the DST over all state STI programmes and initiatives has to be strengthened to eradicate the 'silo' planning with its endemic wastefulness of opportunities and its potential for contradictory policies.
2. The DST has to redefine the 'human capital pipeline' to include all education and training programmes. From this stance it should be an active partner with the Departments

of Education and Labour so as to bring in an overall coordinating structure in education. It should also liaise with the Department of Public Works in its expanded public works programme so as to ensure that the training component generates more of an impact on human capital development than a simple soaking up of unemployment.

3. An indigenous STI component should be built into all government construction and infrastructural programmes. The specific economic and environmental conditions in South Africa offer ample scope for the development of local technologies and an STI requirement in the public tendering processes would constitute a significant demand-led stimulus to local innovation. Insofar as the South African economic and environmental conditions are replicated across a substantial portion of sub-Saharan Africa, there are substantial potential economies of scale for the long-term development of local appropriate technologies. The constitutional commitment for the provision of basic needs, in terms of housing, clean water, energy, communications, health, and education offers a potential for a state-led demand stimulus for innovation that should be substantially stronger and certainly longer lasting than that provided by military expenditure under apartheid.
4. The identification of the S&T areas listed as the 'grand challenges' in the 10-year innovation plan (RSA 2007b) provides a clear signal of a concerted and targeted supply-side STI stimulus programme. Again, this could be substantially complemented by demand-side incentives which would assure the long-term viability of STI initiatives.
5. The provincial map of South Africa has to be revisited in order to eradicate the fundamental historically determined differences in development potential. This redrawing should reduce the number of provinces to a maximum of five and should ensure that those sub-national artificial economies previously designated as *bantustans* or homelands be merged with the historically advantaged sub-national entities within the parameters of viable provincial systems of innovation. The DST can play a crucial role in this reformation through its new mandate to deploy STI planning at the provincial level. The redrawing of the provincial map could actually

ensure that the provincial strategy of the STI generates the maximum returns.

6. The urgent addressing of poverty should be placed at the core of development policy as a strategic tool as well as an objective of development. This, when combined with recommendation (3) should also provide a huge boost to the purchasing power of the internal market. In the current environment of the global financial crisis this would imply a strongly expansionary fiscal policy. The 2001 Human Resource Development Strategy did just that and developed 25 indicators as a means to achieve a comprehensive improvement in the human capital base of the South African economy. This endeavour was, however, bedevilled by poor implementation and faulty monitoring mechanisms. The solution to this failure lies not so much in the articulation of the original vision as in the reform of its implementation.

The shunting of the evolutionary path of the South African system of innovation on to an alternative development track cannot be approached in a piecemeal incremental manner, given the distortions generated during apartheid economic history. It requires a considerable programme of structural development on a broad front and it is the state that has to take on this role with conviction in a concerted and coordinated effort.

The weaknesses and threats identified by the OECD review of innovation policy in South Africa (OECD 2007: 13–17) consist almost entirely of shortcomings of the various determinants of human capital and human capabilities availability and development, as well as inappropriate state STI policy implementation. In the case of the latter factor, poor coordination of STI policy across government ministries and departments is cited as a main source of the implementation failure. In the case of human capital formation requirements the report focuses almost exclusively on the higher education sector. Among the several recommendations, the report drew attention to the requirement that a broad approach to innovation should be adopted, wherein the innovation capabilities are fostered and enhanced across the economy (OECD 2007: 19). The report also notes (ibid.: 80–81) that the knowledge base of the South African economy had not shifted significantly away from a resource-based economy.

The landmark 2012 report of the DST Ministerial Review Committee on the STI landscape in South Africa (RSA 2012) marks a watershed in the state's appraisal of its performance in developing an NSI appropriate to the structural transformation of the South African economy. The review committee accepts the assessment of the 2007 OECD report and elaborates on the shortcomings of the current role of the state in the evolution of the South African system of innovation. The identified problem areas can be summarised as follows (RSA 2012: 10):

- An enduring strong reliance on a resource- and commodity-based economy
- Poor public sector coordination of the planning and implementation of the NSI
- Business was insufficiently involved in building the NSI, at the levels of both large and small firms
- Lack of understanding of the broader definition of the NSI
- Human capital constraints at the higher end of the skills spectrum
- Inadequate capacity for the STI measurement
- Enduring poverty and exclusion

In Section 6.1 of the report of the Ministerial Committee the conceptualisation of the NSI is addressed directly with two broad alternatives on its coordinating form considered — loose or tight coordination (RSA 2012: 96–97). The report offers a 'tripartite' coordination model with a central policy-making core and a coordination structure setting the context within which the 'NSI performing agents', covering the public and private sectors and civil society, operate (RSA 2012: 98–99). The path dependence of an uncoordinated NSI in South Africa is explicitly recognised in the report.[22] The report offers a wide range of recommendations (41 in all) covering the governance of the NSI, business and social innovation, human capital and the knowledge infrastructure, monitoring and evaluation, and the financing of the NSI. The more specific and significant recommendations include:

- With respect to governance, the main recommendation is for a single coordinating body (a National Council on Research and Innovation) established and located in the Office of the President and overseen by the Deputy President. A unitary R&I vote is also proposed to ensure better coordination of the public funding of R&I.

- With respect to the business innovation environment, recommendations are made to strengthen existing funding and coordination mechanisms, such as the Technology and Human Resources for Industry Programme (linking industry, HEIs and the state in innovation projects), as well as establishing funding mechanisms specifically designed to enable the access of small- and medium-sized enterprises to technology and scientific knowledge.
- Human capacity development is assigned a high priority as a major obstacle in the development of the NSI. However, the specific recommendations in the report focus on post-schooling education with an envisaged large expansion in technical colleges, curricula revisions at HEIs and measures to ensure a higher rate of reproduction of young academics. The placement of social innovation as a separate vaguely specified category, along with the scant attention to the pre-matriculation school sector does however place limits on the eventual efficacy of human capacity development policy as recommended in the report.
- Monitoring, evaluation and learning enhancement, expansion and centralisation covering system-mapping, analysis, building, steerage, evaluation, learning, and foresight exercises. The proposals should lead to an enhanced coordination and collation of reports from the various state agencies in the NSI.
- In the case of the financing of the NSI, it is proposed that R&I funding for the HEI sector should be significantly increased, that current business R&I-oriented incentive schemes should be enhanced, and that incentives for innovation-intensive foreign direct investment should be put in place.

The report of the Ministerial Review Committee marks a watershed in the evolution of the role of the state in the South African system of innovation. Its candid assessment of the failure of the state to transform the NSI on a number of crucial fronts, along with an explicit acceptance of the path-dependent nature of an unplanned NSI, sets the basis for a new and more appropriate coordination regime of the system. The recognition of the statutory limits to the ability of the DST, in isolation, to alter the shape of the NSI and the proposed elevation of the required coordination role to a supra-ministerial level augurs well for the development of a more coherent innovation strategy. This also opens up the policy formulation space for core areas, especially in the case of human capabilities formation, which are still only partially addressed in the report.

Notes

1. The term 'black' is here used in the way that liberation movements used it as representing all the disenfranchised populations regardless of race or ethnicity.
2. This is documented in detail in Fine and Rustomjee (1996: chapter 7).
3. See Adelzadeh (1996) for an orthodox economic critique of GEAR.
4. The employment of low-skilled labour in South Africa has no significant effect on the long-term prospects for human capital development. As Altman (2006: 6) puts it: 'There is evidence to show that the wages of low skill and semi-skill formal sector workers is stagnant or falling and that these jobs are becoming increasingly precarious in character. This is consistent with the path of industrial development, which has increasingly leaned to the outsourcing, the real expansion of services, and of the informal sector.'
5. See Maharajh (2011: chapter 9) and Nattrass (2011) for a review and discussion of the contradictions in the NGP document.
6. '[T]he New Growth Path document . . . says little about innovation, R&D and technology, instead being content, with one exception, to repeat the indicators of the Ten-Year Innovation Plan. This is insufficient to build a prosperous state whatever its design may be, and would position South Africa outside mainstream thought on the importance of innovation' (RSA 2012: 123).
7. The 1996 White Paper was the second of the two official national STI policy documents in the history of South Africa. The first was legislated in 1916, as part of the move to formalise S&T planning across the British Empire during World War I (Scerri 2009).
8. '[W]e have in place an ailing national system of innovation. It is fragmented and is neither coordinated within itself nor within national goals; innovation capacity is not being built but is being eroded; national investment in R&D is not increasing relative to GDP, but falling' (RSA 1996b: 46).
9. Lall (1993) argued that the tariff system under apartheid was perverted in that it protected mature industries with limited potential for technological advance while exposing emerging industries with a high technology potential to international competition. From this perspective, trade liberalisation would have removed the distortion effects of tariffs. However, the rapid removal of protection for labour-

intensive low-skilled industries such as textiles and clothing caused the collapse of specific sectors and an increase in unemployment. Of course the more appropriate policy would have been to re-draw the tariff regime on the basis of some version of the 'infant industry' argument.

10. '[I]ndividual institutions trying to adapt are doing so in a policy vacuum at the highest levels of the present South African government. It may be that in the past, during the days of the National Party government's "Total Strategy", there was strong coordination and shared purpose among the institutions of the white dominated state. *If that was the case then*, we found no evidence of it being the case now . . . (r)ather, we saw a series of institutions, each trying to define for itself a role in a "new" South Africa' (IDRC 1993: 5).

    'There are no articulated economic or social goals towards which various institutions could apply their efforts . . . as a consequence of the policy vacuum, resource allocations are essentially frozen, subject only to minor variations approved by officials within a system which is non-consultative and non-transparent, even to other high-level government officials' (IDRC 1993: 22–23, emphasis added).

11. The White Paper was clear on the need to integrate S&T policy within the overall national planning framework. Governments of the industrialised countries recognised, at the beginning of the 1980s, that one of the challenges of promoting technological innovation was in devising means to ensure that government actions across all fields — in trade, education, labour laws, environmental protection, to name but a few — be taken with due consideration of how these actions would affect the climate for innovation. (RSA 1996b: 22)

12. 'Section five of the Document (GEAR), on "Trade, Industrial and Small Enterprise Policies", is thin on what the proposed trade policies, industrial policy and small enterprises are to be. On trade, the proposals appear to do away with any policies, as fast as possible. Some small enterprise policies are listed and there is a complete absence of any proposal for an industrial policy or strategy' (Adelzadeh 1996: 81, parentheses added).

    The formulation in labour policy was caught up in the dual trap of low skills and high unemployment. In the absence of an overall policy which placed human capital development as a top priority in economic planning, labour market liberalisation became the only apparently logical tool to address unemployment.

13. 'The evidence to support the proposition that import liberalization is automatically good for growth is weak — almost as weak as the opposite proposition that protectionism is good for growth' (UNDP 2005: 119).

14. 'The government intends to create the following outputs related to human resource development:
    - A human resource development investment strategy which would be an integrated and affordable five-year HRD plan.
    - A training strategy which details sectoral investment programmes for the National Training Strategy, with a priority on immediate investment strategies.
    - Restructuring education through improving the quality of education within the prevailing fiscal constraints with the priority on skills for employment, growth and democracy and a plan for effective backlog provision.
    - Social partnerships in human resource development with specific reference to partnerships with the private sector on education, health and training. This also proposes a training investment target of five per cent of the salary bill' (RSA 1996b: 71).
15. Under apartheid, four 'independent' *bantustans* were created along ethnic lines. These were Transkei (Xhosa), declared independent on 26 October 1976, Bophuthatswana (Tswana), declared independent on 6 December 1977, Venda (Venda), declared independent on 13 September 1979, and Ciskei (also Xhosa), declared independent on 4 December 1981. The other six homelands — Gazankulu (Tsonga [Shangaan]), KaNgwane (Swazi), KwaNdebele (Ndebele), KwaZulu (Zulu), Lebowa (Northern Sotho or Pedi) and QwaQwa (Southern Sotho) — were assigned partial administrative autonomy.
16. These were the Cape, Natal, the Orange Free State, and the Transvaal.
17. However, the ratio of gross expenditure on R&D relative to the GDP has been rising steadily since 1997–98 and is comparable to that of Poland, Portugal and Hungary (Kahn and Blankley 2006).
18. 'This issue has become so pressing that it will be necessary to increase "out-of-school" programmes to support mathematics, science and computer education. A number of pilot programmes, run by dedicated volunteers in many cases, have shown excellent results. In addition, specific consideration should be given to incentivising schools to produce more black and more female Mathematics and Science matriculants at the higher grade. For example, private schools that successfully produce higher-grade Mathematics and Science matriculants from designated groups could be retrospectively paid the equivalent of the education subsidy' (RSA 2002a: 55).
19. 'So far the effect of TIA on the innovation landscape has not been apparent. On the contrary, quite a number of funding initiatives incorporated into the TIA have been abruptly ended, leaving research institutions responsible for personnel and running costs and in some cases even resulting in the loss of highly skilled personnel. In addition,

the payments of many research contracts are in arrears, leaving institutions liable for payments to subcontractors and international collaboration partners. Apart from the financial implications, this situation has serious international reputational risks for the South African innovation system' (van Zyl 2011).

20. See http://www.dst.gov.za/media-room/press-releases/sadc-ministers-sign-protocol-to-improve-science-and-technology-cooperation/?searchterm=SADC%20protocol%20on%20STI (accessed 2 December 2011).
21. See http://www.dst.gov.za/other/icr/products?submen=1#flagship (accessed 2 December 2011).
22. 'Where innovation has been left free to proceed along trajectories defined by historical precedent, it becomes a dynamic that inadvertently has the effect of deepening inequalities and imbalances, rather than ameliorating them' (RSA 2012: 110).

References

Adelzadeh, A., 1996. 'From the RDP to GEAR: The Gradual Embracing of Neoliberalism in Economic Policy', *Transformation*, 31(4): 66–95.

African National Congress (ANC), 1994. *Reconstruction and Development Programme*. Johannesburg: Umyanyano Publication.

Altman, M., 2006. 'Low Wage Work in South Africa', Paper presented to IZA/World Bank Conference on Employment & Development Berlin, Germany, 25–27 May, Human Resources Development Council, Cape Town.

Barnard, G., 2009. 'Realising South Africa's Employment Potential', Working Paper no. ECO/WKP (2009)3, Economics Department, Organisation for Economic Co-operation and Development.

Bowles, S. and H. Gintis, 1975. 'The Problem with Human Capital Theory — A Marxian Critique', *American Economic Review*, 65(2): 74–82.

Bundy, C., 1988. *The Rise and Fall of African Peasantry*. London: Currey.

Centre for Science, Technology and Innovation Indicators (CeSTII), 2005. *Main Results of the South African Innovation Survey 2005 (Covering the Period 2002–2004)*. Pretoria: Department of Science and Technology.

Fine, B. and Z. Rustomjee, 1996. *The Political Economy of South Africa: From Minerals-Energy Complex to Industrialisation*. Johannesburg: University of the Witwatersrand Press.

International Development Research Centre (IDRC), 1993. *Towards a Science and Technology Policy for a Democratic South Africa*. Ottawa: International Development Research Centre.

Kahn, M., 2008. 'Science and Technology Policy', in A. Kraak and K. Press (eds), 2008. *Education, Employment and Skills in South Africa*. Cape Town: Human Resources Development Council, 134–60.

Kahn, M. and W. Blankley, 2006. 'The State of Research and Experimental Development: Moving to a Higher Gear', in S. Buhlungu, J. Daniel, R. Southhall, and J. Lutchman (eds), *State of the Nation: South Africa 2005–2006*. Cape Town: Human Resources Development Council, 270–98.

Lall, S., 1993. 'What Will Make South Africa Internationally Competitive?', in P. Baker, A. Boraine and W. Krafchik (eds), *South Africa and the World Economy in the 1990s*. Washington DC: Brookings Institution, 50–70.

Maharajh, R., 2011. 'Innovating beyond Racial Capitalism', Ph.D. Dissertation, Lund University.

Maharajh, R. and T. Pogue, 2006. 'A Representation to the African Peer Review Mechanism on Assessment of South Africa's Socio-Economic Development', African Peer Review Mechanism (APRM) National Secretariat and Institute for Economic Research on Innovation, Tshwane University of Technology, Pretoria.

———, 2008. 'South African Science, Technology and Industry Scoreboard 2008', *Cooperation Framework on Innovation Systems between Finland and South (COFISA)*, Department of Science and Technology, Tshwane University of Technology, Pretoria.

———, 2009. 'Transforming South Africa's National System of Innovation for Accelerated and Shared Growth and Development', Country Report for Comparative BRICS Study, Rede de Pesquisa em Sistemas e Arranjos Produtivos e Inovativos Locais (RedeSist) and International Development Research Centre (IDRC), Rio de Janeiro.

Masilela, T., 2008. 'Governance Challenges: Considerations in Structuring Agencies to Support Innovation', Faculty Seminar Paper, Faculty of Economics and Finance, Tshwane University of Technology, Pretoria.

Muchie, M., P. Gammeltoft and B.-Å. Lundvall (eds), 2003. *Putting Africa First: The Making of African Innovation Systems*. Aalborg: Aalborg University Press.

Nattrass, N., 2011. 'The New Growth Path: Game Changing Vision or Cop-out?' *South African Journal of Science*, 107(3/4): 1–8.

New Partnership for Africa's Development (NEPAD), 2006. *Africa's Science and Technology Consolidated Plan of Action*. Midrand: New Partnership for Africa's Development (NEPAD) Office of Science and Technology.

Organisation for Economic Cooperation and Development (OECD), 2007. *OECD Reviews of Innovation Policy: South Africa*. Paris: Organisation for Economic Cooperation and Development.

Republic of South Africa (RSA), 1996a. *Growth, Employment and Redistribution: A Macroeconomic Strategy*. Pretoria: Department of Finance, Republic of South Africa.

Republic of South Africa (RSA), 1996b. *White Paper on Science and Technology: Preparing for the 21st Century*. Pretoria: Department of Arts, Culture, Science and Technology, Republic of South Africa.

———, 2000. *Towards a National Skills Development Strategy: Skills for Productive Citizenship for All*. Pretoria: Department of Labour, Republic of South Africa.

———, 2001. *Human Resource Development Strategy for South Africa*. Pretoria: Department of Education and Department of Labour, Republic of South Africa.

———, 2002a. *South Africa's National Research and Development Strategy*. Pretoria: Department of Science and Technology, Republic of South Africa.

———, 2002b. *Accelerating Growth and Development: The Contribution of an Integrated Manufacturing Strategy*. Pretoria: Department of Trade and Industry, Republic of South Africa.

———, 2003. *Towards a Ten Year Review: Synthesis Report on Implementation of Government Programmes*. Cape Town; Pretoria: Office of the Presidency, Republic of South Africa.

———, 2004. *Accelerated and Shared Growth Initiative for South Africa-AsgiSA*. Cape Town; Pretoria: Office of the Presidency, Republic of South Africa.

———, 2005a. *National Skills Development Strategy, 1 April 2005–31 March 2010*. Pretoria: Department of Labour, Republic of South Africa.

———, 2005b. *National Survey of Research & Development 2003/2004*. Pretoria: Department of Science and Technology, Republic of South Africa.

———, 2006a. *National Framework for Local Economic Development (LED) in South Africa (2006–2011)*. Pretoria: Department of Provincial and Local Government, Republic of South Africa.

———, 2006b. *Joint Initiative on Priority Skills Acquisition —JIPSA*. Cape Town; Pretoria: Office of the Presidency, Republic of South Africa.

———, 2007a. *Development Indicators — Mid-term Review*. Cape Town; Pretoria: Office of the Presidency, Republic of South Africa.

———, 2007b. *Innovation towards a Knowledge-based Economy Ten-Year Plan for South Africa (2008–2018)*. Pretoria: Department of Science and Technology, Republic of South Africa.

———, 2008a. *National Survey of Research and Experimental Development (R&D) 2006*/2007. Pretoria: Department of Science and Technology, Republic of South Africa.

———, 2008b. *Towards a Fifteen Year Review*. Cape Town; Pretoria: Office of the Presidency, Republic of South Africa.

———, 2009. 'The New Growth Path: The Framework', South Africa Government Online. http://www.info.gov.za/view/DownloadFileAction?id=135748 (accessed 2 December 2011).

Republic of South Africa (RSA), 2010. *Development Indicators — Mid-term Review*. Cape Town; Pretoria: Office of the Presidency, Republic of South Africa.

———, 2011. *National Survey of Research & Experimental Development: Main Results 2008/2009*. Pretoria: Department of Science and Technology, Republic of South Africa.

———, 2012. *Department of Science and Technology Ministerial Review Committee on the Science, Technology and Innovation Landscape in South Africa (Final Report)*. Pretoria: Department of Science and Technology, Republic of South Africa.

Scerri, M., 1990. 'R&D and the International Competitiveness of the South African Manufacturing Sector', *South African Journal of Economics*, 58(4): 341–56.

———, 2003. 'The Competitiveness of the Southern African Customs Union within the Context of the Indian Ocean Rim', in G. Campbell (ed.), *The Indian Ocean Rim: Southern Africa and Regional Co-operation*. London; New York: Routledge-Curzon, 123–42.

———, 2009. *The Evolution of the South African System of Innovation since 1916*. Cambridge: Cambridge Scholars Publishing.

———, 2010. 'Provincial Systems of Innovation and Globalisation in South Africa', in B. Dallago and C. Guglielmetti (eds), *Local Economies and Global Competitiveness*. New York: Palgrave Macmillan, 75–94.

Sen, A., 1999. *Development as Freedom*. New York: Anchor Books.

United Nations Development Programme (UNDP), 2005. *Human Development Report 2005*. New York: United Nations Development Programme.

———, 2009. *Human Development Report 2009*. New York: Palgrave Macmillan.

———, 2011. 'Human Development Indicators', Human Development Report Office, United Nations Development Programme. http://hdrstats.undp.org/en/countries/profiles/ZAF.html (accessed 2 December 2011).

Van Zyl, A., 2011. 'Innovation in South Africa — The Role of the Technology Innovation Agency', *South African Journal of Science*, 107(1/2).

Annexure

Annexure A: Selected Macroeconomic Indicators for South Africa

Figure A6.1: *Real South African GDP Growth Rate*

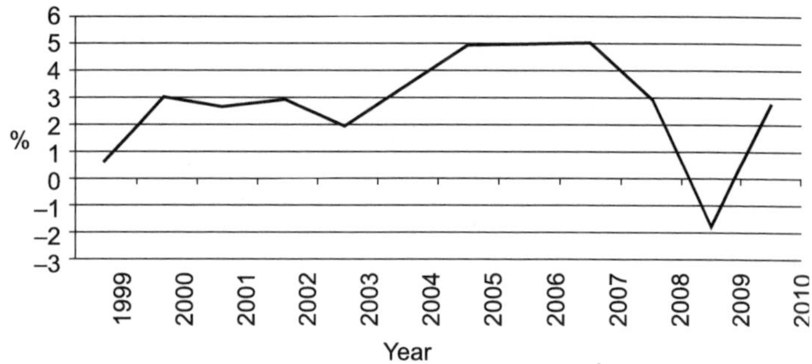

Source: Maharajh (2011: 244), http://www.indexmundi.com/g/g.aspx?c=sf&v=66 (accessed 2 December 2011).

Figure A62: *South African GDP Per Capita (PPP US$)*

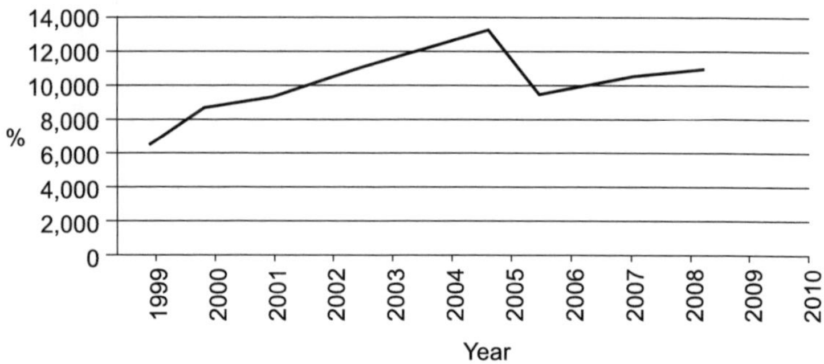

Source: RSA, 2005b and RSA, 2011, http://www.indexmundi.com/g/g.aspx?c=sf&v=67 (accessed 2 December 2011).

Figure A6.3: *South African Unemployment Rates (2001–2007)*

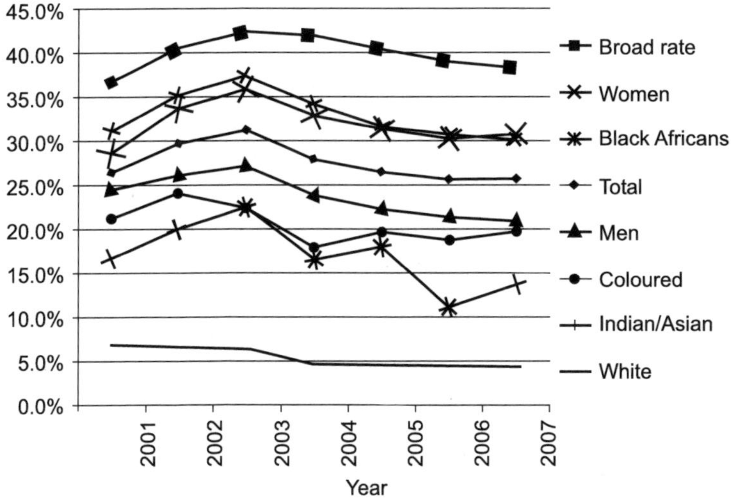

Source: Maharajh and Pogue (2008: 33).

Figure A6.4: *Income Inequality in South Africa: Gini-coefficient*

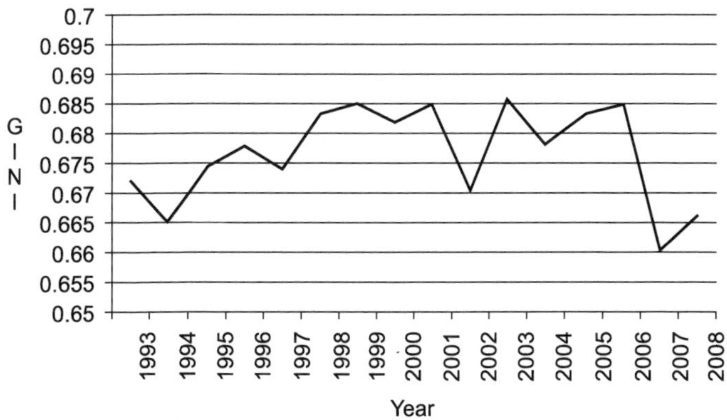

Source: RSA (2010).

Figure A6.5: *Composition of Exports, 2003–2007*

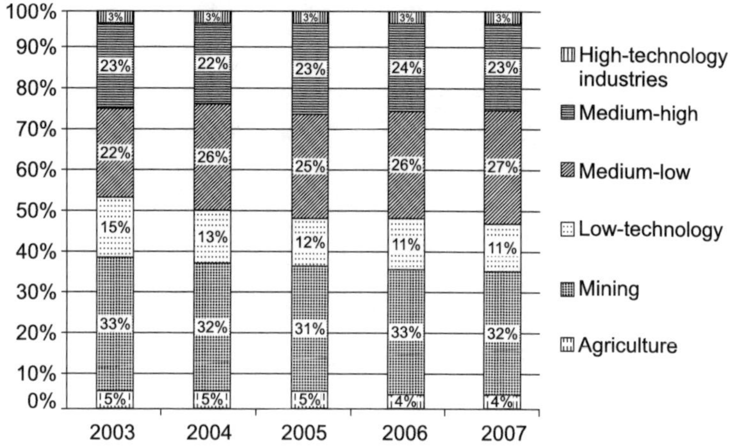

Source: Maharajh and Pogue (2008:18).

Figure A6.6: *Comparative HDI Trends*

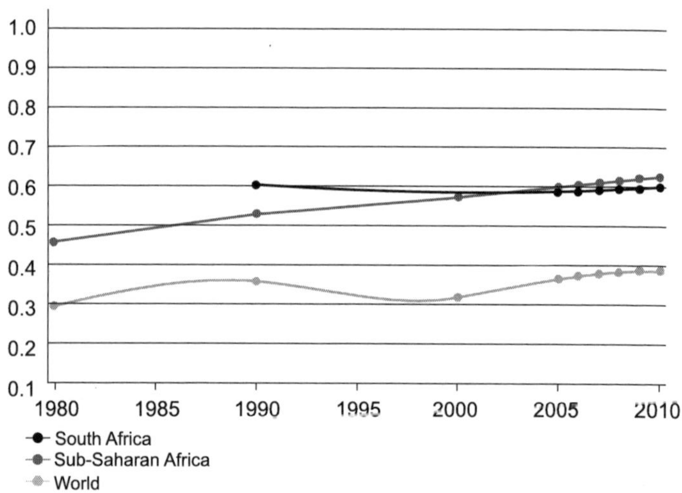

Source: UNDP (2011).

Table A6.1: *Composition of South African GDP by Sector*

Industry	*Relative Size 2010 (per cent)*
Agriculture, forestry and fishing	2.2
Mining and quarrying	5.5
Manufacturing	15.3
Electricity, gas and water	1.9
Construction	3.2
Wholesale and retail trade, hotels and restaurants	11.9
Transport, storage and communication	9.1
Finance, real estate and business services	21.0
General government services	13.7
Personal services	5.6
Total value added	89.4
Taxes less subsidies on products	10.6
GDP at market prices	100.0

Source: Statistics South Africa — Statistical Release P0411 (Table D).

Table A6.2: *Percentage contribution to South African Industrial Output by Sector and Province (2010)*

Industrial Sector	*Province*								
	W. Cape	North West	Mpumalanga	Limpopo	KZN	Free State	Gauteng	E. Cape	N. Cape
Primary industries	3.7	32.7	26.4	29.7	5.7	19.6	3.8	1.9	32.2
Mining and quarrying	0.2	30.7	23.6	27.2	1.9	13.6	3.4	0.4	26.2
Secondary industries	19.9	9.2	21.2	8.3	23.1	14.9	22.4	17.1	7.3
Manufacturing	13.0	4.9	12.6	2.6	16.8	9.4	15.0	12.6	2.3
Tertiary industries	67.1	48.6	43.0	52.6	62.0	58.0	64.4	71.5	51.0
Wholesale and retail trade; hotels and restaurants	15.7	10.3	9.7	10.3	13.6	11.4	13.2	13.7	10.8

(*Cont.*)

(*Cont.*)

Industrial Sector	*Province*								
	W. Cape	North West	Mpumalanga	Limpopo	KZN	Free State	Gauteng	E. Cape	N. Cape
Finance, real estate and business services	27.8	11.9	11.4	14.3	17.7	14.7	23.0	18.9	12.5
Community, social and other personal services	5.5	7.9	5.4	4.8	6.1	11.6	4.5	10.8	8.8
General government services	10.0	11.7	10.0	17.1	13.3	14.0	16.5	21.0	12.3

Source: Statistics South Africa — Statistical Release P04411 (Table I).

Annexure B: Selected Human Capital Indicators

Figure B6.1: *Demographics of Research Personnel*

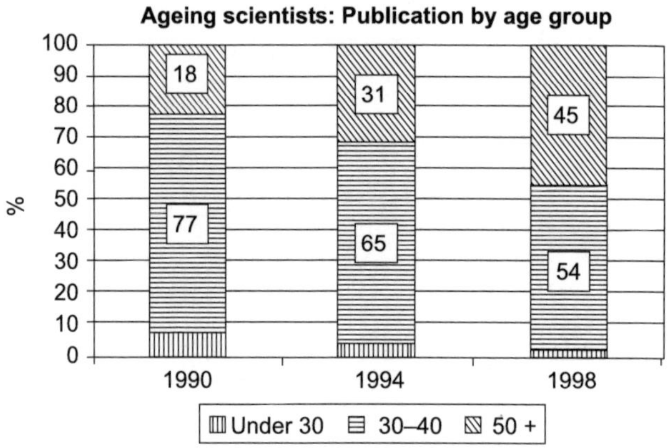

Figure B6.2: *Scientific Publication by Race*

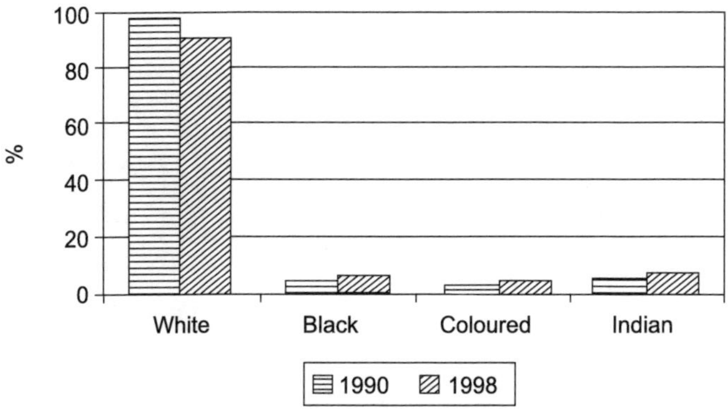

Source: RSA (2002a: 53).

Annexure C: HEI Enrolments

Figure C6.1: *Total HEI Enrolments in South Africa*

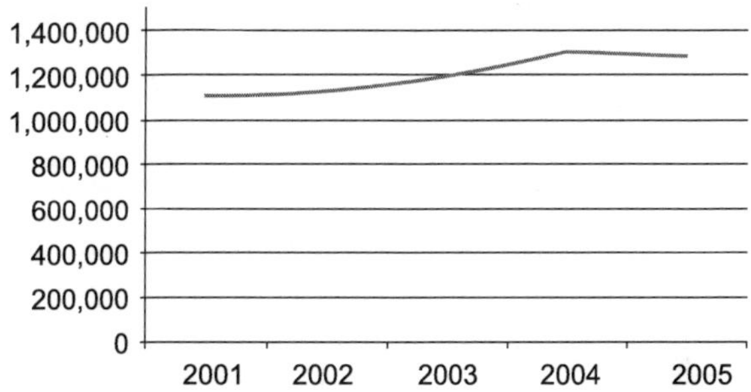

Source: Maharajh and Pogue (2008: 56).

Figure C6.2: *Contact HEI Enrolments in South Africa*

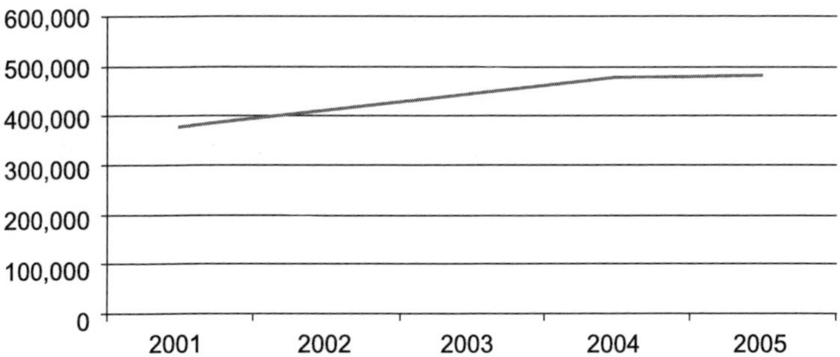

Source: Maharajh and Pogue (2008: 56).

Annexure D

Figure D6.1: *International Tests of Scholastic Achievement*

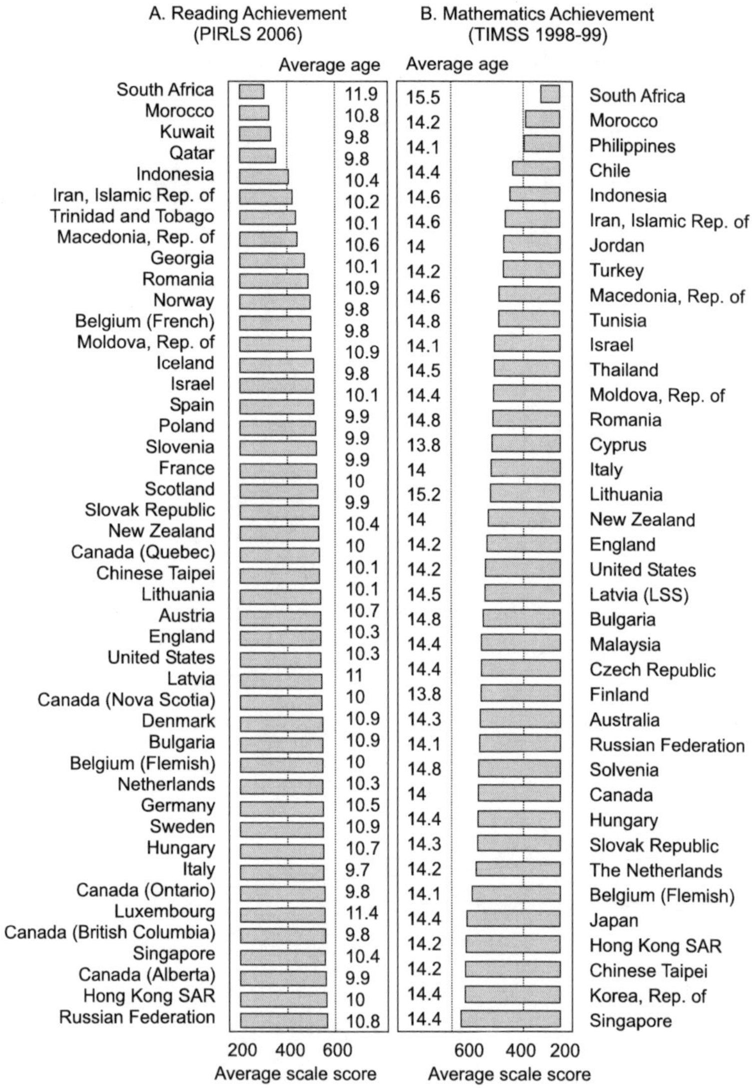

Source: International Association for the Evaluation of Educational Achievement (IEA), Progress in International Reading Literacy Study (PIRLS) 2006 and IEA, Trends in International Mathematics and Science Study (TIMSS), 1998–99, in Barnard (2009).

About the Series Editors

José E. Cassiolato teaches Innovation Studies and is the coordinator of RedeSist (Research Network on Local Productive and Innovation Systems) at the Institute of Economics, Federal University of Rio de Janeiro, Brazil. During 2011–2012 he was the President of the Scientific Board of Globelics, Global Research Network on the Economics of Learning, Innovation and Capacity building Systems where he coordinated the Research Project — A Comparative Study of the National Systems of Innovation of BRICS Countries. He has been Visiting Professor at the Université de Rennes (since 2001) and teaches at the Globelics Academy—School on National Systems of Innovation and Economic Development, Portugal and Finland (since 2004).

Maria Clara Couto Soares is a sociologist and political scientist, and is currently working as Senior Researcher at RedeSist, Institute of Economics, Federal University of Rio de Janeiro, Brazil. She was previously Science and Technology Policy Researcher at the Ministry of Science and Technology and at CNPq-National Council for Scientific and Technological Development, Brazil. Her main areas of interest are in national innovation systems, S,T&I policies, social innovation and sustainable development.

About the Editors

Mario Scerri is Professor of Economics and Senior Research Fellow, Institute for Economic Research on Innovation (IERI) at the Tshwane University of Technology, South Africa. He is also Director of the Institute for Comparative Studies in Local Development based in Mozambique. His research focus is on the evolution of innovation systems, specifically within southern Africa, from a political economy perspective. He has worked and written on the measurement of innovation, on the teaching of undergraduate economics and the economics of innovation. He is the author of the book *The Evolution of the South African System of Innovation since 1916* (2009) and co-editor of *Measuring Innovation in OECD and non-OECD Countries* (2006).

Helena M. M. Lastres is Head of the Office for Local Production and Innovations Systems and Regional Development, Brazilian Development Bank (BNDES). Her main areas of interest include development and science, technology & innovation (S, T&I) policies; economics of knowledge and innovation; financing of national/local production and innovation systems in the BRICS nations. Her recent publications include the co-edited volume *Systems of Innovation and Development: Evidence from Brazil* (2003). She has also contributed to the edited book *BRICS and Development Alternatives: Innovation Systems and Policies* (2009) and in the journal *Innovation: Management, Policy and Practice.*

Notes on Contributors

José Luis Gordon is an economist and Associate Researcher at Research Network on Local Productive and Innovative Systems (Redesist). He is currently an advisor to the Brazilian Minister of Science, Technology and Innovation. Before that, he was an economic analyst at the National Confederation of Industry of Brazil in the area of economic policy.

Priscila Koeller is an economist and is currently Analyst at the Directorate of Surveys at the Brazilian Institute of Geography and Statistics (IBGE) and Associate Researcher at the Research Network for Local Production and Innovations Systems (RedeSist). She was previously the Adviser to the Executive Secretariat at the Brazilian Ministry of Science and Technology. She has published articles related to Innovation Policy and Systems, Economic Statistics and Innovation Indicators which are her research focus.

V. V. Krishna is Professor of Science Policy at the Jawaharlal Nehru University, New Delhi. He has published 40 research papers and five books. He is the founder-editor and currently Editor-in-Chief of international journal *Science, Technology and Society*. He is consultant to EU and has visiting positions at University of New South Wales, Sydney and Institute of Advanced Study, United Nations University, Japan.

Tatiana Kuznetsova is Director of the Centre for Science and Innovation Policies (Higher School of Economics, Moscow). Her research competence covers studies on S&T and innovation policy and indicators, etc. She has authored over 350 publications and has taken part in different international projects, acting as a consultant to government agencies and is part of the editorial board of journal *Foresight* (Russia).

Lv Ping is Associate Professor at the University of Chinese Academy of Sciences in China. Her research interests include international business strategy, globalization and innovation in the context of emerging markets, and regional innovation system. She has published a number of articles and chapters in books. She has taken part in various research projects sponsored by the EU, NNSF (China), Riksbankens Jubileumsfond, Swedish Research Council, among others.

Index